A
Egyptian Galleries

E. A. Wallis Budge

978-1-63923-047-1

A Guide to the Egyptian Galleries

Printed June, 2016

Published and Distributed By:

Lushena Books, Inc 607 Country Club Drive,
Unit E
Bensenville, IL 60106

www.lushenabks.com

Printed in the United States of America

Cover art by Amit Paul.

A GUIDE

TO THE EGYPTIAN GALLERIES

(SCULPTURE).

BRITISH MUSEUM.

A GUIDE

TO THE

EGYPTIAN GALLERIES

(SCULPTURE).

WITH 39 PLATES AND 46 ILLUSTRATIONS IN THE TEXT.

PRINTED BY ORDER OF THE TRUSTEES.

1909.

PRICE ONE SHILLING AND SIXPENCE.

HARRISON AND SONS,
PRINTERS IN ORDINARY TO HIS MAJESTY,
ST. MARTIN'S LANE, LONDON.

PREFACE.

THIS Guide contains descriptions of the Egyptian Sculptures and other Egyptian Antiquities which are exhibited on the Ground Floor, in a series of Galleries extending from north to south on the west side of the British Museum.

The arrangement is, as far as possible, chronological. The monuments of the Ancient Empire are placed chiefly in the Vestibule; those of the Middle Empire will be found in the Northern Gallery and Central Saloon; and in the Southern Gallery are the Antiquities of the New Empire, and of the Saïte, Ptolemaïc, Roman and Christian Periods.

For convenience of reference the monuments have been renumbered consecutively with numbers painted in the top centre of the plinths and frames. The old numbers are in the left-hand lower corners. Indexes to the two sets of numbers will be found on pp. 307 ff.

E. A. WALLIS BUDGE.

DEPARTMENT OF EGYPTIAN AND ASSYRIAN ANTIQUITIES, BRITISH MUSEUM.

January 20, 1909.

CONTENTS.

LIST OF PLATES.

LIST OF ILLUSTRATIONS IN THE TEXT.

LIST OF BENEFACTORS.

1766-1802. His Majesty King George III.

Intercolumnar slabs of Nekht-neb-f	Nos. 926, 927
Portion of a kneeling statue of an official	No. 904
The "Rosetta Stone"	No. 960
Two black basalt obelisks of Nekht-Heru-ḥebt	Nos. 919, 920
Granite statue of the goddess Sekhet	No. 405
Head of a ram-headed Sphinx	No. 550
Left fist from a colossal statue of Rameses II.	No. 596
Seated figure of Rui, high-priest of Àmen	No. 638
Granite figure of Amen-mes	No. 756
Intercolumnar slab of Psammetichus I	No. 800
Grey granite sarcophagus of Ḥāp-men	No. 826
Portion of a granite sarcophagus	No. 882

1767. John, 3rd Earl of Bute, K.G.

Limestone relief from the wall of a tomb at Gîzah	No. 70
Portion of a seated figure of an official	No. 867

1771. Matthew Duane, Esq.

Kneeling statue of Henta, a prefect of the temple of Neith, at Saïs	No. 819

1805. George John, 2nd Earl Spencer, K.G., F.R.S.

Black basalt slab inscribed with a mythological text	No. 797
Lower portion of a granite statue of Rameses II	No. 580
Capital of a basalt pillar	No. 1080

T. Philipe, Esq.

Colossal limestone hawk	No. 898

1807. Dr. Bancroft, Junr.

Pillar altar dedicated to Serapis . . . No. 1086

1814–17. Captain Caviglia.

Portion of the uraeus of the Sphinx . . No. 20
Portion of the beard of the Sphinx . . No. 21
Head of a limestone Sphinx . . . . No. 945
Portion of a stele of Rameses II . . . No. 591
Headless statue of an official . . . No. 34
Stele of the sixth year of Marcus Aurelius and Lucius Verus . . . . No. 1058
Limestone slab . . . . No. 1079

Louis Burckhardt and Henry Salt, Esqs.

Upper portion of a colossal statue of Rameses II . . . . No. 576

1820. The Earl of Belmore.

Sandstone coffin and cover . . . . No. 913

1834. Sir J. Gardner Wilkinson.

Sandstone pyramid of Ḥeru-nefer . . . No. 699
Limestone libation tablet . . . . No. 1043

Sir Henry Ellis, K.H.

Portion of a wall-painting from a tomb . . No. 515

1835. Algernon, Baron Prudhoe, afterwards 4th Duke of Northumberland.

Stele describing an expedition of Åmen-ḥetep III, B.C. 1450, into the Sûdân . . No. 411
Red granite lion of Åmen-ḥetep III . . No. 430
Red granite lion of Tut-ānkh-Åmen . . No. 431

1836. J. B. Collings, Esq.

Stele of the reign of Åmen-em-ḥāt III . . No. 181
Stele of Tetåthi, a scribe . . . . . No. 534
Stele of Thuå . . . . No. 535
Stele of Nub-Nefert . . . . . . No. 542

1838–39. Colonel Howard Vyse.

Three casing stones from the Great Pyramid . . . Nos. 10–12
Sarcophagus of Nes-qetiu . . . . . No. 825
Portion of a granite statue of Nekht-neb-f . No. 924

1838–40. William Richard Hamilton, Esq.

Upper portion of a statue of Sekhet . . No. 399
Head of a granite sphinx . . . . . No. 531
Portion of a statue of Rameses II . . . No. 582
Portion of a statue of Psammetichus I . . No. 801
Sandstone libation tank . . . . No. 909

1844. E. Fletcher, Esq.

Kneeling statue of Uaḥ-âb-Rā . . . No. 818

1847–48. Robert Goff, Esq.

Sepulchral stele of Àru . . . . No. 296
Basalt libation bowl . . . . . No. 822

1848–54. Sir J. Bowring.

Slab from the tomb of Peṭā-Àmen-âpt . . No. 839
Stele of Khā-em-âpt . . . . . No. 845
Sepulchral stele of George, a Monk . . No. 1130

1852. The Marquis of Northampton.

Cover of the coffin of Peṭā-Ḥeru-Ḥap-ḥap . No. 934
Limestone stele of the Roman Period . . No. 1056

J. Scott Tucker, Esq.

Fragment of the obelisk of Thothmes III . No. 364

1854. Her Majesty Queen Victoria.

Head of a statue of a king of Egypt, perhaps one of the Ptolemies . . . . . . No. 947

Lyttleton Annesley, Esq.

Stele of the reign of Àmen-ḥetep I . . No. 350
Stele of Àmen-em-âpt . . . . . No. 354
Stele of Nefer . . . . . . No. 356
Stele of Rā-mes . . . . . . No. 426

Lyttleton Annesley, Esq.—*continued.*

Portion of a bas-relief . . . . . . No. 479
Stele of Pen-neferu . . . . . . No. 506
Stele of Àri-nefer . . . . . . No. 536
Stele of a judge . . . . No. 663
Stele of Takhāt . . . . No. 698
Stele with figures of Menu and Qetshet . . No. 702
Stele in the form of a shrine . . . . . No. 1085
Stele of Mena . . . . No. 1093
Stele of Aideosa . . . . No. 1095
Stele of Nikea . . . . No. 1096

1858. **Sir Thomas Phillips.**

Stele of Naia, an ambassador . . . . No. 656

1861–85. **Sir Augustus Wollaston Franks, K.C.B.**

Stele of Nekhtà . . . . No. 294
Stele mentioning Queen Merseḳer . . . No. 330
Stele of Mentu . . . . No. 488

1862. **The Rev. T. R. Maynard, Chaplain of the Forces.**

Base of a statue of Àmen-ḥetep IV . . . No. 436

1863. **A. H. Rhind, Esq.**

Altar inscribed in the Meroïtic character . No. 1050

1864. **Colonel T. P. Thompson.**

Angle slab from the tomb of Seti I . . . No. 569

1865. **The Trustees of the Christy Collection.**

Kneeling figure of Ḥui . . . . . . No. 530

J. Manship Norman, Esq.

Sepulchral stele of John the Deacon . . . No. 1105

1866. **Samuel Sharp, Esq.**

Statue of Khā-em-Uast, a son of Rameses II . No. 615

1869. **H. Danby Seymour, Esq.**

A series of wall-paintings from an Egyptian tomb . . . . Nos. 517–520

1870. **The Royal Institution.**

Stele of Ḥetep-neb-su . . . . . . No. 314
Stele inscribed in Greek . . . . No. 1094

F. T. Palgrave, Esq.

Stele of Ȧāḥmes . . . . No. 491

Society of Antiquaries.

Cast of the inscription of Psemthek . . . No. 808

1871. **H.H. Isma'il Pâshâ, Khedive of Egypt.**

Cast of a stele inscribed with a copy of the decree of the priests of Canopus, B.C. 238 . No. 957

1875. **Wentworth Huyshe, Esq.**

Stele of Ȧthu . . . . No. 734

1882. **F. G. Hilton Price, Esq., Dir. S.A.**

Stele of the Ptolemaïc Period . . . No. 1044

1883–1905. **The Egypt Exploration Fund.**

Portion of a stele of Sa (?) . . . . . No. 2
Reliefs from the tomb of Suten-ȧbu . . . Nos. 5, 6
Statue of Ȧn-kheft-ka . . . . . . No. 33
Decree of King Tetȧ . . . . . . No. 74
Stone lintel of a door . . . . . . No. 77
Stele of Nefer-sennȧ . . . . . . No. 78
Limestone roof slab . . . . . . No. 90
Stele of Merer-Ȧqer . . . . . . No. 91
Stele of Menȧ . . . . No. 92
List of offerings . . . . No. 119
Relief from Denderah . . . . . . No. 125
Stele of En-Ȧntef-ȧqer . . . . . . No. 135
Portion of a seated statue of Hathor . . No. 149
Three grey granite statues of Usertsen III Nos. 158–160
Head of a statue of Usertsen III . . . No. 162
Lower portions of four quartzite statues of Usertsen III . . . . . Nos. 162–165

1883-1905. The Egypt Exploration Fund—*continued.*

A series of granite slabs inscribed with royal names from the temple of Osorkon II at Bubastis . . . No. 167, 339, 771, 772, 773

Four painted reliefs from the tomb of Ṭeḥuti-ḥetep . . . . Nos. 198–201

Sandstone obelisk from Ṣarâbît al-Khâdim . No. 202

Stele of the reign of Rā-sekhem-ṭā . . . . . No. 282

Stele of Sekhem-khu-taui-Rā . . . . . No. 284

Limestone statue of Åmen-ḥetep I . . No. 346

Limestone stele of Åmen-ḥetep I . . . . No. 347

Statue of Pa-ser . . . . No. 427

Statue of Åmen-ḥetep . . . . . . No. 448

Portion of a stele . . . . No. 470

Pyramid of Tcha-nefer . . . . . . No. 559

Relief of Seti I . . . . No. 571

Statue of a king . . . . No. 585

Portion of a statue of Rameses II . . . No. 587

Granite hawk . . . . No. 596

Two red granite columns of Rameses II Nos. 598, 599

Stele of Ṭāṭā-åa . . . . No. 652

Hathor-headed capital of a pillar . . . No. 768

Granite reliefs from the temple of Osorkon II Nos. 769, 770

Head and lower portion of a seated colossal statue of Åmen-em-ḥāt III, usurped by Osorkon II . . . . . . No. 774, 775

Seated figure of the "Recorder of Pithom" . No. 776

Stele of King Uaḥ-åb-Rā . . . . . No. 804

Altar of Åāḥmes II . . . . No. 807

Basalt coffin of Psemthek . . . . . No. 829

Inscription of Ptolemy I . . . . . No. 951

Relief of Ptolemy I . . . . . . No. 952

Relief of Ptolemy II . . . . . . No. 953

Stele of Ptolemy II . . . . . Nos. 954, 955

1885–86. The Rev. Greville J. Chester, B.A.

Stele of Rā-nefer . . . . No. 87
Altar inscribed in the Meroïtic character . No. 105

1886. Captain Handcock, R.E.

Mural ornament from a Coptic church . . No. 1152
Stone sculptured with a rosette . . . No. 1167

1887. Field Marshal the Lord Grenfell.

Statue of Sa-Renput . . . . . . No. 157

General Sir C. Holled Smith, K.C.M.G.

Jamb of a door of Thothmes III . . . No. 365
Portion of a stele of Thothmes III . . No. 368
Stele of Thothmes III . . . . . . No. 370
Portion of a seated figure of Kamesu . . No. 452
Stele of Seti I . . . . No. 574
Sandstone relief of Setau, a governor of the Sûdân . . . . No. 608
Sepulchral stele of Mer-netchem . . . No. 645

General G. F. Plunkett, R.E.

Granite stele with figures of Menu and Khnemu No. 784

1888. H. Martyn Kennard, Esq.

Stele of Pa-áu . . . . No. 847

1890. The Egyptian Government.

Cast of a figure of the goddess Smeṭsmeṭ . No. 824
Cast of the Cow of Hathor . . . . . No. 823

1894. Captain H. G. Lyons, R.E.

Stele of Erṭā-Ántef-Ṭāṭāu . . . . . No. 196

1896–99. Somers Clarke, Esq., F.S.A.

Portion of a grey granite statue of a king . No. 453
Granite figure of Māiu . . . . . . No. 721
Stele from Semnah . . . . . . No. 176

1897. G. Willoughby Fraser, Esq.

Door socket . . . . No. 148

1898. **George Page, Esq.**

Seated figure of Åāḥmes . . . . . No. 653

Morgan S. Williams, Esq.

Stele of Ānkhu . . . . No. 302
Stele of Sabu . . . . No. 317
Stele of Åntef . . . . No. 325
Stele of Unenkhu. . . . . . . No. 507

1901. **Mrs. Hawker.**

Stele of Usertsen . . . . No. 235
Relief from the wall of a tomb . . . . No. 661

1903. **His Majesty King Edward VII.**

Papyrus inscribed in hieroglyphic characters with a series of chapters from the Theban Recension of the Book of the Dead for Queen Netchemet, B.C. 1050 . . . . No. 758

Colonel W. Hayes-Sadler.

Stele of User-satet, governor of the Sûdân . No. 512

1904. **Professor Golénischeff.**

Cast of a seated figure of Åmen-em-ḥāt III . No. 172

1905. **The Government of the Egyptian Sûdân.**

Relief from the south wall of the funerary chapel of one of the queens called "Candace," at Meroë . . . . . No. 1049

Robert Mond, Esq.

Sandstone lintel from the tomb of Pa-åri . No. 424

1908. **The Egyptian Research Account.**

Limestone door-post from a temple of Meneph-thah at Memphis . . . . . . No. 1169
Limestone cornice slab of Sa-Åmen . . No. 1170
Two stelæ on which are sculptured ears Nos. 1171, 1172

A GUIDE

TO THE EGYPTIAN GALLERIES

(SCULPTURE).

ANCIENT EMPIRE.

THIRD DYNASTY.

1. (*Vestibule. South Wall.*)—Sandstone **relief** from the tomb of **Sherȧ**, a priest. On the lower half of the slab is sculptured a figure of the deceased, seated on a chair of state of archaïc form, and holding a staff. The inscription shows that Sherȧ was a "superintendent and priest of the *ka*," or "double," of **Senṭ**, a king of the IInd dynasty, who reigned about B.C. 4000. His duty was to perform commemorative services for the king at regular intervals. From Ṣakkârah. IInd or IIIrd dynasty, about B.C. 4000–3800. Height 4 ft. 9 in., width 1 ft. 8 in. [No. 1192.]

2. (*Vestibule. South Wall.*)—Portion of a **stele** sculptured with a figure of a king who wears the Crown of the North, and is represented in the act of smiting his foes; the reading of his Horus name (**Sa**), which is above him, is doubtful. From Ṣarâbît al-Khâdim in the Peninsula of Sinai. IIIrd dynasty, about B.C. 4000. Height 1 ft. 1 in, width 1 ft. 7 in. [No. 691.]

Presented by the Egypt Exploration Fund, 1905.

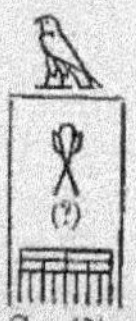

SA (?)

3. (*Vestibule. East Doorway.*)—Red granite **statue of Betchmes**, a *suten rekh*, or "royal kinsman." The deceased is supposed to be seated on a stool of state, the shape of which resembles the stools of chiefs in the Southern Sûdân at the present time. His right hand rests on his knee, and in his left he carries an axe, with a long handle, which rests on his left shoulder. On his left knee is the inscription—

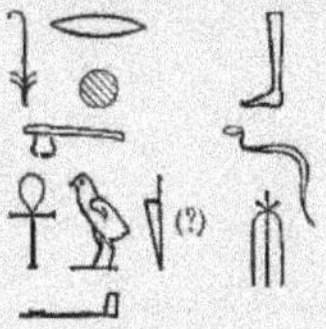

The work of this statue is very archaïc in character. IIIrd dynasty, about B.C. 3800. From a tomb near the Pyramids of Gîzah. Salt Collection. Height 2 ft. 2 in.

[No. 171 (70 A).]

4. (*Vestibule. South Wall.*)—Rectangular limestone **tablet** covered with hieroglyphics cut in relief, which form a prayer on behalf of the deceased **Ḥes**, that a "royal table of offerings" may be prepared for him, that offerings may be made to him at certain festivals of the year, and that he may have a "happy burial" in Semt-Ȧmentet, *i.e.*, the Mountain of Ȧmentet. The deceased was a "royal kinsman," and a loyal devotee of the "Great God." The text is not divided by lines, and it was probably cut under the IIIrd dynasty. From Gîzah. Length 1 ft. 5½ in., breadth 11 in.

[No. 1212.]

5. (*Vestibule. South Wall.*)—Limestone **relief,** sculptured with figure of **Suten-ȧbu,** a royal kinsman and priest of the goddess Hathor. The deceased wears a panther skin, fastened round his waist by a girdle. In his right hand he holds the *kherp* sceptre, and in the left he grasps some object made of cord, or strips of leather, which falls over his left shoulder. From Denderah. IIIrd or IVth dynasty, about B.C. 3700. Height 2 ft. 5 in., width 1 ft. 8 in. [No. 1267.]

Presented by the Egypt Exploration Fund, 1898.

6. (*Vestibule. South Wall.*)—Portion of a limestone **relief** from the wall of the tomb of **Suten-àbu** 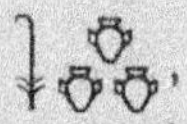, a royal kinsman and priest, sculptured with a representation of a false door of a tomb. From Denderah. IIIrd or IVth dynasty, about B.C. 3700. Height 1 ft. 8 in., width 1 ft. 4 in. [No. 1266.]

Presented by the Egypt Exploration Fund, 1898.

FOURTH DYNASTY.

7. (*Vestibule. North Wall.*)—Limestone **sepulchral stele** in the form of a door from the tomb of the "royal kinswoman," Queen **Mert-tefs** 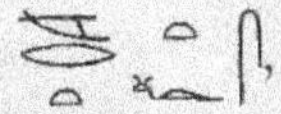, who flourished during the reigns of **Seneferu, Khufu** (Cheops), and **Khā-f-Rā** (Chephren). On the upper portion, in relief, is the queen seated at a table of offerings, and below this is a line of inscription containing her name, and stating that she was the "loyal servant of her husband." On the lower part are figures of her daughters, Ḥetep-sekher 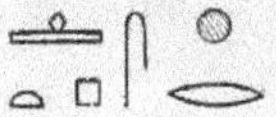 and Seshsesht 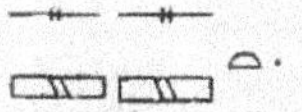. From Gîzah. IVth dynasty, about B.C. 3660. Height 4 ft. 2 in., breadth 1 ft. 5 in. [No. 1228.]

8. (*Vestibule. North Wall.*)—Limestone **sepulchral stele** in the form of a door from the tomb of **Prince Ka-nefer,** , who flourished in the reign of **Seneferu,** king of Egypt, about B.C. 3760. The deceased held a number of high civil and ecclesiastical offices, and was the governor of the pyramid tomb which the king built at Mêdûm. On the right side of the doorway is sculptured, in low relief, a figure of the prince wearing a panther skin, emblem of his office of *kher ḥeb*, and on the left is a similar figure wearing a tunic. By his side stands his son Ka-āb, a "royal kinsman." Below, on the right, are figures of three of his sons who are called Seneferu-Ṭuat, Seneferu-Khāf, and Seneferu-baf

respectively. On the left are: 1. The royal kinsman Ka-āb, . 2. The priest of the *ka* Àthà, 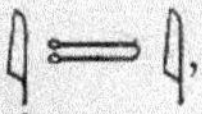, carrying a goose. 3. The priest of the *ka* Àuà, . Between the legs of the large figures of the deceased are the names of Ptaḥ-shepses, priest of the *ka*, and Ka-nefer, his son, the royal kinsman, the superintendent of the priests of the *ka*. From Gîzah. IVth dynasty, about B.C 3760. (**Plate I.**) Height 8 ft. 8 in., width 4 ft. [No. 1324.]

Sepulchral stele of Ka-nefer.
[Vestibule, North Wall, No. 8.]

9. (*Vestibule. North Wall.*)—Limestone **memorial tablet,** sculptured in low relief, with the figure of a tablet for offerings, and inscribed with a text mentioning the "old prince, the offspring of his body, loving him, the *smer uăt,* director of the priests of **Seneferu** (king of Egypt, about B.C. 3760), the councillor of Horus." The second portion of the inscription states that this slab was dedicated to "father **Ka-nefer**" by his son. Found in the tomb of Ka-nefer (see No. 1324). From Gîzah. IVth dynasty, about B.C. 3760. Length 3 ft. 7 in. breadth 1 ft. 2 in. [No. 1345.]

10–12. (*Vestibule. North Wall.*)—Three of the **casing-stones** from the **Great Pyramid,** built at Gîzah, by Khufu (Cheops), king of Egypt, about B.C. 3730, showing the angle of inclination to have been 51° 20′ 25″. They were found on the north side of the pyramid among an accumulation of sand and fragments of limestone, etc. No. **10** measures 2 ft. by 1 ft. 6 in. by 11 in.; No. **11,** 2 ft. 4½ in. by 1 ft. 3 in. by 1 ft. 5 in.; No. **12,** 1 ft. 11½ in. by 1 ft. 3½ in. by 11 in. [Nos. 490, 491, 492.]

Presented by Colonel Howard Vyse, 1838.

13. (*Vestibule. South Wall.*)—Plaster **cast** of a seated stone **statue of Khufu,** the Cheops of Greek writers, and builder of the Great Pyramid at Gîzah, king of Egypt, about B.C. 3730. The king wears a square beard and a full wig, and over his forehead is the uraeus , emblematic of sovereignty. The original is in the Egyptian Museum in Cairo. Height 2 ft. 1 in. [No. 1114.]

14. (*Vestibule. East Doorway.*)—Painted limestone seated **figures of Ka-ṭep** 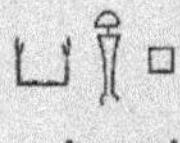, and his wife, **Ḥetep-ḥeres,** 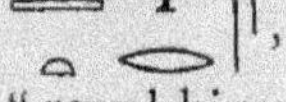, who are described as "royal kinsman," and "royal kinswoman;" Ka-ṭep was also a "royal libationer," and he held other offices of a priestly character , etc. He wears a deep white collar and a short tunic, and his wife wears a garment which extends nearly to her ankles; on her breast is the figure of a triangle inverted . From Gîzah. IVth dynasty, about B.C. 3730. Height 1 ft. 7 in. [No. 1181.]

15. (*Vestibule. South Wall.*)—**Sepulchral stele** in the form of a door from the tomb of **Ka-ṭep** , a "royal kinsman," royal libationer, and leader of certain ceremonies in the funerary chapel attached to the Great Pyramid, who flourished in the reign of **Khufu** (Cheops), king of Egypt, about B.C. 3730. For the statues of Ka-ṭep and his wife, see No. **14**. From Gîzah. IVth dynasty. Height 3 ft. 11 in., width 3 ft. [No. 1288.]

16. (*Vestibule. South Wall.*)—Limestone **relief** from the tomb of **Ka-ṭep** . On the left is cut in outline a figure of the deceased, seated on a chair of state, and the accompanying text enumerates some of the offices which he held, among them being that of . For the statues of Ka-ṭep and his wife Ḥetep-ḥeres, see No. 14. From Gîzah. IVth dynasty. Length 2 ft. 2 in., breadth 11 in. [No. 1173.]

17. (*Vestibule. South Wall.*)—Upper portion of a limestone **sepulchral stele** in the form of a door from the tomb of **Ka-ṭep** , a royal libationer and royal kinsman, who flourished in the reign of **Khufu,** or Cheops, king of Egypt, about B.C. 3730. Two priests of the *ka*, Sennu  and Àkhu , are mentioned. For the statues of Ka-ṭep and his wife, see No. 14. From Gîzah. IVth dynasty. Length 2 ft. 9 in., breadth 1 ft. 8 in. [No. 1174.]

18. (*Vestibule. North Wall.*)—Limestone **sepulchral stele,** in the form of a door from the tomb of **Sheshà** 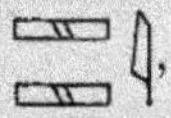, a royal scribe and overseer of the libationers, who flourished in the reign of **Khufu,** or **Cheops,** king of Egypt, about B.C. 3730. On the upper part, upon a raised, rectangular tablet, are cut figures of the deceased and his wife, **Khentet-ka** 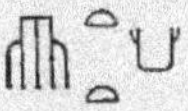, a royal kinswoman, seated with tables of offerings before them. On the right side of the door, on the lower portion, are figures of his wife and daughter, Nub-ḥeset

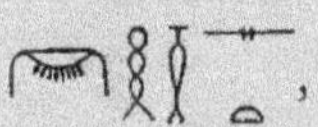, and on the left, figures of himself and his son. From Gîzah. IVth dynasty. Height 4 ft. 3 in., width 2 ft. 4 in. [No. 1282.]

19. (*Vestibule.*)—**Cast** of the massive, rectangular granite **sarcophagus** of **Khufu-ānkh** , a high official who flourished in the reign of Khufu, or Cheops, the builder of the First Pyramid, about B.C. 3730. The deceased held a number of important offices at court, and he was also steward of the temple, clerk of the works, chancellor  (*khetemet*), etc.; his rank was that of *smer uāt*, and he performed duties in connection with the legal and ecclesiastical institutions of the period. The text running round the upper edge of the sarcophagus contains prayers that the deceased may enjoy a "happy burial," and receive offerings at the chief festivals of the year. The ornamentation of the sarcophagus is interesting, and is one of the best examples of the funerary sculpture of the period known. The original is in the Egyptian Museum at Cairo. Length 8 ft. 3 in., breadth 3 ft. 3½ in., height 4 ft. 5 in. [No. 1111.]

20. (*Vestibule. North Wall.*)—Portion of the limestone **uraeus**, or serpent, the symbol of sovereignty, which stood above the forehead of the **Sphinx** at Gîzah. Traces of the red colour with which it was painted are still visible. Length 2 ft. 2 in., breadth 1 ft. 1½ in. [No. 1204 (443*).]

Presented by Captain Caviglia, 1817.

21. (*Vestibule. North Wall.*)—Portion of the limestone **beard of the Sphinx** at Gîzah, sculptured with diagonal bands which are intended to represent plaits of hairs; traces of the red colour with which it was painted are still visible. Length 2 ft. 7 in. [No. 58.]

Presented by Captain Caviglia, 1817.

22. (*Vestibule. South Wall.*)—Portion of an **inscription** from a wall of the tomb of **Rutchek** , who flourished in the reign of Khā-f-Rā (Chephren), king of Egypt, about B.C. 3660. The deceased was a "royal kinsman," and a libationer, and held a priestly office in connection with the funerary chapel of Khā-f-Rā. From Gîzah. IVth dynasty. Length 2 ft. 3 in., breadth 5 in. [No. 1269.]

23. (*Vestibule. North Wall.*)—Limestone **architrave** from the door of the tomb of **Rutchek**, a "friend of Pharaoh", *smer en Per-āa*, and priest and inspector of the libationers in the funerary temple of **Khā-f-Rā,** king of Egypt, about B.C. 3660, and "beloved of his lord." From Gîzah. IVth dynasty. Length 3 ft. 6 in., breadth (at ends) 11 in. [No. 1268.]

24. (*Bay* 1. *North Wall.*)—Massive limestone **door** from the tomb of **Thethȧ,** a royal kinsman and overseer of the pyramid of King **Khā-f-Rā** at Gîzah. This door was probably an exact duplicate of No. 25, when it was complete. In the inscriptions on each side of the lintel is given a list of the offices held by the deceased, *i.e.*, overseer of the pyramid of Khā-f-Rā, overseer of the throne of Pharaoh, president of the mysteries and magical ceremonies performed in Khā-f-Rā's pyramid, priest of Hathor, lady of the Sycamore, and priest of Neith, to whom Khā-f-Rā dedicated a temple. On the left flank of the door are figures of the deceased and his sons, and on the right, when complete, were figures of his wife Ṭebt, and daughters. On the sloping sides of the framework are cut figures of altars, stands for lights, incense, etc. Salt Collection, 1835. From Gîzah. IVth dynasty, about B.C. 3660. Height 8 ft., breadth 6 ft. 10 in. [No. 157B.]

25. (*Bay* 1. *North Wall.*)—Massive limestone **door** from the tomb of **Thethȧ**, a royal kinsman, and overseer of the pyramid which was built by king **Khā-f-Rā** (Chephren) at Gîzah. Above the lintel of the door is a flat, raised tablet, whereon is sculptured a scene representing the deceased and his wife **Ṭebt,** seated at a table of offerings, a list of which is given above it. Immediately below this is inscribed a full list of the offices held by the deceased, who was a councillor, priest, and overseer in the royal palace. On the left flank of the doorway is a figure of Thethȧ, and on the right figures of his wife and five of their daughters. Salt Collection. From Gîzah. IVth dynasty, about B.C. 3660. Height 8 ft., breadth 7 ft. 2 in. [No. 157A.]

26. (*Bay* 1. *North Wall.*)—Sandstone **door-jamb** from the tomb of the royal kinsman **Thethȧ**; see Nos. 24

and 25. The text, which is cut in fine bold hieroglyphics, states that the deceased provided a tomb for his father and his mother, and performed their funeral ceremonies in a suitable manner 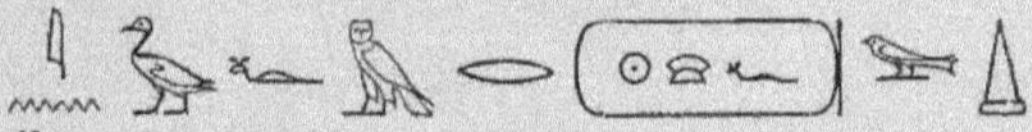
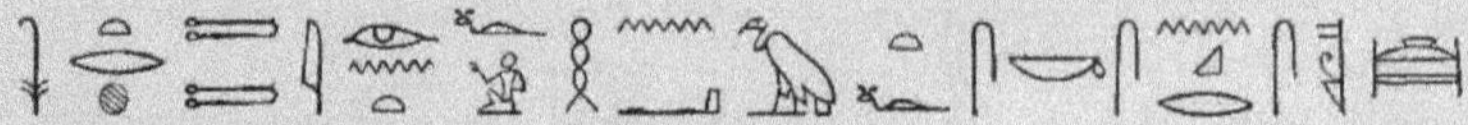
. Salt collection. From Gîzah. IVth dynasty. Length 7 ft. 10 in., breadth 7 in. [No. 157C.]

27. (*Vestibule.*)—**Cast** of a hard stone **statue of Khā-f-Rā,** or Chephren, king of Egypt, and builder of the Second Pyramid at Gîzah, about B.C. 3660. The original is in the Egyptian Museum at Cairo. The king is seated on a throne, the front of which is ornamented with the fore-parts of lions; on the sides, in relief, are designs symbolic of the union of Upper and Lower Egypt . The king wears a wig characteristic of the period, and on his forehead is the uraeus, emblem of sovereignty; behind his head is the hawk of Horus, with outstretched wings. At each side of his feet are cut the Golden Horus and Suten Bât names of the king:

Height of seated figure, 4 ft. 6 in. [No. 1110.]

28. (*Vestibule. South Wall.*)—**Cast** of a seated stone **statue of Khā-f-Rā,** the Chephren of Greek writers, builder of the Second Pyramid at Gîzah, and king of Egypt, about B.C. 3660. The original is in the Egyptian Museum in Cairo. The king has a large, square beard, and wears a full wig, and his tunic extends from his waist to his knees. On the right and left sides of the throne are inscribed his Horus and Suten Bât names thus:

USR-ÀB.

KHĀ-F-RĀ.

On the step, in front of his feet, is inscribed 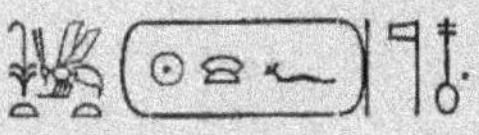
Height 2 ft. 7 in. [No. 1113.]

29. (*Vestibule. South Wall.*)—**Cast** of a seated stone figure of an **early king,** who is represented in the form of Osiris. He wears the Crown of the South ; in his right hand is the whip , and in his left the sceptre , emblematic of authority and rule. The original is in the Egyptian Museum in Cairo. Height 1 ft. 8 in. [No. 1117.]

30. (*Vestibule. South Wall.*)—**Cast** of a seated stone statue of **Men-kau-Rā,** the Mykerinos of Greek writers, and builder of the Third Pyramid at Gîzah, king of Egypt, about B.C. 3630. The king wears a full wig, and over his forehead is the uraeus , emblematic of sovereignty; his beard is square. On the front of the throne are inscribed the Horus and Suten Bât names of the king thus:—

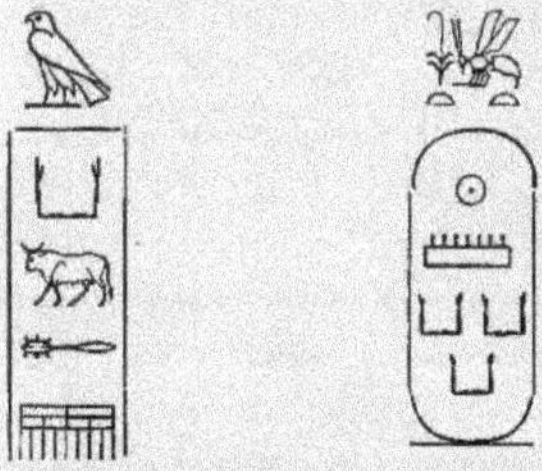

The original is in the Egyptian Museum in Cairo. Height 1 ft. 3 in. [No. 1115.]

31. (*Vestibule. South Wall.*)—**Sepulchral stele** in the form of a door from the tomb of **Khennu** , a "royal kinsman," priest, libationer, councillor, etc., who flourished in the reign of **Men-kau-Rā** (Mykerinos), king of Egypt, about B.C. 3630, whose prenomen appears on the monument. On the rectangular panel at the top are sculptured figures of Khennu and his wife, seated at a table of offerings, and on the slab below and on the raised sides are sculptured lists of the offices and titles held by the deceased. From Gîzah. IVth dynasty. Height 6 ft., width 3 ft. 7 in. [No. 1272.]

32. (*Vestibule. North Wall.*)—**Sepulchral stele** in the form of a door, from the inside of the tomb of **Ptaḥ-shepses,** , who flourished under Men-kau-Rā, a king of the IVth dynasty, about B.C. 3630, and the six or seven kings who succeeded him. Ptaḥ-shepses was educated with the royal children at the court of **Men-kau-Rā** (Mykerinos), the builder of the Third Pyramid at Gîzah, and he married the princess **Maāt-khā** , the eldest daughter of the king. He was a "royal kinsman," and performed duties in connection with the personal service of the king, and attended in the palace. He was high priest of Memphis , high priest of the cult of Rā, chief libationer, superintendent of the royal storehouses and temple property, royal barge-master, priest of the gods Seker and Ṭeṭ, clerk of the works in the palace and temples, and the inscription states that in the performance of these offices he gave great satisfaction to the kings his lords. On the façade are four lines of text wherein the deceased prays that a "royal offering" may be granted to him at all the great festivals of the year, and that after a happy old age he may receive honourable burial; the inscription ends with an enumeration of his titles. To the left, in sunk relief, is a seated figure of Ptaḥ-shepses, holding a staff. On each side of the monument is a series of panels in which are sculptured, in low relief, representations of vases and vessels of oil, milk, wine, etc., bowls of flowers and fruits, etc. The columns of text on each side of the false door contain lists of the offices which he held under the various kings in whose reigns he lived. Length (façade) 13 ft. 6 in., height 11 ft. 9 in.; doorway, 9 ft. 3 in. by 3 ft. From Ṣaḳḳârah. IVth and Vth dynasties. [No. 682.]

33. (*Bay* 1.)—Painted limestone **portrait statue of Ankheft-ka** , a royal kinsman. The deceased wears a wig, a collar, and tunic, which is fastened at the waist by a knotted belt. Very fine work. From Dahshûr. IVth dynasty, about B.C. 3700. Height 4 ft. 3 in. [No. 1239.]

Presented by the Egypt Exploration Fund, 1897.

34. (*Vestibule.*)—Headless **statue** of a priestly official wearing a tunic, which is fastened round the waist by a belt with a double knot in front. When found the statue was in two pieces, and near them was a stone head, which is, however, the product of a later period. Found in a tomb near the Pyramids of Gîzah. IVth dynasty, about B.C. 3700. Height 5 ft. [No. 35.] *Presented by Captain Caviglia*, 1817.

35. (*Vestibule.*)—Painted plaster cast of a wooden figure of a high Egyptian official who flourished under the IVth or Vth dynasty, about B.C. 3700. The original, which is now in the Egyptian Museum in Cairo, was found in a tomb at Ṣaḳḳârah, and on account of its likeness to the local shêkh of the neighbouring village was called **Shêkh al-Balad,** or "Chief of the village." The left hand grasped a staff of office. Height of figure 3 ft. 8 in. [No. 1144.]

36. (*Vestibule.*)—Cast of a seated stone **figure of a scribe** of the Ancient Empire, who is represented cross-legged. He wears a full wig of a very early form, and holds in his hands an unrolled papyrus. The original is in the Egyptian Museum in Cairo. Height 1 ft. 7 in. [No. 1116.]

37. (*Vestibule. South Wall.*)—Painted limestone **relief** from the wall of a tomb sculptured with figures of attendants bearing offerings of cakes, birds, etc., for a funerary feast to be held at the tomb in commemoration of the deceased. From Gîzah. IVth dynasty. Length 10 in., breadth 6 in. [No. 993.]

38. (*Vestibule. South Wall.*)—Portion of an inscribed limestone **sepulchral stele** from the tomb of an official who flourished under the Ancient Empire. The work is somewhat archaic in character. IVth dynasty, about B.C. 3700. Height 2 ft. 2 in., width 1 ft. 3 in. [No. 1185.]

39. (*Vestibule. South Wall.*)—Fragment of an **inscription** from the wall of the tomb of an official who was a councillor, and had the rank of *smer uāt;* he was a votary of the god Anubis. The hieroglyphics are in low relief, and were probably cut under the IVth dynasty. From Gîzah. Height 1 ft. 2 in.; width 8 in. [No. 992.]

40. (*Vestibule. South Wall.*)—**Bas-relief** from the tomb of **Rā-ḥetep** 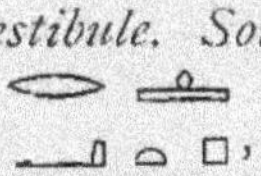, a priestly official. The deceased is seated before a tablet for offerings, to the right of which is a tabular list of the various kinds of food and wine, incense, changes of apparel, etc., which he prays that he may enjoy in the Other World. He held high, priestly rank at Memphis. This relief is one of the finest pieces of funerary sculpture in the British Museum, and the delicate work of the hieroglyphics is remarkable. From Mêdûm. IVth or Vth dynasty. Length 3 ft. 9 in., breadth 2 ft. 7 in. [No. 1242.]

Bas-relief from the tomb of Rā-ḥetep at Mêdûm.
[Vestibule, South Wall, No. 40.]

41. (*Vestibule. South Wall.*)—Painted limestone **relief** from the tomb of **Ȧri,** , a "royal kinsman" and "royal libationer." Below the inscription stands a figure of the deceased, wearing a necklace with pendant, a bracelet on his right wrist, and a white linen tunic; in one hand he holds a staff, and in the other the sceptre . Good work. From Gîzah. IVth dynasty, about B.C. 3700. Height 3 ft. 9 in., width 1 ft. 7 in. [No. 1169.]

42. (*Vestibule. South Wall.*)—Fine hard limestone **slab,** sculptured in low relief with figures of **Ȧri** , and his wife **Ant** , seated at a table of offerings. Àri's wig and Ànt's head-dress are painted black, and each holds some cord (?) object, emblematic of a priestly office. The side-bars of the frame of the stools terminate at one end in lotus-shaped objects. From Gîzah. IVth dynasty, about B.C. 3700. Height 2 ft. 4 in., width 2 ft. 1 in. [No. 1171.]

Relief from the tomb of Àri.
[Vestibule, South Wall, No. 41.]

43. (*Vestibule. South Wall.*)—Fine hard limestone **slab** from the tomb of **Àri** , a royal libationer, sculptured in low relief with figures of the deceased and his five sons. Àri's wig is painted black, and he holds a staff and the sceptre . The names of the sons are Nenek , Nefer-suten- . . . . , Ka-nefer , Àtheḥ , and Àri-netches . From Gîzah. IVth dynasty, about 3700. Height 3 ft., width 1 ft. 7 in. [No. 1168.]

44. (*Vestibule. South Wall.*)—Limestone **relief** from the hall of the tomb of **Åfå**, a "royal kinsman," superintendent of the palace, and overseer of the gardeners and labourers of the king's orchard. On the upper portion is sculptured in low relief a scene wherein the deceased and his wife **Unten** are seated at a table of offerings, and below is a line of hieroglyphics recording the name and titles of the deceased. On each side of the door are figures of the deceased and his wife, accompanied by sons and daughters, namely, Erṭā-en-åf-s, Ḥet-Ḥeru-Nefer-ḥetep, Sestu, Āper-s, Thenthå, Betå, etc., , , , , , . From Gîzah. IVth dynasty. Salt Collection, 1835. Height 2 ft. 2 in., width 2 ft. 4 in. [No. 130.]

45. A–H. (*Vestibule. North Wall.*)—A series of eight **fragments of inscriptions,** and portions of stelae in the form of doors, from the tomb of **Ānkh-ḥa-f**, a royal kinsman and scribe of the treasure-house of one of the kings of the IVth dynasty. **A** is inscribed with a prayer to Ånpu for sepulchral offerings; **B** contains the name and titles of the deceased, and the name of his wife, Nefert-Setchet; **C** is sculptured with figures of the deceased and his wife seated at a table of offerings; **D** is sculptured with figures of his sons Kapå, and Ḥep; **E** shows the deceased burning incense; **F** and **G** are sculptured with figures of censers; and **H,** an architrave of a door, is inscribed with the names and titles of the deceased. From Gîzah or Ṣaḳḳârah. IVth dynasty, about B.C. 3700. Salt Collection, 1835. [Nos. 527, 529, 530, 532, 533, 534, 535, 538.]

46. (*Vestibule. North Wall.*)—**Sepulchral stele,** in the form of a door, from the tomb of a high official who flourished under one of the kings of the IVth dynasty. On the upper part are sculptured figures of the deceased and his wife seated at a table of offerings, and of two members of their family.

On the lower portion, on each side of the door, is a figure. The inscription contains a prayer to Ȧnpu, or Anubis, for funerary offerings, but the name of the deceased is illegible. From Gîzah or Ṣaḳḳârah. IVth dynasty, about B.C. 3700. Salt Collection, 1835. [No. 531.]

47. (*Vestibule. North Wall.*)—Portions of a **sepulchral stele** in the form of a door from the tomb of **Ru-mu** (?) a royal kinsman. On **A** are inscribed the name of the deceased, and that of his wife **Thentet**, a royal kinswoman and priestess of Hathor. On **B** are sculptured figures of the deceased and his wife seated at a table of offerings; on **C** is a figure of his son K-khent, and on **D** are figures of Thentet and "her daughter's son" Nefer. From Gîzah or Ṣaḳḳârah. IVth dynasty, B.C. 3700. Salt Collection, 1835. [No. 528.]

FIFTH DYNASTY.

48. (*Vestibule. South Wall.*)—Lower portion of a seated, black granite **statue of User-en-Rā Ȧn,** a king of Egypt of the Vth dynasty, about B.C. 3430. On each side of the throne are four lines of hieroglyphics, which say that the statue was made in honour of the king by a royal successor , *i.e.*, **Usertsen I,** a king of the XIIth dynasty, about B.C. 2430. On the left side is User-en-Rā's prenomen:

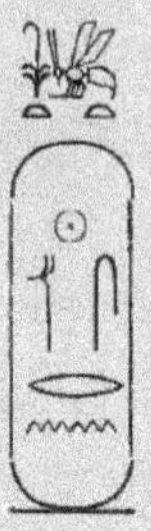 , and on the right his nomen: .

On the king's girdle the name **Ȧn** is repeated. From the Collection of Chevalier Bunsen. Height 1 ft. 1 in.

[No. 870. (54-7-22, 1.)]

49. (*Vestibule. South Wall.*)—**Cast** of a seated stone **statue of User-en-Rā,** king of Egypt, about B.C. 3430. The king wears a full wig, and over his forehead is the uraeus, , emblematic of sovereignty. His short tunic extends from the waist to the knees; he is here beardless. On the step of the throne, near his right foot, is the name of the king as Suten Bȧt, *i.e.*, King of the South and North:

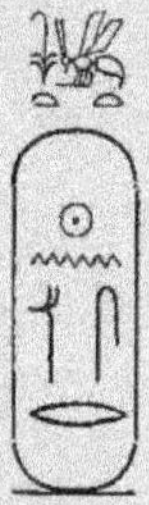

The original is in the Egyptian Museum in Cairo. Height 2 ft. 3 in. [No. 1112.]

50. (*Vestibule.*)—**Granite column,** with palm-leaf capital, from the portico of the **Pyramid of Unȧs,** king of Egypt, about B.C. 3330. From Ṣaḳḳârah. Vth dynasty. A portion of the shaft has been restored. Height 18 ft. 6 in., weight about 7 tons 17 cwt. [No. 1385.]

51. (*Vestibule. East Wall.*)—**Sepulchral stele** in the form of a door from the tomb of **Khnemu-ḥetep** 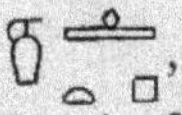, a high official who flourished in the reign of **Userkaf** 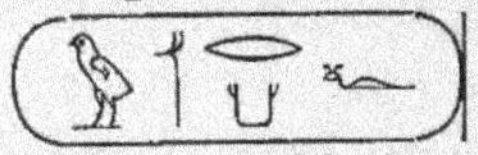, king of Egypt, about B.C. 3566. The deceased held the rank of *smer uāt*, and was a libationer and councillor, and performed administrative duties in connection with the palace. The hieroglyphics are in low relief, and are well cut. From Gîzah. Vth dynasty. Height 3 ft. 7 in., width 3 ft. [No. 1143.]

52. (*Vestibule. North Wall.*)—Limestone **lintel of a door** from the tomb of **Neka-ānkh** , a priest of the goddess Hathor, and of the tomb of **Userkaf,** king of Egypt, about B.C. 3560. The deceased, a figure of whom is cut at one end of the slab, held the rank of *smer*, and was a councillor, etc. The text records the names and titles of the deceased, and contains a prayer that funerary offerings may be brought to his tomb at the principal statutory feasts of the year. From Gîzah. Vth dynasty, about B.C. 3560. Length 12 ft., width 1 ft. 6 in. [No. 1275.]

53. (*Vestibule. South Wall.*)—Massive limestone **sepulchral stele,** in the form of a door, from the *maṣṭaba* tomb of **Ȧsȧ-ānkh** 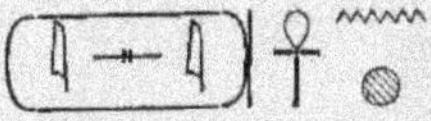, an *Utcheb* priest of Horus , a *smer uāt*, a councillor of the Ṭuat Chamber of Pharaoh , and a highly trusted and confidential servant 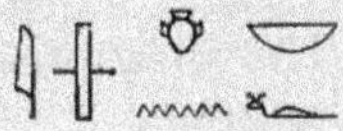 of King **Ṭeṭ-ka-Rā Ȧssȧ,** who reigned about B.C. 3360. On the upper portion of the stele is an inscription containing a prayer to Anubis, and below this is a tablet on which is sculptured a figure of the deceased, with a table of offerings before him and his name and chief titles cut above it. On the right and left are perpendicular lines of text containing prayers to Anubis and Ȧsa-ānkh's name and titles, and below these are figures of the deceased sculptured in low relief. From Ṣaḳḳârah. Vth dynasty. Height 10 ft. 6 in., width 5 ft. 5½ in., weight about 4¾ tons. [No. 1383.]

54–59. (*Vestibule. North and South Walls.*)—A series of fragments of limestone **reliefs**, from the tomb of a high official at Memphis, which are sculptured with scenes representing the preparation of food and the slaughter of a bull for a funeral feast, ministrants bearing offerings to the hall of the tomb, etc. From Gîzah. IVth or Vth dynasty, about B.C. 3600.

54.	Length	1 ft. 5 in.,	width	1 ft. 4 in.	[No. 864.]
55.	„	2 ft. 6 in.,	„	1 ft. 4 in.	[No. 865.]
56.	„	4 ft. 2 in.,	„	1 ft. 4 in.	[No. 866.]
57.	„	5 ft. 4 in.,	„	1 ft. 6 in.	[No. 867.]
58.	„	3 ft. 6 in.,	„	1 ft. 5 in.	[No. 868.]
59.	„	3 ft. 7 in.,	„	1 ft. 4 in.	[No. 869.]

60. (*Vestibule. South Wall.*) — Hard limestone **relief** sculptured with a figure of the royal kinswoman **Thethȧ** 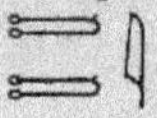. Very fine work. From Gîzah. Vth dynasty, about B.C. 3450. Height 2 ft. 5 in., breadth 1 ft. 2 in. [No. 1161.]

61. (*Vestibule. North Wall.*)—Limestone **relief** from the tomb of **Khnemu-ḥetep** 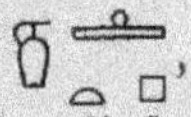, a *smer uāt* and chief of Nekheb, sculptured in sunk relief with a figure of the deceased, painted, seated before . Fine work. From Gîzah. Vth dynasty, about B.C. 3560. Length 2 ft. 5 in., breadth 2 ft. 2 in. [No. 1166.]

62. (*Vestibule. North Wall.*)—Portion of a limestone **relief** from the wall of a tomb of a councillor who flourished under the Ancient Empire. The inscription, which is formed of large hieroglyphics, cut in low relief, contains the names of a number of substances which were offered to the "double" of the deceased at funerary feasts. From Gîzah. Vth dynasty, about B.C. 3500. Height 3 ft. 7 in., width 2 ft. 1 in. [No. 1277.]

63. (*Vestibule. North Wall.*)—Limestone **sepulchral stele,** in the form of a door, from the tomb of **Uash-ka**, a priest of Rā-Harmachis and the governor of the granary of Memphis (?). On the upper part of the stele is sculptured a figure of the deceased, who is seated with his wife Tchefat, at a table of offerings, and on the sunk sides are figures of the sons and daughters of the deceased. From Gîzah. Vth dynasty, about B.C. 3400. Height 5 ft., width 1 ft. 10 in. [No. 1156.]

64. (*Vestibule.*)—Massive **sepulchral stele,** in the form of a door, from the tomb of **Tetȧ**, a priest and official of high rank. Within the doorway is a figure of the deceased who wears a wig, deep necklace or collar, and tunic, in the band of which is a dagger. Originally there was an inscription, traced in black ink, on each side of the doorway, but only a few signs are now legible. Fine work. From Ṣaḳḳârah. Vth dynasty, about B.C. 3500. Height 4 ft. 3 in., width 2 ft. 3 in. [No. 1165.]

65. (*Vestibule. South Wall.*)—Portion of a **sepulchral stele,** in the form of a door, from the tomb of **Utchu-ānkh**, a "royal kinsman" and inspector of the royal cattle. In the upper portion the deceased is seen seated with a table of offerings before him. On the right are five panels on which figures of offerings are sculptured, and on the left is a small false door, with elaborate decorations of the style of the IVth dynasty. The inscriptions record the name and titles of the deceased, and contain prayers for funerary offerings. From Gîzah. IVth or Vth dynasty. Length 3 ft. 11 in., breadth 2 ft. 11 in. [No. 1223.]

66. (*Vestibule. North Wall.*)—Limestone **relief** from the tomb of **Ptaḥ-uash**, a *smer uāt*, and *kher ḥeb* priest. The inscription, in large deeply-cut hieroglyphics, contains a prayer that sepulchral offerings may be provided at all the chief festivals throughout the year. On the left is sculptured in relief a figure of the deceased seated at a table of offerings. From Gîzah. IVth or Vth dynasty, about B.C. 3560. Length 5 ft. 10 in., breadth 1 ft. 3 in. [No. 1278.]

67. (*Vestibule. South Wall.*)—Pyramidal limestone **stele of Khuu**, a high official who held the rank of *kher ḥeb, smer uăt*, etc. Sams Collection. From Gîzah (?). IVth or Vth dynasty. Height 1 ft. 6 in. [No. 199.]

Sepulchral stele, with a figure of Tetà in high relief. [Vestibule, No. 64.]

68, 69. (*Vestibule. South Wall.*)—Portions of two limestone **reliefs** from the wall of a tomb of a high official at Memphis. The hieroglyphics, which are sculptured in relief, record the name of the "royal kinswoman" and princess **Bu-Nefer,** or **Bu-Nefer-f**. From Gîzah. IVth or

Vth dynasty. Length (No. 1273) 1 ft. 10 in., breadth 1 ft. 10 in.; (No. 1274) length 2 ft., breadth 1 ft. 10 in. [Nos. 1273, 1274.]

70. (*Vestibule. North Wall.*)—Limestone **relief** from the wall of a tomb of a high official, sculptured with figures of priests, ministrants, etc., bearing offerings for the funeral feast, and with a representation of the slaughter of a bull for the performance of the ceremony of "Opening the Mouth." From Gîzah or Ṣaḳḳârah. IVth or Vth dynasty, about B.C. 3560. Length 4 ft. 8 in., breadth 1 ft. 6 in. [No. 430.]

Presented by the Earl of Bute, 1767.

71. (*Vestibule. North Wall.*)—Portion of a **relief** from a wall of the tomb of an official, whose name is lost, sculptured with a scene in which the deceased, who is seated on a chair of state, is receiving offerings from his wife, who stands before the tablet for offerings, with her four children. IVth or Vth dynasty, about B.C. 3560. Length 1 ft. 10 in., breadth 1 ft. 4 in. [No. 1186.]

72. (*Bay* 2.)—Portion of a painted **relief** from the tomb of a high official on which are sculptured figures of the workmen, field labourers, and others who were employed on the estate of the deceased, engaged in the work of boat-building, harvesting, fishing, etc. In the second register is a representation of the women's quarters, and a number of men are seen running or dancing; among them is a male figure with pointed lions' ears on his head. From Gîzah. IVth or Vth dynasty, about B.C. 3560. Length 2 ft. 10½ in., breadth 1 ft. 7 in. [No. 994.]

73. (*Vestibule. North Wall.*)—Limestone **relief** from the tomb of **Ȧnt** , a royal kinswoman, sculptured with two lines of text and figures of her four children, three daughters and one son, whose names are: 1. Ȧnteth-sherȧu, 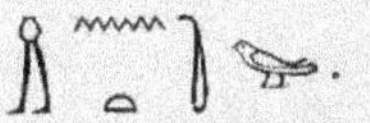. 2. . . . . . . Kheptȧ 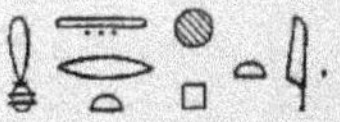. 3. Khent-kau-s . 4. Suten-kap . From Gîzah. Vth dynasty, about B.C. 3560. Height 3 ft. 8 in. width 1 ft. 8 in. [No. 1170.]

Sepulchral stele of Qarta, priest, chancellor, and librarian of Pepi I, king of Egypt, about B.C. 3230.

[Vestibule, North Wall, No. 75.] VIth dynasty.

SIXTH DYNASTY.

74. (*Vestibule. South Wall.*)—Limestone **stele** inscribed with a text, perhaps a decree, of the "Horus, **Seḥetep-taui,**"

i.e., of TETÀ, king of Egypt, about B.C. 3266. The hieroglyphics are so much decayed that it is impossible to give a connected rendering of the inscription, but it seems to refer to the granting of some land to the local god Khenti Àmenti by the king. The "chancellor and overseer, **Àssà-nekau,**(?)" 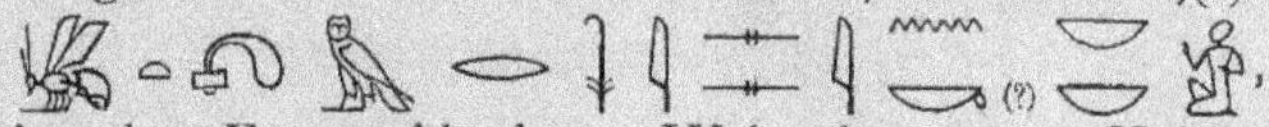, is mentioned. From Abydos. VIth dynasty. Height 4 ft. 7 in., width 1 ft. 11 in. [No. 626.]

Presented by the Egypt Exploration Fund, 1903.

75. (*Vestibule. North Wall.*)—Massive limestone **sepulchral stele** with cornice, in the form of a door from the tomb of **Qarta** , who flourished in the reign of **Pepi** (I), king of Egypt, about B.C. 3230, and was surnamed **Pepi-nefer** 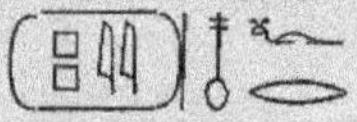 and **Rā-meri-nefer** 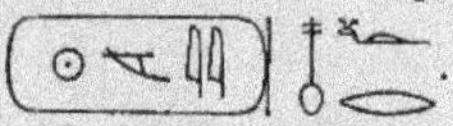. The deceased held the offices of governor of the temple, *smer uāt*, priest (*kher ḥeb*), keeper of the seal, and overseer of the library (?). The inscriptions contain prayers to Anubis and Osiris for funerary offerings. From Gîzah. VIth dynasty, about B.C. 3230. (**Plate II.**) Height 7 ft., width 4 ft. 3 in. [No. 1341.]

76. (*Vestibule. North Wall.*)—Limestone **sepulchral stele** in the form of a door, with a massive cornice, and thick, raised border, from the tomb of **Qarta** , who flourished in the reign of **Pepi I,** king of Egypt, about B.C. 3230, and was surnamed Pepi-nefer and Rā-meri-nefer. From Gîzah. VIth dynasty, about B.C. 3230. (See No. 75.) Height 4 ft. 10 in., width 2 ft. 10 in. [No. 1342.]

77. (*Vestibule. South Wall.*)—Stone **lintel** of a door, on which is sculptured the solar disk with wings and uraei.

Below is a line of inscription containing the prenomen of **Pepi II**, king of Egypt, about B.C. 3160. This slab was obtained from the temple of Osiris at Abydos. VIth dynasty. Length 4 ft. 10 in., breadth 10 in. [No. 627.]

Presented by the Egypt Exploration Fund, 1903.

78. (*Vestibule. South Wall.*)—Limestone **sepulchral** stele of **Nefer-Sennȧ**, a *smer uāt, kher ḥeb*, councillor, and keeper of the seal, who flourished in the reign of **Pepi II.** On the right is a figure of the deceased holding a staff and bearing the *kherp* sceptre in his left hand. From Denderah. VIth dynasty, about B.C. 3160. Length 1 ft. 8 in., width 1 ft. 5 in. [No. 1263.]

Presented by the Egypt Exploration Fund, 1898.

79. (*Vestibule. North Wall.*)—Small limestone **sepulchral stele,** in the form of a door, with a cornice ornamented with representations of palm leaves, from the tomb of **Heb-peri** (?), a high priestly official. The deceased held the rank of *smer*, and was a member of the company of priests whose duty it was to perform services of commemoration in the chapel attached to the pyramid of **Pepi II**, king of Egypt, about B.C. 3160. The text contains a prayer to Ȧnpu (Anubis) for sepulchral meals. From Ṣakḳârah (?) VIth dynasty. Height 2 ft. 2 in., width 1 ft. 5 in. [No. 212.]

80. (*Assyrian Saloon.*)—**Maṣṭaba tomb** of **Ur-ȧri-en-Ptaḥ**, a royal kinsman, royal scribe, royal libationer, and councillor who flourished in the reign of **Pepi Nefer-ka-Rā,** about B.C. 3160. On each side of the doorway is cut a figure of the deceased standing and holding a staff, and above these is a long limestone slab inscribed with a prayer that sepulchral offerings may be given to the deceased at all the great festivals of the year. The inside of the tomb is ornamented with the following scenes:

North Wall: The deceased inspecting the work of ploughing and reaping on his farm, servants fishing, carpenters making a pillow, donkeys carrying farm produce to the barns.

Sepulchral stele of Ur-àri-en-Ptaḫ, a scribe and libationer of Pepi II, king of Egypt, about B.C. 3160.

[Assyrian Saloon, No. 80.] VIth dynasty.

Sepulchral stele, in the form of a door, of Sennu, an inspector of agriculture.
[Bay 1, No. 81.] VIth dynasty, B.C. 3200.

South Wall: 1. The deceased and his wife Khent-kaut-s 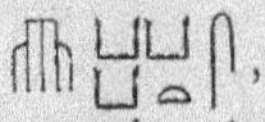, seated with offerings set before them and round about them. 2. Men-servants bringing offerings. 3. Butchers slaughtering cattle. 4. First "false door" inscribed with the names of about 90 offerings, and prayers to Osiris and Ànpu on behalf of the deceased; on the lower portion are sculptured in relief figures of the deceased. 5. The deceased and his wife seated as before, but facing in the opposite direction. 6. A harper, and a player on the pipes. 7. Dancing women. 8. Men-servants bearing offerings, birds, joints of meat, cakes, etc. 9. The slaughter of the cattle offered for sacrifice. 10. Second "false door," inscribed with prayers to Anubis on behalf of the wife of the deceased. On the upper portion Khent-kaut-s is represented seated at a table of offerings, and on the lower are figures of her, sculptured in relief.

East Wall: The deceased seated; men carrying to him offerings of birds, cattle, etc.

West Wall: The scenes are obliterated. From Ṣaḳḳârah. VIth dynasty. (**Plate III.**) [No. 718.]

81. (*Bay* 1.)—Limestone **sepulchral stele,** in the form of the door of a tomb, from the tomb of **Sennu** 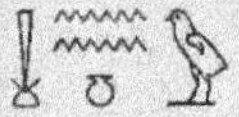, an inspector of agriculture. In the centre of the upper portion are figures of the deceased and his wife **Thentets** 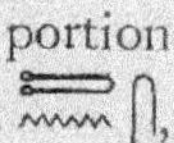, seated at a table of offerings, and on each side is a panel in which two of their children are bringing offerings. On the lower portion are figures of Sennu and Thentets, and of five of their children, three daughters and two sons. From Gîzah. VIth dynasty, about B.C. 3200. (**Plate IV.**) Height 2 ft. 10½ in., width 2 ft. [No. 1136.]

82. (*Vestibule.*)—Massive limestone **sepulchral stele,** on which is cut in outline and painted the representation of a "false door" of a tomb, with a palm-leaf cornice and a figure of the deceased seated with a tablet for offerings before him, hieroglyphic texts, etc. This slab was set up in memory of **Ptaḥ-ḥetep** 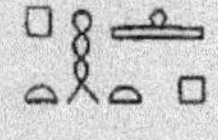, a *smer uāt* and priest, who prays to Ànpu for sepulchral offerings, and declares his devotion to Osiris. From Ṣakkârah. VIth dynasty, about B.C. 3200. Height 3 ft. 2½ in., width 2 ft. 8 in. [No. 1287.]

83. (*Vestibule. North Wall.*)—Inscribed limestone **relief** from the right side of the door of the tomb of **Erṭā-en-ānkh**, a royal kinsman, who held the offices of inspector, councillor, etc. The text contains the names and titles of the deceased, and a list of the offerings which were to be made to him on the great festivals throughout the year. On the lower portion of the slab is cut a figure of the deceased holding a staff and the *kherp* sceptre. From Gîzah. VIth dynasty, about B.C. 3333. Height 2 ft. 11 in., width 1 ft. 5 in. [No. 658.]

84. (*Vestibule. North Wall.*)—Limestone **relief** from the tomb of **Uthenȧa**, whose "good name" was **Penȧ**. Within a rectangular panel is cut in low, flat relief a figure of the deceased, wearing a deep collar. In his right hand he grasps a club or mace, and in his left, a bow, which was probably nearly six feet long. From Gîzah. VIth dynasty. Height 1 ft. 3½ in., width 9½ in. [No. 647.]

85. (*Vestibule. North Wall.*)—Massive limestone **sepulchral stele,** in the form of a door, from the tomb of **Ȧṭu**, a royal scribe, and priest, and libationer of the goddess Maāt, and superintendent of the Great House of Six. The text contains a prayer to Ȧnpu (Anubis), for a "royal table of offerings." On the flat surface in the middle of the doorway are the utchats. From Ṣakkârah. VIth dynasty, about B.C. 3200. Height 4 ft. 10 in., width 3 ft. 6 in. [No. 1191.]

86. (*Vestibule. South Wall.*)—Rectangular **sepulchral stele** of **Meṭu** (?), a *smer uāt*, and scribe, and civil and ecclesiastical official 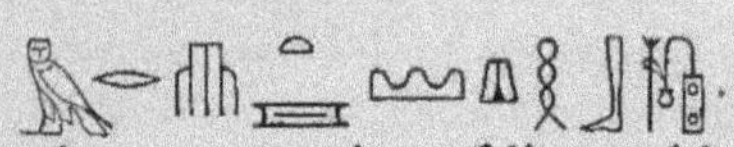. On the upper portion of the stele are a number of lines which are intended to represent a cornice of uraei, and below these are five lines of hieroglyphics in which the deceased is made to pray to Anubis and to Osiris Khenti-Amenti, for "a royal "table of offerings"; and to the "Great God" for sepulchral meats as a "lord of Abydos," and also for a "happy burial" in his sepulchre in Neter-Khert, *i.e.*, the Other World. Finally he is described as being a loyal devotee of "the Great God, the lord of Abydos." Below, in sunk relief, are figures of the deceased and the "son who loveth him"; the latter was, like his father, a *kher ḥeb*, or priest. From Ṣaḳḳârah. VIth dynasty. Height 3 ft., width 1 ft. 7 in. [No. 128.]

87. (*Vestibule. North Wall.*)—Portion of the upper part of a **sepulchral stele,** in the form of a door, from the tomb of the royal kinsman and scribe **Rā-nefer** 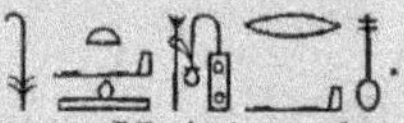. From Gîzah. VIth dynasty, about B.C. 3200. Height 7 in. width 10½ in. [No. 1011.]

Presented by the Rev. Greville Chester, B.A., 1886.

88. (*Vestibule. North Wall.*)—Massive limestone **sepulchral stele,** with cornice and raised, rounded band, in the form of a door, from the tomb of **Behennu** , a priestess of Hathor , and a royal favourite . On the upper part of the stele the deceased is seen seated with a table of offerings before her. From Gîzah. VIth dynasty. Height 6 ft. 7 in., width 3 ft. 7 in. [No. 1330.]

89. (*Vestibule. North Wall.*)—Limestone **sepulchral stele,** in the form of a door, from the tomb of **Pepi-seṭ** (?) 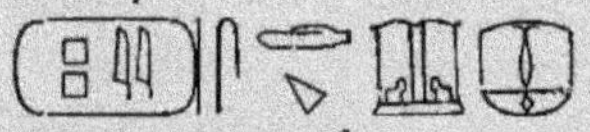, an official who held the rank of *smer uāt*, and was a superintendent of scribes. The text contains a prayer to Ȧnpu (Anubis) for a "royal table of offerings" and a happy burial. The cornice is painted in alternate stripes of green and red. From Gîzah. VIth dynasty, about B.C. 3200. Height 4 ft. 4 in., width 1 ft. 10 in. [No. 112.]

90. (*Vestibule. East Wall.*)—Portion of a limestone **roof-slab** from a tomb, the under surface of which is fluted, and is probably intended to imitate the wooden beams, or small tree trunks, of which roofs were formerly made. VIth dynasty (?), about B.C. 3200. Length 1 ft. 8 in., width 1 ft. 4 in. [No. 1293.] *Presented by the Egypt Exploration Fund*, 1899.

91. (*Vestibule. South Wall.*)—Limestone **sepulchral stele** of **Merer-Åqer**, an overseer of the priests. From Denderah. VIth dynasty, about B.C. 3200. Length 2 ft. 1 in., breadth 1 ft. 3 in. [No. 1264.]
Presented by the Egypt Exploration Fund, 1898.

92. (*Vestibule. South Wall.*)—Limestone **sepulchral stele** of **Menȧ**, a seal-bearer and governor of the palace. From Denderah. VIth dynasty, about B.C. 3200. Length 2 ft. 3 in., width 1 ft. 8 in. [No. 1262.]
Presented by the Egypt Exploration Fund, 1898.

93. (*Bay* 14.)—Limestone **libation tank** of the lady **Ȧntḳes**, inscribed with a prayer to Anubis for sepulchral offerings. From Gîzah. VIth dynasty. Length 1 ft., breadth 8½ in. [No. 1175.]

94. (*Bay* 14.)—Limestone **libation tank** of the lady **Khart-en-Khennu**, inscribed with a prayer to Anubis that funerary offerings may be made to her on the chief festivals of the year. From Gîzah. VIth dynasty. Length 1 ft., breadth 8½ in. [No. 1176.]

95. (*Bay* 14.)—Limestone **tablet for offerings** of **Senb**, on which are sculptured two circular flat bowls, between which is a standing figure of the deceased; below are two rectangular tanks. The text contains a prayer to Anubis that sepulchral offerings may be given to the deceased on several of the great annual festivals. From Ṣaḳḳârah. VIth dynasty. Length 1 ft. 2½ in., breadth 1 ft. 3½ in. [No. 1179.]

96. (*Vestibule. East Wall.*)—Limestone **sepulchral stele,** with rounded top, of **Rutch-āḥau**, a superintendent of priests. In the first register the preparation of the table of offerings is represented; in the second the deceased and his wife **Áṭena**  are seated, with a table of offerings before them, while priests and members of the family bear sepulchral gifts. In the third register are the cow and calf for sacrifice, and ministrants bearing offerings of unguents in vases, etc. Below are twelve lines of text which contain short speeches by various gods, and a declaration in which Rutch-āḥau affirms that he has neither committed sin nor spoken words of wickedness. This stele probably belongs to the period between the VIth and XIth dynasties. From Abydos. Salt Collection. Height 5 ft. 2 in., width 3 ft. 2 in. [No. 159.]

97. (*Vestibule. North Wall.*)—Limestone **sepulchral stele,** of pyramidal form, of **Sekheref** . On two sides of its lower portion are cut, in outline, figures of the deceased seated with a table of offerings before him; he holds a lotus flower to his nose. The text contains a prayer for funerary offerings. From the Salt Collection. VIth to XIth dynasty. Height 1 ft. 10 in., breadth at base 9 in. [No. 203.]

98. (*Vestibule. South Wall.*)—Limestone **sepulchral stele,** in the form of a door, from the maṣṭaba tomb of **Rā-en-ānkh** , on the jambs of which are inscribed the names of forty-eight offerings. Above is sculptured a seated figure of the deceased with a draught-board and offerings before him. From Ṣaḳḳârah. VIth dynasty. Height 2 ft. 6 in. [No. 1429.]

ELEVENTH DYNASTY.

99. (*Bay* 4.)—Rectangular limestone **sepulchral stele** of **Ȧntef** , an official who flourished in the reigns of the three following kings:—

Uaḥ-ānkh Ȧntef-āa .

Nekht-neb-ṭep-nefer Ȧntef 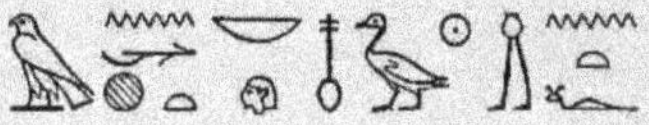.

Sānkh-ȧb-taui Menthu-ḥetep 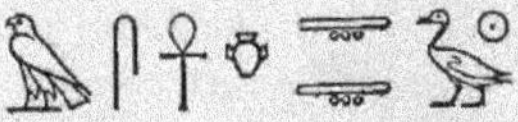

.

Below the text is sculptured a scene wherein a priest is represented making offerings to the deceased, who is followed by his three wives. The style of the work is of a most unusual character, and the mention of three successive kings of the XIth dynasty makes the monument one of first class importance for the history of the period. From Ḳûrnah. XIth dynasty. Length 3 ft. 3 in., breadth 2 ft. 3 in.

[No. 1203.]

100. (*Bay* 4.)—Rectangular limestone **sepulchral stele** of **Thethȧ** , a man of high rank, who filled several offices at Thebes in the reign of **Uaḥ-ānkh Ȧntef** 

, king of Egypt, about B.C. 2600. On the upper half of the stele are fourteen lines of text in which the deceased is made to describe his career, and his devotion and fidelity to his royal master. On the lower are five perpendicular lines of text and figures of the deceased and two of his sons, offerings, etc. The work is fine and good, and this stele is an excellent example of the best sculptor's work of the period. From Ḳûrnah. XIth dynasty. Height 5 ft., width 3 ft. 7 in. [No. 614.]

101. (*Bay* 4.)—Long, narrow piece of limestone, which formed the **over-lintel** of the tomb of **Thethȧ**, inscribed with a prayer that sepulchral offerings might be brought to his tomb at the great festivals of the year, and that he might possess the power of travelling happily over the ways of Amentet, and enjoy felicity therein. From Ḳûrnah. XIth dynasty. Length 4 ft. 7 in. [No. 614C.]

102. (*Bay* 4.)—Limestone **relief** from the side of the tomb of **Thethȧ** on which are sculptured figures of a daughter and two sons of the deceased who are bearing offerings of food to the tomb. From Ḳûrnah. XIth dynasty. Height 5 ft. 4 in., width 1 ft. [No. 614B.]

103. (*Bay* 4.)—Portion of a limestone **relief** from the tomb of **Thethȧ,** on which is sculptured a figure of a woman bearing on her head a vessel containing food for the deceased, and holding a duck in her left hand. From Ḳûrnah. XIth dynasty. Height 1 ft. 9 in., width 11 in. [No. 614A.]

104. (*Bay* 3.)—Painted limestone **head of a statue** of **Neb-ḥapt-Rā Menthu-ḥetep,** king of Egypt about B.C. 2600. The king is represented in the form of Osiris, and wears the White Crown, or Crown of the South; above the forehead is an uraeus. From the temple of Menthu-ḥetep at Dêr al-Baḥarî. XIth dynasty. Height 1 ft. 10 in. [No. 720.]

105. (*Bay* 3.)—Portion of a **painted relief** with a representation of King **Neb-ḥapt-Rā Menthu-ḥetep** embraced by the god Rā. From the temple of Menthu-ḥetep at Dêr al-Baḥarî. XIth dynasty. Height 2 ft. 4 in., width 1 ft. 8 in. [No. 1397.]

106. (*Bay* 3.)—Limestone **relief** sculptured with a figure of King **Neb-ḥapt-Rā Menthu-ḥetep,** seated on his throne; in front of him is his prenomen . XIth dynasty, about B.C. 2600. Height 1 ft. 9 in., width 1 ft. 9 in. [No. 721.]

107. (*Bay* 3.)—Portion of a **relief** with a painted portrait, in relief, of **Neb-ḥapt-Rā Menthu-ḥetep.** XIth dynasty, about B.C. 2600. Length 1 ft. 9 in. [No. 722.]

108. (*Bay* 3.)—Portion of a **relief** sculptured with a figure of the king grasping an **Āamu,** or Semite, by one leg. XIth dynasty, about B.C. 2600. Length 2 ft. 1 in. [No. 731.]

109. (*Bay* 3.)—Portion of a **relief** sculptured with a painted **figure of an Āamu,** or Semite. XIth dynasty, about B.C. 2600. Height 1 ft. 3 in., width 1 ft. 0½ in. [No. 730.]

110. (*Bay* 3.)—**Relief** sculptured with a painted figure of a **hippopotamus.** XIth dynasty, about B.C. 2600. Length 1 ft. 6 in. [No. 752.]

111. (*Bay* 3.)—Portion of a **relief** sculptured with a **figure of a prince** named Menthu-ḥetep , holding a bow and arrow. XIth dynasty, about B.C. 2600. Height 1 ft. 9½ in. [No. 729.]

112. (*Bay* 3.)—Limestone slab from the **lining of a wall,** with painted frieze and a figure of the vulture-goddess Nekhebit, in relief. XIth dynasty, about B.C. 2600. Height 1 ft. 10½ in., width 1 ft. 3 in. [No. 750.]

113. (*Bay* 3.)—Limestone slab from the **lining of a wall** sculptured, in relief, with painted figures of **herdsmen.** XIth dynasty, about B.C. 2600. Length 2 ft. 5 in. [No. 742.]

114. (*Bay* 3.)—Limestone **relief** sculptured with figures of **slaughtered Āamu** (Semites). XIth dynasty, about B.C. 2600. Height 1 ft. 8½ in., width 2 ft. 1½ in. [No. 732.]

115. (*Bay* 3.)—Fragment of a **relief** on which are sculptured the ram-headed bow of a **boat** and the figure of a man holding a whip in his hand. XIth dynasty, about B.C. 2600. Length 1 ft. 3 in. [No. 745.]

116. (*Bay* 3.)—Limestone slab from the **lining of a wall** on which are sculptured figures of high officials in procession; in the centre is **Bebȧ,** a judge. XIth dynasty, about B.C. 2600. Length 3 ft. 5 in. [No. 724.]

117. (*Bay* 3.)—Slab from the **lining of a wall** inscribed **Sma Taui** , "Uniter of the Two Lands," *i.e.*, Uniter of Upper and Lower Egypt, the *ka*-name of King Neb-ḥapt-Rā Menthu-ḥetep. XIth dynasty, about B.C. 2600. Length 1 ft. 3½ in. [No. 753.]

Stele set up by Seḥetep-âb to the memory of his father Khensu-user and his mother Nekhtâ-Ânkh.

[Bay 3, No. 121.] XIth or XIIth dynasty.

118. (*Bay* 3.)—Portion of an **inscription** referring to the **overthrow of the Āamu** (Semites) by King **Neb-ḥapt-Rā Menthu-ḥetep**; on the left is his prenomen *Neb-ḥapt-Rā* . XIth dynasty, about B.C. 2600. Length 1 ft. 6½ in. [No. 754.]

Nos. 104–118 all came from the temple of Menthu-ḥetep at Dêr al-Baḥarî.

Presented by the Egypt Exploration Fund, 1906.

119. (*Bay* 4.)—Sandstone slab inscribed with a **list of the offerings** made to the statue of King **Neb-ḥapt-Rā**  **Menthu-ḥetep.** From the temple of Osiris at Abydos. XIth dynasty, about B.C. 2600. Length 3 ft. 4 in., breadth 1 ft. 3 in. [No. 628.]

Presented by the Egypt Exploration Fund, 1903.

120. (*Bay* 4.)—White limestone **sepulchral stele** of **Sebek-āa** , an overseer of transport, inscribed with a prayer to Ȧnpu and Osiris, the great god Khenti Ȧmenti, for sepulchral offerings. On it, cut in relief, are the following scenes:—1. A youth pouring out a libation before Sebek-āa. 2. The deceased seated receiving a leg of beef. 3. Women making bread for the funeral feast. 4. Sebek-āa lying on his bier and embracing a child. 5. Sebek-āa standing with his wife and children whilst men bring offerings of a goat, a bull, and numbers of different kinds of geese and feathered fowl. The figures in relief are painted, and there are traces of colour in the hieroglyphics. From Thebes (Ḳûrnah). XIth dynasty, about B.C. 2600. Height 2 ft., width 1 ft. 10 in. [No. 1372.]

121. (*Bay* 3.)—Rectangular limestone **stele,** set up by **Seḥetep-ȧb** to the memory of his father **Khensu-user** , his mother **Nekhtȧ-Ānkh,** and other relatives. In the first register Seḥetep-ȧb is seen pouring out a libation before his father and mother, and in the three other registers various members of the family are making offerings to their deceased relatives. XIth dynasty (?) (**Plate V.**) Height 1 ft. 9¼ in., width 10 in. [No. 643.]

C

122. (*Bay* 2.)—White limestone **sepulchral stele,** in the form of a door of a tomb, with palm-leaf cornice and a raised, rounded border, within which are cut, in outline, figures of the deceased **Menthu-sa**, who is sitting in a chair of state, with a table of offerings before him. By the side of the table stands a woman. The text contains a prayer to Menthu for sepulchral offerings, and mentions the mother of the deceased Menthu-su (?) and the "lady of the house," Neter-mesu, daughter of Merit-àtefs . XIth dynasty. Height 1 ft., width 9 in. [No. 1313.]

123. (*Vestibule. North Wall.*)—Dark granite **stele inscribed with prayers** to "Osiris, lord of Ṭaṭṭu, great god, "lord of Abydos," for sepulchral offerings on behalf of **Mentu-ḥetep**, the son of the lady Neferttu, the overseer of the office wherein the share of the crops claimed by the Government was assessed. On the left, in sunk relief, is sculptured a figure of the deceased, who holds a staff and the sceptre in his hands. From the Sams Collection, 1835. XIth dynasty, about B.C. 2500. Height 1 ft 11 in., width 1 ft. 3 in. [No. 187.]

124. (*Bay* 2.)—White limestone **sepulchral stele,** in the form of a door of a tomb, with palm-leaf cornice, and raised, rounded border. On it are cut, in outline, scenes representing **Shesu-Ḥeru-mer** and **Seānkhȧ**, "the life of the city," seated with a table of offerings between them, and **Nekhtȧ** seated at a table of offerings. The text contains a prayer for the usual sepulchral offerings. The first named sits on a chair of state, and holds a whip. Above the cornice is the name of the artisan (?) who cut the stone—Ren-senb. From Akhmîm. XIth dynasty (?) Height 1 ft. 6½ in., width 11 in. [No. 1312.]

125. (*Vestibule. South Wall.*)—Portion of a **relief** from the wall of a tomb, on which is sculptured the figure of a man leading an ox for sacrifice at the funeral feast; behind follows a man who urges on the animal with a stick. Above the ox are inscribed the words which are addressed to the deceased: "driving an ox to thy double." From Denderah. XIth dynasty, about B.C. 2600. Length 2 ft. 7 in., breadth 1 ft. 4 in. [No. 1260.]

Presented by the Egypt Exploration Fund, 1898.

126. (*Bay* 5.)—Portion of a **relief** from the wall of a tomb, on which are sculptured figures of a **herdsman, a cow,** etc. XIth dynasty, or earlier. Height 1 ft. 3 in., width 1 ft. 2 in. [No. 451.]

127. (*Vestibule.*)—Black granite seated statue of **Menthu-āa,** the son of the lady Mert  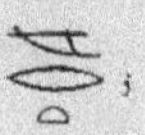; an Erpā and Hā prince, a councillor and priest, who probably flourished at the end of the XIth or beginning of the XIIth dynasty. The sides of the rectangular throne on which he sits are inscribed with his name and titles, in large, bold hieroglyphics. XIth or XIIth dynasty, about B.C. 2500. Height of figure 3 ft. 2 in., with throne 3 ft. 7 in. [No. 100.]

Seated statue of Menthu-āa, a prince, priest, and councillor.
XIth or XIIth dynasty.
[Vestibule, No. 127.]

128. (*Bay* 1.)—**Sepulchral stele,** with rounded top, set up by **Menthu-ḥetep** , the overseer of the priests, in honour of his mother **Nefertut** , who was surnamed **Neferu-**

enen , so that "her name might live upon "earth." On the upper portion is inscribed a prayer to Osiris Khenti Àmenti and Àp-uat for funerary offerings, and on the lower is a scene in which the family of the deceased are represented bringing offerings to her. The whole is enclosed within a border. Salt Collection. From Abydos. XIth or XIIth dynasty. About B.C. 2500. Height 2 ft. 10 in., width 1 ft. 7 in. [No. 152.]

129. (*Bay* 1.)—Rectangular limestone **sepulchral stele** of **User-ur** , son of the lady Sat-nebt-nut (?) , a sculptor. On the upper portion are five lines of text containing prayers to the chief gods of the dead, and an address to the living to pray that an abundant supply of funerary food may be provided for him. Below are:—1. Figures of the deceased and his wife seated at a table of offerings, "his wife Amenàsat," his son Senefer, and two relatives.—2. Figures of one son and seven daughters offering lilies (?) The cutting of the figures was not finished; see the left-hand bottom corner. This stele is of special interest because the red lines of the canon to which the mason worked are in many places still visible. XIth or XIIth dynasty. Height 1 ft. 8½ in., width 1 ft. 6½ in. [No. 579.]

130. (*Bay* 1.)—White limestone **sepulchral stele,** with palm-leaf cornice and raised border, set up in honour of **Àqer-ur,** or **Àqer the Elder,** , the son of Pert. In the first division are sculptured, in low relief, figures of the deceased seated at tables of offerings, and figures of his children standing before him. In the four following divisions are figures, in sunk relief, of the sons and daughters of the deceased by his three wives, seated and smelling lotus flowers. From Abydos. XIth or XIIth dynasty, B.C. 2500. Height 2 ft. 7 in., width 1 ft. 7 in. [No. 131.]

131. (*Vestibule. South Wall.*)—Portion of a large limestone tablet inscribed with **a list of offerings** which were to be made to a tomb or temple. From Denderah. XIth or XIIth dynasty, about B.C. 2500. Height 3 ft. 0½ in., width 2 ft. 2 in. [No. 1172.]

132. (*Bay* 4.)—Portion of a painted limestone **relief** on which is sculptured a figure of **Nekhtà**, the son of Ḥeteptu, who is represented making sepulchral offerings to his father. XIth or XIIth dynasty. Height 10¾ in., width 10 in. [No. 1315.]

Sepulchral stele of Àqer-ur, sculptured with figures of his three wives, and his sons and daughters.
XIth or XIIth dynasty.
[Bay 1, No. 130.]

133. (*Vestibule. East Wall.*)—Limestone **sepulchral stele** of **Àntef,** the son of the lady **Qeḥet**, a "real kinsman "of the king", who was attached to the service of the king's sanctuary, and superintended the royal preserves of water-fowl and cattle. Below the text the deceased and his wife, **Àmen-Sat** , are seen seated at a table of offerings, and in the lower register are figures of his four daughters and one son. Across the tablet below these is a red and yellow band. XIth or XIIth dynasty. Height 2 ft. 5 in., width 1 ft. 8 in. [No. 582.]

134. (*Bay* 4.)—Rectangular **limestone stele** from the tomb of **Àntef,** the son of the lady **Màit** 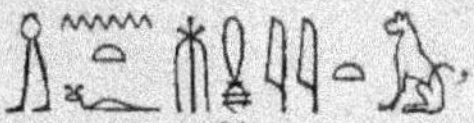, an Erpā and official who held several important offices under one of the kings of the XIth or XIIth dynasty. On the right is sculptured a figure of the deceased holding a staff and the *kherp* sceptre, receiving offerings from his son, and to the left are fourteen lines of hieroglyphic texts wherein his virtues and devotion are set forth. From Ḳûrnah. XIth or XIIth dynasty. Length 3 ft. 10 in., breadth 2 ft. 6¾ in. [No. 1164.]

135. (*Vestibule. North Wall.*)—Limestone slab, inscribed with a text in deeply cut hieroglyphics, containing a **prayer to Ànpu** (Anubis), lord of the city of Sepau , on behalf of **En-Àntef-àqer** , that sepulchral offerings may be provided for him. From Denderah. XIth or XIIth dynasty, about B.C. 2500. Length 3 ft. 8 in., breadth 1 ft. 3 in. [No. 1261.]

Presented by the Egypt Exploration Fund, 1898.

MIDDLE EMPIRE.

TWELFTH DYNASTY.

136. (*Bay* 5.)—Massive red granite **stele,** with rounded top, on which are sculptured a winged disk, figures of the gods Khnemu and Sati, the Horus name of **Usertsen I,** B.C. 2430, and six lines of hieroglyphic text recording the benefactions of the king to the gods of the First Cataract. From Philae. XIIth dynasty. Height 3 ft. 7 in., width 2 ft. 1 in. [No. 963.]

Stele of Usertsen I, king of Egypt, B.C. 2430. [Bay 5, No. 136.]

137. (*Bay* 1.)—Red granite **head of a** colossal **statue of Usertsen I** (?), king of Egypt, about B.C. 2430, wearing the *Ḥetch* or White Crown [hieroglyph], of Upper Egypt. Above the forehead is the uræus [hieroglyph], symbol of sovereignty. From Memphis. XIIth dynasty. Height 2 ft. 6 in. [No. 615.]

138. (*Bay* 3.)—Rectangular, painted **limestone stele** of **Àthi** [hieroglyphs], the son of the lady Sebek-sat, which was set up in his tomb in the fourteenth year of the reign of

Usertsen I , king of Egypt, about B.C. 2430. On the upper portion are four lines of text recording the services of the deceased to his king, and below are scenes in which the sons and daughters of the deceased and his wife, Àurâ , are making offerings to their parents. Fine, carefully executed work. The text contains no prayer for sepulchral offerings. Belmore Collection. XIIth dynasty. **(Plate VI.)** Height 2 ft. 1 in., width 1 ft. 6 in. [No. 586.]

139. (*Bay* 3.)—Rough sandstone **sepulchral stele,** with rounded top, of **Neferu** , the son of the lady Merrt 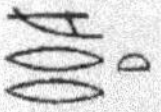, overseer of the boats or barges  at Behen (Wâdî Ḥalfah), who flourished in the reign of **Usertsen I,** king of Egypt, about B.C. 2430. In the centre of the upper portion is cut the prenomen of Usertsen I ; on the right is the hawk of Horus, lord of Behen, and on the left the hawk of Horus, lord of the mountains. The inscription contains a prayer for funerary offerings. From Wâdî Ḥalfah. XIIth dynasty. Height 1 ft. 10 in., width 1 ft. 1 in. [No. 489.]

140. (*Bay* 1.)—Rectangular **limestone stele** of **Àntef** , the son of Sebek-unnu , and the lady Sent 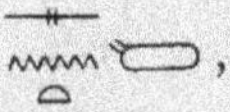, an overseer of the private apartments of the royal palace. On the upper half of the stele are fourteen lines of text, containing prayers for sepulchral offerings, and a description of the good works of the deceased. Below these are reliefs in which the deceased and his father and mother are seen seated with a table of offerings before them, and rows of figures of the principal members of their family. The stele is dated in the thirty-ninth year of **Usertsen I,** king of Egypt, about B.C. 2430 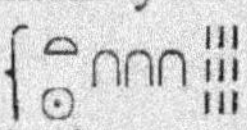 . . . . . 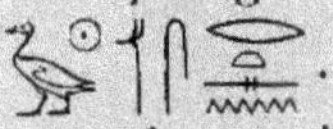. See also stele No. 141 and the statue No. 142. Anastasi Collection. XIIth dynasty. Heigth 3 ft. 7 in., width 1 ft. 6 in. [No. 572.]

141. (*Bay* 3.)—Lower portion of a rectangular limestone **sepulchral stele** of **Àntef** , the son of the lady Sent

Sepulchral stele of Åthi, who died in the fourteenth year of the reign of Usertsen I.

[Bay 3, No. 138.] XIIth dynasty

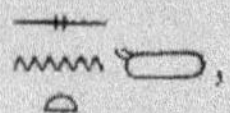, an overseer of certain royal apartments, inscribed with fifteen lines of well-cut hieroglyphics, wherein he describes his virtues and the fidelity of his service to his king. In the left bottom corner is a figure of the deceased leaning upon a staff; he appears to have been lame. Ȧntef flourished in the reign of **Usertsen I,** about B.C. 2430. For another stele from his tomb see No. **140** (572), and for his statue see No. **142** (461). Anastasi Collection. XIIth dynasty. Height 1 ft. 11½ in., width 1 ft. 7½ in. [No. 562.]

142. (*Bay* 3.)—Seated limestone **statue,** with a deep base, of **Ȧntef,** the son of the lady Sent; from the stele No. 140 (572) we learn that the name of his father was **Sebek-unnu,** and that he flourished in the reign of **Usertsen I.** He was the overseer of a portion of the royal apartments, and he holds in his right hand the symbol of his office, in the form of a cord (?) doubled. The inscriptions contain a dedication to Osiris and Anubis. From the Anastasi Collection. XIIth dynasty, about B.C. 2430. Height 2 ft. 1½ in. [No. 461.]

143, 144. (*Bay* 1.)—Rectangular **limestone stele,** with painted palm-leaf cornice, of **Ḥet-ḥert-sa,** or **Sa-Hathor,** , a high official who flourished in the reign of **Ȧmen-em-ḥāt II** 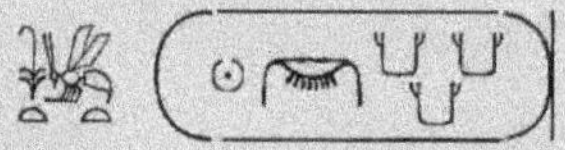, about B.C. 2400. On the upper portion of the stele are four lines of text containing prayers for sepulchral offerings, and below this is a relief in which the deceased is seen seated at a table of offerings. Opposite to him is his mother Ȧst-meri, daughter of Ḥetepi. Below, in a niche, the sides of which are decorated with painted figures of Sa-Hathor and texts, is a **seated figure** (No. 144) of the deceased. To the right and left of the niche are lines of hieroglyphics which state that Sa-Hathor went several times to the Sûdân, where he superintended the working of the mines and the washing of the gold. Anastasi Collection. XIIth dynasty. Height 3 ft. 9 in., width 2 ft. 1 in. [Nos. 569, 570.]

145. (*Bay* 6.)—Fine painted **limestone stele** of **Sa-Menthu** 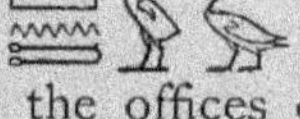, an Erpā, Ḥā prince, and *Smer uāt*, who held the offices of royal scribe and overseer of works. In his inscription he says that he was born in the reign of

Åmen-em-ḥāt I, that he was appointed scribe by **Usertsen I**, and was promoted by him to other offices; the stele is dated in the third year of the reign of **Åmen-em-ḥāt II**, when, presumably, Sa-Menthu died. Anastasi Collection. XIIth dynasty. Height 4 ft. 5 in., width 1 ft. 7½ in. [No. 828.]

146. (*Bay* 1.)—Fine white limestone **sepulchral stele,** with rounded top, of **Khenti-em-semti**, son of the lady Åst-Åthi, an official of Åmen-em-ḥāt II, king of Egypt, about B.C. 2400. On this stele are twenty-two lines of hieroglyphic text in which the deceased enumerates the services which he rendered to his sovereign, and the works which he carried out in connection with the restoration of the temples of the gods. On the rounded portion of the stele is sculptured a winged disk, and in the left bottom corner are figures of the deceased and his mother. Anastasi Collection. XIIth dynasty, about B.C. 2400. (**Plate VII.**) Height 3 ft., width 1 ft. 7¼ in. [No. 574.]

147. (*Bay* 1.)—Fine white limestone **sepulchral stele,** with rounded top, of **Khenti-em-set (semt)-ur**, a royal kinsman, a councillor, and priest of the pyramid of king **Åmeni (Åmen-em-ḥāt II)**. Below the eleven lines of text are figures of the deceased, his wife Hathor-em-ḥāt, his daughter Semti-seneb, and his brother, Ba[k]-en-re-Mut. Anastasi Collection. XIIth dynasty, about B.C. 2300. Height 2 ft. 9 in., width 1 ft. 3 in. [No. 839.]

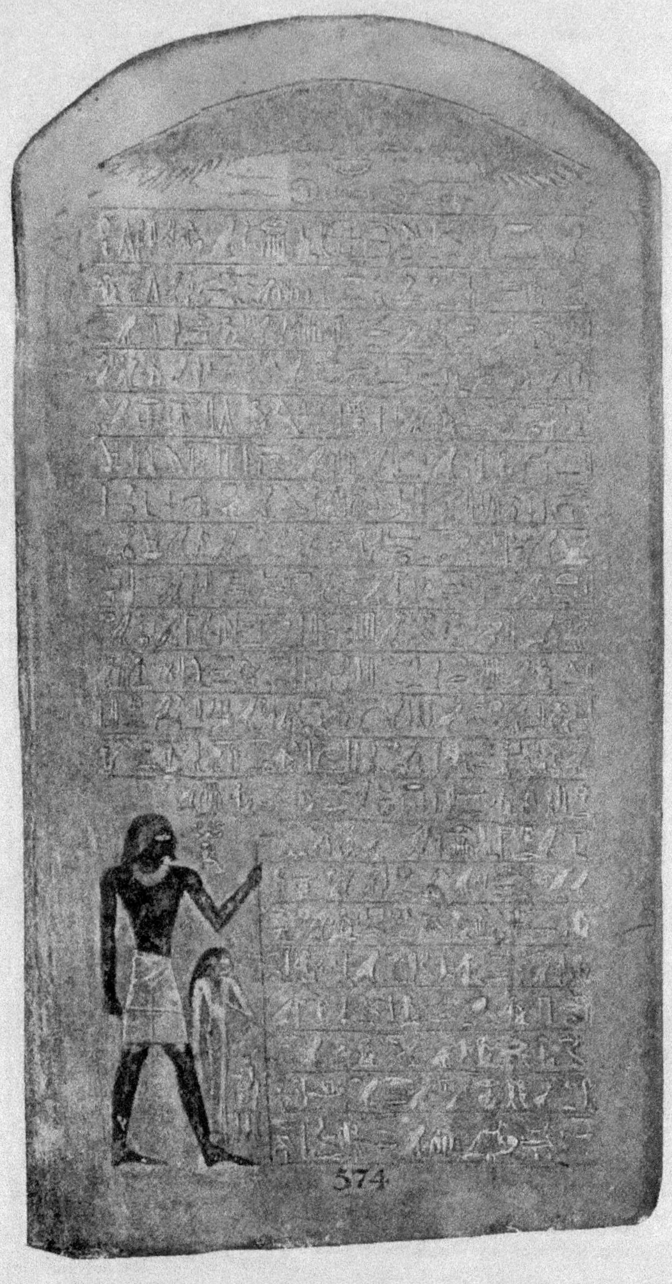

Sepulchral stele of Khenti-em-semti, a builder and architect who flourished in the reign of Ȧmen-em-ḥāt II, about B.C. 2400.
[Bay 1, No. 146.]

148. (*Bay* 5.)—Limestone **door-socket,** dated in the thirtieth year of **Ȧmen-em-ḥāt II** 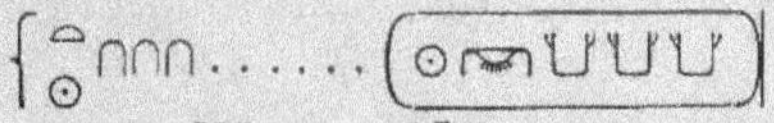. XIIth dynasty. 1 ft. 2 in. square. [No. 1236.]

Presented by G. Willoughby Fraser, Esq., 1897.

149. (*Bay* 1.)—Lower portion of a red sandstone seated **figure of** the goddess **Hathor** (?), which was dedicated by the captain of the boats, **Seneferu,** the son of Māket  , who flourished in the reign of **Ȧmen-em-ḥāt II** 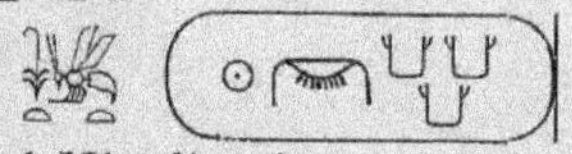, about B.C. 2400. From Ṣarâbît al-Khâdim, in the peninsula of Sinai. XIIth dynasty. Height 1 ft. 1 in. [No. 497.]

Presented by the Egypt Exploration Fund, 1905.

150. (*Bay* 1.)—Fine limestone **sepulchral stele,** with rounded top, of **Ȧmen-em-ḥāt** , an official,[1] inscribed with twenty-seven lines of hieroglyphic text containing prayers to Osiris, Anubis, Ḥeqt, and Khnemu, for funerary offerings and for happiness in the Other World. On the left-hand bottom corner is sculptured in low relief a figure of the deceased. This stele is dated in the thirteenth year of **Ȧmen-em-ḥāt II,** king of Egypt about B.C. 2400

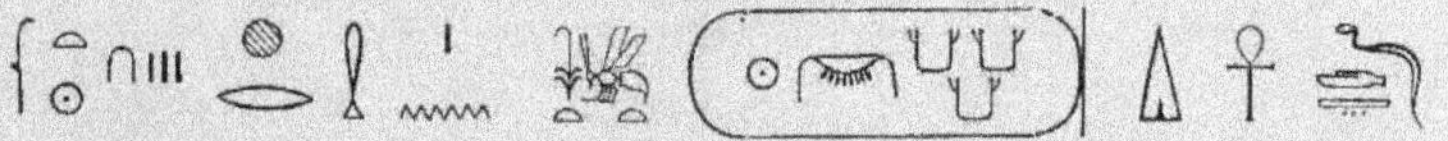.

Anastasi Collection. XIIth dynasty. Height 3 ft. 5 in., width 2 ft. 1 in. [No. 567.]

151. (*Bay* 7.)—White limestone **sepulchral stele,** with rounded top, set up to commemorate **Seḥetep-ȧb** 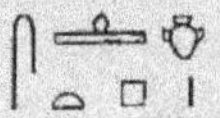, the son of Sat-Nefert, and his wife Ren-s-ānkh, and **Rāu,** (or Erṭāu) , son of Senȧ, and his wife Sat-nefert, in the nineteenth year of the reign of **Ȧmen-em-ḥāt II** 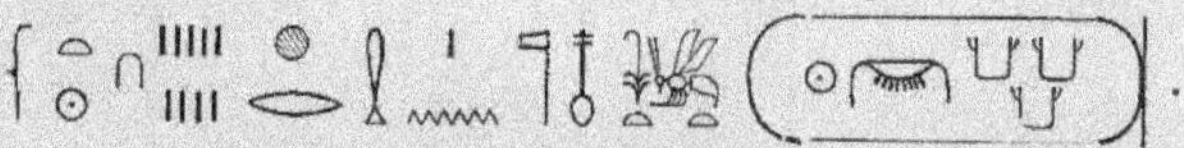. On the

[1] 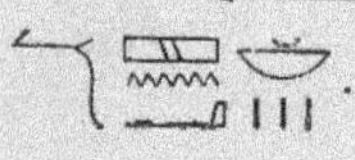.

upper portion is cut a winged disk, with pendent uræi, and below are:—1. A text giving the date of the stele. 2. A list of the various objects of a "Table of Offerings" arranged in rows. On each side of this are figures of relatives of Seḥetep-àb and Rāu, and on the lower portion are figures of the deceased seated in pairs, with a table of offerings before them. Seḥetep-àb and Rāu were each the governor of a temple, and each was . Anastasi Collection. XIIth dynasty, about B.C. 2400. Height 2 ft. 2 in., width 1 ft. 7½ in. [No. 583.]

152. (*Bay* 5.)—Rectangular painted limestone **sepulchral stele** of **Menu-Nefer** 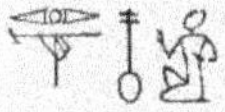, an overseer of the private apartments of the palace, inscribed with an address in which the living are entreated to pray that sepulchral offerings may be given to the deceased. On the lower portion is a scene representing the sons and daughters of Menu-nefer performing ceremonies of adoration and bearing offerings to him, and behind him stands his mother Ànnu . The stele is dated in the twenty-ninth year of the reign of **Àmen-em-ḥāt II** 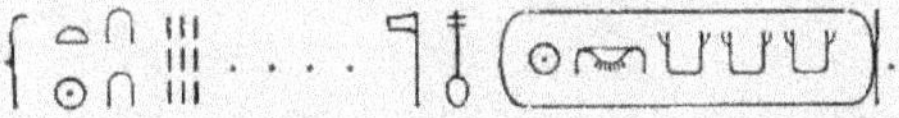. Anastasi Collection. XIIth dynasty. Height 2 ft. 1 in., width 1 ft. 9 in. [No. 829.]

153. (*Bay* 3.)—Limestone **sepulchral stele,** with rounded top, of **Seneferu** , the son of Sat-àfu 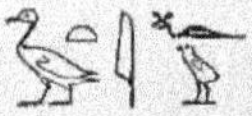, an overseer of certain royal apartments, and prefect of the temple of **Àmen-em-ḥāt II** 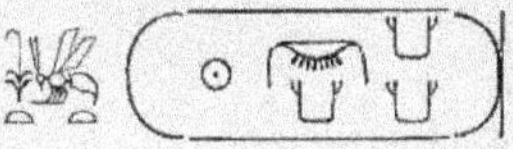, king of Egypt, about B.C. 2400. The text contains a prayer to Khenti Àmenti that sepulchral offerings may be given to the deceased, and, presumably, to thirteen of his relatives whose names, with those of their mothers, are inscribed above. On the lower portion of the stele is a figure of Seneferu receiving offerings from the principal members of his family. Sams Collection. XIIth dynasty. Height 1 ft. 5¼ in., width 1 ft. 2½ in.

[No. 256.]

154. (*Bay* 1.)—Fine limestone **sepulchral stele** of **Sen-àtef**, son of the lady **Reḥu-ānkh,** overseer of the private royal apartments in the palace of king **Àmen-em-ḥāt II.** On the rounded portion are cut in outline representations of offerings, and below are:—1. A figure of the deceased holding a staff and the sceptre; near his head is the prenomen of the king **Nub-kau-Rā**, and before him are his two brothers bearing offerings; 2. Figures of his wife, son, and three daughters. XIIth dynasty, about B.C. 2400. Height 1 ft. 11½ in., width 1 ft. 2 in.

[No. 576.]

155. (*Bay* 9.)—Limestone stele, in the form of a **table of offerings,** of **Sebek-ḥetep**, a boat-builder, inscribed with a prayer to Osiris for sepulchral offerings. Below are figures of the deceased and his wife Ken, seated, with a table of offerings before them, and to the right are figures of their sons, Mentu and Àmen-em-ḥāt, paying homage to their parents. This stele was set up in the sixth year of the reign of **Usertsen II** .... Sams Collection. XIIth dynasty. Height 1 ft., width 9 in.

[No. 257.]

156. (*Bay* 1.)—Fine limestone **sepulchral stele,** with rounded top, of **Tchaa**, a guardian of the palace (?). The upper portion is inscribed with thirteen lines of hieroglyphic text containing prayers to Osiris, Ḥeqt, and Khnemu for funerary offerings. Below these is a relief wherein the deceased is seen seated at a table of offerings, and figures of his mother, brethren, and sisters are represented bringing offerings to him. This stele is dated in the sixth year of the reign of **Usertsen II,** about B.C. 2360

Anastasi Collection. XIIth dynasty. Height 3 ft. 8 in., width 1 ft. 11 in. [No. 573.]

157. (*Vestibule. East Doorway.*)—Lower portion of a black granite seated **statue of Sa-Renput** *i.e.*, "the Child of the Years," the son of Satet-ḥetep, the governor-general of Ta-Kenset, *i.e.*, of Northern Nubia, under the XIIth dynasty, about B.C. 2300. The deceased held the rank of *Erpā*, *Ḥā*, *Smer-uāt*, and *Khetemet*, or "Chancellor," and he was the "Superintendent of the prophets of Satet," or Sati, a goddess of the region of the First Cataract and Ābu, or Elephantine, *i.e.*, the modern Aswân. He is described as, and he was especially a devotee of "Anpu (Anubis) on his hill." His tomb is on the west bank of the Nile at Aswân, and is one of the finest of those of the governors of Elephantine. Height 2 ft. 3 in. [No. 1010.]

Presented by Field Marshal Lord Grenfell, 1887.

58. (*Bay* 1.)—Fine dark grey granite **statue of Usertsen III,** king of Egypt, about B.C. 2330, as a young man (?). He wears the full wig with a plaited tail, which is characteristic of the period, a necklace with pendant, and a closely pleated tunic which projects over his knees; from his girdle hangs a long lappet, ornamented with uraei at the end. The handle of a dagger is seen projecting from the belt, in the centre of which is the king's prenomen Khā-kau-Rā . On the plinth at the back of the statue are cut the king's Horus name and his name as king of the South and North. Found in the south court of the temple of Menthu-ḥetep (Neb-ḥapt-Rā) at Dêr al-Baḥarî. XIIth dynasty. Height 4 ft. 11 in. [No. 684.]

Horus name of Usertsen III.

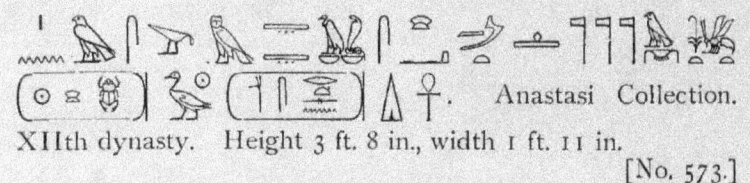

Presented by the Egypt Exploration Fund, 1905.

159. (*Bay* I.)—Fine dark grey granite **statue of Usertsen III,** king of Egypt, about B.C. 2330, as a young man (?). This statue is similar to No. 160, but the king's name of Usertsen , instead of his prenomen, appears on his belt. Found in the south court of the temple of Menthu-ḥetep (Neb-ḥapt-Rā) at Dêr al-Baḥarî. XIIth dynasty. Height 4 ft. 11 in. [No. 685.]

Presented by the Egypt Exploration Fund, 1905.

160. (*Bay* 3.)—Fine, dark grey granite **statue of Usertsen III,** king of Egypt, about B.C. 2330; the sculptor appears to have intended to represent the face of a man who is no longer young. This statue is similar to No. 159. Found in the south court of the temple of Menthu-ḥetep (Neb-ḥapt-Rā) at Dêr al-Baḥarî. XIIth dynasty. Height 4 ft. 7 in. [No. 686.]

Presented by the Egypt Exploration Fund, 1905.

161. (*Bay* I.)—Red granite **head of** a colossal **statue of Usertsen III,** king of Egypt, about B.C. 2330, wearing the *Ḥetch*, or White Crown , of Upper Egypt. Above the forehead is the uraeus , symbol of sovereignty. From Abydos. XIIth dynasty. Height 2 ft. 8 in. [No. 608.]

Presented by the Egypt Exploration Fund, 1902.

162. (*Bay* I.)—Lower portion of a sandstone seated **statue of Usertsen III,** king of Egypt, about B.C. 2330. The inscription states that it was dedicated to the goddess Hathor, the lady of the land of the copper and turquoise, by some of the officers of the king who were stationed in the peninsula of Sinai. From Ṣarâbît al-Khâdim. XIIth dynasty. Height 1 ft. 9 in. [No. 692.]

Presented by the Egypt Exploration Fund, 1905.

163. (*Vestibule. West Doorway.*)—Lower portion of a quartzite sandstone seated **figure of Usertsen III,** king of Egypt, about B.C. 2330. The style and ornamentation are the same as those of No. 165. From the Delta. XIIth dynasty. Height 4 ft. 6 in. [No. 1145.]

Presented by the Egypt Exploration Fund, 1888.

164. (*Vestibule. West Doorway.*)—Lower portion of a quartzite sandstone seated **statue of Usertsen III**

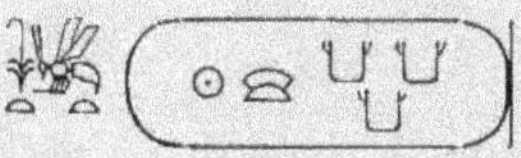, king of Egypt, about B.C. 2330. The style and ornamentation are the same as those of No. 165. On one side of the base is an inscription containing the cartouches—

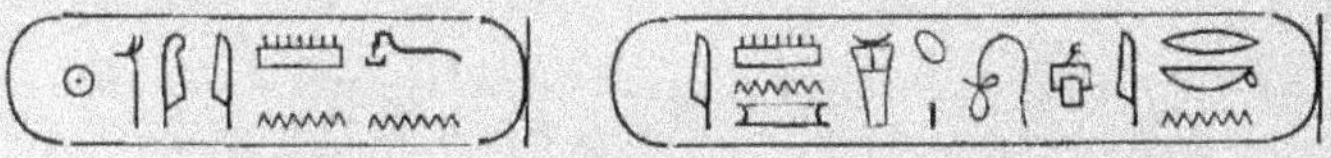

which prove that the statue was "usurped" under the XXIInd dynasty by "**Uasàrken**, son of Bast, beloved of Àmen," *i.e.*, **Osorkon II**. From the Delta. XIIth dynasty. Height 3 ft. 6 in. [No. 1146.]

Presented by the Egypt Exploration Fund, 1888.

165. (*Vestibule. East Doorway.*)—Lower portion of a quartzite sandstone seated **statue of Usertsen III** 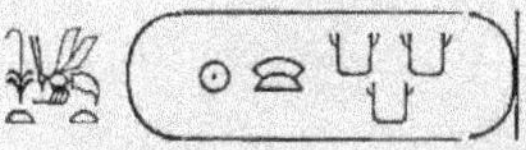, king of Egypt, about B.C. 2330. On each side of the legs is a mutilated figure of a royal lady; the figure on the right is probably that of the queen, and that on the left the king's mother. On each side of the throne is an allegorical representation of the uniting of the two Egypts. In the centre is the sign  *sma*, *i.e.*, "union"; on the right side is the god of the South, and on the left the god of the North, and each god has one foot resting on the lower portion of the symbol, and is helping his fellow to tie a knot round the shaft. Below is the ornament . The feet of the king are supposed to rest on nine bows, typifying the Nine Tribes of the Sûdân, who were conquered by him. From the Delta. Height 3 ft. 3 in. [No. 1069.]

Presented by the Egypt Exploration Fund, 1888.

166. (*Bay* **23.**)—Portion of a red granite **slab** on which is cut 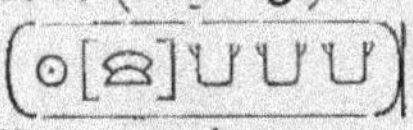 the prenomen of **Usertsen III,** king of Egypt, about B.C. 2330. From the temple at Bubastis. Height 1 ft. 10 in., width 3 ft. 3 in. [No. 1099.]

167. (*Bay* **23.**)—Portion of a red granite slab on which the name of **Rameses II** has been cut over a part of the prenomen of **Usertsen III** . From the temple at Bubastis. XIIth and XIXth dynasties. Height 3 ft. 3 in. width 3 ft. 3 in. [No. 1102.]

Presented by the Egypt Exploration Fund, 1891.

168. (*Bay* 1.)—Limestone **sepulchral stele,** with rounded top, of **Ȧn-ḥer-nekht** , an overseer of the revenue . The inscription of eleven lines is inlaid with blue paste, and contains prayers for sepulchral means and happiness in the Other World. Below these is a rectangular cavity in the stele, in which a small statue was placed originally ; on each side of it is a figure of the deceased, painted red. The stele is dated in the seventh year of **Usertsen III,** king of Egypt, about B.C. 2330

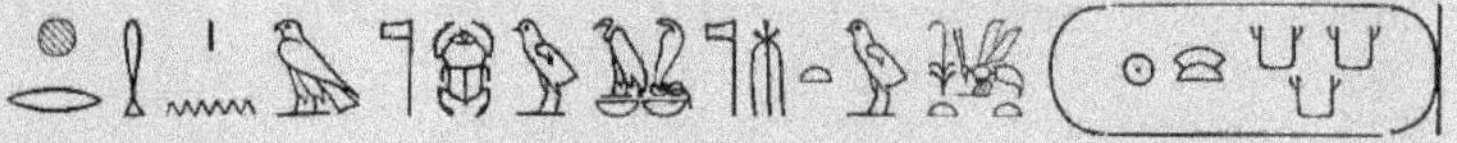

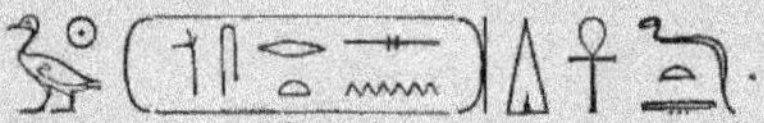

. Anastasi Collection. XIIth dynasty. Height 3 ft. 1 in., width 1 ft. 7 in. [No. 575.]

169. (*Bay* 3.)—Sandstone **sepulchral stele,** with rounded top, dated in the eighth year of **Usertsen III,** king of Egypt, about B.C. 2330 . On the upper portion are cut his Horus name and his name as king of the South and North, etc. The six mutilated lines of text mention that the king despatched an official named **Ȧmeni** , to Ābu, or Elephantine, to carry out certain building operations in connection with his expedition into Nubia, "to overthrow the detestable people of Kash" (Cush). In the last line is the name of the Ḥā prince **Rā-nub-kau** . From Elephantine. XIIth dynasty. Height 1 ft. 2½ in., width 11 in. [No. 852.]

170. (*Bay* 5.)—Limestone **sepulchral stele,** in the form of a door of a tomb, with palm-leaf cornice and raised rounded border, ornamented with a linear design, dated in the thirteenth year of the reign of King Khā-kau-Rā, *i.e.*, **Usertsen III,** B.C. 2330. Within the border is cut a prayer to Osiris Khenti Ȧmenti that sepulchral offerings may be given by him to the deceased **Sebek-ḥetep**, a warder of the temple and a royal officer, to Usertsen, his father, and to Ȧtau, his mother. Below are two registers, in which Sebek-ḥetep is seen seated at a table of offerings with his father, and at another table with his mother. The names of several brothers and sisters are enumerated at the bottom of the stele. Anastasi Collection. XIIth dynasty. Height 1 ft. 4½ in., width 1 ft. 1½ in. [No. 831.]

Sepulchral stele of Sebek-ḥetep, inscribed with the text of a prayer to Osiris.
[Bay 5, No. 170.] XIIth dynasty.

171. (*Bay* 5.)—Rectangular limestone **inscribed slab** on which are cut in low relief, with the Horus name, the Suten Bȧt name, the son of Rā name, and certain titles of **Ȧmen-em-ḥāt III,** king of Egypt, about B.C. 2300. From the king's pyramid at Ḥawârah. Length 7 ft. 9 in., breadth 2 ft. 11 in. [No. 1072.]

172. (*Bay* 2.)—**Cast** of a **portrait statue of Ȧmen-em-ḥāt III,** king of Egypt, about B.C. 2300, in the Hermitage at St. Petersburg. He wears a heavy head-dress, the lappets of which fall over his shoulders, and over his forehead is the uraeus 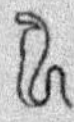, symbol of sovereignty. On each side of the legs are cut the king's names and titles 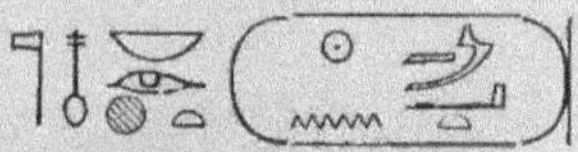 . This cast is important, for a comparison of it with the grey granite statue No. 774 suggests that the latter was made for Åmen-em-ḥāt III, and if this be the case, the inscription of Osorkon II was added to it at a much later period. Height 2 ft. 10 in. [No. 688.]

Presented by Professor Golénischeff, 1904.

173. (*Central Saloon.*)—**Cast** of a bearded, man-headed **Sphinx,** inscribed with the cartouches of:

1. **Rameses II** . (On front and right side of pedestal.)

2. **Mer-en-Ptaḥ I** 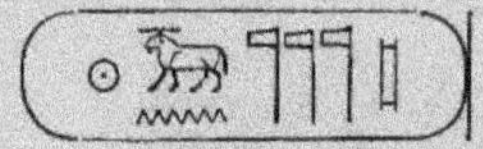. (On front and left side of pedestal, and on left shoulder.)

3. **Paseb-khā-nut** . (On the breast.)

This Sphinx is much older than the kings who had their names cut on it, and was probably made in the reign of Åmen-em-ḥāt III, about B.C. 2300. The original was found at Ṣân (Tanis), and is now in the Egyptian Museum in Cairo. Length 6 ft. 10 in. [No. 1120.]

174. (*Bay* I.)—White limestone **shrine,** in the shape of a funeral chest, made to commemorate **Pa-suten-sa** 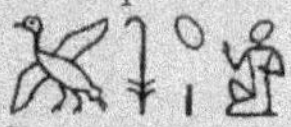 a "scribe of the offerings of all the gods," who flourished in the reign of **Åmen-em-ḥāt III,** king of Egypt, about B.C. 2300. On the top of the shrine is a figure of the hawk of Horus, and on the front of it, sculptured in high relief, is a figure of Osiris, wearing the Atef Crown and holding the crook and whip in his hands. On the sides and back are the following scenes: 1. Pa-suten-sa making offerings to Ptah-Tanen. 2. Pa-suten-sa making offerings to Osiris Khenti Ȧmenti. 3. Horus standing between Isis and Nephthys. On the pedestal are prayers to Seker and to Osiris Khenti Ȧmenti. The shrine is hollow, and at one time probably held a figure of the deceased. From Mêdûm. XIIth dynasty. Height 3 ft., width at base 1 ft. 3 in. [No. 1135.]

Shrine dedicated to Osiris and other gods by Pa-suten-sa, an official of Ȧmen-em-ḥāt III, B.C. 2300.
[Bay 1, No. 174.]

175. (*Bay* **2.**)—Rectangular limestone **sepulchral stele** of **Nebpu-Usertsen** , son of the lady Ȧt , in the form of the door of a tomb, with palm-leaf cornice and raised, rounded border ornamented with a linear design. The deceased was a personal attendant of King **Ȧmen-em-ḥāt III,** and having been promoted he took part in celebrating the "festival of the years" 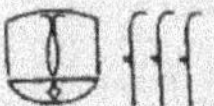; subsequently he received further promotion, and officiated at the celebration of the Seṭ festival. Within the border are cut three figures of the deceased, two standing and one seated at a table of offerings, and a series of short inscriptions which contain prayers to Osiris and Anubis for sepulchral offerings, and mention the duties which he performed. Below the cornice is the prenomen of **Usertsen III**:—

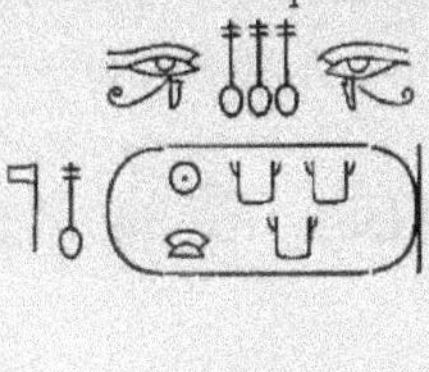

Salt Collection. XIIth dynasty, about B.C. 2330. Height 3 ft. 3½ in., width 2 ft. 2 in. [No. 101.]

176. (*Vestibule. North Wall.*)—Dark-coloured hard stone (quartzite sandstone?) **stele,** on which are inscribed fourteen lines of rudely-shaped hieroglyphics. It is dated in the ninth year of a king whose prenomen appears to read **Maāt-en-Rā** , *i.e.*, **Åmen-em-ḥāt III,** king of Egypt, about B.C. 2300, and it was set up to commemorate an official called **Menthu-sa** . From Semnah, in the Second Cataract. XIIth dynasty. Height 2 ft. 2 in., breadth 1 ft. 3 in. [No. 1290.]

Presented by Somers Clarke, Esq., 1899.

177. (*Bay* 1.)—Painted limestone **sepulchral stele,** with a rounded top, of **Senbu-Userten** 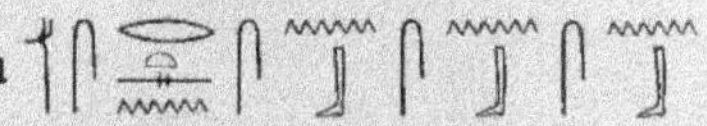, son of the lady Nebt-Ånt 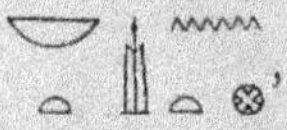, a veritable royal kinsman and the comptroller of a department of revenue. Below the five lines of text, which contains a prayer to Osiris, is a scene wherein the four daughters of the deceased are standing in worship of their father, who is seated at a table of offerings. Below these are figures of his father, mother, and brother, each with the text of the prayer, which he recites, above his head. This stele is dated in the twenty-fifth year of the reign of **Åmen-em-ḥāt III**  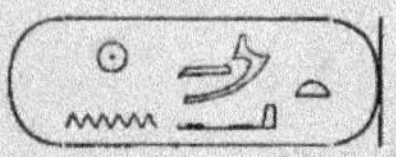. Anastasi Collection. XIIth dynasty, about B.C. 2270. Height 2 ft. 11 in., width 1 ft. 9 in. [No. 557.]

178. (*Vestibule. South Wall.*)—**Sepulchral tablet,** of unusual shape, set up to record the name of **the chief boatman** . . : . . . , the son of the lady **Åsȧ,** and the names of several sons and daughters and those of their mothers. The tablet is dated in the twenty-eighth year of King **Maāt-en-Rā,** *i.e.*, **Åmen-em-ḥāt III** 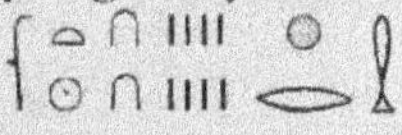

. From the Anastasi Collection, 1857. XIIth dynasty, about B.C. 2270. Height 2 ft. 2 in., breadth 1 ft. 11½ in. [No. 827.]

179, 180. (*Bay* 3.)—Red sandstone **sepulchral stele** and **altar** commemorating **Sebek-ḥer-ḥeb**, an overseer of certain of the royal apartments, and **Kemen**, the son of the lady Ḥetep-ka, a subordinate official in the royal chancery. It is dated in the forty-fourth year of a king, who must be **Ȧmen-em-ḥāt III**, and in the inscription, Hathor, the lady of the Turquoise Land, is entreated to give sepulchral offerings to the deceased persons. The altar in front of the stele was found in the position in which it now is. From Ṣarâbit al-Khâdim, in the peninsula of Sinai. XIIth dynasty, about B.C. 2250. Height of stele 2 ft. 7½ in., width of altar 1 ft. 3 in. [Nos. 694, 695.]

Stele and altar for offerings of Sebek-ḥer-ḥeb, an official who died in the forty-fourth year of the reign of Ȧmen-em-ḥāt III.
[Bay 3, Nos. 179 and 180.]

181. (*Bay* 5.)—Limestone **sepulchral stele,** with rounded top, on the upper part of which are cut the prenomen of

Åmen-em-ḥāt III, and figures of Osiris and the jackal sacred to Anubis. Below these is a text containing an address wherein the living are besought to pray that sepulchral offerings may be given to the metal worker **Ānkef** (?), the son of Tenåuit, Åfret (his wife), daughter of Åmeni, and several of their sons and daughters. Found in Malta in 1823. XIIth dynasty. Height 1 ft., width $10\frac{1}{2}$ in. [No. 233.]

Presented by J. B. Collings, Esq., 1836.

Seated statue of Åmen-em-ḥāt, a royal kinsman, and master of the robes.
[Bay 1, No. 183.] XIIth dynasty.

182. (*Vestibule, South Wall.*) — Limestone **sepulchral stele,** in the form of a door, from the tomb of **Khnemu-ḥetep**, an official who flourished under the XIIth dynasty. The stele is ornamented with a cornice. On the upper part the deceased is seen seated with a table of offerings before him, and immediately below is a raised band, whereon are cut *utchats*, and large flat leaves. The inscription is lightly cut, and, in places, almost illegible. A son or brother, called Åmeni, and a lady, Hehet (?) are mentioned. From Beni Hasan in Upper Egypt. About B.C. 2300. Height 3 ft. 6 in., width 2 ft. [No. 625.]

Presented by the Beni Hasan Excavation Fund, 1903.

183. (*Bay* I.)—Black basalt **seated statue of Åmen-em-ḥāt**, a "veritable royal kinsman", who held the office of superintendent of the private apartments of the royal palace and of master of the robes. On the sides, front, and base of the seat are inscriptions recording the name and titles of the deceased. XIIth dynasty, about B.C. 2400. From the Anastasi Collection. Height 1 ft. 8 in. [No. 462.]

184. (*Bay* I.)—Dark basalt **seated figure of Åmeni,** the son of Åmeni, inscribed with a prayer for sepulchral offerings. XIIth dynasty, about B.C. 2400. Height 1 ft. 3 in. [No. 777.]

Inscribed seated figure of Åmeni, son of Åmeni.
[Bay 1, No. 184.] XIIth dynasty.

185. (*Bay* I.)—Painted limestone **sepulchral stele,** in the form of a door, with raised, rounded edges, surmounted by a palm-leaf cornice; it was made for the Ḥā prince **Nekhtå**, son of the lady Nekhtå. Below the three lines of text is a scene in which the deceased is represented seated on a chair of state, with a table of offerings before him. Below, in three panels, are seated figures of Nekhtå, his mother, Net-nub his wife, and Åst his nurse. Salt Collection. From Abydos. XIIth dynasty, about B.C. 2300. Height 2 ft. 8 in., width 1 ft. 8½ in. [No. 143.]

186. (*Bay* I.)—Sandstone **sepulchral stele,** with rounded top, of **Ån-ḥer-nekht**, an Erpā, and Ḥā prince, who held the offices of chancellor, *smer uāti*, and chief of the accounts connected with the grain supply of the district in which he lived. On the lower part of the stele is a painted figure of the deceased making offerings to the god Osiris; he is accompanied by his wife and son. Anastasi Collection. XIIth dynasty, about B.C. 2250. Height 2 ft. 9½ in., width 1 ft. 3 in. [No. 559.]

187. (*Bay* 1.)—Limestone **sepulchral stele,** with rounded top, of **Àntef**, an overseer of the priests, who prays that Osiris, the lord of Àmenti, will give him funerary offerings, and that he "may look upon the beauties (or "bounteous acts) of the great god, the lord of Abydos." Below the text are figures of the deceased and his son Sebek-sen, the son of the lady Bebà, each holding a staff and a sceptre. The father and son were Ḥā princes, and each was an Erpā. This tablet was set up by Sebek-sen to make his father's name to live upon the earth. Anastasi Collection. XIIth dynasty. Height 2 ft., width 1 ft. 8 in. [No. 577.]

188. (*Bay* 1.)—Limestone **sepulchral stele** of the steward **Ànà**, son of the lady Nubi, in the form of a door, with a palm-leaf cornice. Within the raised border is sculptured a series of scenes in which the children of the deceased and his wife are performing acts of worship of their parents. The surface of the stele has suffered from damp, and the work is poor. XIIth dynasty. Height 1 ft. 11 in., width 1 ft. 2½ in. [No. 774.]

189. (*Bay* 1.)—Limestone **sepulchral stele,** with rounded top, of **Àn-ḥer-sa,** or **Sa-Àn-ḥer**, an official who was subordinate to the overseer of the seal. The inscription contains a prayer to Osiris, Rā, and Sab, or Ḳeb ( ) for funerary offerings. Below the text are two scenes. In the one we see the deceased standing at a table of offerings, behind him being his mother Kek, and his brother Àṭeṭa, and on the other side of the table is a kher ḥeb priest; in the other are figures of eighteen of his children and relatives, some bearing offerings. Many of the figures are coloured. Anastasi Collection. XIIth dynasty. Height 3 ft. 6 in., width 1 ft. 8½ in. [No. 568.]

190. (*Bay* 1.)—Rectangular limestone **sepulchral stele,** commemorating the lady **Khu** , and her husbands **Sa-Hathor** , and **Sa-Ȧmen** 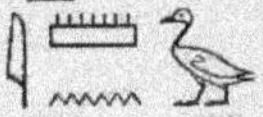, each of whom held the office of steward. In the first relief Khu and Sa-Hathor are seated with a table of offerings before them, and their children are bearing gifts. In the second, Khu and Sa-Ȧmen are seated as before, and their children are bringing gifts; and in the third are twelve children of Khu and her two husbands, arranged in pairs. Anastasi Collection. XIIth dynasty. Height 4 ft. 1½ in., width 1 ft. 8 in. [No. 571.]

191. (*Bay* 2.)—Limestone **sepulchral stele,** with rounded top, set up to commemorate sixteen persons; it is inscribed with a list of their names and those of their mothers, and with a prayer to Ptaḥ-Seker-Ȧsȧr for sepulchral offerings. The names are: Ȧntef, Ḥeru-em-ḥāt, Maḥes-ḥetep, Khati, Ren-sānkh, I-senb, Ṣa-Ḥetḥert, Ȧn-Metef, Ȧntef, Ḥeru-em-ḥāt Āa, Ḥeru-em-Ḥāt Khartˌ, Sat-Ṭep-neter, Sebek-ḥetep, Ānkh-ren, Ṡatukh, and Ḥāpu-uaḥ. XIIth dynasty. Height 1 ft. 7½ in., width 1 ft. 1 in. [No. 253.]

192. (*Bay* 2.)—Stone **sepulchral stele,** with rounded top, inscribed with two lines of text containing prayers to Osiris and Anubis for sepulchral offerings, set up to commemorate **Ḥeni** and his family. Above these is the name of the city , Shas-ḥetep. Below there is a row of figures of four men and five women, each carrying a lotus in the left hand. The lower portion of the stele is filled by eleven lines of hieratic writing, which contain the names **Ḥeni**, son of Reḥu-ānkh 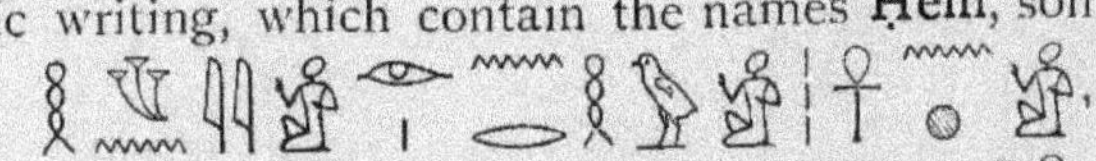, and his wife Ȧṭeni , the daughter of Āāt , his mother and sisters and brothers. Sams Collection. XIIth dynasty. Height 1 ft. 4 in., width 11½ in. [No. 228.]

193. (*Bay* 2.)—Fine white limestone **sepulchral stele,** with rounded top, of **Sebek-ṭāṭāu** (?), an Erpā, and a Ḥā prince, and a *smer-uāt*, who held several high civil and legal offices. On the upper portion of the stele is a raised band, which is unusual, and below this are eleven lines of text and a painted scene, in which the deceased is represented seated with a table of offerings before him, and his wife Ȧi, ministering to him. The hieroglyphics are inlaid with blue paste. The text contains prayers to Osiris and Anubis for funerary offerings, and describes the important offices held by Sebek-ṭaṭāu. Anastasi Collection. XIIth dynasty. Height 2 ft. 9 in., width 1 ft. 7½ in. [No. 566.]

194. (*Bay* 2.)—Limestone **sepulchral stele,** with rounded top, of **Ȧmeni**, the son of Qebu, a commander-in-chief of the bowmen. On the upper portion are cut five lines of text, which follow the curve of the top of the stele: an unusual characteristic. Below these are figures of:—1. His wife Meṭ-ḥu, a priestess of Hathor. 2. Her daughter Khent-khati. 3. His son Sa-Hathor, a chancellor of Hathor. 4. His brother Khenti-khati-ḥetep. 5. The steward, and other officers of the house of the deceased, bearing offerings. The text contains the usual prayer to Osiris Khenti Ȧmenti, *i.e.*, that sepulchral offerings may be made at the chief festivals. XIIth dynasty. Height 3 ft. 6 in., width 2 ft. 4½ in. [No. 162.]

195. (*Bay* 2.)—Rectangular limestone **sepulchral stele** of **Pefes**, a royal kinswoman, and a priestess of Hathor. The first four lines contain a prayer to Osiris Khenti Ȧmenti that she may tread the paths of happiness in the Other World, and may advance among the loyal servants to Osiris "in peace, in peace." Below is a figure of the deceased seated at a table of offerings, and on the lower portion of the stele Pefes is twice represented standing with her "beloved eldest daughter" Ȧrt-nes. Anastasi Collection. XIIth dynasty (?). Height 3 ft. 8 in., width 1 ft. 6 in. [No. 832.]

196. (*Bay* 4.)—Sandstone **stele,** which was set up in a temple at Wâdî Ḥalfah to commemorate the rule of **Erṭā-Àntef-Ṭāṭāu** 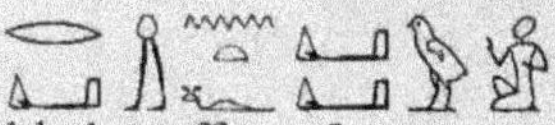, an Erpā and a Ḥā prince, who held the office of governor of the South, *i.e.*, of the Sûdân, in the reign of **Usertsen I,** about B.C. 2430. On the right of the text, which records the titles of the deceased, are cut several of the king's names. From Wâdî Ḥalfah. XIIth dynasty. Length 3 ft. 10 in., breadth 2 ft. [No. 1177.]

Presented by Captain H. G. Lyons, R.E., 1894.

197. (*Bay* 7.)—Rectangular limestone **sepulchral stele of Àntef** , the son of Sent , the superintendent of the royal palace. On the upper portion are cut seven lines of text which refer to the works which the deceased carried out during his lifetime, and a standing figure of him. Below are twenty perpendicular lines of hieroglyphics, each of which begins with the word *nuk* "I," wherein Àntef describes his virtues, qualities, and abilities. Anastasi Collection. XIIth dynasty. Height 2 ft. 2 in., width 1 ft. 2½ in.

[No. 581.]

198. (*Bay* 2.)—Portion of a painted **relief** from a wall of the tomb of **Teḥuti-ḥetep,** on which are sculptured figures of members of the household of the deceased bearing to his tomb his bow and arrows, litter (?), staff, box, shield and sword, axe, sandals, etc. By the side of the litter is Teḥuti-ḥetep's favourite dog. From Al-Barshah, in Upper Egypt. XIIth dynasty, about B.C. 2400. Length 5 ft. 5 in., breadth 1 ft. 2 in. [No. 1147.]

Presented by the Egypt Exploration Fund, 1894.

199. (*Bay* 2.)—Portion of a painted **relief** from a wall of the tomb of **Teḥuti-ḥetep,** on which are sculptured figures of field-labourers who are engaged in ploughing and sowing the lands on the estate of the deceased. From Al-Barshah in Upper Egypt. XIIth dynasty, about B.C. 2400. Length 2 ft., breadth 1 ft. 8 in. [No. 1152.]

Presented by the Egypt Exploration Fund, 1894.

200. (*Bay* 2).—Portion of a painted **relief** from a wall of the tomb of **Teḥuti-ḥetep,** on which are sculptured kneeling figures of men bearing vases of unguents, etc., as sepulchral offerings. From Al-Barshah in Upper Egypt. XIIth dynasty, about B.C. 2400. Length 2 ft. 3 in., breadth 1 ft. 8 in. [No. 1151.]

Presented by the Egypt Exploration Fund, 1894.

201. (*Bay* 7.)—Portion of a **relief** from a wall of the tomb of **Teḥuti-ḥetep,** on which is a sculptured and painted figure of a woman. From Al-Barshah. XIIth dynasty. Height 2 ft. 4 in., width 1 ft. [No. 1150.]

Presented by the Egypt Exploration Fund, 1904.

202. (*Bay* 1.)—Small red **sandstone obelisk,** set up in memory of an Egyptian official, or soldier, who was stationed at the copper and turquoise mines at Ṣarâbît al-Khâdim in the peninsula of Sinai. On two of the sides are the names of two of his loving sons, **Àqen** , the soldier, and **Àhenem** , the soldier. The third name is illegible, but the last two signs of it appear to be  *shà*. From Ṣarâbît al-Khâdim. XIIth dynasty, about B.C. 2400. Height 1 ft. 8½ in. [No. 693.]

Presented by the Egypt Exploration Fund, 1905.

203. (*Vestibule. North Wall.*)—Rectangular limestone **sepulchral stele** from the tomb of **Sebek-sen** 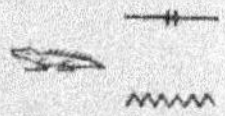, who held the rank of Ḥā , the son of Beb 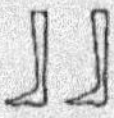. On the left is sculptured a relief, wherein the deceased is seen standing, with his hands raised in adoration, before a table of offerings; behind him stands his wife Ià, the daughter of Àtu 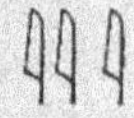
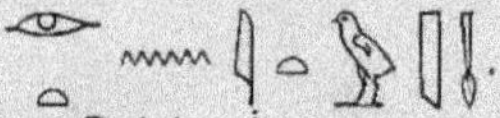. The text is a formula of praise addressed to Osiris, Àp-uat, and Un-nefer. From the Anastasi Collection. XIIth dynasty. Length 2 ft. 6 in., breadth 1 ft. 7 in. [No. 580.]

204. (*Vestibule. South Wall.*)—**Sepulchral stele** of **Àmen-em-ḥāt** , a superintendent of a portion of the palace. On the right is a figure of the deceased, sculptured in low relief, painted flesh-colour, and seated on a chair of state with a table of offerings before him. The text contains a prayer for sepulchral offerings. XIIth dynasty. Anastasi Collection. Length 2 ft. 2 in., breadth 1 ft. 10 in. [No. 587.]

205. (*Vestibule. South Wall.*) — Rectangular limestone **sepulchral stele** of **Ḥeru-Nekht** , the son of Sekhet-Usert 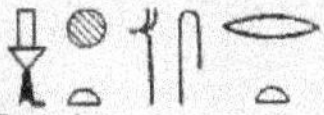, an overseer of builders, or architect, . In the upper portion is a figure of the deceased standing with his wife Uatchet-ḥetep 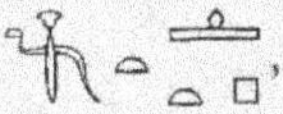, on one side of him, and his daughter Sekhmet-Usert 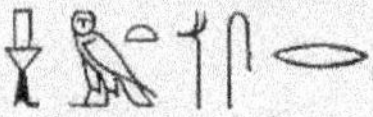, on the other. In the lower portion of the stele is also a figure of the deceased, and before him stand his wife, a son, and two daughters. XIIth dynasty. Anastasi Collection. Height 2 ft. 2 in., width 1 ft. 4 in. [No. 560.]

206. (*Vestibule. South Wall.*)—Limestone **fragment** of a sepulchral stele, with inscription " . . . . beloved of the "great goddess, lady of Bāḥet." XIIth dynasty (?) Height 1 ft., breadth 9 in. [No. 1149.]

207. (*Bay* 1.)—Limestone **sepulchral stele,** with rounded top, inscribed with a prayer for funerary offerings to Osiris, Anubis, and Khenti Àmenti, on behalf of **Às-āb** (?) , a Ḥā prince and overseer of the priests, or prophets. His mother's name appears to have been Tef-ābt 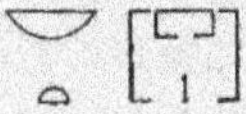 . On the left are figures of the deceased and his son (?), and on the right is a table of offerings. XIIth dynasty, about B.C. 2400. Height 2 ft. 5 in., breadth 1 ft. 4 in. [No. 193.]

208. (*Bay* 1.)—White limestone **sepulchral stele,** with palm-leaf cornice and raised border, set up in memory of **Àqer,** a steward , the son of Pert 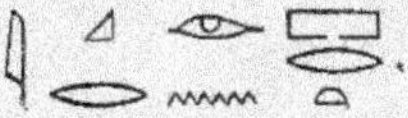.

The tablet is divided into sections wherein the various members of the family of the deceased are seen engaged in doing reverence to their kinsman. XIIth dynasty. About B.C. 2400. Height 2 ft. 9 in., width 1 ft. 7 in. [No. 129.]

209. (*Bay* I.)—Rectangular limestone **sepulchral stele** of **Khen-bȧk-Ḥeru**, the son of the lady Rerut, a master builder or chief mason, which was set up by one of his sons "to make his name to live." The six lines of text contain prayers to Osiris, Khenti Ȧmenti, Anpu, Khnemu, Ḥeqt, and all the gods for sepulchral meals. Below these is a figure of the deceased seated at a table of offerings; behind him is his wife Mes-en-maȧ-en-Ḥeru, and to the right of the table are figures of his two sons, En-Ptaḥ-kau and Ptaḥ-ḥetep. Anastasi Collection. XIIth dynasty. Height 1 ft. 8½ in., width 1 ft. 8½ in. [No. 584.]

210. (*Bay* I.)—Rectangular, limestone **sepulchral stele** of **Ḥer-ȧp** (?), the son of Āakas. On the upper portion of it is inscribed a prayer to Osiris Khenti Ȧmenti, and on the lower are figures of the deceased and his son Ȧp-ānkh, standing before a table of offerings. Sams Collection. XIIth dynasty. Height 1 ft. 7½ in., breadth 1 ft. 4 in. [No. 578.]

211. (*Bay* I.)—Limestone **sepulchral stele,** with a rounded top, of **Sa-ȧst**, son of the lady Ȧsenes, a veritable royal kinsman, who held the offices of governor of the South and the North, and overseer of the private royal apartments in the palace. Below the four lines of text are figures of the deceased and his father and mother standing at a table of offerings, and three brothers and three sisters. Anastasi Collection. XIIth dynasty. Height 1 ft. 10 in., width 1 ft. 2 in. [No. 561.]

212. (*Bay* **1.**)—Rectangular, painted limestone **sepulchral stele** of **Ānkh-ren** 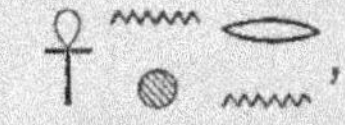, the son of Mest-tekhȧ , a veritable royal kinsman, and overseer of a department of the Treasury. Below the inscription are sculptured :—1. A figure of the deceased, painted red, seated before a table of offerings. 2. His wife, a son and a daughter, and a kinswoman. Text and scenes are enclosed within a painted border. Anastasi Collection. XIIth dynasty. (**Plate VIII.**) Height 2 ft. 7 in., width 1 ft. 8½ in. [No. 564.]

213. (*Bay* **1.**)—Painted limestone **sepulchral stele** of **Ȧmeni** 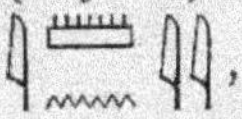, the son of the lady Sat-Sekhemet , the guardian of the royal palace, and a royal kinsman. Below the four lines of text, which contain prayers to the chief gods of the dead, are sculptured figures of the deceased, his mother, father, sisters and brothers. The rounded portion of the stele is ornamented with red and yellow bars, and text and figures are enclosed within a plain red border. Anastasi Collection. XIIth dynasty. (**Plate IX.**) Height 2 ft. 7 in., width 1 ft. 9 in. [No. 565.]

214. (*Bay* **1.**)—Rectangular limestone **sepulchral stele** of **Nemki**  (or Uḥemki), the son of the lady Mertȧ 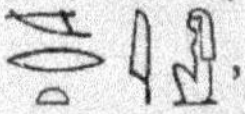, a royal kinsman. On the upper portion of the stele are six lines of text containing prayers by the deceased to Osiris, the chief god of the dead, and below is a figure of the deceased standing before a table of offerings. Anastasi Collection. XIIth dynasty. Height 2 ft. 8 in., width 1 ft. 5½ ins. [No. 558.]

215. (*Bay* **2.**)—Sandstone **sepulchral stele** in the form of the door of a tomb, with palm-leaf cornice and a raised rounded border, set up to commemorate: 1. **Senbsu-em-ḥāt** , an Erpā, and Ḥā prince, chancellor, keeper of the seal, etc., and his wife **Ȧthȧ** . 2. **Renpet** 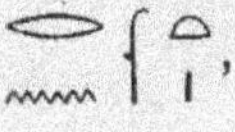, the overseer of the throne, and his wife **Pu-ḥer**

Sepulchral stele of Ānkh-ren, an overseer of a department of the Treasury.
[Bay 1, No. 212.] XIIth dynasty.

Sepulchral stele of Àmeni, a royal kinsman and warden of the palace.

[Bay 1, No. 213.] XIIth dynasty.

3. **Ṭāṭā**, "a follower of the prince," and his wife **Åpu**. The texts contain prayers to Osiris and Anubis for sepulchral offerings. XIIth dynasty. Height 2 ft., width 1 ft. 2½ in. [No. 252.]

216. (*Bay* **2.**)—Painted limestone **sepulchral stele** in the shape of a door of a tomb, with palm-leaf cornice and raised rounded border; it was made to commemorate **Khenemes**, the son of the lady Ki, the overseer of the throne, and **Autiḥi**, the son of the lady Khert-åb, the overseer of the seal. Below the text, which contains prayers to Ptaḥ-Seker-Åsår and Sab for funerary offerings, is a scene wherein the deceased persons are seen to be receiving worship from their sons. In the two lower registers are figures of eight other members of their families. XIIth dynasty. Height 1 ft. 8½ in., width 1 ft. 1 in. [No. 903.]

217. (*Bay* **2.**)—Sandstone **sepulchral stele,** with rounded top, of **Ånå**, the son of Åtau, a high official, inscribed with twenty lines of text, three horizontal and seventeen perpendicular. In the first register is a figure of the deceased, in the second are figures of his wife **Kemtet**, daughter of Ben[r]åt, and **Åmen-em-ḥāt**, the scribe of the wine-cellar, and in the third is a figure of his brother. Poor work, and hieroglyphics shallow. D'Athanasi Collection. From Abydos. XIIth dynasty. Height 1 ft. 5 in., width 11½ in. [No. 334.]

218. (*Bay* **2.**)—Limestone **sepulchral stele,** with rounded top, of **Khenti-khathi-åm-ḥāt**, a guardian of a portion of the royal palace, inscribed with sixteen lines of text containing a prayer to Osiris for sepulchral offerings. On the left is a figure of the deceased cut in outline.

The hieroglyphics are ill-shaped and shallow; the left bottom corner and a portion of the base of the stele are wanting. XIIth dynasty. Height 1 ft. 3 in., width 1 ft. [No. 243.]

219. (*Bay* 3.)—Limestone **sepulchral stele,** with rounded top, of **Åu-nef** (or **Set-nef**) (or), a high official, who flourished in the joint reign of **Åmen-em-ḥāt III** and **Åmen-em-ḥāt IV,** whose prenomens are cut on the upper portion of it. In rude outline are also seen figures of Osiris, Anubis, the deceased, and several members of his family. Salt Collection. XIIth dynasty, about B.C. 2300. Height 1 ft. 1 in., width 8 in. [No. 258.]

220. (*Bay* 3.)—Limestone **sepulchral stele,** in the form of a door of a tomb with palm-leaf cornice and raised, rounded border. On the upper part we see the deceased seated at a table of offerings; before him stands his son. The text contains a prayer to Osiris, Åp-uat, and Un-Nefer, that sepulchral offerings may be given to the deceased, whose name was written in red ink but is now illegible, and to the lady Neferiu, and to other kinsfolk. Very rough, poor work. Sams Collection. XIIth dynasty. Height 1 ft. 5 in., width 11 in. [No. 205.]

221. (*Bay* 3.)—Limestone **sepulchral stele,** with rounded top, of **Kemef** , the son of Åtau-enen , inscribed with prayers to Osiris on behalf of himself, and to Hathor, on behalf of his wife Peri , for sepulchral offerings. Below the text are figures of the deceased and his wife, and of various members of their family. XIIth dynasty. Height 1 ft. 3½ in., width 10½ in. [No. 222.]

222. (*Bay* 3.)—Limestone **sepulchral stele,** with rounded top, of **Maḥesa-user** , inscribed with a prayer to the "great god, the lord of Abydos," for sepulchral offerings. In the upper register are figures of the sons of the deceased making offerings to their father, and in the lower, one son and four daughters making offerings to Khenti-khat-sa, their mother. XIIth dynasty. Height 1 ft. 5½ in., width 1 ft. 2½ in. [No. 971.]

Painted sepulchral stele of Usertsen, a high official.
[Bay 3, No. 224.] XIIth dynasty.

223. (*Bay* 3.)—Limestone **sepulchral stele,** with rounded top, of **Renpif** , a keeper of the seal, inscribed with an address to those who pass by his tomb exhorting them to pray that sepulchral offerings in thousands may be given to his *ka*, or double, and "the gifts of heaven, and the products "of the earth, and the things which the Nile-god bringeth "forth, whereon the god liveth." On the upper portion are cut the two symbolic eyes, with the emblem of eternity between them , and the jackals (?) of Ànpu and Àp-uat; below are cut figures of **Renpif** and his wife Athà, offerings, etc. Sams Collection. XIIth dynasty. Height 1 ft. 8 in., width 1 ft. 1 in. [No. 240.]

224. (*Bay* 3.)—Painted limestone **sepulchral stele,** with rounded top, of **Usertsen** , a high official, inscribed with a prayer to Osiris for sepulchral offerings. Below are figures of Usertsen and his wife Sat-Hathor, seated at a table of offerings, and of his sister, father, mother, and two brothers. Sams Collection. XIIth dynasty. (**Plate X.**) Height 1 ft. $5\frac{1}{2}$ in., width 1 ft. [No. 198.]

225. (*Bay* 4.)—Limestone **monolithic shrine,** with palm-leaf cornice, of the royal scribe **Ān-àbà** 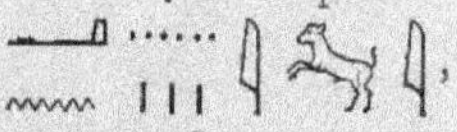, the son of Sebek - ṭāṭāu - ṭetà , a priest of Menthu. Above the opening are four lines of text which contain an address to the living, whom the deceased asks to pray that sepulchral meals may be given to him, and a prayer to Osiris Khenti Àmenti and Àp-uat. On the right is a prayer to Osiris, and on the left a prayer to **Menu-Ḥeru-nekht** 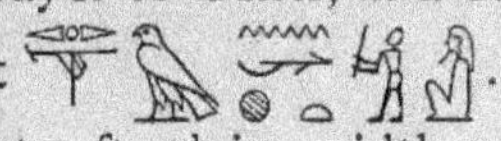. Salt Collection. XIIth dynasty. Height 2 ft. $5\frac{1}{2}$ in., width 1 ft. 6 in. [No. 471.]

226. (*Bay* 4.)—Limestone **sepulchral stele,** with rounded top, set up by Menthu-em-ḥeb , in memory of his brother **Smen-nu** 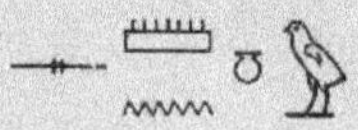. On it is cut a figure of the deceased, and the text contains a prayer to Osiris for sepulchral offerings. Sams Collection. XIIth dynasty. Height 10 in., width 5½ in. [No. 362.]

227. (*Bay* 4.)—Limestone **sepulchral stele**, with rounded top, set up by **Ȧmeni** 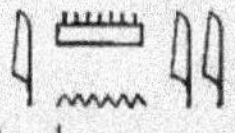 to make to live the name of his father **Sabu** 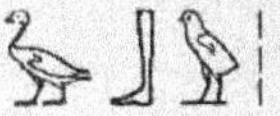; both father and son held some office in connection with the king's crown 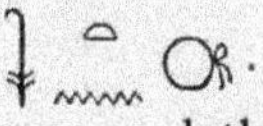. On the upper portion of the stele are the sacred eyes and the symbol of eternity , and below these is a request to "those "who live upon the earth" to say a prayer to Osiris Khenti Ȧmenti on behalf of the deceased. This is followed by a scene representing the deceased seated with a table of offerings before him; by it stands his son, and close by is a seated figure of his wife Karu. Below these are the names of several relatives of the deceased. XIIth dynasty. Height 1 ft. 4 in., width 10 in. [No. 223.]

228. (*Bay* 4.)—Limestone **sepulchral stele**, with rounded top, made to commemorate a family of nine persons, whose names and figures are cut upon it. On the upper portion, in **hieratic characters**, is a prayer to Osiris and Anubis for sepulchral offerings. Salt Collection. XIIth dynasty. Height 1 ft., width 8½ in. [No. 230.]

229. (*Bay* 4.)—Limestone **sepulchral stele** of the lady **Māthȧ** 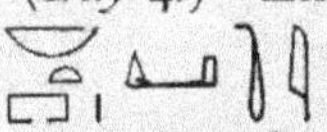 inscribed with  and a prayer to Osiris for sepulchral offerings; it was set up to her memory by her son Menthu-sa . Below are figures of the deceased and two of her sons. Sams Collection. XIIth dynasty. Height 10 in., width 5½ in. [No. 232.]

230. (*Bay* 4.)—Limestone **sepulchral stele**, with rounded top, made to commemorate a family of eight persons, whose names and figures are cut upon it. On the upper portion, in **hieratic characters**, is a prayer to Osiris and Anubis for sepulchral offerings. Salt Collection. XIIth dynasty. Height 11½ in., width 8½ in. [No. 219.]

231. (*Bay* 4.)—Limestone **sepulchral stele**, with rounded top, of **Ȧmeni** , on which are cut figures of himself, his brother, wife, and other members of his family. A portion of the tablet is painted green. XIIth dynasty. Height 8½ in., width 5½ in. [No. 788.]

232. (*Bay* 4.)—Rectangular limestone **sepulchral stele,** in the form of a door of a tomb, with palm-leaf cornice and raised, rounded border, of **Senb-su-em-ḥā** , treasurer and keeper of the seal. On the upper portion are a seated figure of the deceased, and the figures of five members of his family, who are bringing to him offerings of eye paint, unguents, linen, etc. Of these the first was the overseer of the royal couch, the second a guardian of a private chamber in the palace, the third and fourth were overseers, and the fifth was a scribe. From Abydos. XIIth dynasty. Height 1 ft. 7 in., width 11 in. [No. 215.]

233. (*Bay* 4.)—Portion of a painted limestone **relief,** on which is sculptured the figure of a man seated in a boat and rowing. The details of the work are good. XIIth dynasty. Height 7½ in., width 5½ in. [No. 914.]

234. (*Bay* 4.)—Sandstone **sepulchral stele,** with a rounded top, of **Senb-sen** , the son of the lady Maa, scribe of the *Khent*, on which is inscribed a prayer to Osiris and Ȧp-uat for sepulchral offerings. Below the text are cut figures of the deceased and various members of his family. XIIth dynasty. Height 1 ft. 5½ in., width 10½ in. [No. 225.]

235. (*Bay* 4.)—Rectangular limestone **sepulchral stele** of **Usertsen** , son of the lady Satȧ, inscribed with a prayer to Osiris and Khenti Ȧmenti for sepulchral offerings. In the first register are painted figures of Ȧmen- . . . . and Menthu-user making offerings to their father Usertsen and their mother; in the second are figures of "his brother Ȧmen-em-ḥāt," and a son and a daughter, making offerings to their father Menthu-user and his wife Ment-ȧshetek . Below these are daughters and servants bearing offerings. XIIth dynasty. Height 1 ft. 10½ in., width 1 ft. 1½ in. [No. 1322.]

Presented by Mrs. Hawker, 1901.

236. (*Bay* 5.)—Limestone **sepulchral stele,** with rounded top, of **Ȧp-uat-ḥetep**, a Ḥā prince, chancellor, etc., the son of Khnemu-ḥetep, a Ḥā prince and chancellor of the god, inscribed with adorations to Osiris Khenti Ȧmenti. On the upper portion are the utchats and the symbol of "life", and on the lower is a well-sculptured figure of the deceased. From Thebes. XIIth dynasty. Height 1 ft. 7 in., width 1 ft. [No. 1367.]

237. (*Bay* 5.)—Limestone **sepulchral stele,** with rounded top, of **I-kher-nefert**, an Erpā, a Ḥā prince, a councillor, keeper of the seal, etc., inscribed with a prayer to Osiris Khenti Ȧmenti, Ȧp-uat, Ȧnpu, Menu, Ḥeqt, Khnemu, Ḥeru-netch-ḥrȧ-ȧtef, and the gods and goddesses of Abydos for sepulchral offerings. Below are cut figures of the deceased and his father seated at a table of offerings, and of twenty-four relatives. XIIth dynasty. Height 1 ft. 9½ in., width 1 ft. 2 in. [No. 202.]

238. (*Bay* 5.)—Limestone **sepulchral stele,** with rounded top, of **Pa-enti-en**, a councillor, inspector of scribes of the land of the South, the son of the lady Ȧnȧ. On the upper portion are cut in outline, a palm-leaf cornice, and the text of a prayer to Osiris Khenti Ȧmenti, Ptaḥ-Seker-Ȧsȧr, Ȧnpu, and Ȧp-uat for sepulchral offerings. Below are well-cut figures of the deceased and his wife (?) Neferu-nubu, the daughter of Senb, table of offerings, etc. XIIth dynasty. Height 1 ft. 9½ in., width 11 in. [No. 254.]

239. (*Bay* 5.)—Limestone **sepulchral stele,** with rounded top and raised, inscribed border, of **Teḥuti**, the son of Teḥuti-ḥetep, a veritable royal kinsman, overseer of the royal throne, libationer, ministrant to the king's *ka*, or double.

Within the border are nine lines of well-cut hieroglyphics, containing a prayer to Osiris Khenti Ȧmenti, Ȧnpu, Khnemu, Ḥeqt, and Ḥeru-netch-tef-f for sepulchral offerings, and below are figures of the deceased and members of his family, a table of offerings, etc. XIIth dynasty. Height 1 ft. 8½ in., width 1 ft. 2½ in. [No. 805.]

240. (*Bay* 5.)—White limestone **sepulchral stele** of **Usertsen-senb** , the son of Renf-senb and Ptaḥ-neferu, in the form of the door of a tomb, with palm-leaf cornice and a raised, rounded border; the deceased was a scribe and governor of the city. Two lines of text contain a prayer to Osiris, "lord of life of the two lands," and to Ȧp-uat for sepulchral offerings, and below these, cut in outline, are figures of several members of the family of the deceased. Sams Collection. XIIth dynasty. Height 1 ft. 8½ in., width 1 ft. 1 in. [No. 209.]

241. (*Bay* 5.)—White limestone **sepulchral stele,** with rounded top, of **User** , the son of a father and mother who bore the same name, **Meshthȧ** , inscribed with a prayer to Osiris that funerary offerings might be brought to his tomb at the chief festivals of the year. Below the text, in sunk relief, is the figure of User seated, with a table of offerings before him, and his **dog Ṭeb** (?) at his feet; at the table stands his son, and near him are his mother and two sisters. Anastasi Collection. XIIth dynasty. Height 1 ft. 7½ in., width 1 ft. [No. 237.]

242. (*Bay* 5.)—Rectangular limestone **sepulchral stele,** set up to commemorate **Nekhtȧ** , an Erpā and a Ḥā prince, and his wife Emsas , and Khenti-khathi-ḥetep and his wife Sat-Hathor, and others. From Abydos. D'Athanasi Collection. XIIth dynasty. Height 1 ft. 5½ in., width 1 ft. [No. 241.]

243. (*Bay* 5.)—Limestone **sepulchral stele,** with rounded top, of **Sukhenemes** , the son of Ki . On the upper portion are cut figures of the jackal-gods Ȧnpu and Ȧp-uat, and below are figures of thirteen members of a family, including one of the deceased, who is seated with a table of offerings in front of him. Two lines have been left blank for the usual formula concerning sepulchral offerings. D'Athanasi Collection. XIIth dynasty, or later. Height 1 ft. 9 in., width 1 ft. 3 in. [No. 238.]

244. (*Bay* 6.)—Upper portion of a black granite bearded **statue** of a high official. XIIth dynasty (?). Height 1 ft. 6 in. [No. 98.]

245. (*Bay* 7.)—Rectangular limestone **sepulchral stele** of **Ȧmeni** , a governor of the South, in the form of a door of a tomb, with palm-leaf cornice and raised, rounded border. Within the border is a figure of Ȧmeni, seated at a table of offerings, and above are two lines of text wherein the deceased is made to pray to "the gods and goddesses who "dwell in Abydos" for strength and power in the Other World. D'Athanasi Collection. XIIth dynasty. Height 1 ft. 3 in., width 10½ in. [No. 235.]

246. (*Bay* 7.)—Limestone **sepulchral stele,** with rounded top, of **Usertsen-senbu** (*sic*), the son of Nebt-ȧnt, on which are cut figures of the deceased and his three daughters, seated at a table of offerings, a prayer to Osiris for sepulchral offerings, and . XIIth dynasty. Height 1 ft. 3½ in., width 1 ft. 0½ in. [No. 247.]

247. (*Bay* 7.)—**Sepulchral stele,** with rounded top, of **Ānkhu-usert** , the son of Ḥepi , a libationer, inscribed with a prayer to Ȧsȧr-Ap-uatu , lord of Abydos, for sepulchral offerings.

Below are cut figures of the deceased and his wife, and a list of names of relatives, Ȧtef-ānkh, Mentu-āa, Mentu-shrȧue, Nefer-sānkh, Ṭetȧ, Nebt-ḥeḥ, etc. XIIth dynasty. Height 1 ft., width $7\frac{1}{2}$ in. [No. 220.]

248. (*Bay* 7.)—Limestone **sepulchral stele,** with rounded top, of **Kheper-ka**, the son of Bebu, warder of the hall of the royal palace, inscribed with a prayer to Osiris Khenti Ȧmenti for sepulchral offerings. Below, cut in outline, are series of figures paying homage to the deceased. Sams Collection. XIIth dynasty. Height 1 ft. 3 in., width $9\frac{1}{2}$ in. [No. 227.]

249. (*Bay* 7.)—Limestone **sepulchral stele,** with rounded top, of **Sebek(?)-ṭāu** (?), son of Ȧt, an Erpā, a Ḥā prince, and a Smer, inscribed with prayers to Osiris Khenti Ȧmenti, Ȧp-uatu, Ḥeru-netch-tef-f, Ḥeqt, Khnemu, Anubis, Hathor, and other gods, for sepulchral offerings. The "beautiful name" of the deceased was **Tchaa**. On the right are inscribed seven lines of text, wherein the deceased describes his merits and addresses the living, entreating them to pray that offerings may be made to him. On the left are cut four scenes, in which the deceased is seated at a table of offerings, etc. From Abydos. XIIth dynasty. Height 1 ft. 3 in., width $9\frac{1}{2}$ in. [No. 1213.]

250. (*Bay* 7.)—Rectangular limestone **sepulchral stele** of Kharṭ, a Ḥā prince, chancellor, Smer-uāt, and Kher ḥeb priest. On the upper portion are cut a prayer to Ȧnpu for sepulchral offerings and a statement to the effect that [the king] bestowed upon him favours greater than those which his fathers had enjoyed. On the lower portion is cut an address to the living, in which the deceased beseeches them to pray that sepulchral offerings may be given to him, and by the side are figures of the deceased and his wife **Mert-ȧtef-s**, a priestess of Hathor. XIIth dynasty. From the neighbourhood of Akhmîm. Height 2 ft. 1 in., width 1 ft. 4 in. [No. 1059.]

251. (*Bay* 7.)—Rectangular limestone **sepulchral stele,** set up to commemorate **Àtfà**, the son of Àbà, his wife **Àner,** daughter of Ḥepi, and **Menthu-nekhtà,** the son of Ṭuṭuà, and his wife **Àbà,** the daughter of Ḥi. Above is a prayer to Osiris for sepulchral offerings, and below are sculptured figures of the four persons whose names are recorded on the stele. XIIth dynasty. Height 1 ft. 2½ in., width 1 ft. 3½ in. [No. 1201.]

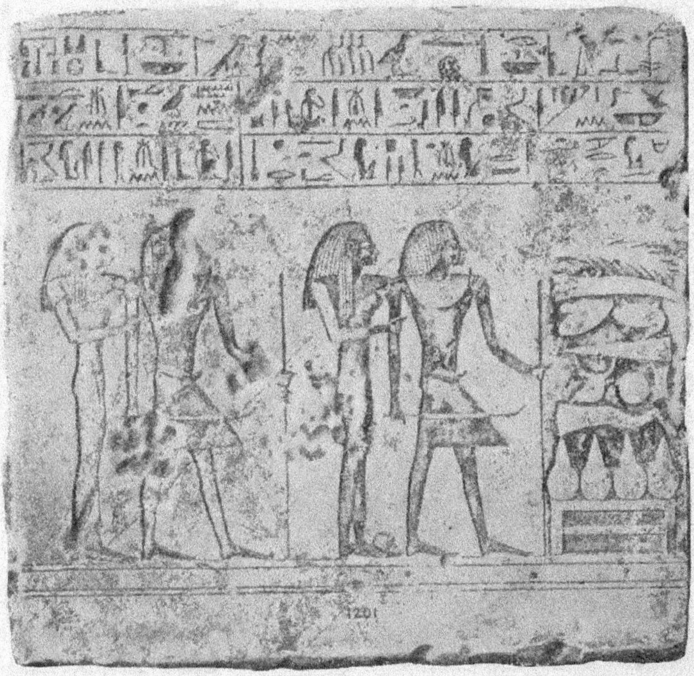

Sepulchral stele of Àtfà and Menthu-nekhtà.
[Bay 7, No. 251.] XIIth dynasty.

252. (*Bay* 7.)—Limestone **sepulchral stele,** with rounded top, of **Bebà**, the son of Ànnu. On the upper portion is cut a prayer to Osiris for sepulchral offerings, and below it is a figure of the deceased, in outline, seated with a table of offerings before him. The inscription on the lower portion of the stele is obliterated. XIIth dynasty. Height 1 ft. 1½ in., width 8 in. [No. 244.]

253. (*Bay* 7.)—Limestone **sepulchral stele**, with rounded top, of **Senb**, son of Uaḥ-ka, the overseer of the temple of Nefer-ruṭ. On the upper portion are cut a prayer to Osiris for funerary offerings and figures of the deceased and his son Uaḥ-ka-ḥetep, seated, with a table of offerings before them. Below are two groups, the first containing figures of two men and one woman, and the second, figures of two women and one man, all of whom represent relatives of the deceased. Sams Collection. XIIth dynasty. Height 10½ in., width 7½ in. [No. 363.]

254. (*Bay* 7.)—Rectangular limestone **sepulchral stele** of **Sa-rennutet**, the son of Ba-māket, steward of the palace, keeper of the offerings made to the gods, and treasurer of the double storehouse. On the upper portion is a prayer to Osiris for funerary offerings, and below is a figure of the deceased seated with a table of offerings before him. Anastasi Collection. XIIth dynasty. Height 1 ft. 8½ in., width 1 ft. 8 in. [No. 585.]

255. (*Bay* 7.)—Rectangular limestone **sepulchral stele,** with a raised band at the top, of **Sebek-āāui, or Sebek-ṭāṭāu**, a veritable royal relative, who held the rank of Erpā, Ḥā prince, chancellor, Smer-uāt, judge of Nekhen, chief of the South, and overseer of the *Shent*. Below the text are:—A figure of the deceased, seated with a table of offerings before him, a figure of his mother (?) Ȧi, and figures of members of his family. The stele was set up by **Sebek-āāui,** the overseer of the "House of the Six" in Ḥet-Thet-taiu, and overseer of the *Shent*. Anastasi Collection. XIIth dynasty. Height 2 ft. 2½ in., width 1 ft. 7 in. [No. 830.]

256. (*Bay* 9.)—Limestone **sepulchral stele**, with rounded top, of **Senb-ān** (?), inscribed with a prayer to Osiris. In the upper register the deceased and his wife

Ren-senb, are seen seated, with two stands between them, one with a draught-board (?) upon it, and the other bearing offerings. In the lower register are a stand with a draught-board upon it and a vessel of wine on each side of it. Here also are two figures of Sa-Ptaḥ, the son of Ren-senb. Sams Collection. XIIth dynasty. Height 9 in., width 5½ in. [No. 361.]

257. (*Bay* 9.)—Painted limestone **sepulchral stele**, with rounded top, of **Khati**, inscribed with prayers to Osiris and Seb for sepulchral offerings. On the upper portion are the two *utchats* and below these is a list of offerings. We next see the deceased (?) offering incense to two of his relatives and their wives, and in the lower register are figures of Khati and his wife Ȧp-Ḥerui (?), and their eight children. From Asyût. XIIth dynasty. Height 1 ft. 6½ in., breadth 1 ft. 2½ in. [No. 928.]

258. (*Bay* 6.)—Limestone **seated figure** of **Menth-ḥetep**, the governor of the western district of Memphis, which was made to his memory by his sister Neḥsit, *i.e.*, "the Negress," a priestess of Ȧmen. The deceased is represented holding before him a shrine, on the front of which is a sculptured figure. The work is poor, and the figure appears to be in an unfinished state. Anastasi Collection. XIIth dynasty. Height 1 ft. 9½ in. [No. 469.]

259. (*Bay* 14.)—Limestone **tablet for offerings** of **Nefer**, inscribed with prayers to Osiris and Anubis for funerary offerings. In the face of the tablet are cut three rectangular tanks, with sloping sides. Sams Collection. XIIth dynasty. Length 11½ in., breadth 6½ in. [No. 413.]

260. (*Bay* 14.)—Dark granite **tablet for offerings** of **Ȧmen-em-ḥāt**, a scribe of the bowmen, sculptured in relief with figures of cakes, vases, etc., and inscribed with prayers to Rā and Sab for sepulchral offerings. Anastasi Collection. XIIth dynasty. Length 1 ft., breadth 9½ in. [No. 553.]

261. (*Bay* 14.)—Limestone **tablet for offerings** of **Åmen-ḥāt** 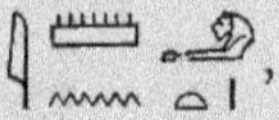, on which are sculptured figures of bread-cakes, libation vases, a bull's head, a leg of beef, etc.; near the spout are cut two rectangular tanks. On the tablet are cut the following names: Sebek-sa , wife of the deceased, Åmen-ḥetep, and Menthu-ḥetep. XIIth dynasty. Length 9½ in., breadth 7 in. [No. 414.]

262. (*Bay* 14.)—Limestone **tablet for offerings** of **Åpit** 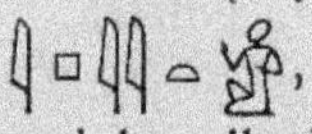, sculptured in relief with figures of offerings, and inscribed with prayers to Osiris and Ånpu for sepulchral offerings. From Asyût. XIIth dynasty. Length 8½ in., breadth 7 in. [No. 980.]

263. (*Bay* 14.)—Limestone **tablet for offerings,** in which are cut two rectangular tanks. On the face, in the place of the usual sculptured figures, are cut the name of the deceased **Sebek** , a scribe, his wife Nefertu, his daughters Åst-Ḥet-Ḥert and Åmḥāt, and his son Ḥeru-nefer. Next come the names of the scribe Nekhtå, his wife Åṭenå, and his daughter Qa-åat, Åmenemḥāt, and his wife Ḥetchert 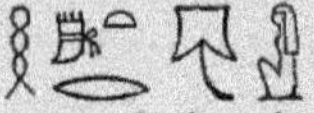. This tablet was dedicated by Nefer-Tem, a son of the deceased Sebek. Salt Collection. XIIth dynasty. Length 1 ft. 2 in., breadth 12½ in. [No. 417.]

264. (*Bay* 14.)—Limestone **tablet for offerings** of **Åpai** , sculptured in relief with figures of offerings, and inscribed with prayers to Osiris and Ånpu for sepulchral offerings. From Asyût. XIIth dynasty. Length 1 ft. 4 in., breadth 1 ft. [No. 976.]

265. (*Bay* 16.)—Limestone **tablet for offerings** of **Àpai**, sculptured in relief with figures of libation vases, cakes, etc., and inscribed with prayers to Osiris and Ànpu for sepulchral offerings. From Asyût. XIIth dynasty. Length 1 ft. 1 in., breadth 1 ft. 2 in. [No. 973.]

266. (*Bay* 16.)—Limestone **tablet for offerings** of **Āḥa-khu**, sculptured in relief with figures of offerings; in front are cut two tanks. From Asyût. XIIth dynasty. Length 12½ in., breadth 12½ in. [No. 974.]

267. (*Bay* 16.)—Limestone **tablet for offerings,** sculptured in relief with figures of libation jars, haunches of beef, geese, etc. In it are cut three tanks, *i.e.*, one for each of the three persons whose names are inscribed upon it, viz., **Ḥetep-à**, **Ḥep-tchefà**, and **Ànt**. The text contains prayers to Osiris and Ànpu for sepulchral offerings. From Asyût. XIIth dynasty. Length 9½ in., breadth 9½ in. [No. 990.]

268. (*Bay* 14.)—Limestone **tablet for offerings** of **Ḥeru** (?) **seḥt**, sculptured in relief with figures of libation vases, cakes, etc., and inscribed with prayers to Osiris and Ànpu for sepulchral offerings. From Asyût. XIIth dynasty. Length 1 ft. 2½ in., breadth 10½ in. [No. 929.]

269. (*Bay* 17.)—Rectangular limestone **tablet for offerings,** on four legs; made for **Usertsen**, a Ḥā prince and superintendent of the prophets, and inscribed with prayers on behalf of the deceased for sepulchral offerings, and the names of his father Ānkhet, his mother, and various near relations. On the face of the tablet are sculptured figures of two vases, etc., and at each end is a rectangular tank; in front is a deep channel. On the spout is cut the text of an address to the living, in which the deceased beseeches them to pray that he may receive sepulchral offerings. Anastasi Collection. XIIth dynasty. Length 1 ft. 10 in., breadth 1 ft. 7 in., height 8 in. [No. 590.]

270. (*Bay* 14.)—Limestone **tablet for offerings,** uninscribed, sculptured in relief with figures of offerings; in the front are cut two tanks. From Asyût. XIIth dynasty. Length 11 in., breadth 10½ in. [No. 975.]

271. (*Bay* 14.)—Limestone **tablet for offerings,** uninscribed, sculptured in relief with figures of sepulchral offerings; in the front are cut two tanks. From Asyût. XIIth dynasty. Length 10½ in., breadth 8½ in. [No. 997.]

272. (*Bay* 14.)—Limestone **tablet for offerings,** sculptured with figures of bread cakes, etc., and inscribed with prayers to Ȧp-uat and Osiris Khenti Ȧmenti, on behalf of a person whose name has been erased. XIIth dynasty, or later. Length 1 ft. 2½ in., breadth 1 ft. 1 in. [No. 420.]

273. (*Bay* 14.)—Limestone **tablet for offerings,** uninscribed, sculptured in relief with figures of libation vases, geese or ducks, etc.; at each end is cut a small tank. From Asyût. XIIth dynasty. Length 1 ft. 1 in., breadth 8 in. [No. 991.]

274. (*Bay* 16.)—Limestone **tablet for offerings,** sculptured in relief with figures of vases, etc., and inscribed with prayers to Osiris and Ȧnpu for sepulchral offerings. From Asyût. XIIth dynasty. Length 1 ft., breadth 1 ft. 2 in. [No. 977.]

275. (*Bay* 16.)—Portion of an uninscribed **tablet for offerings,** in which is cut a tank. From Asyût. XIIth dynasty. Length 7 in., breadth 7½ in. [No. 978.]

THIRTEENTH-SEVENTEENTH DYNASTIES.

276. (*Bay* 1.)—Red granite **seated statue** of **Sekhem-uatch-taui-Rā**, a king of the XIIIth or XIVth dynasty. The king is bearded, and wears a heavy wig, with an uræus over his forehead, and a close-fitting tunic. Both hands rest on the knees, and in the left the king holds an object which has not yet been identified. On the back of the throne are cut in outline the figures of two winged lions placed back to back; above them are the signs which probably refer to the "fluid of life," which animates and protects the king. On one side of the throne are the king's titles, "Giver of life," etc. About B.C. 2000. Height 7 ft. 6 in. [No. 871.]

277. (*Bay* 2.)—Limestone **sepulchral stele**, with rounded top, of Prince **Pau-ḥeru-á**, an Erpā, and Ḥā prince, who flourished in the reign of **Sekhem-ka-Rā**, a king of the XIIIth dynasty. On the upper portion is a winged disk, and below is a figure of Ḥāpi, the Nile god, making an offering to the *Serekh*, or Horus name of the king, "S-ānkh taui," *i.e.*, "Vivifier of the Two Lands." From the ruins of Athribis, near Benha. XIIIth dynasty. Height 3 ft. 10 in., width 2 ft. 2 in. [No. 1346.]

S-ānkh taui.

278. (*Bay* 5.)—Portion of a limestone **stele** inscribed with a text mentioning **Khā-nefer-Rā Sebek-ḥetep**, a king of the XIIIth dynasty. Height 1 ft. $3\frac{1}{2}$, width 1 ft. $6\frac{1}{2}$ in. [No. 1060.]

279. (*Bay* 5.)—Fine limestone **sepulchral stele,** with rounded top, of Ḥet-Ḥeru-sa, or **Sa-Hathor**, the son of Usertsen-Usá, inscribed with a prayer to Ptaḥ-[Seker-Ásár] and Ámen-Rā for funerary offerings. Below this is a list of the names of the relatives of Sa-Hathor and the offices which they held. On the upper portion are cut 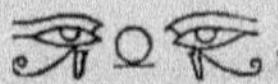, and in the left bottom corner are sculptured in low relief figures of the deceased and his wife Senb-sen 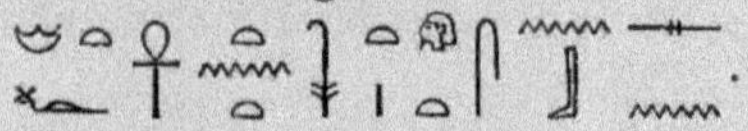. This stele was made in the reign of **Ab-åā** 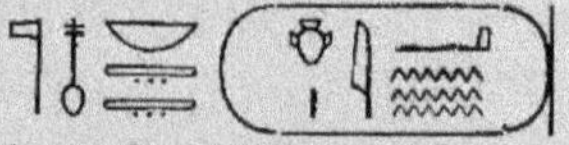, a king of the XIIIth dynasty. Height 1 ft. 10½ in. width 1 ft. 2½ in. [No. 1348.]

280. (*Bay* 1.)—White limestone **memorial cone** of **Sebek-ḥetep** , a scribe of the temple, son of Sebek-nekht, 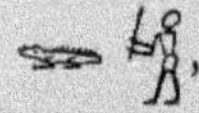, a scribe of the temple, and of the lady Sebek-ḥetepet, who flourished in the reign of **Sebek-em-sa-f,** king of Egypt, about B.C. 2000 . On the sides are the following scenes:—1. Sebek-ḥetep and his wife, Princess Åuḥetåb , standing before a table of offerings. 2. Sebek-ḥetep and his wife. 3. Sebek-ḥetep and his son standing before a table of offerings. From Thebes. XIIIth dynasty. Height 2 ft. 4 in., width at base 1 ft. 4½ in. [No. 1163.]

281. (*Bay* 3.)—Limestone **stele** with rounded top, on which is cut a scene representing King **Nefer-sekhem-khāu-Rā Åp-uat-em-sau-f** standing in adoration before the god Anubis. On the upper portion is a winged disk, with pendent uraei, and below this are six short lines of text containing the king's names and titles 

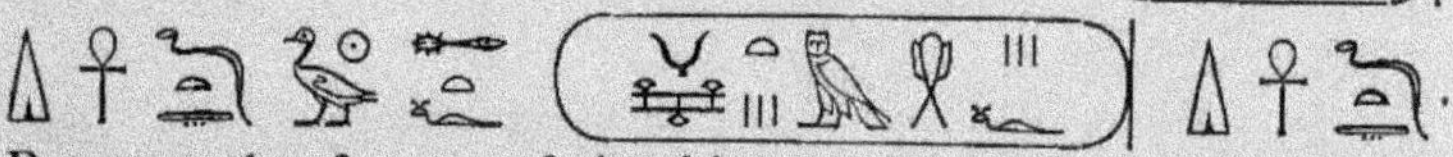.

Between the figures of the king and god is a line of text reading: "Adoration be to Åp-uat, the lord of Abydos, [every] "day." Harris Collection. XIIIth dynasty. Height 11 in. width 8 in. [No. 969.]

282. (*Bay* 4.)—White limestone **sepulchral stele,** with rounded top, inscribed with prayers for sepulchral offerings on behalf of the Princess **Teḥuti-āa** , and Prince **Ḥetep-neteru.** On the upper portion of it are the prenomen and nomen of King **Rā-sekhem-ṭā- . . . . . Pen- . . . .-then** (?). . The figure of the prince is sculptured in low relief, within a panel, and that of the princess is cut in outline. From Abydos. XIIIth dynasty. Height 1 ft. 3 in., width 10½ in. [No. 630.]

Presented by the Egypt Exploration Fund, 1903.

283. (*Bay* 5.)—Upper portion of a limestone **sepulchral stele,** with rounded top, on which are cut the figure of a winged disk, with pendent uraei, and a scene representing three men, one of whom is called **Besȧ** 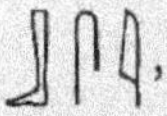, making offerings to Osiris Khenti Ȧmenti. Below these are three mutilated lines of text, in the first of which it is said that the "Ȧm-khent" priest **Ptaḥ-S-ānkh** 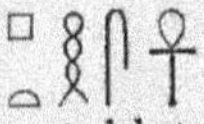, "offereth praise to Osiris, lord "of Abydos." This tablet was set up in the reign of **Sekhem-uatch-khā-Rā Rā-Ḥetep** . On the edge to the left are cut in outline figures of a man and two women. Anastasi Collection. XIIIth dynasty. Height 1 ft. 7 in., width 1 ft. 3½ in. [No. 833.]

284. (*Bay* 23.)—Red granite **slab** on which is cut the prenomen of King **Sekhem-khu-taui-Rā** 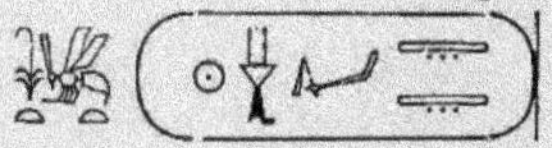, a king of the XIIIth or XIVth dynasty. Height 2 ft. 6 in., width 5 ft. 11 in. [No. 1100.]

Presented by the Egypt Exploration Fund, 1891.

285. (*Bay* 1.)—Limestone **sepulchral stele,** in the form of a door of a tomb, with palm-leaf cornice, dedicated to Osiris, lord of Tattu and Khenti Amenti, on behalf of **Nebȧ** , an inspector of the North and South. Within a raised border, which is decorated with zig-zag lines, are cut in outline figures of Men-nefer, his wife, his daughter Åru, and his sons Renås and Nekhti, who set up this tablet. Salt Collection. XIIth or XIIIth dynasty. Height 2 ft. 1 in., breadth 1 ft. 2 in. [No. 201.]

286. (*Bay* 2.)—Rectangular limestone **sepulchral stele,** in the form of a door of a tomb, with palm-leaf cornice and raised, rounded border, within which are five lines of hieroglyphic text and a scene wherein the deceased and his wife are represented, standing at a table of offerings. The text contains prayers to Osiris, lord of Ānkh-taui 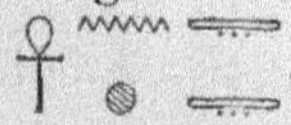, on behalf of a land inspector called **Iusenb** , the son of the lady **Åbeb** 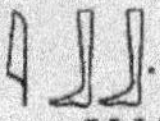. His wife Ṭep-åḥet was the daughter of Ren-senb. XIIth or XIIIth dynasty. Height 1 ft. 4 in., width 10½ in. [No. 861.]

287. (*Bay* 2.)—Rectangular painted limestone **sepulchral stele** of **Renf-senb** 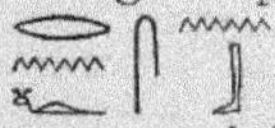, the son of Ḥāpu , with two lines of text, containing a prayer to Osiris for funerary offerings and a figure of the deceased standing with a table of offerings before him. Figures of two members of his family stand near. Text and scene are enclosed within a deep line border. From Thebes. XIIth or XIIIth dynasty. Height 1 ft. 1½ in., width 1 ft. [No. 636.]

288. (*Bay* 2.)—Grey granite uninscribed **portrait figure** of an ecclesiastical or civil official of high rank, who served in the city of Ḥet-ta-ḥer-åbt, or Athribis. He wears a heavy wig, and is draped in a long, cloak-like garment, which reaches to his feet and resembles the loose cloak worn by Egyptians at the present day. From Benha. XIIth or XIIIth dynasty, about B.C. 2266. Height 2 ft. 1 in. [No. 1237.]

289. (*Bay* 2.)—Rough-hewn granite **statue of Nefer-åri** , a high, priestly official, with shaven head and face. Before him he holds a shrine, on the front of which is inscribed a prayer to the god Ånpu (Anubis) for sepulchral offerings; below, in outline, are two roughly cut figures of the deceased facing each other, and each holding a staff and the *kherp* sceptre . The cutting and polishing of the figure were not completed. From Bubastis (Zaḳâzîḳ). XIIth or XIIIth dynasty. Height 2 ft. 11 in. [No. 1229.]

Statue of Nefer-âri, a priest, holding a shrine.
[Bay 2, No. 289.] XIIIth dynasty.

290. (*Bay* 3.)—Dark sandstone **sepulchral stele,** with rounded top, inscribed with a prayer to Osiris for funerary offerings on behalf of **Sebek-ḥetep** , the son of Atepi, Ḥeq-âb, the son of Atep, Tapi, the son of Ḥeq-âb, etc. Anastasi Collection. XIIth or XIIIth dynasty. Height 1 ft. 5 in., width 1 ft. 1 in. [No. 507.]

291. (*Bay* 3.)—White limestone **sepulchral stele,** with rounded top, which was set up by **Mentu-user-senb-f** in memory of his brother **Ānkhef** , the son of the lady Mert-nefer and Ānkh-ren, the superintendent of the revenue. The text contains a prayer to Osiris Khenti Àmenti for sepulchral offerings. XIIth or XIIIth dynasty. Height 1 ft. 6 in., width 1 ft. [No. 208.]

292. (*Bay* 3.) — Limestone **sepulchral stele,** in the form of a door of a tomb, with a palm-leaf cornice and a raised, rounded border. On the upper part is an inscription containing a prayer to Osiris that sepulchral offerings may be given to **Sebek-ḥetep,** an overseer, to **Nekhtenen** , and to the lady **Net-ḥetchet**, figures of whom are seen seated at a table of offerings. Below these is a list of the names of eight of their kinsfolk and those of their parents. XIIth or XIIIth dynasty. Height 1 ft. 2½ in., width 9 in. [No. 904.]

293. (*Bay* 3.)—Limestone **sepulchral stele**, with rounded top of **Àuà** (?), the son of the lady Kasen. On the upper portion are cut figures of the jackals of Ànpu and Àp-uat, and below these are two lines of text containing a prayer to Osiris for sepulchral offerings. On the central portion are figures of the deceased and his mother. The lower lines of text commemorate the mother, father, brothers, and sisters of the deceased. XIIth or XIIIth dynasty. Height 1 ft. 6 in., width 11 in. [No. 224.]

294. (*Bay* 4.)—Painted limestone **sepulchral stele**, with rounded top, of **Nekhtà**, a scribe. On it are cut the sacred eyes, the names and figures of Nekhtà, his wife Ḥekui, and their sons and daughters, and a prayer to Osiris, "lord of life and prince of the everlasting-"ness," for sepulchral offerings. XIIth or XIIIth dynasty. Height 11½ in., width 8 in. [No. 851.]

Presented by Sir A. Wollaston Franks, K.C.B., 1861.

295. (*Bay* 4.)—Rectangular limestone **sepulchral stele**, in the form of a door of a tomb, with painted palm-leaf cornice and a raised decorated border, of **Khenti-khathi-ur**, an official, the son of Aben and the lady Rent. This stele also commemorates his wife (?) Àthi and his mother Rent, and is inscribed with a prayer to Ànpu (Anubis), and to Ptaḥ-Seker-Àsàr for sepulchral offerings, figures of which are cut on its lower part. XIIth or XIIIth dynasty. Height 1 ft. 10½ in., width 1 ft. 2½ in. [No. 239.]

296. (*Bay* 4.)—Limestone **sepulchral stele**, with rounded top, of **Àru** (?), an official. On the upper portion are cut figures of the jackals of Ànpu and Àp-uat, and below are three scenes:—1. The deceased seated at a table of offerings, with his wife Ṭā-Ptaḥ-ānkh-s 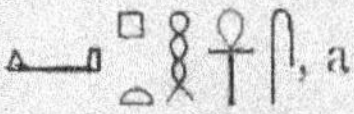, and his son before him. 2. His father, mother, and another member of his family. 3. His brother, with his son and wife. Below is inscribed an address to those who are on the earth, every priest and libationer, to pray to Osiris Khenti Àmenti that sepulchral offerings may be given to the deceased. XIIth or XIIIth dynasty. Height 1 ft. 8½ in., width 11 in. [No. 504, formerly 216.*]

Presented by Robert Goff, Esq., 1847.

297. (*Bay* 4.)—Limestone **sepulchral stele,** with rounded top, of **Menthu-ḥetep** , a worshipper of Khenti Àmenti, inscribed with a prayer to Osiris for funerary offerings, and for felicity in the Other World. Below the text is a scene in which the deceased and his wife Ḥāpi are seated on one side of a table of offerings, and his father and mother on the other. On the lower portion are figures of thirteen relatives and members of his family. XIIth or XIIIth dynasty. Height 2 ft. 1 in., width 1 ft. 3 in. [No. 213.]

298. (*Bay* 7.)—Portion of a hard stone **stele** on which are sculptured a figure of a god and a portion of the prenomen of a king . The inscription refers to the "Spirits of Ànnu" (Heliopolis). Found at the base of the column at Alexandria commonly known as "Pompey's Pillar." XIIth or XIIIth dynasty. Length 4 ft. 4 in., width 1 ft. 9 in. [No. 145.]

Presented by Earl Spencer, 1805.

299. (*Bay* 7.)—Limestone **sepulchral stele,** with rounded top, of **Pai-neḥsi** 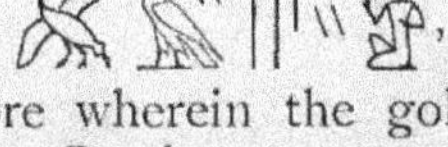, *i.e.*, "the Negro," a chief officer of the store wherein the gold from the Sûdân was stored, or worked. On the upper portion is a scene in which the ceremony of setting up on a standard the box containing the head of Osiris is represented; on one side stands Isis, and on the other are Horus and the cow-headed goddess Hathor. To the right and left are kneeling figures of the deceased. Below are two rows of figures, the first being those of seven male and the second those of eight female relatives, and an

Sepulchral stele of Ȧntef-ȧqer-Ānkh-khu, a priestly official.
[Bay 7, No. 301.]

inscription and figure of **Àni**, "the master-"craftsman of the house of gold, wherein the figures of the "gods are made." XIIth or XIIIth dynasty. Height 2 ft. 6 in., width 1 ft. 3 in. [No. 141.]

300. (*Bay* 7.)—Rectangular sandstone **sepulchral stele,** with raised border, set up to commemorate **Nefer-iu**, an overseer of the palace, **Àmeni,** and several of their relatives. On the upper portion are two lines of text containing a prayer to Ptaḥ-resu-àneb-f and Osiris Khenti Àmenti for funerary offerings. Below are sculptured three figures of the deceased persons, and a series of texts recording the names and titles of all those who are mentioned on the stele. XIIth or XIIIth dynasty. Height 2 ft. 5½ in., width 1 ft. 8 in. [No. 905.]

301. (*Bay* 7.)—Limestone **sepulchral stele,** with rounded top, of **Àntef-àqer-Ānkh-khu**, the son of Sen-ānkh, the texts and sculptures of which are enclosed within a double line border. On the upper part are cut, and below them are:—1. A prayer to Osiris on behalf of the deceased (who held the rank of chancellor, royal relative, and overseer of the palace) for sepulchral offerings. 2. A figure of the deceased seated with a draught-board and a table of offerings before him. 3. Figures of Usertsen-nefer-renput, Nebesu, Ṭāṭāt-nubt, Ḥeru, Menthu-em-ḥāt, Sen-Ānkh, Ḥeru-shere, Sāntef-ānkh, and Seḥāpi, relatives of the deceased. Anastasi Collection. XIIth or XIIIth dynasty. (**Plate XI.**) Height 2 ft. 3 in., width 1 ft. 3½ in. [No. 563.]

302. (*Bay* 7.)—Limestone **sepulchral stele,** with rounded top, on which are cut, set up to commemorate **Sen-bebà**, and **Ānkhu**, **Āqu**, **Senb**, and other relatives of the family of Sen-bebà.

On the upper portion are cut prayers to Osiris, Ȧp-uat, and Ptaḥ-Seker-Ȧsȧr for funerary offerings, and below, seated at two tables of offerings, are figures of four husbands and their wives. All the men appear to have been employed in the cemetery of Abydos (?). XIIth or XIIIth dynasty. Height 2 ft., width 1 ft. 2 in. [No. 1246.]

Presented by Morgan S. Williams, Esq., 1898.

303. (*Bay* 7.)—Limestone **sepulchral stele**, with rounded top, set up to commemorate **Ḥeq-hau** , a libationer, **Ȧmen-em-ḥāt-senb-f,** an inspector of the royal bodyguard , and **Usertsen,** the son of Sen-Ānkh. Below, sculptured in relief, are scenes where the deceased persons are seated at tables of offerings, and a list of names of members of their families cut in the hieratic character. The figures and some of the offerings are painted red. Salt Collection. XIIth or XIIIth dynasty. Height 1 ft. 4½ in., width 10 in. [No. 226.]

304. (*Bay* 7.)—Limestone **sepulchral stele,** with rounded top, of **Seḥetep-ȧb** 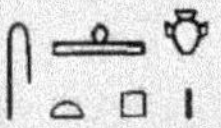, the son of Ḥer-seḥetep-ȧb , a councillor of the city of Nekhen, inscribed with a prayer to Osiris Khenti Ȧmenti for sepulchral offerings. On the upper portion, cut in outline, are figures of the gods Ȧp-uatu, and , and below are figures of the deceased, his son, and his wife. XIIth or XIIIth dynasty. Height 1 ft. 3 in., width 10½ in. [No. 221.]

305. (*Bay* 7.)—Limestone **sepulchral stele,** with rounded top, on which are inscribed 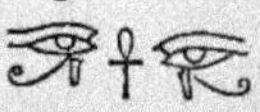, of the governor **Iuf-senb,** , a scribe and overseer; it was set up to his memory by his brother **Sa-Hathor,** warder of the bow. Below are cut figures of the deceased, his mother, grandmother, wife, daughter, etc. XIIth or XIIIth dynasty. Height 1 ft. 5 in., width 9½ in. [No. 255.]

306. (*Bay* 9.)—Rectangular limestone **sepulchral stele** of **Menthu-em- . . . . . ṭu** , his wife **Ren-sānkhu** (?) , painted figures of whom are cut below the inscription. Sams Collection. XIIth or XIIIth dynasty. Height 11 in., width 8 in. [No. 206.]

307. (*Bay* 3.)—Rectangular, limestone **sepulchral stele** of the lady **Seur-resht-ḥennut** 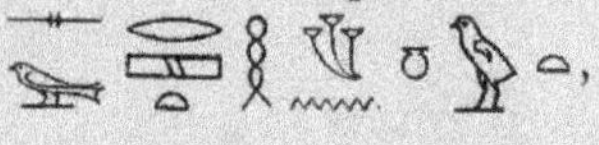, and her son **Ḥenḳȧ** ; below the text are figures of the deceased persons sitting at a table. XIIIth dynasty. Height 1 ft. 8 in., width 1 ft. 4½ in. [No. 1061.]

308. (*Bay* 3.)—Limestone **sepulchral stele,** with rounded top, of **Kherti-em-sa-f** , on which are cut a prayer to Osiris for sepulchral offerings and a series of figures of members of the family of the deceased bringing offerings to him. Sams Collection. XIIIth dynasty. Height 1 ft. 1½ in., width 8½ in. [No. 196.]

309. (*Bay* 3.)—White limestone **sepulchral stele,** with rounded top, of **Ānkh-Ḥeru** , son of Sat-nekht, and his wife **Āamu,** daughter of Merses, on which are cut, in sunk relief, figures of the same and of offerings, etc. Sams Collection. XIIIth dynasty (?). Height 9½ in., width 5½ in. [No. 195.]

310. (*Bay* 4.)—Limestone **slab,** of irregular shape, on which are traced in black ink the figures and names of **User** 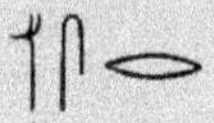, the son of Em-sa-s, and members of his family. On the upper portion several of the hieroglyphics and the table of offerings have been cut with a chisel. XIIIth dynasty (?). Height 9 in., width 8 in. [No. 207.]

311. (*Bay* 4.)—Limestone **sepulchral stele** of **Ȧmen-em-ḥāt** 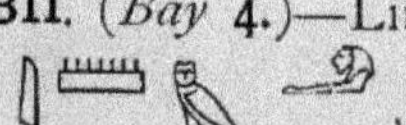, a seal bearer (?) and overseer, inscribed

with , and a prayer to Osiris for sepulchral offerings; below are figures of the deceased and his son. This stele was set up by Ȧmen-em-ḥāt's brother. XIIIth dynasty. Height 10 in., width 5½ in. [No. 231.]

312. (*Bay* 4.)—Limestone **sepulchral stele,** with rounded top, of **Ȧmeni** , a chancellor of Osiris, and son of Khenemesu , who was also a "divine "chancellor," and the lady Kaȧ . On the upper portion of the stele are figures of the jackals of Ȧnpu and Ȧp-uat, with the symbol of "life" between them, and a prayer to Osiris for sepulchral offerings, and below are figures of the deceased and his wife and other members of his family. Sams Collection. XIIIth dynasty or later. Height 1 ft. 6 in., width 1 ft. [No. 204.]

313. (*Bay* 4.)—Limestone **sepulchral stele,** with rounded top, of **Sheps** , a governor of the private apartments in the royal palace, son of Ḥennu . On the upper portion are cut the eyes of Horus , a prayer to Osiris and Ȧp-uat for sepulchral offerings, and figures of the deceased and members of his family; below are the names of several brothers, their mothers Rens-senb , and Ȧnȧ , etc. XIIIth dynasty. Height 1 ft. 6 in., width 1 ft. [No. 249.]

314. (*Bay* 4.)—Limestone **sepulchral stele,** with rounded top, of **Ḥetep-neb-su** , an overseer of the grain of the god Menu, or Ȧmsu, inscribed with a prayer to Osiris for sepulchral offerings. On the upper part are the eyes of Horus and Rā , and below the inscription are figures of the deceased, his son, wife, and mother. XIIIth dynasty or later. Height 1 ft. 1½ in., width 9 in. [No. 930.]

Presented by the Royal Institution, 1870.

315. (*Bay* 5.)—White limestone **sepulchral stele**, with rounded top, of **Tcharru** 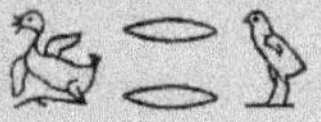, the son of the lady Seḥuri , a keeper of the seal, inscribed with a prayer to Ptaḥ-Seker-Åsår that sepulchral offerings may be given to the deceased and the members of his family, the names and figures of whom are cut on the monument. On the upper portion are cut the utchats and the symbol of "eternity" , and the "north" . XIIIth dynasty. Height 1 ft. 6 in., width 11 in. [No. 242.]

316. (*Bay* 7.)—Rectangular sandstone **sepulchral stele**, in the form of a door of a tomb, with palm-leaf cornice and a raised border, of **Ukheptāu** (?) 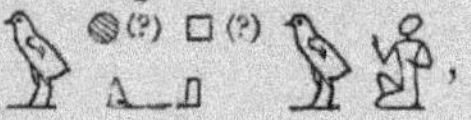, the son of Uatchet (?) , warden of a portion of the palace. The text contains a prayer to Osiris for sepulchral offerings, and mentions the names of the father, sisters, and grandmother of the deceased. XIIIth dynasty. Height 1 ft. 7½ in., width 1 ft. 3 in. [No. 791.]

317. (*Bay* 7.)—Limestone **sepulchral stele**, in the form of the door of a tomb, with palm-leaf cornice and raised border, of **Sabu** 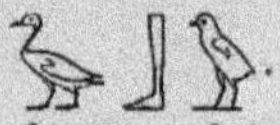. On the upper portion is cut a prayer to Osiris for sepulchral offerings, and below this are painted, sculptured figures of the deceased, his brother, son, wife, and other relatives. The right-hand bottom corner of the stele is wanting. XIIIth dynasty. Height 1 ft. 9½ in., width 10½ in. [No. 1244.]

Presented by Morgan S. Williams, Esq., 1898.

318. (*Bay* 7.)—Limestone **sepulchral stele**, with rounded top, on which are . Below is inscribed a prayer to Seker-Åsår and Hathor for sepulchral offerings on behalf of a prince, or chief, , who appears to have been called

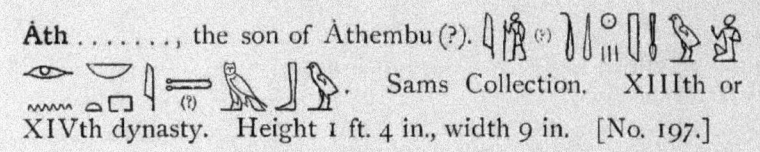

Åth . . . ., the son of Åthembu (?). . Sams Collection. XIIIth or XIVth dynasty. Height 1 ft. 4 in., width 9 in. [No. 197.]

319. (*Bay* 7.)—Limestone rectangular **sepulchral stele,** on the upper part of which is inscribed a prayer to Osiris for sepulchral offerings, on behalf of **Khenti-kha**[**ti**], a royal relative, a steward, and superintendent of the treasury. He was a loyal servant of the god "Ånpu on his hill." Below is a painted figure of the deceased, seated, with a table of offerings before him. XIIth to XVIIth dynasty. Height 1 ft. 7½ in., width 1 ft. [No. 251.]

320. (*Bay* 7.)—Limestone **sepulchral stele,** with rounded top, of **Sabu,** , the son of Keḥer-mert (?), a transport officer, inscribed with a prayer to Osiris for sepulchral offerings. Below this are sculptured five seated figures, representing his father, wife, etc., and 22 lines of text containing the names of male and female relatives. XIIth to XVIIth dynasty. Height 1 ft. 4 in., width 11 in. [No. 248.]

321. (*Bay* 9.)—Rectangular limestone **sepulchral stele,** in the form of the door of a tomb, with a palm-leaf cornice and a raised, rounded border, of **Sebek-ṭāṭā** , an official (?), the son of Khnemet (?). Below the text is a painted figure of the deceased receiving an offering from his son Sebek-ṭāṭā. Sams Collection. XIIth to XVIth dynasty. Height 11 in., width 7 in. [No. 234.]

322. (*Bay* 18.)—Limestone **pyramid,** uninscribed. In two sides are small niches, wherein are small kneeling figures, with hands raised in adoration, of the priest, or official, for whom this monument was made. Anastasi Collection. XIIth to XVIIIth dynasty (?). Height 1 ft. 10 in. [No. 477.]

323. (*Bay* 7.)—Limestone **sepulchral stele,** with rounded top, set up to commemorate **Kemes** , an artisan, his wife, Ren-s-senb, and several members of their family, and relatives. On the upper portion are cut in outline two jackals, and a prayer to Ȧp-uatu for sepulchral offerings. XIIIth to XVIIth dynasty. Height 1 ft. 1½ in., width 9 in. [No. 844.]

324. (*Bay* 7.)—Limestone **sepulchral stele**, with rounded top, on which are cut , set up to commemorate **Ȧtef-ȧi** , and **Nunā-ent-senu** 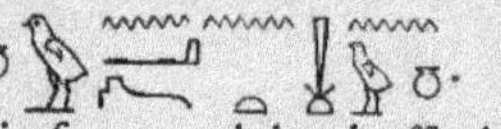. On the upper part are cut prayers to Osiris for sepulchral offerings, and below are sculptured figures of the deceased persons and of various members of their family, Ȧpu, Ānkhu, Khati-ur, Ama, Ȧpepi, and Sper (?). The lower portion of the stele is blank. XIIIth to XVIIth dynasty. Height 1 ft. 9½, width 1 ft. [No. 1245].

Presented by Morgan S. Williams, Esq., 1898.

325. (*Bay* 7.)—Limestone **sepulchral stele,** with rounded top, set up to commemorate **Ȧntef,** the chief libationer of the god Menu, or Ȧmsu, 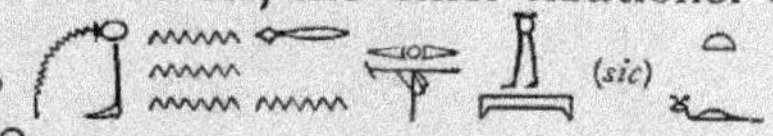, and **Ākub-ānkh** , the overseer of the storehouse of the offerings to the gods, by his brother **Menu-Nekht** (?) , a libationer of Menu, or Amsu. On the upper portion are cut prayers to Osiris and Ȧnpu for sepulchral offerings, and below are figures of Ȧntef, Menu-nekht, four wives, two brothers, a sister, and a priest. XIIIth to XVIIth dynasty. Height 1 ft. 7 in., width 11½ in. [No. 1247.]

Presented by Morgan S. Williams, Esq., 1898.

326. (*Bay* 7.)—Limestone **sepulchral stele**, with rounded top, on which are sculptured, in low relief, figures of a man and his wife, seated on chairs of state, receiving homage and offerings from members of their family. Above are . The stele is without inscription. XIIIth to XVIIth dynasty. Height 1 ft. 6½ in, width 12½ in. [No. 806.]

327. (*Bay* 9.)—Limestone **sepulchral stele,** with rounded top, set up by the lady **Ḥāpu** , in honour of her father **Nefer-ḥetep** 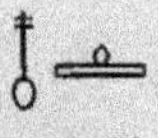, and her mother **Sebek-ḥetep** 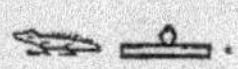. On the upper part are , and below, sculptured in relief, are figures of the deceased persons, who are seated with a table of offerings before them, and their daughter Ḥāpu, pouring out a libation. The text contains a prayer to Osiris for sepulchral offerings. XIIIth to XVIIth dynasty. Height 1 ft. 1 in., width 9 in. [No. 1370.]

328. (*Bay* 9.)—Limestone **sepulchral stele,** with rounded top, of **Uas (?) -ḥetep**, a warden of a portion of the palace, inscribed with a prayer to Osiris and Ȧp-uat for sepulchral offerings. On the upper portion are cut figures of jackals, and on the lower are figures of the deceased and his wife, and of kinsfolk seated. D'Athanasi Collection. XIIIth to XVIIth dynasty. Height 1 ft. 5 in., width 9½ in. [No. 236.]

329. (*Bay* 9.)—Sandstone **sepulchral stele,** with rounded top, of **Bebȧ-res**, a builder, inscribed with a prayer to Horus of Edfu, Ptaḥ-Seker, Ptaḥ of the Southern Wall, and Osiris for sepulchral offerings. On the upper portion are, and below the inscription are rudely cut figures of Bebȧ-res and his wife Neferu, receiving the offerings and homage of their five sons. From Thebes. XIVth to XVIIth dynasty. Height 1 ft. 4½ in., width 1 ft. 1 in. [No. 1371.]

330. (*Bay* 9.)—Upper portion of a limestone **stele,** with rounded top, on which are sculptured portions of the figures of . . . . . **kau,** a king, the period of whose reign is uncertain, and Queen **Merseḳer**. The king wears the White Crown, and the queen the vulture head-dress. Before the XVIIIth dynasty. Height 11½ in., width 10 in. [No. 846.]

Presented by Sir A. Wollaston Franks, K.C.B., 1861.

331. (*Bay* 9.)—Limestone **sepulchral stele,** with rounded top, of **Pa-enti-en**, the scribe of the robes

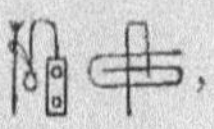, inscribed with a prayer to Osiris for sepulchral offerings. On the upper portion are the Utchats , and between them is cut a prayer on behalf of **Keki** 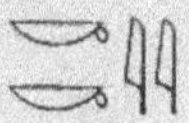 (?), a scribe of the wardrobe. On each side of a perpendicular line of hieroglyphics are cut figures of twelve seated women, each in a panel with her name. They represent the kinsfolk of the two scribes. XIIIth dynasty. Height 1 ft. 6½ in., width 1 ft. [No. 250.]

332. (*Bay* 9.)—Limestone **sepulchral stele,** with rounded top, of **Senbu** , a doorkeeper of some building of Osiris and Horus, inscribed with a prayer to Ptaḥ-Seker and Anubis for sepulchral offerings. On the lower portion of the tablet is a figure of Senbu seated with a table of offerings before him, and above are cut figures of four unguent vessels, with the names of their contents in hieroglyphics over them. XIIIth dynasty. Height 8½ in., width 6 in. [No. 246.]

333. (*Bay* 9.)—Limestone **sepulchral stele,** with rounded top, set up to commemorate **Ptaḥ-Sekri** 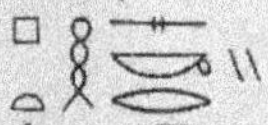, by his brother **Sebek-ḥetep,** the chief of the Southern Ten (?). On the upper portion are cut the utchats and symbol of eternity , and a prayer to Osiris for sepulchral offerings; below is a figure of the deceased standing, smelling a flower, with a table of offerings before him. Sams Collection. XIIIth dynasty. Height 8½ in., width 5 in. [No. 245.]

334. (*Bay* 9.) —Limestone **sepulchral stele,** with rounded top, of **Ki** , the son of the lady Sebek-ḥetep 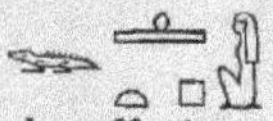, inscribed with a prayer to Osiris for sepulchral offerings. Below are cut figures of the deceased, adoring the rising sun, and his wife Āāḥ-Sat . On the right are ten lines of text which contain the names of his father, sisters, and other relatives. The hieroglyphics are well cut, and appear to have been inlaid with green colour. Sams Collection. XIIIth dynasty. Height 11 in., width 10 in. [No. 229]

335. (*Bay* 11.)—Limestone **sepulchral stele,** with rounded top, of a chancellor and overseer of the seal, the son of the lady Meru, inscribed with a prayer to Osiris for funerary offerings. On the upper portion are cut figures of Anubis of Ta-tchesert, and Anubis of the mummy chamber, and below are figures of the deceased and ten kinsfolk, each in a small panel, with his, or her, name in front. Sams Collection. XIVth to XVIIth dynasty. Height 1 ft. 8 in., width 1 ft. 2 in. [No. 210.]

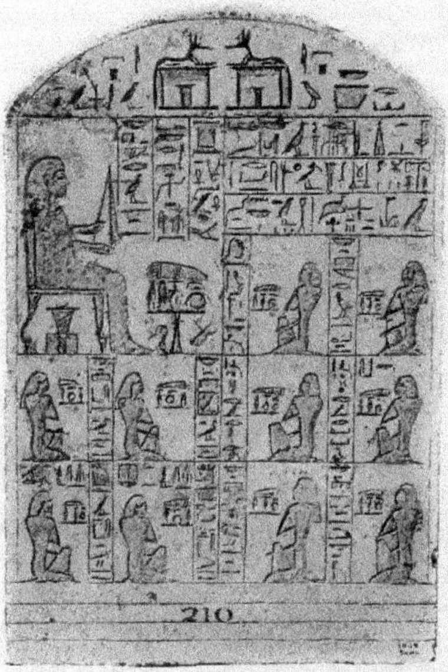

Sepulchral stele of a chancellor and overseer of the seal.
[Bay 11, No. 335.] XIVth to XVIIth dynasty.

336. (*Bay* 9.)—Limestone **sepulchral stele,** with rounded top, of **Āāḥmes**, a scribe, the son of the lady Āāḥmes, inscribed with a prayer to Ptaḥ-Seker-Āsār for sepulchral offerings. On the upper portion is cut a winged disk, with pendent uraei, and below the inscription is a figure of the deceased, who is accompanied by his wife Sab (?), receiving the homage of his father Åpumes, his mother, and son (?). XVIIth dynasty. Height 1 ft. 1 in., width 10 in. [No. 1314.]

337. (*Bay* **11.**)—Limestone **sepulchral stele,** with rounded top, of **Nekht**. On the upper portion are, and below is sculptured a scene in which Åāḥmes, an officer, son of Nekht, is represented pouring out a libation and making offerings to his father, and his mother Åāḥmes. XVIIth or XVIIIth dynasty. Height 1 ft. 3 in., width 11½ in. [No. 1318.]

338. (*Bay* **11.**)—Limestone **sepulchral stele,** with rounded top, of **Rei**, a temple official, inscribed with a prayer to Osiris for sepulchral offerings. On the upper portion are, and below is a scene in which Åmenḥetep, son of Rei, is represented, standing at a table of offerings making offerings to his father and his mother **Takmāi**. XVIIth or XVIIIth dynasty. Height 1 ft. 4½ in., width 1 ft. 3½ in. [No. 310.]

339. (*Bay* **23.**)—Red granite **slab,** on which are cut the name and part of an inscription of **Åpepå**, a Hyksos king. From the temple at Bubastis. Height 3 ft. 11 in., width 2 ft. 9 in. [No. 1101.]

Presented by the Egypt Exploration Fund, 1891.

340. (*Bay* 5.)—Granite **lion** inscribed on the breast "Beautiful god, **S-user-en-Rā**," , *i.e.*, with the prenomen of the Hyksos or "Shepherd" king, **Khian.** Purchased in Baghdad, Turkey-in-Asia. XVth or XVIth dynasty, about B.C. 1800. Length 1 ft. 7 in., height 10 in. [No. 987.]

341. (*Vestibule. South Wall.*)—Portion of a small stone memorial **pyramid** inscribed with the names of **Åntef-āa**

Åp-Maāt , king of Egypt, about B.C. 2600 (?), as the representative of Horus, as king of the South and North, and as son of Rā. XIth to XVIIth dynasty. Height 9½ in., base 1 ft. 2 in. square. Sams Collection. [No. 478.]

342. (*Bay* 4.)—Upper portion of a painted limestone **relief,** on which was sculptured a figure of **Nub-kheper-Rā**  **[Åntef].** On the right a portion of the White Crown of the king is visible, and in front are cut his titles and his prenomen; to the left is the vulture-goddess Nekhebit. From the temple of Osiris at Abydos. XIth–XVIIth dynasty, after B.C. 2000. Length 3 ft. 5 in., breadth 1 ft. 5 in. [No 631.]

EIGHTEENTH DYNASTY.

343. (*Bay* 16.)—Massive red granite **tablet for offerings,** which was dedicated to the temple of Ȧmen-Rā, at Karnak, by **Ȧāḥmes I,** king of Egypt, about B.C. 1600. On the face are sculptured in relief figures of bread cakes, a goose, haunch of beef, etc., and on the edges are cut the names and titles of the king. On the flat surface, on each side of the spout, is a deeply cut kneeling figure of the king. From Karnak. XVIIIth dynasty. Length 2 ft., breadth 1 ft. 6½ in. [No. 1142.]

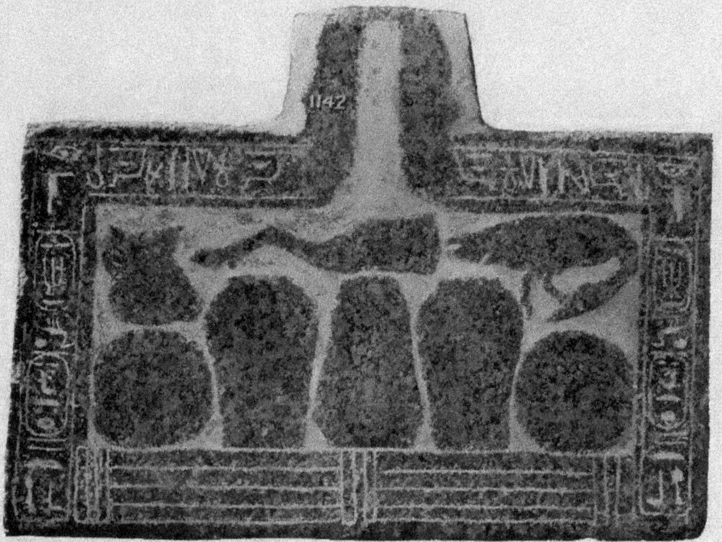

Red granite tablet for offerings of Ȧāḥmes I, B.C. 1600.
[Bay 16, No. 343.]

344. (*Bay* 12.)—Head from a black granite **seated figure** of **Queen Nefert-ȧri,** "the chief royal wife, and Lady of the "Two Lands," wife of Ȧāḥmes I, king of Egypt, about B.C. 1600 (?). From Thebes. XVIIIth dynasty. Height 11 in., width 7½ ins. [No. 1133.]

345. (*Bay* 20.)—Limestone **stele,** with rounded top, of **Pen-Åmen** (?) , a judge, on which are cut figures of the deceased and the Queen **Åāḥmes-nefert-åri,** who wears plumes and the solar disk  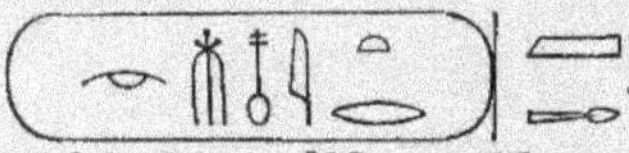. XVIIIth dynasty. Height 8 in., width 6 in. [No. 916.]

346. (*Bay* 3.)—White limestone **statue of Åmen-ḥetep I,** king of Egypt, about B.C. 1600, having the form and attributes of Osiris. The king wears the crowns of the South and North; above his forehead is the uraeus, symbol of sovereignty, and his arms are crossed over his chest. Down the plinth, at the back, is inscribed a line of large well-cut hieroglyphics, which contains some of the royal names and titles. From Dêr al-Baḥarî. XVIIIth dynasty. Height 9 ft. 2 in. [No. 683.]

Presented by the Egypt Exploration Fund, 1905.

347. (*Bay* 9.)—Upper portion of a fine white limestone **stele,** with rounded top, on which are sculptured the figures of four royal personages. In the centre is a table of offerings, and above it are written twice the prenomen and nomen of **Åmen-ḥetep** (I) . On the right of it is a figure of this king wearing the crowns of the South and North, and behind him is a figure of one of the **Menthu-ḥetep** kings, whose prenomen is 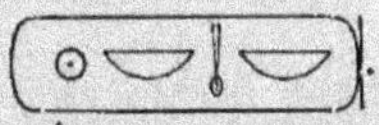. To the left of the table is another figure of Åmen-ḥetep I, wearing the crown of the South, and behind him is a figure of a king, whose name is not given. Above the group is a winged solar disk. From Dêr al-Baḥarî. XVIIIth dynasty, about B.C. 1600. Height 1 ft. 1½ in., width 1 ft. 4 in. [No. 690.]

Presented by the Egypt Exploration Fund, 1905.

348. (*Bay* 7.)—Portion of the upper part of a sandstone **relief,** with cornice and raised band, on which are cut in outline a figure of the judge , **Pa-sheṭ,** accompanied by his sister Makhai , "giving praise" to King **Åmen-ḥetep I**  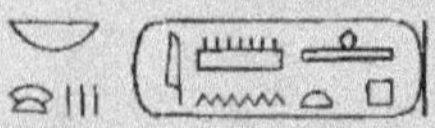, and his queen **Åāḥmes-nefert-åri** . XVIIIth dynasty, about B.C. 1600. Length 2 ft. 8 in., breadth 1 ft. 7 in. [No. 598.]

349. (*Bay* 9.)—Upper portion of a limestone **stele**, with rounded top, on which are cut seated figures of **Åmen-ḥetep I** 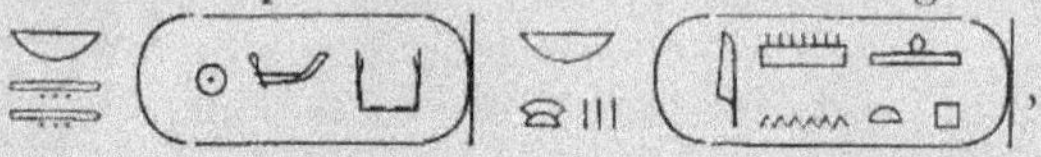, and his queen **Åāḥmes-nefert-åri** 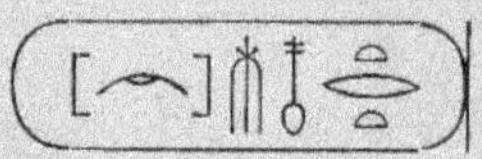. Belmore Collection. XVIIIth dynasty, about B.C. 1600. Height 8½ in., width 1 ft. 1 in. [No. 277.]

350. (*Bay* 10.)—Limestone **stele,** with rounded top, on which are sculptured figures of the cow of Hathor, Osiris wearing the Atef crown and holding the flail and sceptre, and **Åmen-ḥetep I,** with his right hand raised in adoration. The stele was made by a "sceptre bearer" in the "seat of "law," called **Qen** . . . . the son of Tchanefer and Nefert-åri. XVIIIth dynasty, about B.C. 1600. Height 1 ft. 3½ in., width 1 ft. 1½ in. [No. 815.]

Presented by Lyttleton Annesley, Esq.

351. (*Bay* 11.)—Portion of a **door-jamb** from the tomb of **Pa-Shuti** 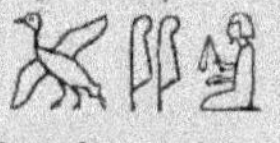, a scribe of the Place of Maāt, who flourished in the reign of **Åmen-ḥetep I** 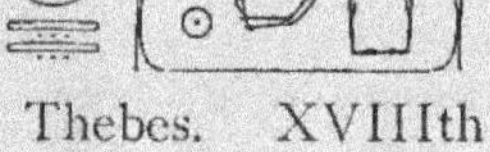 the son of Rā-ḥetep 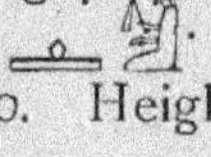. From Thebes. XVIIIth dynasty, about B.C. 1600. Height 2 ft. 11 in., width 1 ft. 1½ in. [No. 186.]

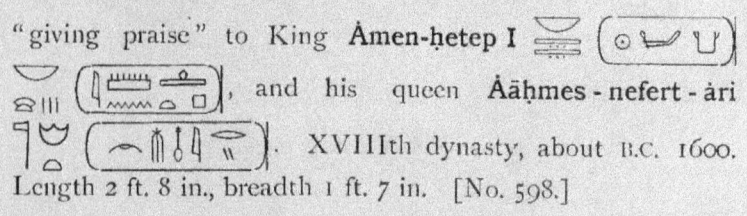

352. (*Bay* 8.)—Limestone **relief** from the tomb of **Ḥui**, a judge, and his wife, sculptured with two scenes in which the deceased is seen adoring Åmen of Thebes and his consort Mut, and **Åmen-ḥetep I** and his wife **Åāḥmes-nefert-åri.** XVIIIth dynasty, about B.C. 1600. Length 3 ft. 6 in., breadth 11 in. [No. 448.]

353. (*Bay* **8.**)—Limestone **stele,** with rounded top, of **Pa-ren-nefer** , a judge in the

Door-jamb from the tomb of Pa-Shuti, a scribe of Åmen-ḥetep I, B.C. 1600.

[Bay 11, No. 351.]

"seat of Maāt" in Western Thebes. Below a winged disk, with uraei, are cut figures of the deceased, who stands with his right hand raised, offering a cup of wine to **Åmen-ḥetep I**

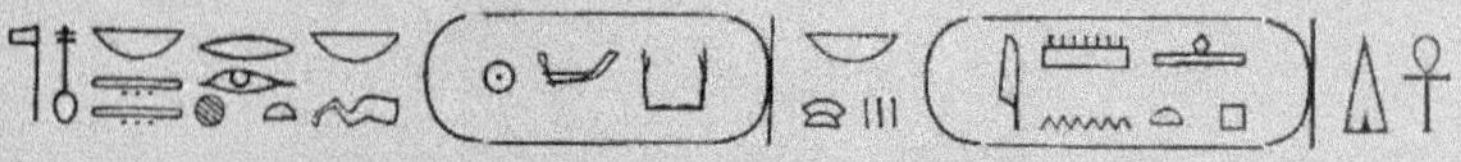
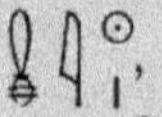, and his queen **Àāḥmes-nefert-àri** 
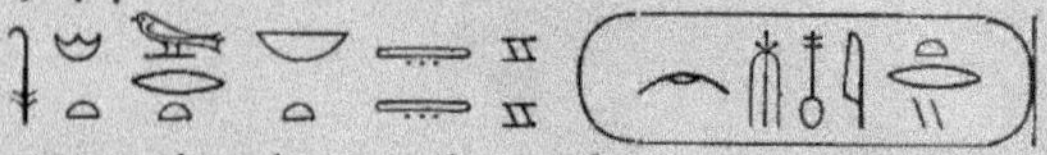. In the lower scene the deceased stands at a table of offerings facing his wife Mut-em-uáa, who is making an offering to him; behind him stand two sons, and behind his wife two daughters. XVIIIth dynasty. Height 1 ft. 10½ in., width 1 ft. 6 in.

[No. 1347.]

354. (*Bay* 10.)—Portion of a limestone **stele,** with rounded top, of **Àmen-em-àpt** 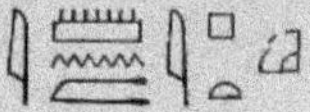, a judge. On the upper portion is sculptured a scene in which the deceased is represented standing at a table of offerings, and burning incense before Àmen-Rā, Mut, and **Àmen-ḥetep I** 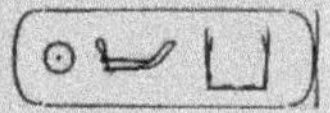 who reigned about B.C. 1600. From Thebes. XVIIIth dynasty. Height 11 in., width 11 in. [No. 816.]

Presented by Lyttleton Annesley, Esq., 1854.

355. (*Bay* 10.)—Painted limestone **stele,** with rounded top, of **Àmen-men** 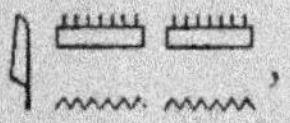, a judge. In the upper register is cut a figure of the deceased, standing at a table of offerings and making adorations to Osiris, Isis, and Horus, son of Isis. In the lower he is seen standing in adoration before **Àmen-ḥetep I** 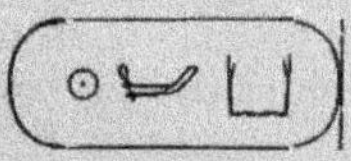, and the queens **Àāḥmes-nefert-àri**  and **Satkames** . Salt Collection. XVIIIth dynasty. Height 1 ft. 2½ in., width 9½ in. [No. 297.]

356. (*Bay* 10.)—Limestone **stele,** with rounded top, of **Nefer** 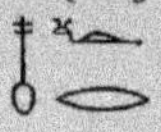, a judge. In the upper register is a figure of

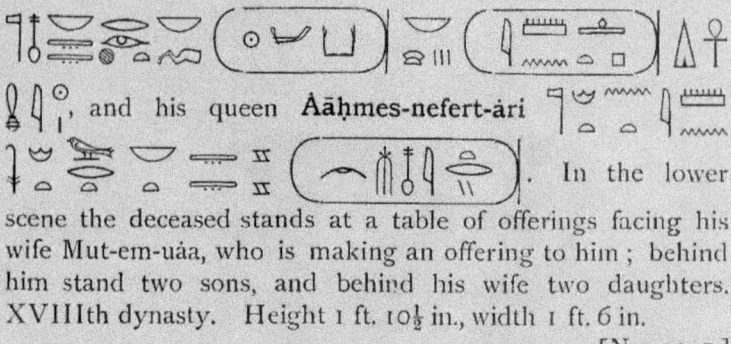

the deceased making an offering to **Ȧmen-ḥetep I** and his queen **Ȧāḥmes-nefert-ȧri,** who are seated on thrones, and in the lower are cut figures of Nefer, his sister, his son Pen-ur , and a daughter, seated, with hands raised in adoration. XVIIIth dynasty. Height 1 ft. 1 in., width 9½ in. [No. 811.]

Presented by Lyttleton Annesley, Esq., 1854.

357. (*Bay* 11.)—Portion of a limestone **sepulchral stele,** inscribed with five lines of hieroglyphic text containing prayers to the gods Osiris Khenti Amentet, Un-nefer, Ptaḥ-Sekri, Hathor, Ḥeru-sa-Ȧst, son of Ȧmen, and to King **Ȧmen-ḥetep I** and Queen **Ȧāḥmes-nefert-ȧri,** that sepulchral offerings may be made to **Ḥui,** a judge 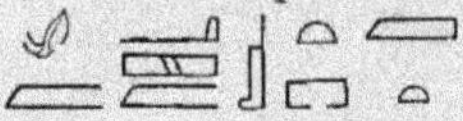 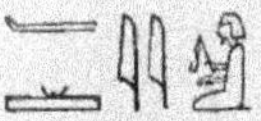, the son of the lady of the house Nefert-ithȧ. XVIIIth dynasty, about B.C. 1600. Height 9½ in., width 1 ft. 11 in. [No. 446.]

358. (*Bay* 13.)—Limestone **sepulchral stele,** with rounded top, of **Qaḥa** 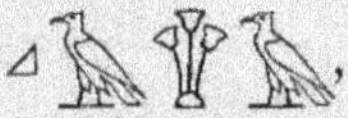, a judge, sculptured with a figure of the deceased making an offering to **Ȧmen-ḥetep I** , who wears the triple crown, and holds the sceptre , and the ṭeṭ , in his hands. XVIIIth dynasty. From the Belmore Collection. Height 7 in., width 4½ in. [No. 274.]

359. (*Bay* 14.)—Limestone **tablet for offerings** of **Rā-uben** , on which are sculptured in relief figures of bread-cakes, etc.; it is inscribed with a prayer on behalf of the deceased addressd to King **Ȧmen-ḥetep I** , and Queen **Aāḥmes-nefert-ȧri** 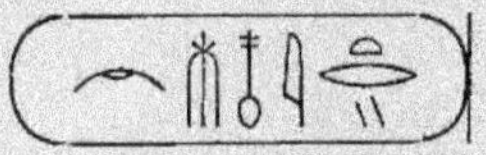, who are entreated to give him funerary offerings. XVIIIth dynasty. Length 1 ft. 2½ in., breadth 11½ in. [No. 594.]

360, 361, 362. (*Northern Gallery.*)—Red granite head from a colossal statue of an Egyptian king, wearing the crowns of the South and the North and the uraeus, symbol of sovereignty. It was found by Belzoni in 1817 at Karnak, near the remains of a granite building of Thothmes III, and for this reason has been regarded as the head of a statue of **Thothmes III**. For the left arm of the statue see No. 301 (**Bay 5**), and for a portion of the left leg see No. 362 (**Bay 5**). Salt Collection. XVIIIth dynasty, about B.C. 1550. Total height 9 ft. 5 in., height of the White Crown 4 ft. $3\frac{1}{2}$ in., diameter of Red Crown 4 ft. 7 in., length of ear 1 ft. $3\frac{1}{4}$ in., length of nose $11\frac{1}{2}$ in., width of face 2 ft. $7\frac{1}{2}$ in., weight 4 tons 1 cwt. [No. 15.]

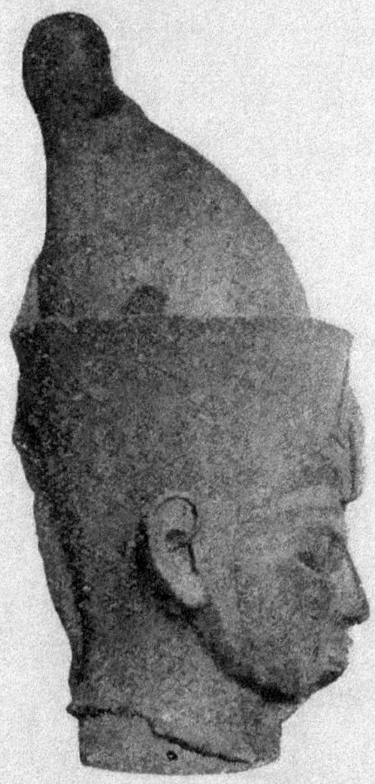

Head from a colossal statue of Thothmes III, B.C. 1550. [Northern Egyptian Gallery, No. 360.]

363. (*Bay* **2.**)—Massive **granite monument** set up at Karnak by **Thothmes III,** king of Egypt, about B.C. 1550. On the east and west sides, in high relief, are figures of Thothmes III, and the god Menthu-Rā, with hands touching. Those of the king are headless, but his identity is proved by the inscriptions over his shoulders  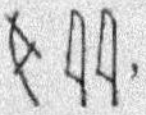, and on his belt 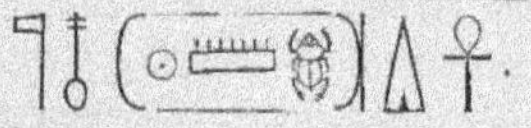. The god "Menthu-Rā, dweller in Thebes," is hawk-headed, and he wears on his head the solar disk, uraei, and plumes. On the north and south sides, also in high relief, are figures of the goddess "Hathor, lady of heaven, mistress of all the gods," 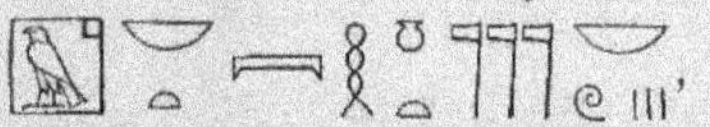, wearing the lunar disk and horns. This object was placed on a white stone base, and stood in a small temple in the north-east angle of the wall enclosing the temple of Àmen-Rā. It was acquired by Signor Belzoni for Mr. Henry Salt. XVIIIth dynasty. Height 5 ft. 10 in., base 4 ft. 3 in. by 2 ft. 6 in. [No. 12.]

E 3

364. (*Bay* 12.)—Fragment of the granite **obelisk** which was made for **Thothmes III,** about B.C. 1550, and set up at Heliopolis. It was removed to Alexandria during the Roman Period, and placed in the Hippodrome, but whether it was re-erected is not known. There it lay until 1878, when, at the cost of Sir Erasmus Wilson, it was brought to London. This obelisk is commonly known as "Cleopatra's Needle," and it now stands on the Thames Embankment. (From Heliopolis.) XVIIIth dynasty. Height 1 ft. 2 in., width 1 ft. [No. 943.]
Presented by J. Scott Tucker, Esq., 1852.

365. (*Bay* 10.)—Sandstone **jamb of a door,** inscribed with the prenomen of **Thothmes III** 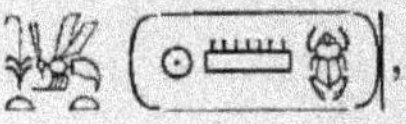, who is styled "Beloved of Horus of Behen, the Lord of the Land of the South" . It was found built into the wall of a modern house on the east bank of the Nile at Wâdî Ḥalfah. XVIIIth dynasty. Height 4 ft. 9½ in. [No. 1019.]
Presented by Major-Gen. Sir C. Holled Smith, K.C.M.G., 1887.

366. (*Bay* 6.)—Painted plaster **cast** of a red granite **Sphinx** on the breast of which, and in the space between the fore-paws, are cut titles and the prenomen of **Thothmes III** 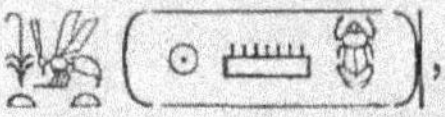, king of Egypt, about B.C. 1550. The original is in the Egyptian Museum at Cairo. Length 8 ft. 11 in. [No. 1109.]

367. (*Central Saloon.*)—**Cast** of a massive **stele** inscribed with a text, in which the god Àmen-Rā, the king of the gods, and lord of the thrones of the lands, enumerates the various countries which he has given into the possession of his chosen son, **Thothmes III.** On the upper portion, beneath the winged disk, are sculptured two scenes in which the king is represented making offerings of incense and unguent to Àmen-Rā. Behind him, in each scene, stands the goddess of Thebes, holding a bow and arrows in one hand. The original is in the Egyptian Museum in Cairo. Height 5 ft. 6 in.
[No. 1108.]

368. (*Bay* 11.)—Portion of a large handsome painted limestone **stele,** with rounded top, on which are sculptured in relief a figure of **Thothmes III** and a number of his titles.

The king is in the act of making an offering to a god, and he holds in his left hand a long staff and a mace . From the first few words left of the inscription we learn that the tablet was dated in the thirty-fifth year of the king's reign. From Wâdî Ḥalfah. XVIIIth dynasty. Height 1 ft. 11½ in., width 10 in. [No. 1021.]

Presented by Major-Gen. Sir C. Holled Smith, K.C.M.G., 1887.

369. (*Bay* 12.)—Rectangular sandstone **relief** on which are cut in outline the following scenes: 1. **Ȧmen-ḥetep I** 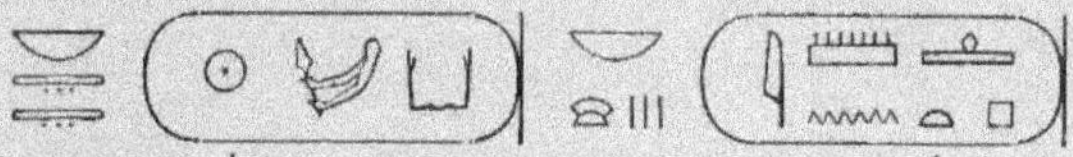, offering two vases to Ȧmen-Rā, lord of the South Ȧpt (Luxor), Khnemu, Sati, and Ānqet. 2. **Thothmes III** making an offering of Māat  to Ȧmen-Rā, of the North Ȧpt (Karnak), Mut, Khensu, and Hathor. Belmore Collection. XVIIIth dynasty. Height 1 ft. 11 in., width 4 ft. 5 in. [No. 153.]

370. (*Bay* 11.)—Portion of a sandstone **sepulchral stele,** with rounded top, which was set up in a temple at Wâdî Ḥalfah by an official of **Thothmes III,** who styles himself the "two eyes and the two ears" of the king, who held the rank of Ḥā prince and chancellor, and who was the governor of the Sûdân. Two figures and a cartouche have been erased; the remaining cartouche is that of Thothmes III . From Wâdî Ḥalfah. XVIIIth dynasty, about B.C. 1550. Height 1 ft. 7 in., width 1 ft. 1 in. [No. 1015.]

Presented by Major-Gen. Sir C. Holled Smith, K.C.M.G., 1887.

371. (*Bay* 10.)—Fine limestone **sepulchral stele,** with rounded top, of **Neb-uāui** , the first prophet of Osiris, god of Abydos, who flourished in the reign of **Thothmes III,** from whom he received many favours

On the upper portion are cut the utchats, and below are eighteen lines of well-cut hieroglyphics (portions of some, however, are defaced), in which the deceased enumerates the favours and promotions which he received from the king, and he seems to have held a position in connection with the memorial chapel (?) of **Āāḥmes I**. From Abydos. XVIIIth dynasty. Height 2 ft. 7 in., width 1 ft. 6½ in. [No. 1199.]

372. (*Bay* 8.)—Hard limestone **inter-columnar stele,** in the form of the door of a tomb, with palm-leaf cornice and raised, rounded border, set up to commemorate **Messuáu**, a priest of the temple of Thothmes III. On the obverse are the following scenes:—1. The deceased adoring Osiris, who is seated in a shrine. 2. The sons of the deceased making offerings to their father and mother. On the reverse are the following scenes:—1. The deceased adoring Rā-Ḥeru-khuti. 2. A son of the deceased making an offering to his father, who is seated on a chair. This stele is a rare example of the intercolumnar stelae of the XVIIIth dynasty. From Ṣaḳḳârah. Height 3 ft. 6 in., width 1 ft. 4 in. [No. 701.]

Seated statue of Netchem. [Bay 9, No. 373.] XVIIIth dynasty.

373. (*Bay* 9.)—Painted limestone **seated statue of Netchem**, an official, inscribed with prayers to Ȧmen-Rā, Mut, Osiris, Anubis, Hathor, and the royal Ka of Thothmes III for sepulchral offerings. Anastasi Collection. From Thebes. XVIIIth dynasty. Height 1 ft. 6½ in. [No. 840.]

374. (*Bay* 9.)—Limestone **seated statue of Ȧnebni** , a prince who was in charge of the king's bow and other weapons of war and the chase, who was a member of the royal bodyguard, and who followed his lord on his expeditions through the deserts and mountains in the South and in the North. It was set up in honour of the deceased, as a mark of their favour, by Queen **Ḥātshepset** and her "brother" **Thothmes III** 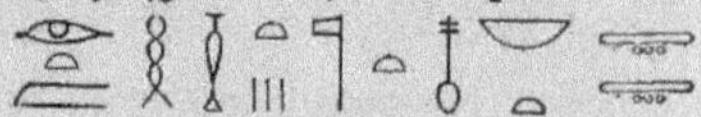 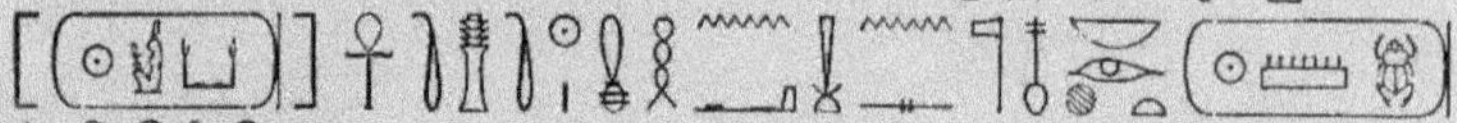 . The text, which is inlaid with blue paste, contains a prayer to Ȧmen-Rā, Osiris, and Anubis for sepulchral offerings. Salt Collection. XVIIIth dynasty. Height 1 ft. 8½ in. [No. 1131, formerly 51*a*.]

375. (*Bay* 4.)—Painted limestone **seated statues of Ȧthu** 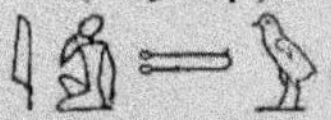, an Ȧm-khent priest, a libationer of Ȧmen, a warden of the palace, and an overseer of the treasury, and **Ḥent-ur** , "his beloved sister," priestess of Ȧmen, and their son **Nefer-ḥeb-f.** The group was dedicated to the memory of his parents by Nefer-ḥeb-f 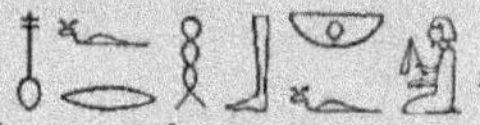, second priest of **Ȧmen-ḥetep II,** king of Egypt, about B.C. 1500. 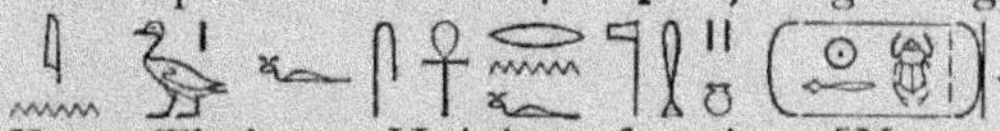. Salt Collection. From Thebes. Height 2 ft. 5 in. [No. 31.]

376. (*Bay* 12.)—Portion of a grey **granite bowl** made for **Teḥuti-mes** 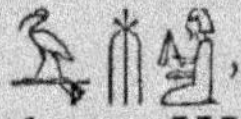, a royal scribe, who flourished in the reigns of **Thothmes III** and **Ȧmen-ḥetep II,** whose cartouches appear on it side by side, thus:—

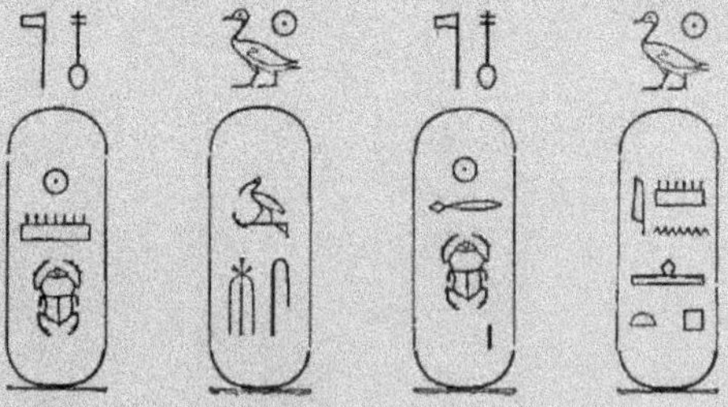

From Coptos. XVIIIth dynasty. Height 1 ft. 6½ in., diameter 1 ft. 6½ in. [No. 890.]

377. (*Bay* 11.)—Fine white limestone **sepulchral stele,** with rounded top, of **Åmen-ḥetep** 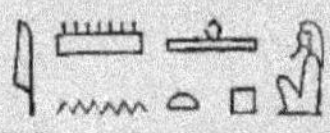, a member of the body-guard of **Thothmes IV**, who accompanied the king on his expeditions into Northern Mesopotamia and into the Southern Sûdân. On it are sculptured the following scenes:—1. The winged disk, beneath which are the cartouches of Thothmes IV, flanked by the jackal-gods Ånpu and Åp-uatu. 2. Figures of the deceased worshipping Osiris Khenti Åmenti and Åp-uatu, who are seated within a shrine with a cornice of uraei. 3. The deceased and his wife Ån-Ḥer-ḥent 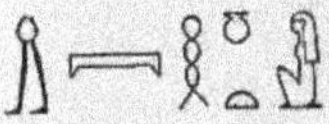, receiving offerings from their son Ḥāt . 4. The deceased and his mother Ri 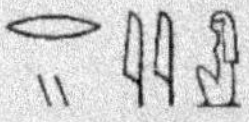 receiving offerings. The text contains a prayer for sepulchral offerings. Fine work. XVIIIth dynasty. (**Plate XII.**) Height 2 ft. 10 in., width 1 ft. 11 in. [No. 902.]

378. (*Bay* 8.)—Limestone **sepulchral stele**, with rounded top, of **Nefer-ḥāt** 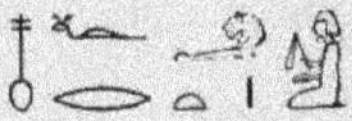, a Superintendent of the Works of the Temple in Abydos, who flourished in the reign of King **Thothmes IV** 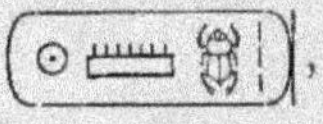, about B.C. 1450. On the upper portion are two jackals, two utchats,  and , and the deceased is standing in adoration before Menu, Osiris, and Isis, and below, in two registers, he is receiving adoration and offerings from his kinsfolk. At the bottom of the stele are four lines of text containing a prayer of the deceased to Osiris and Anubis for sepulchral offerings. Salt Collection. XVIIIth dynasty. Height 3 ft., width 2 ft. [No. 148.]

379. (*Bay* 7.)—Black granite model of a **ceremonial boat,** with the lower portion of a seated figure of the "Chief Wife and Royal Mother," **Mut-em-uȧa** , queen of Thothmes IV

Sepulchral stele of Ȧmen-ḥetep, a member of the body-guard of Thothmes IV, B.C. 1450.

[Bay 11, No. 377.]

and mother of Amen-ḥetep III, in the character of Mut, the consort of Åmen-Rā, the great god of Thebes. At the feet of the queen are cut her name and titles and a table of offerings, and on each side of the boat are an *utchat* 𓂀, and a long cartouche containing the queen's names and titles. The prow is sculptured on the back and front with heads of the goddess Hathor, above which rises the base of a sistrum; in the panels of this are cut the prenomen and nomen of Åmen-ḥetep III, and on the flat upper surface is a cartouche, partly obliterated. For the head of the seated figure of the queen in the boat see No. 380 (1434). From the Belmore Collection. XVIIIth dynasty, about B.C. 1450. Length 7 ft. 4 in. [No. 43.]

380. (*Bay* 7.)—Portion of the **head of the** black granite **seated figure] of Mut-em-uåa**, queen of Thothmes IV and mother of Åmenḥetep III, from the model of the ceremonial boat of the goddess Mut, described in the preceding number. The queen wears a crown of uraei inscribed with her name 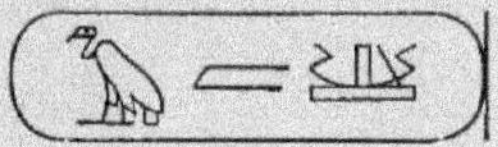, and a heavy wig, and on her forehead is a uraeus. The lower portion of the face is restored. Height 6 in. [No. 1434.]

381–404. A series of black granite **statues,** seated and standing, and portions of statues of the lioness-headed **Fire-goddess Sekhet,** who symbolized the fierce destructive heat of the sun. She wears the solar disk and uraeus, and holds in one hand the symbol of "life" 𓋹, and in the other the papyrus sceptre 𓇅. These statues came from the temple of Mut at Thebes, built by **Åmen-ḥetep III,** about B.C. 1450:—

381. (*Bay* 1.)—Statue of Sekhet. Feet wanting. Height 7 ft. 10 in. [No. 76.]

382. (*Bay* 1.)—Statue of Sekhet. Feet wanting. Height 7 ft. 6 in. [No. 80.]

383. (*Bay* 1.)—Statue of Sekhet. Feet wanting. Height 4 ft. [No. 50.]

384. (*Bay* 1.)—Statue of Sekhet. Feet wanting. Height 3 ft. 8 in. [No. 71.]

385. (*Bay* 2.)—Statue of Sekhet. Feet wanting. Height 5 ft. 9 in. [No. 72.]

386. (*Bay* 2.)—Statue of Sekhet. Feet wanting. Height 5 ft. 5 in. [No. 60.]

387. (*Bay* 3.)—Statue of Sekhet. Feet wanting. Height 5 ft. [No. 53.]

388. (*Bay* 5.)—Statue of Sekhet. Feet wanting. Height 7 ft. [No. 49.]

389. (*Bay* 6.)—Statue of Sekhet. Feet wanting. Height 3 ft. 10 in. [No. 69.]

390. (*Bay* 7.)—Seated statue of Sekhet. Height 4 ft. 9 in. [No. 65.]

391. (*Bay* 10.)—Seated statue of Sekhet. Height 7 ft. 2 in. [No. 62.]

392. (*Bay* 7.)—Statue of Sekhet. Feet wanting. Height 6 ft. 6½ in. [No. 45.]

393. (*Bay* 8.)—Statue of Sekhet. Feet wanting. Height 6 ft. [No. 84.]

394. (*Bay* 9.)—Statue of Sekhet. Feet wanting. Height 5 ft. 4 in. [No. 41.]

395. (*Bay* 12.)—Statue of Sekhet. Feet wanting. Height 5 ft. 4 in. [No. 519.]

396. (*Bay* 13.)—Statue of Sekhet. Feet wanting. Height 4 ft. 10 in. [No. 520.]

397. (*Bay* 10.)—Upper portion of a statue of Sekhet. Height 3 ft. [No. 87.]

398. (*Bay* 10.)—Upper portion of a statue of Sekhet. Height 2 ft. 7 in. [No. 85.]

399. (*Bay* 15.)—Upper portion of a statue of Sekhet. Height 3 ft. [No. 599.]

Presented by W. R. Hamilton, Esq., 1838.

400. (*Bay* 11.)—Head of a statue of Sekhet. Height 2 ft. 6 in. [No. 521.]

401. (*Bay* 11.)—Head of a statue of Sekhet. Height 2 ft. 3 in. [No. 77.]

402. (*Bay* 13.)—Head of a statue of Sekhet. Height 1 ft. 10 in. [No. 522.]

403. (*Bay* 16.)—Head of a statue of Sekhet. Height 3 ft. 4 in. [No. 52.]

404. (*Bay* 4.)—Head of a statue of Sekhet. Height 2 ft. 3 in. [No. 79.]

405. (*Bay* 4.)—Black granite **seated statue** of the lioness-headed **Fire-goddess Sekhet**; she wears the solar disk and holds in her right hand the symbol of "life" . On the front of her throne are inscribed the names and titles of **Neb-Maāt-Rā Åmen-ḥetep (III)**, prince of Thebes, and on each side is cut in outline a design representing the union of the papyrus and lily, *i.e.*, the South and the North . From Karnak. About B.C. 1450. Height 6 ft. 9½ in. [No. 88.]
Presented by King George III, 1801.

406. (*Bay* 5.)—Black granite **seated statue** of the **Fire-goddess Sekhet,** wearing the solar disk and holding the symbol of "life" in her left hand. On each side of the throne is the design , symbolizing the union of the Lands of the South and North, and on the front is cut an inscription which contains names and titles of **Åmen-ḥetep III,** and indicates that the statue was dedicated by the king to the goddess in her character of "Smiter of the Ånti" . From Karnak. XVIIIth dynasty, about B.C. 1450. Height 6 ft. 9 in. [No. 57.]

407. (*Bay* 8.)—Black granite **seated statue** of the **Fire-goddess Sekhet,** wearing the solar disk and holding the symbol of "life" in her left hand. It was dedicated to Sekhet in her character of Ḥert-en-qef, by **Åmen-ḥetep III,** king of Egypt, about B.C. 1450.

From Karnak. Salt Collection. XVIIIth dynasty, about B.C. 1450. Height 6 ft. [No. 68.]

408. (*Bay* 9.)—Black granite **seated statue** of the **Fire-goddess Sekhet,** holding the symbol of life in her left hand. It was dedicated to Sekhet in her attribute of "Lady of "Sehert" 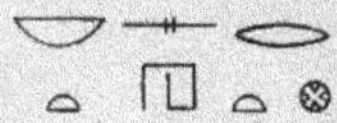, by **Åmen-ḥetep III.** On each side of the throne is cut the symbol of the "union of the South and "North," symbolized by the knotting together of the stems of the papyrus and the lily. Found near the Memnonium, in Western Thebes. XVIIIth dynasty, about B.C. 1450. Height 5 ft. 8½ in. [No. 37.]

409. (*Bay* 11.)—Black granite colossal **seated statue** of the **Fire-goddess Sekhet,** wearing the solar disk and holding the symbol of "life" in her left hand. It was dedicated to the goddess in her character of "Lady of the Two Acacias" 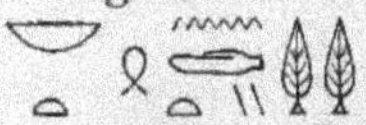, by **Åmen-ḥetep III,** king of Egypt, about B.C. 1450. From Karnak. Belmore Collection. XVIIIth dynasty. Height 6 ft. 8 in. [No. 518.]

410. (*Bay* 6.)—Black granite **seated statue** of the **Fire-goddess Sekhet,** wearing the solar disk and holding the symbol of "life" in her left hand. On each side of the throne is the design , symbolizing the union of the Lands of the South and North, and on the front is cut an inscription which contains names and titles of **Åmen-ḥetep III,** and indicates that the statue was dedicated by the king to the goddess in her character of "crusher of hearts" . From Karnak. XVIIIth dynasty, about B.C. 1450. (**Plate XIII.**) Height 7 ft. 9½ ins. [Nos. 16 and 73.]

411. (*Bay* 6.)—Portion of a sandstone **stele,** inscribed with an account of an expedition which was made by **Åmen-ḥetep III,** king of Egypt, about B.C. 1450, against the country of Åbeh, in the Northern Sûdân. The text states that the king captured 740 slaves, old and young, and mentions "312 hands," which he appears to have cut off. This tablet was set up at Semnah in the Second Cataract by **Meri-mes,** a royal scribe and governor of the Egyptian Sûdân, to commemorate his master's conquests. XVIIIth dynasty. Height 2 ft. 9 in., width 3 ft. [No. 657 (138*).]

Presented by Lord Prudhoe, 1835.

Seated statue of the Fire-goddess Sekhet, dedicated to the goddess by Åmen-ḥetep III, B.C. 1450.

[Bay 6, No. 410.]

412. (*Bay* 8.)—Black granite colossal **seated statue** of a king, wearing the usual heavy wig, with an uraeus over the forehead, which terminates behind in a pig-tail. Round his neck is a deep necklace, and he has about his loins a fluted tunic, which is held in position at the waist by a belt with an oval fastening in front; the belt is ornamented with a wave pattern . Between his legs hangs the tail which was worn by gods and kings from the earliest to the latest times. His throne is of the usual shape, and on its sides are cut the

Stele recording an expedition into the Sûdân by Åmen-ḥetep III, about B.C. 1450.
[Bay 6, No. 411.]

symbol of the union of the South and North . The statue is uninscribed, but, as it was found in the **Memnonium**, it probably represents **Åmen-ḥetep III.** Salt Collection. XVIIIth dynasty. From Thebes. Height 7 ft. 9 in.

[No. 14.]

413. (*Bay* 9.)—Colossal black granite **seated statue** of **Ȧmen-ḥetep III,** wearing the royal head-dress, with an uraeus over his forehead. Round his waist is the royal girdle, inscribed with the king's names and titles, and between his legs falls the animal's tail, which was fastened at the back of the girdle. On the front of the throne are cut the royal names and titles, and on each side of it is the symbol of the Union of the South and North. Down the back of the plinth are cut the king's names as:—1. The successor of Horus. 2. Lord of Nekhebet and Per-Uatchet. 3. King of the South and North. 4. Son of Rā. By the heel of the left foot is cut the name of **BELZONI,** the famous Italian traveller who discovered the statue. Found behind the Memnonium in Western Thebes. Salt Collection. XVIIIth dynasty, about B.C. 1450. Height 9 ft. 6 in. [No. 21.]

414. (*Bay* 11.)—Portion of a grey granite **statue of Ȧmen-ḥetep III,** king of Egypt, about B.C. 1450; on the back are the remains of an inscription containing the king's names and titles. From Thebes. XVIIIth dynasty. Height 1 ft. 7½ in. [No. 105.]

415. (*Bay* 6.)—Upper portion of a colossal bearded **statue of Ȧmen-ḥetep III,** wearing a heavy wig and an elaborate necklace; above his forehead is the uraeus, the symbol of sovereignty. Salt Collection. Found in the ruins between the Memnonium and the temple of Madînat Habû. XVIIIth dynasty, about B.C. 1450. Total height 5 ft., width of shoulders 3 ft. 11 in. [No. 30.]

416. (*Bay* 4.)—Hard sandstone head of a colossal **statue of Ȧmen-ḥetep III,** wearing the uraeus, the symbol of sovereignty, above his forehead. It was found by Mr. Henry Salt during the excavations which he made at a place in a line with the Colossi, or statues of Ȧmen-ḥetep III, and it appears to belong to one of the statues which this king set up before his funerary temple. Salt Collection. From Western Thebes. XVIIIth dynasty, about B.C. 1450. Total height 3 ft. 10 in., length of face 2 ft. 1 in., length of nose 11 in., length of mouth 1 ft. 2 in. [No. 6.]

417. (*Bay* 5.)—Hard sandstone head of a colossal **statue of Ȧmen-ḥetep III,** wearing the uraeus, the symbol of sovereignty, above his forehead. Found by Mr. Henry Salt near

No. **416** (6). Salt Collection. From Western Thebes. XVIIIth dynasty, about B.C. 1450. Total height 3 ft. 6 in. [No. 4.]

418. (*Central Saloon.*)—Grey granite **head** from the **sarcophagus of Åmen-ḥetep III,** king of Egypt, about B.C. 1450. From the tomb of the king at Thebes. Salt Collection. XVIIIth dynasty. Height 2 ft. 9 in. [No. 140.]

419. (*Bay* 7.)—Grey **granite column,** in four sections, from a small temple erected at Memphis (?) by King **Åmen-ḥetep III,** whose cartouche is cut on the north and south sides of the abacus in the following form:  *Neb-Maāt-Rā meri Ḥeru khent peru.* The lower half of the column was destroyed at some period between B.C. 1450 and 1300, but during the reign of **Mer-en-Ptaḥ** (Menephthah I) it was repaired, and this king had his cartouches cut on all the volutes, together with the prenomen of Åmen-ḥetep III, in the following form:  *Mer-en-Ptaḥ ḥetep ḥer Maāt.* About one hundred years later the King **Set-nekht** cut his cartouches 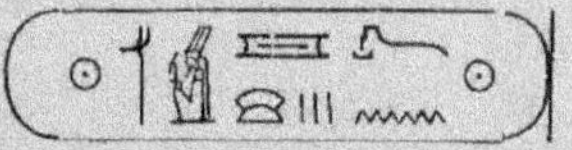  on the abacus and other places on the column. Brought from a house in Cairo. Salt Collection. XVIIIth dynasty, about B.C. 1450. Height 13 ft. 11 in. [No. 64.]

420. (*Bay* 12.)—Black **granite coffin of Meri-mes** 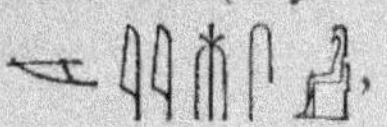, a "prince of Kesh" 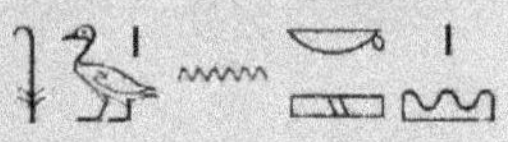, and "Governor of the lands of the South" 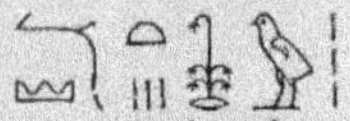, *i.e.*, of the Sûdân, and governor of the gold-producing lands of Åmen 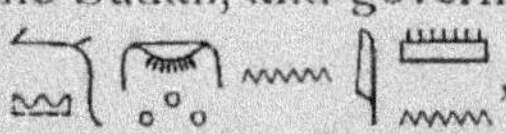, who flourished in the reign of Åmen-ḥetep III. The prince wears the usual head-dress, and a deep elaborately decorated pectoral, beneath which is a kneeling figure of the goddess Nut, whose wings are extended in protection of the deceased. Down the front of the cover is the text of a prayer to this goddess, who is asked to spread her wings over the deceased, and to place him with the everlasting star-gods. The texts on the other portions of the coffin contain the names of the four sons of Horus and of other funerary gods, some of whom address the deceased, and promise him a newly constituted body and happiness. XVIIIth dynasty. Height 6 ft. 6 in. [No. 1001.]

421. (*Bay* 6.)—Lower portion of a **seated figure of Sururu** 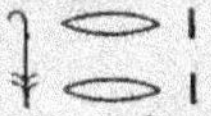, an Erpā, Ḥā prince, real royal scribe, overseer of cattle, superintendent of estates, chief of the Smeru nobles, steward of the king's house, etc. On the right side of the seat is a prayer to Temu for sepulchral offerings, and on the left a prayer to Āmen, king of the gods, for funerary food in perpetuity. XVIIIth dynasty. Feet restored. Height 10 in. [No. 503.]

422. (*Bay* 7.)—Portion of a limestone **statue** of **Āmen-em-ḥāt,** who was surnamed **Sururu**  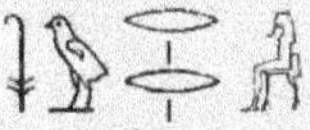, an Erpā, Ḥā prince, Smer-uāt, royal scribe and deputy fan-bearer, and personal attendant on the king, who performed the duties of several high offices, holding a stele, with a rounded top, inscribed with addresses to Āmen-Rā, king of the gods. The deceased flourished in the reign of **Āmen-ḥetep III** 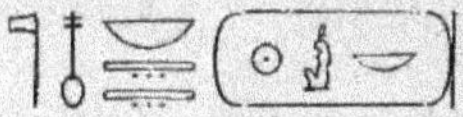, a figure of whom is seen on the upper portion of the stele, making an offering to Āmen-Rā. A full list of the titles of the deceased is given on the back of the statue. Sams Collection. XVIIIth dynasty, about B.C. 1450. Height 1 ft. 11 in. [No. 123.]

423. (*Bay* 5.)—Grey granite **seated figure of Ka-mes** , a "king's messenger by every water, and land, and "mountain," 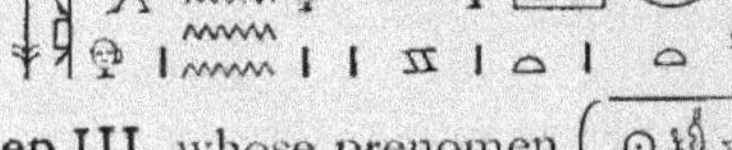, and a fan-bearer of **Āmen-ḥetep III,** whose prenomen 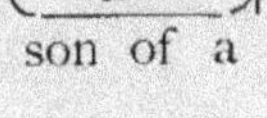 is cut on his right arm. The deceased was the son of a royal envoy

Sepulchral stele of Àpeni, director of the transport of Pharaoh, Àmen-ḥetep III, about B.C. 1450.

[Bay 11, No. 425.]

named Māi 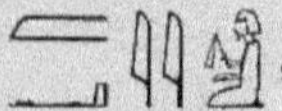, who held high office in the royal chancery. The inscription on the body of the figure contains a prayer by Kames to Menu, or Åmsu, and Isis, that sepulchral offerings may be given to him. XVIIIth dynasty, about B.C. 1450. Height 1 ft. $10\frac{1}{2}$ in. [No. 1210.]

424. (*Bay* 10.)—Massive sandstone **lintel,** with moulded cornice, from the doorway of the tomb of **Pa-åri** 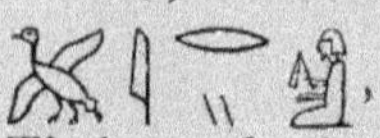, an overseer of the granaries of Åmen-Rā at Thebes. In the centre are the cartouches of **Åmen-ḥetep III,** surmounted by plumes and flanked by the Horus names of the king; below these is the symbol of the union of the Two Lands . On one side is an address of homage to Åmen by the deceased, and on the other an address to Mut. At each end of the slab is a figure of the deceased. From Thebes. XVIIIth dynasty, about B.C. 1450. Length 5 ft. 6 in. [No. 1182.]

Presented by Robert Mond, Esq., 1905.

425. (*Bay* 11.) — Limestone **sepulchral stele,** with rounded top, of **Åpeni** 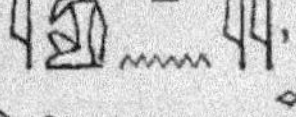, a director of the transport of Pharaoh , who flourished in the reign of **Åmen-ḥetep III.** Below the utchats, etc., are sculptured the following scenes:—1. Åpeni and his father and mother adoring Osiris, Ḥeru-netch-tef, and Isis. 2. Åpeni adoring Ptaḥ-mes and his wife Ia. 3. Åpeni adoring Ānkh and his wife Thåa. 4. Three ladies of the family of Åpeni adoring ancestors. 5. Åpeni's son pouring out a libation to his father and mother. The text contains a prayer to Osiris for sepulchral offerings. Sams Collection. XVIIIth dynasty, about B.C. 1450. (**Plate XIV.**) Height 2 ft. $1\frac{1}{2}$ in., width 1 ft. 5 in. [No. 365.]

426. (*Bay* 12.)—Fragment of a sandstone **stele** of **Rā-mes** 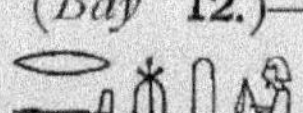, an official, with a portion of a figure of the deceased, who is represented in the act of adoring King

Ȧmen-ḥetep . XVIIIth dynasty. Height 6 in., width 11 in. [No. 813.]

Presented by Lyttleton Annesley, Esq., 1854.

427. (*Bay* 13.)—Painted limestone **statue of Pa-ser** , an Erpā, Ḥā prince, councillor, priest, governor of the city, etc., who flourished in the reign of **Ȧmen-ḥetep III,** whose prenomen and nomen are cut upon his right shoulder. From Thebes (Dêr al-Baḥarî). XVIIIth dynasty. Height 3 ft. 9½ in. [No. 687.]

Presented by the Egypt Exploration Fund, 1905.

Statue of Pa-ser, governor of a city in the reign of Ȧmen-ḥetep III, B.C. 1450. [Bay 13, No. 427.]

428. (*Bay* 12.) — Seated granite **statue of Ȧmen-ḥetep** , an Erpā, and Ḥā prince, judge of Nekhen, deputy of the king, and governor of the city of Bubastis in the reign of **Ȧmen-ḥetep III,** whose prenomen appears on his right shoulder. In his left hand he holds an object like a doubled cord, which appears to be the emblem of one of his offices. From Bubastis. XVIIIth dynasty. Height 2 ft. 10 in. [No. 1068.]

Presented by the Egypt Exploration Fund, 1889.

429. (*Bay* 11.) — Quartzite sandstone, seated **figure** of the **dog-headed ape,** which was sacred to Thoth and Khensu.

Very fine work. Between the hind paws are cut the cartouches of **Åmen-ḥetep III,** king of Egypt, about B.C. 1450—

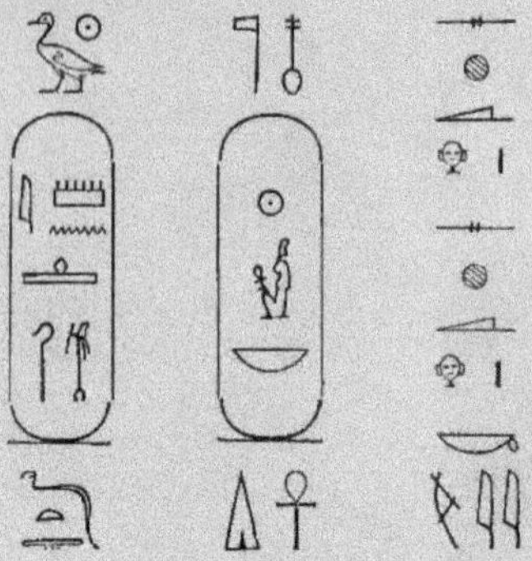

Sams Collection. XVIIIth dynasty. Height 2 ft. 3 in. [No. 38.]

430. (*Bay* 11.)—Red **granite lion,** inscribed on the pedestal with a text containing a statement that it was made by **Åmen-ḥetep III,** king of Egypt, about B.C. 1450, and placed by him in the temple of Ḥet-khā-em-Maāt , which he built in honour of himself as the god of Nubia. The inscription suggests that this lion was placed in the temple at Ṣûlb, an important town situated on the left bank of the Nile, about 150 miles south of Wâdî Ḥalfah, but it was found at Gebel Barkal, about 250 miles further south, whither it may have been taken by **Tut-ānkh-Åmen,** or, more probably, by **Åmen-åsru,** whose cartouches are cut on the neck—

.

XVIIIth dynasty. Length 6 ft. 7 in., height 3 ft. 4 in. [No. 1.]
Presented by Lord Prudhoe, 1835.

431. (*Bay* 10.)—Red **granite lion,** inscribed on the pedestal with a text stating that **Tut-ānkh-Åmen** 

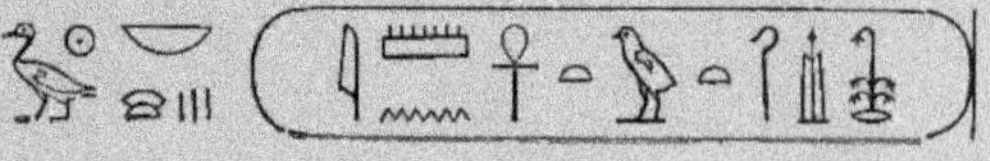, king of Egypt,

about B.C. 1400, restored the buildings of "his father Amen-"ḥetep III" 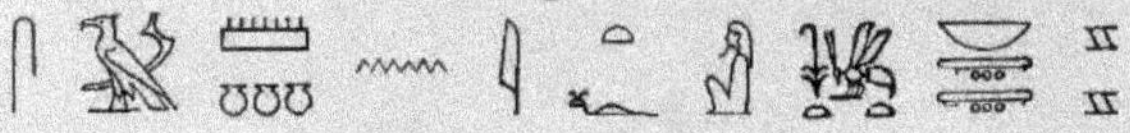 . It is probable that this lion was made by Tut-ānkh-Āmen, and that the lion opposite was his model. On the left shoulder are cut the cartouches of **Āmen-Āsru,** a Nubian king who reigned about one thousand years later. Found at Gebel Barkal. XVIIIth dynasty. Length 7 ft., height 3 ft. 8 in. [No. 34.]

Presented by Lord Prudhoe, 1835.

432. (*Bay* 10.)—Rectangular limestone **stele**, on which is inscribed in the hieratic character a text of nineteen lines, containing a public declaration of the dedication of a KA temple to Āmen-Rā for ever, by **Āmen-ḥetep** 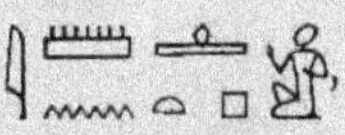, a royal scribe, surnamed **Ḥui**, the son of Ḥāp . Among those present at the dedication were the king, **Āmen-ḥetep III**, the governor of the town, who was also called Āmen-ḥetep, and the governor of the Treasury, Meri-Ptaḥ, and the royal scribes of the army. The document is dated in the **thirty-first year** of the reign of **Āmen-ḥetep III** 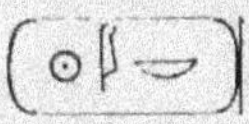. This stele was made in the Ptolemaïc Period, and the text inscribed upon it is only a *copy* of the original document. (**Plate XV.**) Height 2 ft. 8 in., width 2 ft. 0½ in. [No. 138.]

433. (*Bay* 9.)—Portion of a limestone **stele** inscribed with a series of addresses, or prayers, to the goddess Mut, the lady of a portion of Eastern Thebes, called Āsher ; it was set up in the temple of this goddess during the reign of **Āmen-ḥetep III**, about B.C. 1450. At the top left hand corner is cut in outline a series of figures of gods and goddesses, and below these are the remains of a line of hieroglyphic text which seem to say that the composition cut on the stele is of a most unusual and remarkable character, and that the like of it was never seen "since the time of Rā."

(*To face page* 122.)

Stele inscribed with a declaration of the dedication of a Ka-temple to Ȧmen-Rā for ever, by the scribe Ȧmen-ḥetep, surnamed Ḥui.
[Bay 10, No. 432.]

The words of the addresses are divided by lines, and the text can be read both perpendicularly and horizontally. Salt Collection. From Karnak. XVIIIth dynasty. Height 3 ft. 7½ in., width 2 ft. 9 in. [No. 194.]

434. (*Bay* 13.)—Painted limestone **sepulchral stele,** with rounded top, of **Ḥeru-å**, a libationer who flourished at Thebes in the reign of **Åmen-ḥetep III.** On the upper portion of the stele are sculptured figures of Osiris and Isis, and **Åmen-hetep III** and **Queen Thi,** seated at a table of offerings. Below are figures of three men and three women worshipping the deceased and his wife Mut-em-uåa, who are seated on chairs of state. The text of five lines contains praises to the gods and to the king and queen, and a prayer for a happy burial, and other funerary benefits. Anastasi Collection. XVIIIth dynasty. Height 2 ft. 3 in., width 1 ft. 5 in. [No. 834.]

435. (*Bay* 13.)—Rectangular grey granite **base of a statue,** inscribed with names and titles of **Khu-en-Åten**

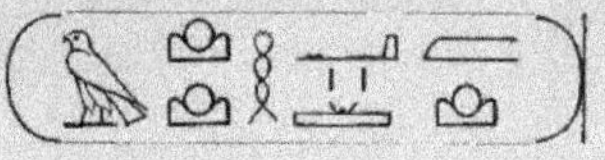 

, king of Egypt, about B.C. 1400. The cartouches which contained his prenomen as **Åmen-ḥetep IV**

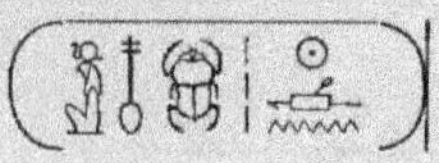 have been mutilated. XVIIIth dynasty. Length 2 ft. 11 in., breadth 1 ft. 8 in., depth 1 ft. [No. 1000.]

436. (*Bay* 13.)—Fine alabaster fragment of the **base of a seated** statue inscribed with the names and titles of **Khu-en-Åten,** *i.e.*, **Åmen-ḥetep IV,** and the name of his queen,

Nefert-ith 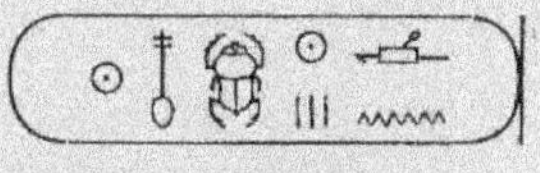 

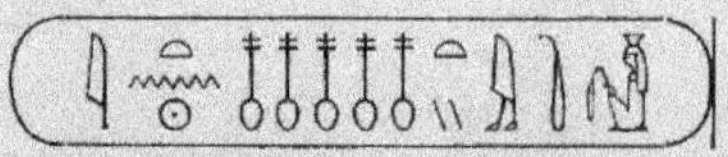. XVIIIth dynasty. From Tell al-Amarna. Height 1 ft. 4 in., width 5 in. [No. 880.]

Presented by the Rev. T. R. Maynard, Chaplain of the Forces, 1862.

437. (*Bay* **13.**)—Portion of a limestone **monument,** on which are inscribed cartouches containing the titles of **Åmen-ḥetep IV, Khu-en-Åten.** From Tell al-Amarna. XVIIIth dynasty. Height 8½ in., width 8½ in. [No. 1083.]

438. (*Bay* **10.**)—Rectangular limestone **sepulchral stele,** in the form of a door of a tomb with palm-leaf cornice and a raised flat border, of **Ptaḥ-māi** 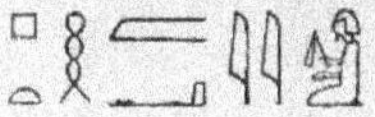, a warder of the Treasury. On the space within the flat border are three scenes: 1. A son and daughter of the deceased making offerings to their father and their mother Ta-khar  . 2. A son and a daughter addressing their father Hui and mother Āb. 3. Rā-mesu and his daughter seated on chairs of state. On the border are cut prayers to **Åten,** lord of eternity, and to **Rā,** governor of the Two Horizons , for sepulchral offerings. Anastasi Collection. End of the XVIIIth dynasty. Height 2 ft. 3 in., width 1 ft. 6½ in. [No. 324.]

439. (*Bay* **12.**)—Limestone **sepulchral stele,** with rounded top, of **Thuthu,** 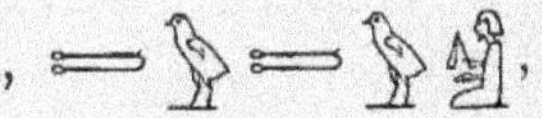, a veritable royal scribe and steward of the palace of King **Åi** , king of Egypt about B.C. 1400. On it is sculptured a scene representing the deceased in adoration before "Seker, the lord of the Hidden House" 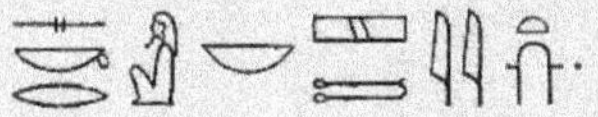. Above and below are prayers to Seker for sepulchral offerings. This stele was set up to the memory of Thuthu by his son **Ptaḥ Khensu** (?). Salt Collection. XVIIIth dynasty. Height 1 ft. 10½ in., width 1 ft. 4½ in. [No. 211.]

440. (*Central Saloon.*)—Portion of a granite **monument** inscribed with the prenomen of **Åi** , king of Egypt, about B.C. 1400. On it are sculptured portions of figures of deities, who appear to be holding a shrine. XVIIIth dynasty. Height 2 ft. [No. 1002.]

441. (*Bay* **13.**)—Grey granite **statue of Ḥeru-em-ḥeb** , the last king of the XVIIIth dynasty, with the attributes of Ḥāpi, the Nile god. Before him he held an altar (now broken away), on which were sculptured the figures of the products of the Nile, *i.e.*, water-fowl, plants, fruits, flowers, etc., and on the pedestal on which it rested are sculptured in relief figures of geese, lilies, etc. From Thebes. XVIIIth dynasty. Height 5 ft. 7 in. (No. 75.)

442. (*Bay* **12.**)—Black granite **statues** of the god **Åmen-Rā,** the "Bull of his mother," with the attributes of the ithyphallic god Menu, or Åmsu, and **Ḥeru-em-ḥeb,** the last king of the XVIIIth dynasty, about B.C. 1400. The king is standing under the uplifted right arm of Menu, and is under the protection of the god, whose son he is said to be. On the belt of the king's girdle is cut his prenomen , and both prenomen and nomen appear in the line of hieroglyphics between the two figures, the former with the addition . From Thebes. XVIIIth dynasty. Height 4 ft. 10½ in. [No. 5.]

443. (*Bay* **2.**)—Painted stone kneeling **figure of Nekht-Menu,** or Nekht-Åmsu , a Ḥā prince, scribe, chief libationer of Isis, etc., holding before him a stele with a rounded top. On the upper portion of the stele is sculptured a figure of the deceased, kneeling in adoration before the Boat of the Sun, on the bows of which is seated a figure of Ḥeru-pa-khart, or Harpokrates. In the boat is the solar disk. Behind the deceased kneels his wife, Muti . Below are thirteen lines of text containing a hymn to the Sun-god. On the flat surface near the face of the statue are cut figures of the deceased and his wife seated at a table of offerings, on the sides of the plinth of the stele are figures of Muti, and on the back of the stele are figures of six of her children. From Thebes. XVIIIth dynasty, about B.C. 1500. Height 1 ft. 7½ in. [No. 1222.]

444. (*Bay* 3.)—Seated, painted limestone **statues of Ȧri-neferu**, a guardian in the service of the Temple of Amen-Rā at Thebes, and his wife **Ȧpu**.

Statues of Ȧri-neferu and Ȧpu. XVIIIth dynasty. [Bay 3, No. 444.]

On the right side of their seat is inscribed a prayer to Ȧmen-Rā, Osiris, and Ȧnpu, for sepulchral offerings, and on the left is a similar prayer addressed to Osiris Khenti Ȧmenti. This monument was made by Mut-khut, the daughter of Ȧri-neferu and Ȧpu, to "keep alive" the names of her parents; her figure is cut on the front of the throne, between the figures of her father and mother. The head of Ȧpu is a restoration. Sams Collection. From Thebes. XVIIIth dynasty. Height 2 ft. [No. 29.]

445. (*Bay* 5.)—Upper portion of a limestone **seated statue** of a priest or civil official. Sams Collection. From Thebes. XVIIIth dynasty. Height 1 ft. 10½ in. [No. 124.]

446. (*Bay* 5.)—Limestone **stele,** with rounded top, of **Ȧnpu-ḥetep**. On the edge of the face of the stele are two prayers addressed by the deceased, one to Osiris and the other to Anubis, and on the upper portion is a prayer to Osiris. Below, in five registers, is a series of figures of the relatives of the deceased, deeply cut and painted. XVIIth or XVIIIth dynasty. (**Plate XVI.**) Height 1 ft. 10½ in., width 1 ft. 3½ in. [No. 200.]

447. (*Bay* 5.)—Limestone **sepulchral stele,** with rounded top, of **Ȧmen-em-ḥāt**, a steward and chan-

Sepulchral stele of Ȧnpu-ḥetep, with scenes representing the worship of the deceased by his family.

[Bay 5, No. 446.]

(*To face page* 127.)

Statue of Åmen-ḥetep, steward of Memphis, and director of the storehouses of gold and silver.

[Bay 6, No. 448.] XVIIIth dynasty.

cellor, inscribed with eighteen lines of hieroglyphic text containing adorations to Osiris, Åp-uat, and Rā, and a prayer for sepulchral offerings. XIIth–XVIIIth dynasty. Height 3 ft. 4 in., width 3 ft. 1 in. [No. 893.]

[This stele was brought from Thebes by Captain R. Bruce, R.N., and presented to the Royal United Service Institution some time before 1838; it was purchased by the Trustees of the British Museum, in 1861, from Messrs. Sotheby and Wilkinson.]

448. (*Bay* **6.**)—Grey granite seated **statue of Åmen-ḥetep** 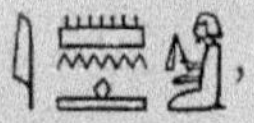, a royal scribe, steward of the royal palace of Memphis, and director of the storehouses of gold and silver. The text contains a list of the offices held by Åmen-ḥetep, praises of Osiris, and a prayer for sepulchral offerings. From Abydos. XVIIIth dynasty. (**Plate XVII.**) Height 2 ft. 4½ in. [No. 632.]

Presented by the Egypt Exploration Fund, 1903.

449. (*Bay* **6.**)—Upper portion of a black granite bearded **figure of a king,** wearing a full wig with uraeus. From Thebes. XVIIIth dynasty, about B.C. 1450. Height 1 ft. 7 in. [No. 1200.]

450. (*Bay* **6.**)—Lower portion of a hard limestone kneeling **figure of Ptaḥ-mes** 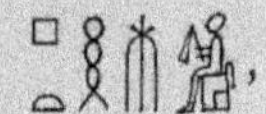, a royal scribe, chief steward of Ptaḥ, and prefect of the House of the Ka of Ptaḥ at Memphis, holding a shrine within which is sculptured a figure of the god Ptaḥ. From Memphis. XVIIIth dynasty. Height 1 ft. 2 in. [No. 1119.]

451. (*Bay* **6.**)—Sandstone **lion,** cut from a bas-relief; the body was coloured yellow and the mane red. XVIIIth dynasty. Length 2 ft. 6 in., width 1 ft. 8 in. [No. 453.]

452. (*Bay* **7.**)—Grey granite, headless **figure of Kamesu** , a Ḥā prince of Behen (Wâdî Ḥalfah), the son of Tennai , and the lady Hurṭ (?) , seated in the usual attitude of the scribe, with an opened roll of papyrus before him. Over his left shoulder is slung a palette. The inscription contains a prayer to Ȧmen-Rā, Khnemu, Satet, Ānqet, [and Horus,] lord of Behen 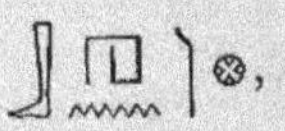, for sepulchral offerings. From Wâdî Ḥalfah. XVIIIth dynasty. Height 1 ft. 6 in. [No. 1022.]

Presented by Major-Gen. Sir C. Holled Smith, K.C.M.G., 1887.

453. (*Bay* 8.)—Portion of a grey granite **statue of a king**, or prince. XVIIIth dynasty. From Al-Ḳâb. Height 2 ft. 6 in. [No. 1195.]

Presented by Somers Clarke, Esq., F.S.A., 1896.

454. (*Bay* 8.)—Portion of a limestone **relief** from the wall of a tomb on which are sculptured standing figures of men, who form part of a procession. XVIIIth dynasty. Height 1 ft. 6 in., width 1 ft. 1 in. [No. 456.]

455. (*Bay* 8.)—Portion of a limestone **sepulchral stele** of **Pa-sheṭ** , "the guardian of the northern lakes of Ȧmen" , and "guardian of the door of the northern pillars (?) of Ȧmen"  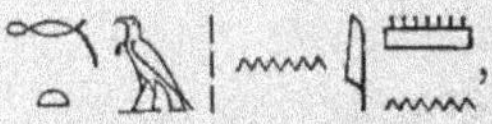, at Thebes. In the first register is a figure of the deceased making offerings to Osiris and Anubis; in the second are figures of the sons of Pasheṭ making offerings to their father and mother Mut-nefert 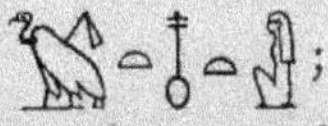; and in the third are figures of three daughters and a son of Pasheṭ. Jervis Collection. XVIIIth dynasty. Height 1 ft. 10 in., width 1 ft. 3½ in. [No. 282.]

456. (*Bay* 8.)—Portion of a limestone **sepulchral stele,** on which are sculptured figures of three priests, who are engaged in performing the ceremony of "Opening the mouth," on behalf of the deceased **Nefer-renpet** 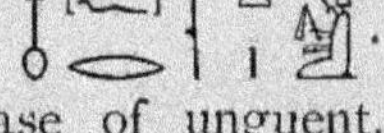. The first is offering to the mummy a vase of unguent, the second is reading from a roll of papyrus, and the third

bears a censer. On the right are the vases of unguents, the feathers, the box, the instruments for opening the mouth, and other objects employed in the ceremony. Fine work. XVIIIth dynasty. Height 1 ft. 8½ in., width 1 ft. 11 in.
[No. 803.]

457. (*Bay* 8.)—Sandstone **sepulchral stele** of **Àpu** , the director of the chamber of the **barge Khā-em-Maāt** . In the upper register is a figure of the deceased adoring Osiris, Horus, and Isis, and in the second is a figure of the deceased offering incense and pouring out a libation to his father, mother, and other members of the family. Below are four lines of text containing a prayer to Osiris Khenti Àmentet, Ḥeru-netch-ḥrà-tef, Isis, and all the gods of Ta-tchesert (the Other World), for funerary offerings. XVIIIth dynasty. Height 1 ft. 7½ in., width 1 ft. 3 in.
[No. 295.]

458. (*Bay* 8.)—Limestone **sepulchral stele,** with rounded top, of **Ḥeq-nefer** 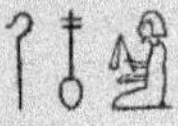, inscribed with a prayer to Osiris for funerary offerings. Under the symbols  is a scene in which the deceased, accompanied by his wife and daughter, stands in adoration before Osiris, and below this are figures of three members of the family of Ḥeq-nefer, making offerings to their father and their mother, who was called **Bàa** 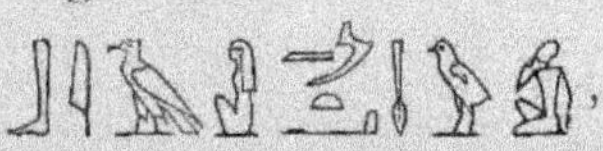, and was a priestess of Àmen. From Akhmîm. Height 1 ft. 5½ ins., width 1 ft.
[No. 1062.]

459. (*Bay* 8.)—Limestone **sepulchral stele,** with rounded top, set up by **Pa-sheṭu** 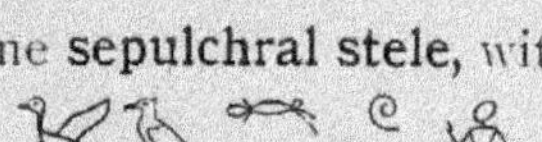, a judge; on it, cut in outline, are figures of Àmen-Rā, "the lord of the "thrones of the world," and the deceased. Below these are two lines of text which refer to the restoration of monuments and a name, and mention a judge called **Pennu** (?)

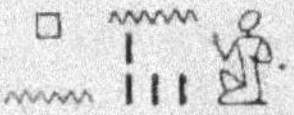 It is possible that the text indicates that Pennu restored the sepulchral monument and inscription of Pa-sheṭu. XVIIIth dynasty. Height 1 ft. 1½ in., width 9 in. [No. 341.]

460. (*Bay* 8.)—Limestone **sepulchral stele,** with rounded top, of **Teḥuti-mes** (Thothmes) 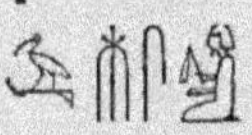, a captain of the keepers of the gate of Memphis 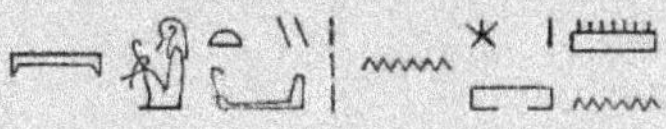 , who flourished under a king of the XVIIIth dynasty. On the upper portion is sculptured a relief in which Thothmes and his brother and sister are represented in the act of making adorations to Osiris and Isis, before whom stands a table of offerings. Below this is cut, in seventeen lines, the text of a hymn and a prayer to Harmachis, Unen-Nefer, Ptaḥ-Seker, and Osiris, for sepulchral offerings. In the left bottom corner is a small relief, in which we see a son pouring out a libation to his father and mother. D'Athanasi Collection. XVIIIth dynasty. (**Plate XVIII.**) Height 3 ft. 10½ in., width 2 ft. 3 in. [No. 155.]

461. (*Bay* 8.)—Massive limestone **sepulchral stele,** with rounded top, of **Ḥeru-em-ḥeb** 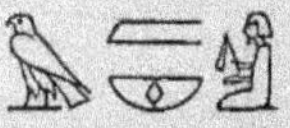, an Erpā, Ḥā prince, chancellor, Smer-uāt, palace-councillor, governor of the country, fan-bearer, general of the king's troops, and veritable royal scribe, who flourished under one of the kings of the XVIIIth dynasty. On the upper portion are sculptured a winged disk and a figure of the deceased, who is seen standing in adoration before Rā, Thoth, and Maāt, and below, in well-cut hieroglyphics, which have been painted yellow, is a hymn to the Sun-god, in twenty-five lines. Salt Collection. XVIIIth dynasty. About B.C. 1500. (**Plate XIX.**) Height 6 ft. 3 in., width 3 ft. 3½ in. [No. 551.]

462. (*Bay* 8.)—Limestone **jamb,** with raised, rounded border, from the right side of the shrine of the tomb of **Ḥeru-em-ḥeb,** whose stele has been described in the preceding paragraph, inscribed with the text of a prayer to Rā, in six lines. Below is sculptured a figure of the deceased, who stands with both hands raised in adoration ; from the fact that

Sepulchral stele of Thothmes, captain of the Gate of Memphis.
[Bay 8, No. 460.] XVIIIth dynasty.

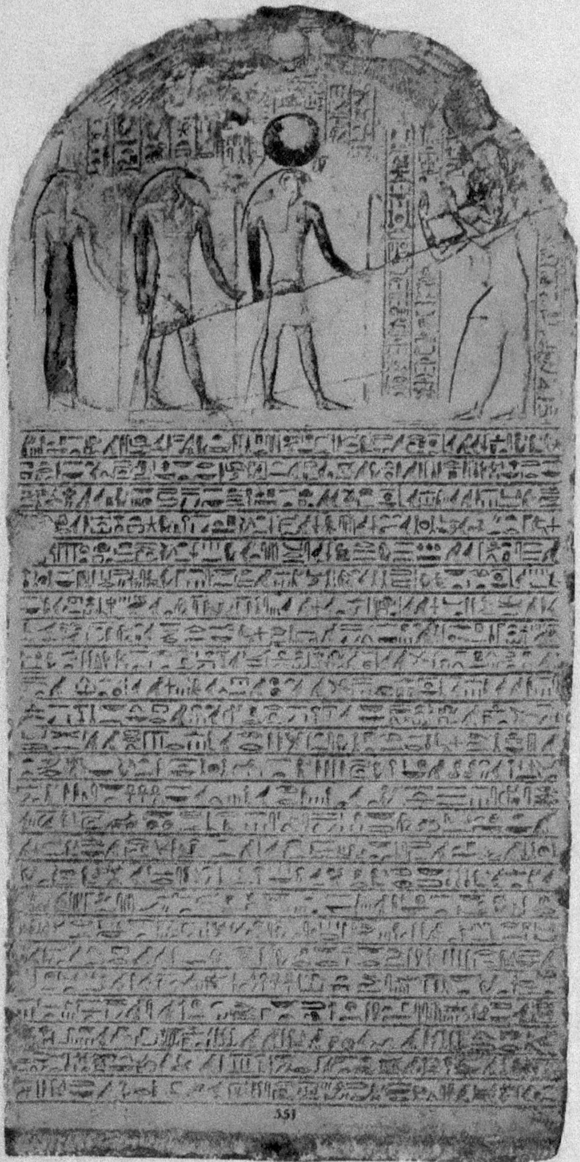

Sepulchral stele of Ḥeru-em-ḥeb, a Prince, Scribe, and Commander-in-Chief.
[Bay 8, No. 461.] XVIIIth dynasty.

he wears an uraeus over his forehead, it appears that Ḥeru-em-ḥeb was a kinsman of the royal family. Salt Collection. XVIIIth dynasty. Height 5 ft. 7 in., width 1 ft. 4½ in.
[No. 552.]

463. (*Bay* 8.)—Limestone **jamb,** with a raised, rounded, border, from the left side of the shrine of the tomb of **Ḥeru-em-ḥeb,** inscribed with the text of a prayer to Rā, in six lines. Below is sculptured a figure of the deceased, wearing a full wig, with an uraeus in front. Salt Collection. XVIIIth dynasty. Height 5 ft. 10 in., width 1 ft. 4½ in.
[No. 550.]

464. (*Bay* 8.)—Limestone **sepulchral stele,** with rounded top, of **Smen-taui** 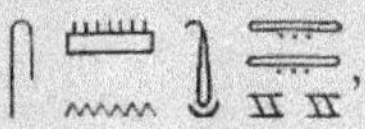, a door-keeper in the "place of Maāt." In the upper register the deceased is represented kneeling and making an offering to Àmen-Rā and his consort Mut, and in the lower are figures of the fan-bearer **Àtef-en-Àtef** 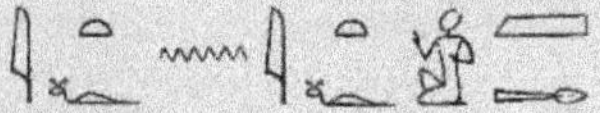, and his sister, Nefer, kneeling, with hands raised in adoration before the goddess "Mer-seḳer, the mistress of Àmentet" 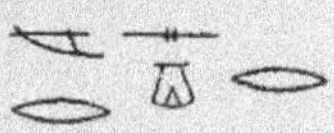 , who is seated on a throne holding a sceptre round which a lotus is twined. Between the figures of the fan-bearer and the sister is the name of another sister. Belmore Collection. XVIIIth dynasty. Height 1 ft. 5½ in., width 11½ in.
[No. 279.]

465. (*Bay* 8.)—Portion of a limestone **relief,** set up in memory of **Bathà** , an official, by his brother Àtu-ennumā 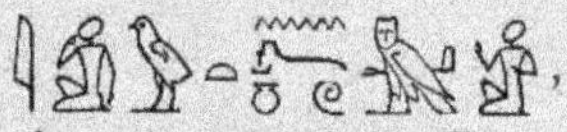, the chief charioteer of the "lord of the two lands." The scene represents a man offering palm branches to two deceased persons, who are seated with a table of offerings before them; behind him are figures of four kinswomen. D'Athanasi Collection. XVIIIth dynasty. Length 2 ft. 1½ in., breadth 11 in. [No. 322.]

466. (*Bay* 9.)—Painted limestone **stele,** with rounded top, of **Āāḥ-mes** , set up by his brother Nekht, a captain of Blacks . On the upper portion are , and below, sculptured in relief, are figures of the deceased, seated, and his brother pouring out a libation. Sams Collection. XVIIth or XVIIIth dynasty. Height 1 ft. 1 in., width 8½ in. [No. 300.]

467. (*Bay* 9.)—Limestone **sepulchral stele,** with rounded top, of **Nebrā** 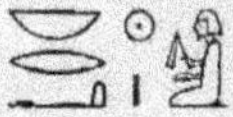, the son of the scribe **Pai.** On the upper portion is sculptured a figure of **Ḥeru-ur** , the lord of heaven and governor of the company of the gods, who wears the Double Crown, and is seated with a table of offerings before him. Behind the figure of the god are four eyes and two ears. Below this are a kneeling figure of Nebrā and four lines of text in which he says: "Praise be to Ḥeru-ur, and homage to "him that heareth petitions; may he grant me eyes to "see the way of truth, and to walk [therein]." From the Belmore Collection. XVIIIth dynasty. Height 10 in., width 6½ in. [No. 276.]

468. (*Bay* 9.)—Portion of a **relief** from the wall of a tomb on which are sculptured the figures of a scribe carrying his palette and ink jar, and a carpenter shaping a frame with an axe. XVIIIth dynasty. Height 8½ in., width 1 ft. 0½ in. [No. 445.]

469. (*Bay* 9.)—Limestone **stele,** with rounded top, on which are sculptured figures of **Ḥeru-em-uȧa** 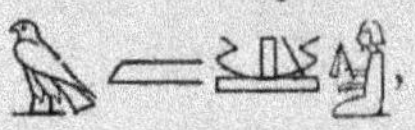, a judge, and his father, **Pa-nefer-em-nekhu**  , kneeling, with their hands raised in adoration before the Ram-god **Baiu-neteru** 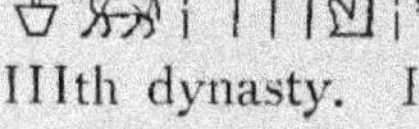, a form of Osiris. Salt Collection. XVIIIth dynasty. Height 11 in., width 7 in. [No. 356.]

470. (*Bay* 9.)—Portion of a limestone **stele,** with rounded top, on which is sculptured a figure of the **Cow of Hathor** coming out of the Theban funeral mountain. Between her horns are a disk and plumes, behind her head is a *menàt*, and under her chin stands the figure of a royal personage, Her titles are: "Lady of the Temple Tchesert, dweller in "Khu-Àst, mistress of the gods"  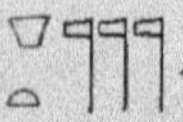. From Dêr al-Baḥarî. XVIIIth dynasty. Height 9 in., width 10½ in. [No. 689.]

Presented by the Egypt Exploration Fund, 1905.

471. (*Bay* 9.)—Rectangular limestone **sepulchral stele,** in the form of a door of a tomb, with palm-leaf cornice and raised flat border, of **Pau** , an officer of the transport of Pharaoh 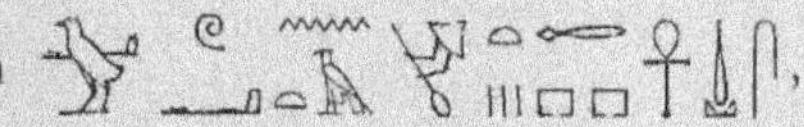, sculptured with the following scenes:—1. Pau, his brother and mother worshipping Osiris. 2. Pau and his sisters making offerings to their mother and father. 3. Eight members of the family seated at a table of offerings. The text on the border contains prayers to Ànpu and Osiris for sepulchral offerings. XVIIIth dynasty. Height 1 ft. 11 in., width 1 ft. 4½ in. [No. 773.]

472. (*Bay* 9.)—Limestone **sepulchral stele,** with rounded top, of **Thuiia** 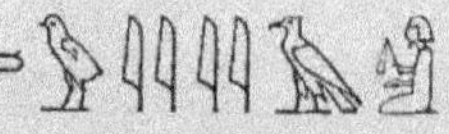, the son of Ṭān , and Taḥunai 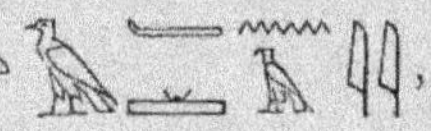, and warden of the king's bow. On the upper portion are , and below, in one register, are sculptured figures of the deceased and his wife seated at a table of offerings, and in the other their father and mother and three brothers and three sisters seated at a table of offerings. The inscription, in four lines, contains a prayer to Osiris and Anubis for sepulchral offerings. XVIIIth dynasty. Height 1 ft. 10 in., width 1 ft. 2½ in. [No. 293.]

473. (*Bay* 9.)—Portion of **relief** from the wall of a tomb, sculptured with the figure of a man and with representations of sepulchral offerings. XVIIIth or XIXth dynasty. Height 1 ft. 5½ in., width 1 ft. 2½ in. [No. 910.]

474. (*Bay* 9.)—Rectangular limestone **sepulchral stele** in the form of a door of a tomb, with palm-leaf cornice and a raised flat border, of **Ban-āa** 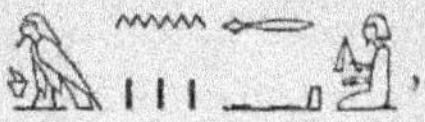, a royal scribe in a department of the government at Memphis. On the top is a flat pyramidal projection, sculptured with the figure of a jackal; on the cornice is a figure of the sun on the horizon , with figures of men in adoration. On the flat border are cut prayers to Osiris for sepulchral offerings. Within the border are cut two scenes:—1. The deceased and his wife Àbuhai , standing in adoration before Osiris, Isis, and Nephthys. 2. **Ḥui** 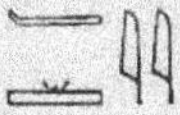, an overseer of the royal washers, and his wife seated, with a table of offerings before them, receiving the adoration of their son Nana , a royal librarian, and their daughter. D'Athanasi Collection. XVIIIth dynasty. Height 3 ft. 11 in., width 2 ft. 4 in. [No. 149.]

475. (*Bay* 9.)—Massive grey granite **sepulchral stele,** in the form of a door of a tomb, with plain cornice and rounded border, set up to commemorate two "Clerks of the Works" called **Ḥeru** , and **Sutui** . On the upper portion of the raised flat surface of the stele are inscribed prayers to Àmen-Rā, Mut, Khensu, Hathor, etc., for sepulchral offerings, and on the sides are prayers to Ḥeru-khuti, Anubis, Queen Nefert-àri, Osiris, Seker, and Isis. On the upper portion of the sunk, rounded stele, cut within the border, are a winged disk and figures of the deceased persons adoring Osiris and Anubis. Below is cut the text of a hymn to Rā-Harmachis, in twenty-one lines, on behalf of Ḥeru. The figures of Ḥeru and Sutui, and the name of Sutui, have in certain places been obliterated. Anastasi Collection. XVIIIth dynasty. (**Plate XX.**) Height 4 ft. 10 in., width 3 ft. [No. 826.]

Stele of the twin brethren Ḥeru and Sutui, overseers of works at Thebes.
[Bay 9, No. 475.] XVIIIth dynasty.

476. (*Bay* **10.**)—Head of a black granite **statue of a king** or prince, wearing the usual heavy wig, with an uraeus over the forehead. Belzoni Collection. XVIIIth dynasty. From Thebes (?) Height 10½ in. [No. 956.]

477. (*Bay* **10.**)—Grey granite standing **figures** of **Ḥeru** . . . . . . , a priest of the god Menu, or Ȧmsu, and his wife, who appears to have been a priestess of Isis. XVIIIth to XXth dynasty. From Ḳûrnah. Height 1 ft. 6 in. [No. 1220.]

478. (*Bay* **10.**)— Lower portion of a rectangular limestone **sepulchral stele of Pa-sheṭ** , a judge, inscribed with a text containing praises of the god **Reshpu,** and prayers for health, strength, and a long life. On the right hand bottom corner is cut a kneeling figure of the deceased, with his hands raised in adoration. Belmore Collection. XVIIIth dynasty. Height 11½ in., width 11½ in. [No. 264.]

479. (*Bay* **10.**)—Portion of a limestone **relief** of an official, on which are cut figures of the deceased and his sister, seated on chairs of state. From Thebes. XVIIIth dynasty. Height 11 in., width 10 in. [No. 819.]

Presented by Lyttleton Annesley, Esq., 1854.

480. (*Bay* **10.**)—Limestone **sepulchral stele,** with rounded top, above which are the shoulders of a male figure who is supposed to hold it before him. On the upper portion are cut , and below it are four lines of text containing an address to Rā when he rises. This tablet was set up in honour of **User-ḥāt,** a judge of Ȧmen, by his son Kati 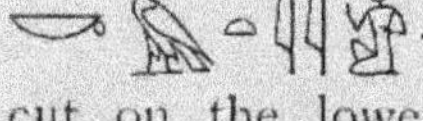. Kneeling figures of father and son are cut on the lower portion of the stele. Sams Collection. XVIIIth dynasty. Height 11 in., width 8 in. [No. 346.]

481. (*Bay* **10.**)—Portion of a limestone **relief** from the wall of a tomb, on which are sculptured figures of the goddess

Hathor and another deity (?). The text gives the name and titles of Hathor. Sams Collection. From Thebes. XVIIIth dynasty. Height 1 ft. 1½ in., width 6 in. [No. 381.]

482. (*Bay* 10.)—Portion of a limestone **shrine of Khā** , a judge. Above the doorway are figures of the deceased kneeling in adoration before Ptaḥ and Sebek, who are seated on thrones, and the goddess Rennut , who appears in the form of a serpent resting on a shrine. On the side is inscribed a prayer to Ptaḥ, the great god, for "life, strength and health," and below it is cut a figure of the wife of Khā. XVIIIth dynasty. Height 1 ft. 3 in., width 9½ in. [No. 597.]

483. (*Bay* 10.)—Sandstone **sepulchral stele,** with rounded top, of **Qaḥa** , a high official. In the upper register the deceased is seen burning incense at a table of offerings before the Ram, symbol of Åmen-Rā of Thebes. In the lower, the deceased is represented pouring out a libation before **Åmen-ḥetep I** 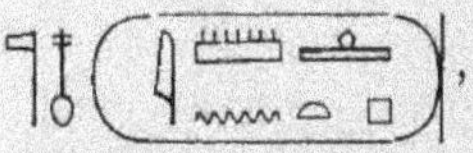, his **queen, Åāḥmes-nefert-åri,** and the goddess Hathor. The figures were originally painted white. XVIIIth dynasty. Height 1 ft. 8½ in., width 1 ft. 1½ in. [No. 291.]

484. (*Bay* 10.)—Limestone **sepulchral stele,** with rounded top, of **Karei** 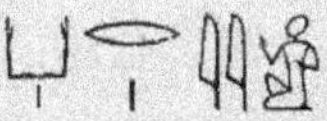, an officer, inscribed with a prayer to Osiris and all the gods of Abydos for sepulchral offerings. On it are cut the following scenes:—1. Karei standing in adoration before Osiris; in front of the god is a table of offerings, and behind him is the symbol of Åmentet . 2. Karei, with his father, brothers and sisters, seated at a table of offerings. 3. Karei and his soul drinking water, which is poured out from vessels by the goddess Hathor or Nut, who appears in a sycamore tree, and hands out to them a table of food. XVIIIth dynasty. Height 1 ft. 11 in., width 1 ft. 2½ in. [No. 294.]

485. (*Bay* 10.)—Painted limestone **sepulchral stele,** with rounded top, on which are cut figures of **Ḥeru-em-uȧa**, a judge in Western Thebes, Baka, a chief of the workmen, Amen-nekht, the chief artificer, Pa-sheṭ, a judge, Ȧmen-mes, the of the lord of the Two Lands, Unen-Nefer, and another person, who stand in adoration before Ptaḥ and Hathor. These deities stand on the emblem *Maāt*, and before them is a pillar altar on which are flowers, a jar of wine, etc. Belmore Collection. From Thebes. XVIIIth dynasty. Height 1 ft. 8 in., width 1 ft. 2 in. [No. 265.]

486. (*Bay* 10.)—Limestone **sepulchral stele,** with rounded top, of **Teḥuti-ḥer-māktu-f**, a judge in Western Thebes. On the upper portion is sculptured the figure of a boat, in which is seated Rā-Ḥeru-Khuti, and before him is seated the dog-headed ape of Thoth, who offers an eye to the god. The text, in ten lines, contains a prayer "to Rā when he riseth," in which the deceased asks that his body may germinate, and that he may see the beauties of the god; to the left is a kneeling figure of the deceased. Belmore Collection. XVIIIth dynasty. Height 1 ft. 8½ in., width 1 ft. 2½ in. [No. 266.]

487. (*Bay* 10.)—Limestone **sepulchral stele,** in the form of a door of a tomb, with palm-leaf cornice and a raised flat border on three sides of the door, which was set up in honour of **Māḥu**, a deputy of the king, and "overseer "of the bow of the lord of the two Lands," by **Ȧmen-em-ȧnt**, the chief of his bodyguard.

On the raised border are cut prayers to Osiris, the Everlasting Governor, and Ptaḥ-seker, and Anpu-ṭep-ṭu-f , for sepulchral offerings, and within it are sculptured the following scenes:—1. Māḥu and his wife making offerings to Ptaḥ-seker and to Ȧnpu-ṭep-ṭu-f. 2. Ȧmen-em-ȧnt making offerings to Māḥu and his wife, who are seated on chairs of state near a tree. D'Athanasi Collection. XVIIIth or XIXth dynasty. Height 2 ft. 3 in., width 1 ft. 6 in. [No. 307.]

488. (*Bay* 10.)—Limestone **sepulchral stele,** with rounded top, of **Mentu** , a scribe and overseer of the granaries, the son of Mentu-sa (?) and the lady Mut-ȧtef-s . On the upper portion are cut , and a scene in which a priest is represented pouring out libations to the deceased Mentu and his wife and daughter, who are seated on chairs of state with a table of offerings before them. Below is a text containing an address to those who live upon earth, in which they are asked to pray for the happiness of the deceased. XVIIIth dynasty. Height 2 ft. 3 in., width 1 ft. 6½ in. [No. 1012.]

Presented by Sir A. Wollaston Franks, K.C.B., 1885.

489. (*Bay* 11.)—Portion of a limestone **sepulchral stele** of **Pa-ren-nefer** , a judge in the "place of Maāt." On the upper portion is sculptured a figure of the Boat of Rā, with the Disk in it, and below is a kneeling figure of the deceased, with his hands raised in adoration to the god. The text contains a prayer to Rā at setting. Belmore Collection. XVIIIth dynasty. Height 9 in., width 8 in. [No. 271.]

490 (*Bay* 11.)—Rectangular limestone **stele** of **Paḥu** on which are sculptured figures of the deceased and his sons Āa-peḥti, the judge, Pa-ḥu, and Āa-ḥiu (?) kneeling, with their hands raised in adoration before a huge serpent (Mer-sekert?) XVIIIth dynasty. From the Belmore Collection. Height 7½ in., width 5½ in. [No. 272.]

491. (*Bay* II.)—Painted limestone **sepulchral stele,** with rounded top, of **Àāḥ-mes** . On the upper portion are , and below, in low relief, is a figure of the deceased seated with a table of offerings before him. This tablet was made by his son, a figure of whom is seen kneeling before him. The text contains a prayer to Osiris for sepulchral offerings, and by the side is a figure of the wife, or daughter, of the deceased bearing cakes and a goose as offerings. XVIIIth dynasty. Height 1 ft., width 9 in. [No. 932.]

Presented by F. T. Palgrave, Esq., 1870.

492. (*Bay* II.)—Painted limestone **sepulchral stele,** with rounded top, of **Bak** , an officer of the Gate of Memphis , sculptured with scenes in which the deceased and his wife are standing in adoration before Osiris, and two daughters are seated in adoration before their father Bak, their grandfather Ta-ur , and a lady called Àmen-em-àt (*sic*) . XVIIIth dynasty. Height 11 in., width 7¾ in. [No. 368.]

493. (*Bay* II.)—Limestone **sepulchral stele,** with rounded top, of **Àpni** , a judge in the "seat of Maāt." On the upper portion is cut a figure of the Boat of Rā, and below is a figure of the deceased kneeling, with hands raised in adoration of the boat. The text contains a hymn to the sun, when he rises and sets. Salt Collection. XVIIIth dynasty. Height 1 ft. 2 in., width 9½ in. [No. 332.]

494. (*Bay* II.)—Painted limestone **sepulchral stele,** with rounded top, of **Tetà** , a fan-bearer , and **Re-Ptaḥ** , and their wives Mut-em-ḥent

, and Then-Menu . Below the are two scenes :—1. The deceased persons sitting with a table of offerings before them. 2. Their families seated in adoration of them. The text contains a prayer to Osiris and Anubis for funerary offerings. D'Athanasi Collection. XVIIIth dynasty. Height 1 ft. 6 in., width 11½ in. [No. 353.]

495. (*Bay* **11.**)—Sandstone **aegis** of the goddess **Hathor,** which probably formed a portion of the capital of a column ; the head of the goddess has the ears of a cow. Traces of the blue paint, with which the face and collar were originally coloured, still remain. Period doubtful. Height 1 ft. 10 in., width 1 ft. 10 in. [No 427.]

496. (*Bay* **11.**)—Limestone **sepulchral stele,** with rounded top, of **Meri-Sekhet** . Below the is cut a figure of the deceased as a child, seated on his mother's knee, by the side of a table of offerings. The text contains a prayer to Osiris Khenti Àmenti for sepulchral offerings. XVIIIth dynasty. Height 9½ in, width 8 in. [No. 804.]

497. (*Bay* **11.**)—Lower portion of a limestone **sepulchral stele** of Nu , dedicated by his son Ànna , a doorkeeper of Amen, "to keep alive the name [s] "of his father, his mother, and his sister" Thuna . The text contains a prayer to Àmen and Osiris for sepulchral offerings. XVIIIth dynasty. Height 9 in., width 11½ in. [No. 1016.]

498. (*Bay* **11.**)—Limestone **stele,** with rounded top, which was set up by **Àp** . . . . . , probably as a thank-offering to Amen-Rā for the recovery of his hearing (?) On the upper portion are one half of a winged disk and an *utchat* . Below is a figure of the deceased kneeling before the god **Menu,** who is here called "Àmen-Rā, the bull of his "mother, king of the gods." Above the deceased are two

Sepulchral stele sculptured with a scene representing the deceased adoring the god Amsu or Menu.

[Bay 11, No. 498.]

ears, and behind the god is a lotus flower, standing on a pedestal. XVIIIth dynasty. (**Plate XXI.**) Height 8 in., width $5\frac{1}{2}$ in. [No. 358.]

499. (*Bay* II.)—Limestone **sepulchral stele,** with rounded top, of the ladies **Bathi** 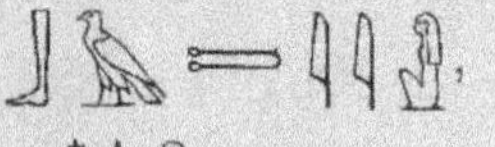, and **Mut-ent-ḥent-nefert** 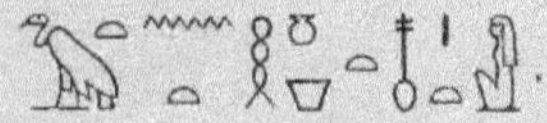. On the upper portion are cut the utchats, etc. , and below is sculptured a scene, in which their father, Àmen-em-ḥāt, is offering incense and pouring out a libation to them. The text contains a prayer to Osiris for sepulchral offerings. Anastasi Collection. XVIIIth dynasty. Height 1 ft. 10 in., width 1 ft. 1 in. [No. 280.]

500. (*Bay* II.)—Unfinished limestone **sepulchral stele,** with rounded top, of an unknown person. On it are sculptured :—1. The winged disk. 2. Osiris and Isis (or Mut?) seated within a shrine in a boat, and a royal personage standing before them. Behind is the hawk of Horus on his stand. 3. The deceased and his wife receiving offerings. The text contains a prayer to Osiris for sepulchral offerings. Salt Collection. XVIIIth dynasty. Height 1 ft. 8 in., width 1 ft. $2\frac{1}{2}$ in. [No. 214.]

501. (*Bay* II.)—Painted limestone **sepulchral stele,** with rounded top, of **Nekht** 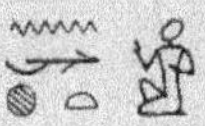 and his father **Khamāi** 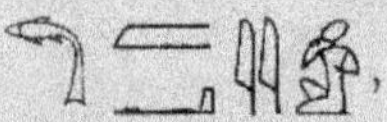, and his mother **Kamā** . On the upper portion is a scene representing the deceased persons worshipping Osiris and Anubis, and below are smaller scenes, in which members of the family of Nekht are adoring their ancestors. The text is a prayer to Osiris Khenti Àmenti for sepulchral offerings. Sams Collection. XVIIIth dynasty. Height 1 ft. $5\frac{1}{2}$ in., width 1 ft. $0\frac{1}{2}$ in. [No. 348.]

502. (*Bay* II.)—Painted limestone **sepulchral stele,** with rounded top, of **Sapa-àr** , on which are sculptured the following scenes :—1. Half of the winged disk and the utchat. 2. The deceased standing in adoration before Osiris Khenti Àmenti. 3. The deceased, and his wife Ḥenti-em-pet 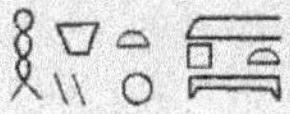, seated with a table of offerings before them, and receiving the adoration of their sons Sesut-em-Àmen , Khā-em-Uast, and Sen-seneb. The text of eight lines contains a prayer to Osiris Khenti Àmenti, Ànpu, Ptaḥ-Sekri, and other gods for funerary offerings. Malcolm Collection. XVIIIth dynasty. Height 3 ft. 5½ in., width 1 ft. 6½ in. [No. 906.]

503. (*Bay* **11.**)—Limestone **sepulchral stele,** with rounded top, of **Ànna** , a priestly official, sculptured with the following :—1. The winged disk. 2. Ànna standing in adoration before a sacred boat containing a shrine, in which are standards surmounted by rams, the standard of Abydos, etc. 3. Ànna and his wife, and two kinsfolk, seated on chairs of state, with tables of offerings before them. The text enumerates the sacred barks, in the making of which Ànna assisted, *e.g.*, the boats of Osiris, Tem, Ptaḥ. Sepi, Iusàs, Nebt-Ḥetep, Thoth, Khensu, Khnemu, Menthu, Sekhet, Sebek, and he describes himself as the "barge-builder of the gods of the "South and the North." XVIIIth dynasty. Height 3 ft. 3½ in., width 1 ft. 9 in. [No. 1332.]

504. (*Bay* **12.**)—Upper portion of a limestone **sepulchral stele,** with rounded top, sculptured with a scene representing the scribe **Pen-màām** 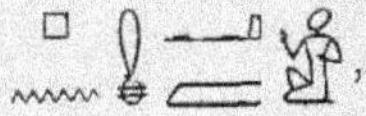, addressing the KA, or double, of Prince **Meri-mes** , and saying "Let "thy Ka be pure. Let thy Ka be pure." The text below contains a prayer to Osiris that sepulchral offerings may be given to Merimes. XVIIIth dynasty. Height 10 in., width 10½ in. [No. 860.]

505. (*Bay* **12.**) — Portion of a rectangular limestone **sepulchral stele,** sculptured with the figures of a priest (?), and his wife and two daughters, adoring Osiris, who is seated with a table of offerings before him. The god wears the Atef crown, and holds and . The stele appears to have been made by the son of the deceased, a judge in the "place of Maāt." Belmore Collection. XVIIIth dynasty. Height 9½ in., width 1 ft. 3½ in. [No. 547.]

506. (*Bay* 12.)—Limestone **sepulchral stele,** with rounded top, of **Pen-neferu** , a door-keeper in the "place of Maāt," sculptured with figures of the ram-headed god Àmen-Rā, and the serpent-goddess Urt-ḥekaut . On the right, below, are cut a kneeling figure of the deceased, with his hands raised in adoration, and a text containing praises of the gods Àmen-Rā and Urt-ḥekau. Following the name of the deceased are the words . XVIIIth dynasty. Height 1 ft., width 8½ in. [No. 812.]

Presented by Lyttleton Annesley, Esq., 1854.

507. (*Bay* 12.)—Limestone **sepulchral stele,** with rounded top, of **Unenkhu** , sculptured with figures of Rā in his boat, and of the deceased and his son Penpa-Khenti , kneeling in adoration before him. XVIIIth or XIXth dynasty. Height 1 ft. 1½ in., width 8½ in. [No. 1248.]

Presented by Morgan S. Williams, Esq., 1898.

508. (*Bay* 12.)—Painted limestone **sepulchral stele,** with rounded top, of a priestly official, sculptured with the following scenes:—1. The deceased and his wife and son adoring Osiris, who is seated with a table of offerings before him. 2. The son of the deceased pouring out a libation to his father and mother, in the presence of two other members of the family. 3. The children of the deceased seated in adoration before a table of offerings. All the names have been erased. D'Athanasi Collection. From Abydos. XVIIIth or XIXth dynasty. Height 1 ft. 3 in., width 10 in. [No. 339.]

509. (*Bay* 12.)—Limestone **sepulchral stele,** with rounded top, of **Ptaḥ-mes**, a priest, sculptured with figures, arranged in three registers, of himself, his wife Ur-nuru, four sons, and six daughters, making adoration and bearing offerings to Osiris and Isis. XVIIIth or XIXth dynasty. Height 1 ft. 11 in., width 1 ft. 2½ in. [No. 366.]

510. (*Bay* 12.) — Limestone **sepulchral stele,** with rounded top, sculptured with figures of **Nefer-Khemennu**, a judge in the "place of Maāt," and his sons **Pa-neb**, a judge, **Āa-peḥti**, a judge, and his grandson **Pa-neb,** kneeling in adoration before the goddess Hathor. From Thebes. XVIIIth dynasty. Height 1 ft. 4½ in., width 11 in. [No. 316.]

511. (*Bay* 12.)—Limestone **sepulchral stele,** with rounded top, of **Tchai**, an official, sculptured with a figure of the Boat of Harmachis and a figure of the deceased ; the text contains a prayer to the god for sepulchral offerings. XVIIIth dynasty. Height 1 ft. 0½ in., width 9 in. [No. 797.]

512. (*Bay* 12.)—Sandstone **sepulchral stele,** with rounded top, of **User-Satet**, an Erpā, and Ḥā prince, and governor of the Sûdân, who had filled high offices. On the upper portion are sculptured a disk with one wing, an utchat, and a figure of the deceased standing in adoration, and pouring out a libation before **Thoth,** lord of **Taȧ-sathȧ**. On the lower portion are cut a prayer to Thoth for sepulchral offerings, and a list of the

names and titles of the deceased. From Wâdi Ḥalfah. XVIIIth dynasty. Height 1 ft. 8 in., width 1 ft. 1 in. [No. 623.]
Presented by Colonel W. Hayes-Sadler, 1903.

513. (*Bay* **12.**)—Painted limestone **sepulchral stele,** with rounded top, of **Sebek-ḥetep** , a scribe of the "House of wine" 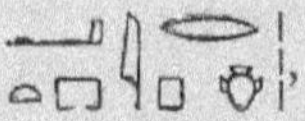, and his sister, **Tchauf** , or Tchefu , a priestess of Hathor, sculptured with the following scenes:—1. The deceased and his sister adoring Osiris. 2. The deceased and his sister adoring Anubis. 3. Four sons of the deceased, Sebek-mes, Neb-nefer, Sebek-em-ḥeb, and Khensu-aȧ (?), making offerings to their father and mother. 4. Nefert-ȧri, a little daughter standing before her mother, and clasping her arm. 5. Shere-mes the younger , making offerings to his father, Shere-mes, accompanied by his sisters Thent-Ȧnt , and Nefert-ari. From Thebes. XVIIIth dynasty. Height 1 ft. 11 in., width 1 ft. 7 in. [No. 1368.]

514. (*Bay* **12.**)—Painted limestone **sepulchral stele,** with rounded top, of **Kaḥu** , the overseer of the building in which the offerings to Ȧmen were stored, sculptured with the following scenes: 1. Kaḥu pouring out a libation before Osiris, the goddess of Ȧmenti, and Anubis; above are 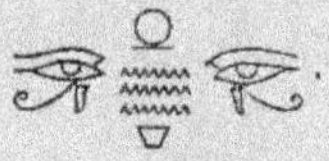. 2. A son of Kaḥu, called Pa-kharu , and thirteen brothers and sisters, bringing offerings to their father and mother, Netchem-peḥi . Anastasi Collection. XVIIIth dynasty. Height 2 ft. 2 in., width 1 ft. 6 in. [No. 303.]

515. (*Bay* **12.**)—Portion of a **wall-painting** from a tomb, on which is represented a group of figures of Egyptian ladies, who are seated on chairs of state. By their side are seated a number of female musicians, one of whom is playing on double pipes, two on harps, whilst one beats the time by clapping her hands. From Thebes. XVIIIth dynasty. Height 2 ft., width 1 ft. 10 in. [No. 175.]

Presented by Sir Henry Ellis, K.H., 1834.

516. (*Bay* 12.)—Portion of a **wall-painting** from a tomb, on which is represented a figure of a high official, who is seated on a high-backed chair, the seat of which is covered with a panther skin. He wears a necklace, bracelets, and a white linen tunic; in his right hand he holds the *kherp* sceptre  and a sort of besom, and in his left a long staff. From Thebes. XVIIIth dynasty. Height 2 ft. 2 in., width 1 ft. 4 in. [No. 173.]

517. (*Bay* 12.)—Portion of a **wall-painting** from the lower part of a wall of a tomb, on which are represented figures of two servants bearing sepulchral offerings, cakes, fruit, flowers, meat, birds, etc. On the left is a line of hieroglyphics, containing a prayer that the deceased may have a safe passage through Re-stau, and enjoy glory in heaven, power upon earth, and triumph in the Other World. From Thebes. XVIIIth dynasty. Height 2 ft., width 2 ft. 3½ in. [No. 919.]

Presented by H. Danby Seymour, Esq., 1869.

518. (*Bay* 12.)—Portion of a **wall-painting** from the upper part of a wall of a tomb, on which are represented figures of workmen seated on stools, working drills, rubbing and polishing beads, fashioning a pectoral, etc. The scene represented is the workshop of a worker in precious stones and metals, and standing near his men are finished and partially finished objects, *e.g.*, rows of beads, vases of various kinds, a small coffer, rings, etc., From Thebes. XVIIIth dynasty. Height 2 ft. 2 in., width 2 ft. 7 in. [No. 920.]

Presented by H. Danby Seymour, Esq., 1869.

519. (*Bay* 13.)—Portion of a **wall-painting** from a tomb, on which is represented a group of Sûdânî men, two of whom are kneeling in adoration before the king's officer, and three are bearing as gifts bowls of some valuable substance and chains of gold "ring money." From Thebes. XVIIIth dynasty. Height 2 ft. 7 in., width 3 ft. 3 in. [No. 921.]

Presented by H. Danby Seymour, Esq., 1869.

520. (*Bay* 13.)—Portion of **wall-painting** from a tomb, on which are represented three figures of men carrying gifts, forming part of a scene in which the payment of tribute from the Sûdân was represented. The first figure carries a bowl in one hand and a chain of gold "ring money" in the other; the second bears a log of wood on one shoulder and a bunch of feathers in one hand; the third brings skins of wild animals, a bowl of some red substance (carnelians?), and has an ape on his shoulders. From Thebes. XVIIIth dynasty. Height 2 ft. 5 in., width 2 ft. 1 in. [No. 922.]

Presented by H. Danby Seymour, Esq., 1869.

521. (*Bay* 12.)—Fragment of a **wall-painting** from a tomb, on which is represented a portion of a figure of a king, or god, holding a sceptre. From Thebes. XVIIIth dynasty. Height 6 in., width $10\frac{1}{4}$ in. [No. 1373.]

522. (*Bay* 12.)—Fragment of a painted **relief** from a tomb, on which are sculptured the hieroglyphics . From Thebes. XVIIIth dynasty. Height $5\frac{1}{4}$ in., width $5\frac{1}{2}$ in. [No. 1374.]

523. (*Bay* 12.)—Fragment of a **wall-painting** from a tomb, on which are painted the heads of a woman and child, the latter having the "curl of youth" on one side of his head. From Thebes. XVIIIth dynasty. Height $7\frac{3}{4}$ in., width 10 in. [No. 1329.]

524. (*Bay* 12.)—Portion of a **wall-painting** from a tomb, on which are represented the heads of two women, who wear necklaces and are arrayed in white linen. From Thebes. XVIIIth dynasty. Height $9\frac{3}{4}$ in., width 11 in. [No. 1291.]

525. (*Bay* 12.)—The **Atef crown,** with plumes, solar disk, horns, uraeus, etc., from a black granite seated statue of the god Osiris, or from the statue of a king who was represented with the attributes of the god. From Thebes. XVIIIth dynasty. Height 1 ft. $1\frac{1}{2}$ in. [No. 876.]

526. (*Bay* 12.)—Head from a black granite seated **statue of a priest,** or high official, wearing a heavy wig. On the plinth behind is cut a portion of a hymn to Rā-Harmachis at sunrise, which forms one of the versions of the XVth Chapter of the Theban Recension of the Book of the Dead. From Thebes. Miss Harris Collection. XVIIIth dynasty. Height 9 in. [No. 968.]

527. (*Bay* 12.)—**Bust** from a grey granite statue of a king, or prince. From Thebes. XVIIIth dynasty. Height 1 ft. 5 in. [No. 1167.]

528. (*Bay* 12.)—**Head** of a porphyry seated figure of a high official wearing a wig. Fine work. XVIIIth dynasty. Height 8 in. [No. 848.]

529. (*Bay* 12.)—**Head** from a black granite statue of a priest, or high official. From Thebes. XVIIIth dynasty. Height 10 in. [No. 120.]

530. (*Bay* 12.)—Portion of a limestone kneeling **figure of Ḥui** , a judge , holding before him a tablet on which are cut a figure of the Boat of Rā, with the solar disk in it, and an extract from a hymn to "Rā "when he riseth in the eastern sky." From Thebes. XVIIIth dynasty. Height $10\frac{1}{2}$ in. [No. 942.]

Presented by the Trustees of the Christy Collection, 1865.

531. (*Bay* 13.)—Grey granite **head of a sphinx.** From Karnak. XVIIIth dynasty. Height 1 ft. 8 in. [No. 526.]

Presented by W. R. Hamilton, Esq., 1839.

532. (*Bay* 13.)—Limestone **sepulchral stele,** in the form of a door of a tomb, with palm-leaf cornice and raised flat border, on which is sculptured a scene representing Nefermut (?) , a high ecclesiastical official  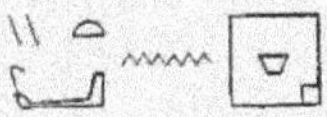 standing in adoration before **Āāḥ-mes,** who is seated with a table of offerings before him. XVIIIth dynasty. Height 9 in., width $5\frac{1}{2}$ in. [No. 275.]

533. (*Bay* 13.)—Upper portion of a limestone **sepulchral stele,** with rounded top, sculptured with a figure of a priest adoring the god Ptaḥ; the names of the deceased and of the judge who set it up in his honour are wanting. Belmore Collection. XVIIIth dynasty. Height 6 in., width $9\frac{1}{2}$ in. [No. 286.]

534. (*Bay* 13.)—Portion of a limestone **sepulchral stele** of **Tetàthi**, a scribe. The text contains a prayer to Osiris Khenti Àmenti for sepulchral offerings. Found in Malta in 1823. XVIIIth dynasty (or later). Height 7 in., width 7 in. [No. 287.]

Presented by J. B. Collings, Esq., 1836.

535. (*Bay* 13.)—Limestone **sepulchral stele,** with rounded top, of **Thuà**. Below the are sculptured figures of the deceased and his wife, or daughter, Àbnes. The text contains a prayer to Osiris for sepulchral offerings. XVIIIth dynasty. Found in Malta in 1823. Height 8 in., width 5½ in. [No. 299.]

Presented by J. B. Collings, Esq., 1836.

536. (*Bay* 13.)—Limestone **sepulchral stele,** with rounded top, of **Àri-nefer**, a judge in the "place of Maāt," on which is sculptured a scene representing the deceased praying at an altar of offerings, placed before a shrine containing the cow-goddess Hathor. Above the shrine is the winged disk. Below are cut a figure of the deceased and a text containing praises of Hathor. XVIIIth dynasty. Height 1 ft. 0½ in., width 8¼ in. [No. 814.]

Presented by Lyttleton Annesley, Esq., 1854.

537. (*Bay* 13.)—White limestone **sepulchral stele**, with rounded top, sculptured with a scene representing **Maa-nà-nekht-f**, and **Nefer-ààb**, adoring Ptaḥ and Maāt. From Thebes. Belmore Collection. XVIIIth dynasty. Height 1 ft. 2 in., width 9½ in. [No. 269.]

538. (*Bay* 13.)—Limestone **sepulchral stele**, with rounded top, of **Àri-nefer**, a judge in the "place of Maāt," sculptured with a scene representing the deceased and his sister Meḥi-Khāthā, seated in adoration before the hippopotamus-goddess **Ta-urt**, the lady of heaven, and mistress of all the gods. Belmore Collection. XVIIIth dynasty. Height 1 ft., width 8½ in. [No. 284.]

539. (*Bay* 13.)—Painted limestone **sepulchral stele,** with rounded top, on which is sculptured a scene representing **Nakhi**, a judge, making offerings to the official **Satpar**. Sams Collection. XVIIIth dynasty. Height 9 in., width 6 in. [No. 360.]

540. (*Bay* 13.)—Painted limestone **sepulchral stele,** with rounded top, on which is painted in outline a scene representing **Nekht-Ȧmen**, and three of his relatives, kneeling in adoration before the snake-goddess with a woman's head, **Mer-Seḳert**, the lady of the Other World. Sams Collection. XVIIIth dynasty. Height 9 in., width 6 in. [No. 371.]

541. (*Bay* 13.)—Limestone **sepulchral stele,** with rounded top, of **Ȧmen-nekhtu**, a scribe in the "place of Maāt," sculptured with a scene representing the deceased kneeling in adoration before Mer-Seḳert, mistress of Ȧmenti (*sic*). XVIIIth dynasty. Height 8 in., width 5½ in. [No. 374.]

542. (*Bay* 13.)—Limestone **sepulchral stele,** with rounded top, sculptured with a scene representing the lady **Nub-Nefert**, making an offering to her sister **Ḥeru-em-ḥent**; above are the utchats, etc. Found in Malta in 1823. XVIIIth dynasty. Height 9 in., width 7 in. [No. 218.] *Presented by J. B. Collings, Esq.,* 1836.

543. (*Bay* 13.)—Limestone **sepulchral stele**, with rounded top, of **Pa-ḥu**, a high official, sculptured with figures of the deceased and his two sons, Ãa-[peḥti (?)] the judge, and Het-nekht, kneeling, with their hands raised in adoration, before the Snake-goddess **Mer-sekert**, the mistress of Åmentet. XVIIIth dynasty. Height 7½ in., width 5 in. [No. 273.]

544. (*Bay* 13.)—Upper portion of a limestone **figure of Maa-nekht-f**, with his hands raised, holding before him a stele inscribed with an address to "Åmen in his rising "and Temu in his setting." The deceased was "superintendent of "the buildings of the South and the "North," and his sister (wife) was called Nefert-khāu. XVIIIth or XIXth dynasty. Height 1 ft. 8 in., width 7 in. [No. 296.]

Figure of Maa-nekht-f holding a stele.
[Bay 13, No. 544.]

545. (*Bay* 13.)—Painted limestone **sepulchral stele**, with rounded top, of **Bakkai**, the overseer of the kitchen of the palace of Queen **Thi**, on which are sculptured two scenes: 1. The deceased and his sister, **Ta-Ån-ḥer**, standing in adoration before Osiris who wears the Atef crown and holds and .

2. **Ḥui**, and his sister Ḥent-nefert receiving offerings from four members of their family, two male and two female. The text contains a prayer to Osiris and Ḥeru-netch-tef-f, and mentions one Bak-en-Åmen. Anastasi Collection. XVIIIth dynasty. Height 1 ft. 8 in., width 1 ft. 2 in. [No. 289.]

546. (*Bay* 13.)—Portion of a **relief** from the wall of the tomb of **Qen-ȧa**. XVIIIth dynasty. Height 1 ft. 10 in., width 5 in. [No. 1243.]

547. (*Bay* 13.)—Portion of a **relief** from the wall of the tomb of **Qen-ȧa**, on which are sculptured figures of the deceased and his wife **Tui**, seated upon chairs of state. XVIIIth dynasty. Height 1 ft. 10 in., width 7½ in. [No. 918.]

548. (*Bay* 13.)—Limestone **sepulchral stele** in the form of a door of a tomb, with palm-leaf cornice and raised flat border, of **Pantu** (?), a priestly official. On the flat border are cut the winged disk and prayers to Osiris for sepulchral offerings, and on the space enclosed by it are scenes representing Tchai, and his wife Rennu, and their children, adoring Osiris Khenti Åmenti. Anastasi Collection. XVIIIth dynasty. Height 1 ft. 10 in., width 1 ft. 4 in. [No. 335.]

549. (*Bay* 13.) — Monolithic **sepulchral monument**, consisting of a stele, with pyramid top and a rectangular libation basin attached, of **Thuthu**, a sandal-maker, and his sister **Mer-seḳer**.

Pyramidal sepulchral stele of Thuthu, with libation tank attached.
[Bay 13, No. 549.]

On the top part are cut the utchats, etc. , and below are scenes representing the deceased persons adoring Osiris, and Neb-Ȧmen and his sister Sti-em-qeb pouring out a libation to their father Thuthu and his sister Bui . A good example of a rare class of stelae. Anastasi Collection. XVIIIth dynasty. (**Plate XXII.**) Height 2 ft. 2 in., width 8½ in. [No. 301.]

550. (*Bay* 14.)—**Head** of a ram-headed **sphinx** from the "Avenue of Sphinxes," by which the pylon at Karnak, built by ḤERU-EM-ḤEB, king of Egypt, about B.C. 1400, was approached. XVIIIth dynasty. Length 3 ft. 10½ in. [No. 7.]
Presented by His Majesty King George III, 1801.

551. (*Bay* 14.) — Limestone **tablet for offerings** of **Rā-uben** , and his wife **Nebt - Ȧnnu** , on which are sculptured figures of fruits, flowers, joints of meat, bread-cakes, etc. Belmore Collection. XVIIIth-XXth dynasty. Length 1 ft. 5½ in., breadth 1 ft. 5 in. [No. 593.]

552. (*Bay* 14.) — Portion of a limestone **tablet for offerings** of **Nefer-ȧāb** , sculptured with figures of bread-cakes, etc.; on one side of the spout is the name of a son of the deceased, Nefer-Renpet ; and on the other, the name of a daughter, Maḥ . XVIIIth dynasty. Length 1 ft. 2½ in., breadth 10½ in. [No. 421.]

553. (*Bay* 14.)—Limestone **tablet for offerings** of **Māia** , a scribe, inscribed with prayers to Ȧmen-Rā and Mut for funerary offerings. In the face of the tablet is a sunk relief, on which offerings of various kinds are represented. XVIIIth dynasty. Length 1 ft. 3 in., breadth 1 ft. 3 in. [No. 422.]

554. (*Bay* 14.)—Limestone **tablet for offerings of Pasheṭ** , a judge in the "place of Maāt," inscribed with prayers to Amen-Rā, lord of the thrones of the Two Lands, and to "the son of Ȧmen," king Ȧmen-ḥetep I, for funerary offerings. In the face of the tablet is a sunk relief, on which offerings of various kinds are represented. Belmore Collection. XVIIIth dynasty. Length 1 ft. 5 in., breadth 1 ft. 4 in. [No. 591.]

555. (*Central Saloon.*)—Lower portion of a black granite seated **figure of Ȧmen-ḥetep** 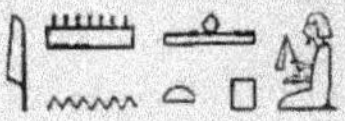, a royal scribe, Erpā, Ḥā prince, chancellor, and fan-bearer, who describes himself as the "eyes of the king of the South, and ears of "the king of the North" . XVIIIth or XIXth dynasty. Height 1 ft.; pedestal 1 ft. 10 in. square. [No. 103.]

556. (*Central Saloon.*)—Black granite seated **figure of Qen-nefer** 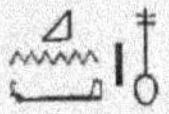, the son of Teḥuti Ḥai , and the lady Teḥuti-sat , an Erpā, Ḥā prince, chancellor, Smer uāt, superintendent-in-chief in the palace, throne attendant, officer in the royal apartments, director of the officials of the court, etc. The inscription contains a prayer to Osiris for sepulchral offerings, and enumerates the various high offices which were held by the deceased. From Thebes. Salt Collection. Found behind the statue of Ȧmen-ḥetep III, commonly called the "Vocal Memnon." XVIIIth dynasty. Height 2 ft. 9 in. [No. 48.]

557. (*Bay* 17.)—Portion of a limestone **relief** from the tomb of **Mer-Uast** 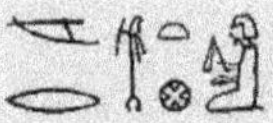, sculptured with the figures of seven priests, Maa-nȧ-nekhtuf, Pui, Ḥui, Ȧpi, Rā-mes, Bak-en-Ȧmen, and Bu-nekht, bearing the Boat of Ȧmen on their shoulders, and the deceased who kneels in adoration before it. XVIIIth or XIXth dynasty. Height 11½ in., width 1 ft. 10 in. [No. 444.]

558. (*Bay* 18.)—White limestone **pyramid** of a priestly official who was the keeper of the temple of Àmen-Rā at Thebes, on which are cut the following scenes:

Side I. The and a figure of the deceased kneeling.

Side II. The and a figure of Osiris.

Side III. The and a figure of the deceased kneeling.

Side IV. The and a figure of the jackal-god Ànpu (Anubis) on a pylon.

From Thebes. XVIIIth dynasty. Height 2 ft. 2 in. [No. 707.]

559. (*Bay* 18.)—Upper portion of a small granite **pyramid**, on two sides of which are cut figures of the solar disk in a boat, and on the other two sides a disk only. The scenes below are mutilated, but the monument appears to have been made for **Tcha-nefer** . XVIIIth or XIXth dynasty. Height 11 in. [No. 493.]

Presented by the Egypt Exploration Fund, 1904.

560. (*Bay* 18.)—Limestone **pyramid**, on the sides of which are cut in outline: 1. Figure of the Sun-god Rā in his boat. 2. Figures of **Àmen-em-ḥeb**, a judge, and his sister Mut-em-uàa. 3. Figure of the Sun-god Rā. 4. Figures of Nefer-Renpit , and his brother Bak-en-Mut . Belmore Collection. XVIIIth dynasty. Height 1 ft. 2 in. [No. 468.]

561. (*Bay* 18.)—Rectangular painted limestone **shrine**, with cornice and pyramidion, of **Àni** , a gardener (?) of Àmen. Within a rectangular niche in each of the four sides, sculptured in relief, is the upper portion of a figure of the deceased holding an inscribed stele before him. The texts on the stelae contain short prayers to Rā, and those on the borders contain prayers to Osiris for funerary offerings. Anastasi Collection. XVIIIth dynasty. Height 1 ft. 8 in. [No. 467.]

Shrine of Àni.
[Bay 18, No. 561.]

562. (*Bay* 20.)—Limestone **relief**, on which are sculptured a figure of Àmen and the figure of a king offering vases to the god. Fine work. This was intended to serve as a sculptor's model. Hay Collection. XVIIIth to XXth dynasty. Height 1 ft. 6 in., width 11 in. [No. 915.]

563. (*Bay* 11.)—Portion of a **bas-relief** on which is sculptured the decoration of the head of a goddess (Hathor?), consisting of a pair of horns, with a disk, surmounted by plumes. XVIIIth or XIXth dynasty. Height 1 ft. 5 in., width 1 ft. [No. 454.]

564. (*Central Saloon.*)—**Cast** of the head of the **statue of a Queen**, who lived under the XVIIIth dynasty, about B.C. 1450. The original is in the Egyptian Museum at Cairo. [No. 179.]

565. (*Bay* 18.)—Fine limestone seated **statues of a priest,** or high state official, and his wife, seated on a chair of state, the legs of which are in the form of the legs of a lion. The priest wears a wig and a sort of cape, or shoulder cloth, a fine linen tunic, and sandals; in his right hand he holds an object, which has not yet been identified, and with his left he clasps the hand of his wife. The lady wears a wig, and is arrayed in a garment of fine linen, which is fastened over her breast and extends to her ankles. She is bare-footed. Anastasi Collection. XVIIIth dynasty. Height (including plinth) 4 ft. 4 in. [No. 36.]

566. (*Vestibule. North Wall.*)—Large **wooden door** from the hall of the tomb of a priestly official called **Khensu-ḥetep** . On it is cut a scene in which the deceased is represented in the act of making offerings to Osiris Khenti Åmenti, in the presence of the goddess Hathor, the lady of the funeral mountain (Åmentet, or Semt Åmentet), on the west bank of the Nile at Thebes. The planks of sycamore wood of which the door is made are fastened to the cross pieces behind with wooden pegs. The door turned in a stone socket on the pivot which is seen projecting downwards on the right. From Thebes (?). About B.C. 1400. Length 8 ft. 4 in., breadth 3 ft. 8 in. [No. 705. (Old number, "H.S. 106.")]

NINETEENTH DYNASTY.

567. (*Central Saloon.*)—**Wooden statue of Seti I,** king of Egypt, about B.C. 1350, from a chamber in his tomb. Salt Collection. XIXth dynasty. Height: figure 6 ft. 5 in., pedestal $9\frac{1}{2}$ in. [No. 854.]

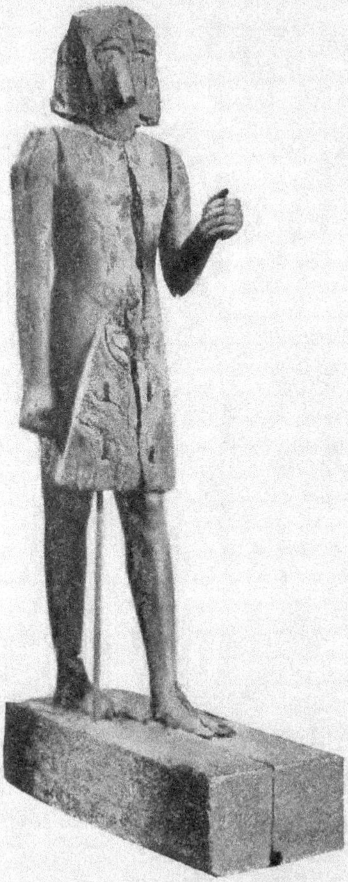

Wooden statue of Seti I, B.C. 1350.
[Central Saloon, No. 567.]

568. (*Central Saloon.*)—Painted limestone **relief** from the tomb of **Seti I,** on which are sculptured a figure of Osiris (?), hieroglyphics, etc. From the Valley of the Tombs of the Kings at Thebes. XIXth dynasty. Height 5 ft. 6 in., width 2 ft. [No. 855.]

569. (*Central Saloon.*)—Fragment of a painted **angle slab,** from a doorway in the tomb of **Seti I,** on which are sculptured in relief a portion of a figure of a goddess, hieroglyphics, and parts of cartouches containing the king's names and titles. From the Valley of the Tombs of the Kings at Thebes. XIXth dynasty. Height 1 ft. $7\frac{1}{2}$ in., width 1 ft. 3 in. [No. 884.]

Presented by Colonel T. P. Thompson, 1864.

570. (*Central Saloon.*)—Two sculptured **fragments of reliefs** from a wall of the tomb of **Seti II** at Thebes. On the upper is a portion of a figure of the king, and on the lower a portion of a figure of the Ȧn-mut-f priest, wearing a panther skin. XIXth dynasty. Height $10\frac{1}{2}$ in., width $10\frac{1}{2}$ in.; height 10 in., width 10 in. [No. 856.]

571. (*Bay* **8.**)—Upper portion of a limestone **relief,** decorated with the *khakeru* ornament , and sculptured with hieroglyphics, in relief, which give some of the titles and the prenomen of King **Seti I,** who makes offerings to the god Horus of Abydos. From Abydos. XIXth dynasty. Height 1 ft. 7 in., width 2 ft. 1 in. [No. 609.]

Presented by the Egypt Exploration Fund, 1902.

572. (*Bay* **18.**)—Grey **granite clamp,** from a wall of a temple built at Abydos by **Seti I,** whose prenomen is cut upon it . XIXth dynasty. Length 1 ft. 9 in., breadth 8 in. [No. 1375.]

573. (*Bay* **11.**)—Limestone **sepulchral stele,** with rounded top, of **Rumā** 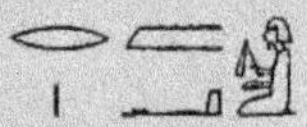, a scribe, and official of the temple of Seti I , at Abydos, sculptured with the following scenes:—1. The standard, or fetish of Osiris of Abydos, with jackal-gods, utchats, offerings, etc. 2. Rumā and members of his family adoring Osiris, Isis, and Horus. 3. Rumā and his wife receiving offerings from his family. XIXth dynasty. From Abydos. Height 3 ft. 1 in., width 2 ft. 1½ in. [No. 146.]

574. (*Bay* **13.**)—Limestone **sepulchral stele,** with rounded top, which was set up by **Seti I,** king of Egypt, about B.C. 1350, in the temple of Thothmes II at Behen, or Wâdî Ḥalfah. On the upper portion is sculptured a scene in which the king is represented making offerings to Àmen, Menu, or Àmsu, Horus, son of Isis, and Isis, and below this is cut an inscription recording the names and titles of the king, and referring to the benefits which he has conferred on his gods and people. The stele was set up in the first year of the king's reign . From Wâdî Ḥalfah. XIXth dynasty. Height 4 ft. 1 in., width 2 ft. 8½ in. [No. 1189.]

Presented by General Sir Charles Holled Smith, K.C.B., 1887.

575. (*Central Saloon.*)—Wooden **statue of Rameses II,** wearing a wig and pig-tail, and a tunic. The legs have been restored. Salt Collection. From the tomb of Rameses II in the Valley of the Tombs of the Kings at Thebes. XIXth dynasty. Height 4 ft. 7 in. [No. 882.]

576. (*Central Saloon.*)—Upper portion of a colossal **granite statue of Rameses II,** wearing a crown formed of uraei, which was one of a pair that were placed in front of a doorway of the Ramesseum in Western Thebes. Down the back are cut in fine, bold hieroglyphics the Horus name, and several of the titles of the king, and a portion of the text of the dedication of the statue to Àmen-Rā. When this object arrived in England, in 1817, there were traces of colour upon it, and it seems that the statue was originally painted red. From Ḳûrnah. XIXth dynasty. Height 8 ft. 9 in., width across shoulders 6 ft. 8 in., weight about 7¼ tons. [No. 19.]
Presented by Henry Salt, Esq., and L. Burckhardt, Esq., 1817.

577. (*Central Saloon.*)—Colossal red granite standing **statue of Rameses II**, wearing the White Crown, or Crown of Upper Egypt. The king's prenomen and nomen are cut upon his shoulders, and upon his breast are cut the pronomen and nomen of **Mer-en-Ptaḥ**, or **Menephtah I.** From Karnak. XIXth dynasty. Height 8 ft. 10 in. [No. 61.]

578. (*Bay* 16.)—Portion of a hard sandstone **slab** on which are cut in large bold hieroglyphics the names and titles of **Rameses II.** It was found at the base of the Column of Diocletian, or "Pompey's Pillar," at Alexandria, and it perhaps once formed part of a statue of Rameses II. XIXth dynasty. Length 3 ft. 3 in., breadth 1 ft. 11 in. [No. 104.]

579. (*Bay* 16.)—Lower portion of a black granite kneeling **statue of Rameses II**, inscribed on the back and pedestal with the king's names and titles. XIXth dynasty. Height 2 ft. 9 in. [No. 42.]
Presented by H.R.H. the Duke of York, 1812.

580. (*Bay* 15.)—Lower portion of a black granite **statue of Rameses II**, who is kneeling and holding before him a shrine, the sides of which are inscribed with the names and titles of the king. On the top of the shrine is sculptured a beetle , symbol of the god Kheperà, whose "beloved one" Rameses II declares himself to be. XIXth dynasty, about B.C. 1330. Height 3 ft. 3 in. [No. 27.]
Presented by Earl Spencer, 1805.

581. (*Bay* 14.)—Upper portion of a black granite seated **statue of Rameses II,** whose prenomen , is cut upon the belt. The feet and legs up to the knees have been restored. XIXth dynasty. Height, with pedestal, 5 ft. [No. 109.]

582. (*Bay* 14.)—Upper portion of a **statue of Rameses II**, bearded and wearing a heavy wig, with an uraeus in front, on which rests the Double Crown of the South and the North. In his right hand he holds the whip , and in his left the sceptre . On the back are two lines of hieroglyphics which contain the names and titles of the king, and state that he was the son of Khnemu, born of Ānqet, Lady of Ta-Kenset, and suckled by Satet, Lady of Elephantine. Found on the Island of Elephantine. XIXth dynasty, about B.C. 1300. Height 5 ft. [No. 67.]

Presented by W. R. Hamilton, Esq., 1838.

583. (*Bay* 12.)—Head from a colossal red granite **statue of Rameses II** (?). From Thebes (?). XIXth dynasty. Height 2 ft. 1 in. [No. 119.]

584. (*Bay* 17.)—Limestone **statue of Rameses II**, kneeling, and holding before him a tablet for offerings on which are sculptured figures of bread-cakes, etc., and a libation vase, on which are cut some of the names and titles of the king 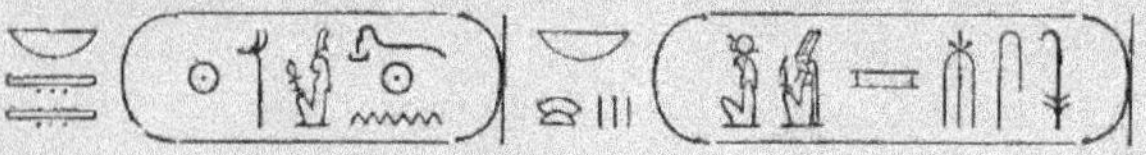. The king's prenomen and nomen are also cut upon his shoulders and on the plinth at the back of the figure. Salt Collection. Found near Abydos. XIXth dynasty. Restored from the waist downwards. Height of figure 4 ft. 3 in. [No. 96.]

585. (*Bay* 16.)—Upper portion of a red granite **statue of a king** holding in his left hand a standard, the head of which was probably in the form of a hawk. It was found at Tall Bastah, among the ruins of the temple of **Osorkon II**, and probably belongs to a statue of **Rameses II.** XIXth dynasty, about B.C. 1300. Height 4 ft. [No. 1066.]

Presented by the Egypt Exploration Fund, 1889.

586. (*Bay* 23.)—Portion of a red granite **slab** on which are cut portions of the cartouches of **Rameses II** and the names of three conquered nations, Keshkesh, Māshauasha, and Atharuta (?). From Bubastis. XIXth dynasty. Height 3 ft., width 1 ft. 8 in. [No. 1104.]

587. (*Central Saloon.*)—Lower portion of a **statue of Rameses II,** the pedestal and plinth of which are inscribed with the names and titles of this king. On one side of the plinth is sculptured a figure of the "royal daughter, great "royal wife, Batautānth" 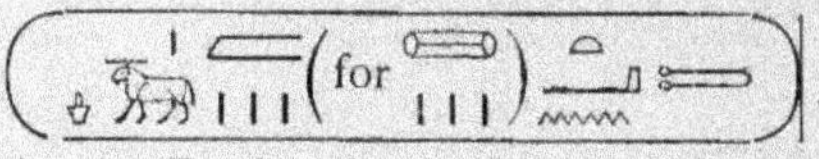.

From Ṣarâbît al-Khâdim, in the Peninsula of Sinai. XIXth dynasty. Height 2 ft. 3 in. [No. 697.]

Presented by the Egypt Exploration Fund, 1905.

588. (*Central Saloon.*)—**Cast** of the head of the colossal **statue of Rameses II,** now lying at Mît Rahînah, a village which marks a portion of the site of Memphis. This statue is supposed to have been one of the two which, according to Herodotus, stood before the great Temple of Ptaḥ, the Hephaisteum of the Greeks, at Memphis, and was presented to the British Nation by Muhammad Ali, Pâshâ of Egypt, in 1820. Height 8 ft. 9 in. [No. 858.]

589. (*Vestibule, over the East Door.*)—**Cast** of the head of one of the four colossal statues of **Rameses II,** which are seated in front of the rock-hewn temple, on the west bank of the Nile, at Abû Simbel, in Nubia. This temple was built by the king, about B.C. 1300, to commemorate his victory over the Kheta, a confederation of tribes in Northern Syria, and to overawe the rebellious tribes of the Northern Sûdân. The following are the principal dimensions of the features:—

	ft.	in.
Width of forehead	7	5
Depth of forehead	3	9
Length of eye	2	4
Length of nose	3	2
Length of mouth	2	8
Length from brow to chin	9	8
Width of face	8	9
Length of ear	3	2

This cast was made by Mr. J. Bonomi, at the expense of Mr. Hay. Total height of cast 10 ft. 4 in. [No. 1071.]

590. (*Bay* 18.)—Rectangular arragonite **base of a statue,** or libation vessel, inscribed on the sides with the principal titles and names of **Rameses II,** king of Egypt, about B.C. 1330. At the bottom is a rectangular projection for insertion into a sub-plinth or base. XIXth dynasty. Length 2 ft. 1 in., breadth 1 ft. 3 in. [No. 681.]

591. (*Bay* 19.)—Upper portion of a slab, or **stele,** inscribed with the opening lines of an official document, drawn up in the reign of **Rameses II,** king of Egypt, about B.C. 1330. The text is dated in the first year of the king's reign, and enumerates his names and titles, wherein he is likened to Menthu, the god of war, and is said to rush among the chiefs of the Nine Tribes who use the bow, and to invade the lands of the East like the god Mau-ḥes, etc. Found in front of the Great Pyramid at Gîzah. XIXth dynasty. Height 1 ft. 5 in., width 4 ft. 7 in. [No. 440.]

Presented by Captain Caviglia, 1817.

592. (*Bay* 6.)—Portions of a series of limestone slabs, on which was sculptured a scene representing **Rameses II,** king of Egypt, about B.C. 1330, making offerings to a number of the kings of Egypt who ruled before him ; the prenomens of these, when complete, were fifty-two in number. Of these the following remain :—Upper Register. 1. . . . . . . ka. 2. Men-ka-Rā. 3. Nefer-ka-Rā. 4. Nefer-ka-Rā Nebi. 5. Teṭ-ka-Rā Maā . . . . 6. Nefer-ka-Rā Khenṭu. 7. Mer-en-Ḥeru. 8. Senefer-ka. 9. Ka-en-Rā. 10. Nefer-ka-Rā Terl (?) 11. Nefer-ka-Ḥeru. 12. Nefer-ka-Rā Pepi-senb. 13. Nefer-ka-Rā-ānnu. Lower Register. 1. Nub-kau-Rā. 2. Khā-kheper-Rā. 3. Khā-kau-Rā. 4. Maāt-en-Rā. 5. Maā-kheru-Rā. 6. Neb-peḥtet-Rā. 7. Tcheser-ka-Rā. 8. Āa-kheper-ka-Rā. 9. Āa-kheper-en-Rā. 10. Men-kheper-Rā. 11. Āa-kheperu-Rā. 12. Men-kheperu-Rā. 13. Neb-Maāt-Rā. 14. Tcheser-kheperu-Rā Setep-en-Rā. 15. Men-peḥtet-Rā. 16. Men - Maāt - Rā. This monument is commonly known as the **Second King List of Abydos.** From the Mimaut Collection. Found in a chamber in the temple of Rameses II, at Abydos, by Mr. Bankes in 1818. XIXth dynasty. Length 12 ft. 2 in. [No. 117.]

593. (*Bay* 14.)—Red **granite lion,** on the back and pedestal of which are inscribed the names and titles of **Rameses II,** king of Egypt about B.C. 1330. Found at

Benha al-'Asal, a place which marks the site of the ancient city of Athribis, about twenty miles north-west of Cairo. XIXth dynasty. Length 5 ft. 10½ in., height 2 ft. 8½ in. [No. 857.]

594, 595. (*Bay* 15.)—A pair of **hawk-headed** sandstone **sphinxes,** symbols of Menthu-Rā, or of one of the forms of Horus which were worshipped in Northern Nubia. They were found, one on each side of a doorway, in the temple of Rameses II at Abû Simbel, by Belzoni. Salt Collection. XIXth dynasty, about B.C. 1300. Length 3 ft. 6 in., height 1 ft. 1 in. [Nos. 11 and 13.]

596. (*Central Saloon.*)—Massive grey **granite hawk,** symbol of Rā-Ḥeru-Khuti, or Rā-Harmachis, "Great "god, lord of heaven." Above the claws is sculptured a cartouche, with plumes, inscribed with the names and titles of **Rameses II,** about B.C. 1330. From Tall al-Maskhûṭah in the Wâdî Ṭûmîlâṭ. XIXth dynasty. Height 2 ft. 10 in. [No. 1006.]

Presented by the Egypt Exploration Fund, 1883.

597. (*Bay* 16.)—**Left fist,** grasping a roll, from one of the two red granite colossal statues of **Rameses II,** which are said to have stood before the temple of Ptaḥ at Memphis. From the ruins of Memphis. XIXth dynasty, about B.C. 1330. Length 4 ft. 3 in., weight about 1 ton 6 cwt. [No. 9.]

Presented by His Majesty King George III, 1802.

598. (*Bay* 18.)—Massive red **granite column,** with palm-leaf capital, on which are cut in fine bold hieroglyphics the names and titles of **Rameses II,** king of Egypt, about B.C. 1330. In several places in the cartouches portions of the king's names have been roughly hammered out, and the name and titles of **Osorkon II,** king of Egypt, about B.C. 860, cut in their stead. From the temple built by Rameses II at Bubastis. XIXth dynasty. Height: abacus 1 ft., capital 4 ft. 6 in., shaft 15 ft. 2½ in., total 20 ft. 9 in., weight 11¼ tons. [No. 1065.]

Presented by the Egypt Exploration Fund, 1889.

599. (*Bay* 17.)—Monolithic, **red granite column,** with palm-leaf capital, from the temple built in honour of the god Heru-shefit at Herakleopolis by **Rameses II,** king of Egypt, about B.C. 1330. On the upper portion are four perpendicular lines of hieroglyphics containing the names and titles of

Rameses II, and beneath these are two scenes in which the king, the "beloved of Ḥeru-shefit," is represented making offerings to Osiris of Ȧn-rer-f. On the lower portion of the column are cut four lines of hieroglyphics, similar to those on the upper portion, and between them are the names and titles of **Mer-en-Ptaḥ**  , or **Menephthah I,** roughly marked out for cutting. From Herakleopolis. XIXth dynasty. Height 17 ft. 2 in., diameter at base 2 ft. 5½ in., weight between 6 and 7 tons. [No. 1123.]

Presented by the Egypt Exploration Fund, 1891.

600. (*Bay* 16.)—Grey granite **tablet for offerings,** made for **Rameses II,** whose names and titles are cut in deep, bold hieroglyphics on the edges. On the face are sculptured in relief figures of bread-cakes, a goose, a haunch of beef, etc., and round all four sides is cut a channel through which the libations ran to the spout of the tablet. From the Ramesseum. XIXth dynasty, about B.C. 1330. Length 2 ft. 10½ in., breadth 2 ft. 2 in. [No. 1355.]

601. (*Central Saloon.*)—Upper portion of a colossal limestone **statue of a queen,** who wears the head-dress characteristic of the goddess Hathor, with an uraeus over the forehead. The lady represented is probably one of the queens of Rameses II. Found by Belzoni in 1817. Salt Collection. XIXth dynasty, about B.C. 1300. Height 3 ft. 8½ in. [No. 93.]

602. (*Central Saloon.*)—Upper portion of a colossal limestone **statue of a queen,** wearing a heavy wig, surmounted by a crown, with an uraeus over the forehead. The lady represented is probably one of the queens of Rameses II. Found by Belzoni. Salt Collection. XIXth dynasty (?) Height 4 ft. 7 in. [No. 948.]

603. (*Central Saloon.*)—Limestone kneeling **statue of Pa-neḥsi** 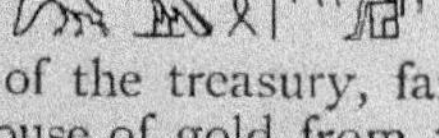, a royal scribe, who was superintendent of the treasury, fan-bearer to the king, overseer of the storehouse of gold from the Sûdân, and controller of the gifts and tribute which were paid to the king of Egypt by the chiefs of the Sûdân. He flourished in the reign of **Rameses II**, whose cartouches are cut upon his right shoulder. Before him he holds a shrine, in the front of which are sculptured figures of Osiris, Isis, and Horus. From Thebes. Barker Collection. XIXth dynasty. Height 3 ft. $7\frac{1}{2}$ in., width 1 ft. $8\frac{1}{2}$ in. [No. 1377.]

Upper portion of a statue of one of the queens of Rameses II, about B.C. 1330.
[Central Saloon, No. 602.]

604. (*Central Saloon.*)—Painted limestone kneeling **statue of Pa-ser**, a prince of Kash , and governor of Ta-Kenset, or Nubia. He holds before him a pedestal of unusual shape, on the top of which is the head of a ram, symbol of the ram of Åmen. The inscriptions contain prayers to Åmsu, or Menu, Isis, and Åmen-Rā, the dweller in Per-Rameses for sepulchral offerings. Belzoni and Salt Collection. XIXth dynasty. Height 2 ft. 4 in. [No. 1376.]

Kneeling statue of Pa-ser, governor of the Sûdân, about B.C. 1350. [Bay 13, No. 604.]

605. (*Bay* 14.)—Rectangular black granite **libation vessel**, dedicated to Åmen-Rā, Ptaḥ, Hathor, and Maāt, by **Nefer-Renpet**, a governor of a city, who flourished in the reign of **Rameses II.** On one end are sculptured figures of the deceased, who is represented in the act of adoring the cartouches of Rameses II, and on the other is a kneeling figure of him. On the sides and flat lip are inscribed prayers to the above-mentioned deities, and in the petition to Ptaḥ the deceased prays that he may live for one hundred and ten years. Salt Collection. XIXth dynasty. Height of kneeling figure 1 ft. 4 in.; length of vessel 2 ft. 1 in. [No. 108.]

606. (*Central Saloon.*)—Lower portion of a seated black granite **figure of Pa-ser**, an Erpā, Ḥā prince, and governor of a city. On the sides and back of the seat are inscribed prayers to Åmen-Rā Harmachis, Mut, Maāt, Thoth, Urt-ḥekau, and other gods for sepulchral offerings. XIXth dynasty. Height 1 ft. 4 in. [No. 954.]

607. (*Bay* 11.)—Limestone **sepulchral stele,** with rounded top, of **Åmen-em-ånt**, the son of Nesi-pa-qa-Shuti, priest of Åmen-Rā, priest of the third order of Khensu in Thebes Nefer-ḥetep, priest of Menthu, and chief military scribe. His father held several priestly offices and was Setem priest in the chapel of Rameses II , in the temple of Ȧmen-Rā at Thebes. The sculptured scene on the upper portion of the stele is obliterated. The text of twenty lines contains a list of the offices held by Ȧmen-em-ȧnt and his father, and a prayer to Osiris for sepulchral offerings, etc. XXth dynasty. Height 3 ft. 5 in., width 2 ft. 1½ in. [No. 645.]

608. (*Bay* 17.)—Sandstone **relief** sculptured with a figure of **Setau** , a prince of Kash, *i.e.*, governor of Nubia, standing in adoration before the goddess **Rennut** , "lady of food, manifold of things," , and the prenomen of **Rameses II.** From Wâdi Ḥalfah. XIXth dynasty. Height 1 ft. 8 in., width 1 ft. 5½ in. [No. 1055.]

Presented by General Sir C. Holled Smith, K.C.B., 1887.

609. (*Bay* 24.)—Painted limestone **relief**, with rounded top, on which are sculptured figures of Rameses II, the governor of Thebes, the judge **Kar** , and his son **Ḥui-nefer** , adoring Ptaḥ "Lord of Maāt, "king of the Two Lands." XIXth dynasty. Height 1 ft. 1½ in., width 9 in. [No. 328.]

610. (*Bay* 19.)—Limestone **sepulchral stele**, with rounded top, of **Ȧmen-ḥetep** , a royal envoy , who was surnamed **Ḥui** , the son of Hau-neferu 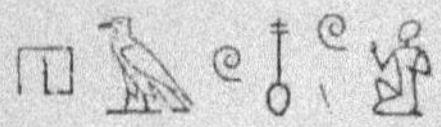, and the lady Rā-mert 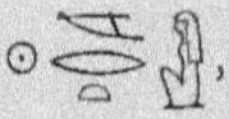, who flourished in the reign of **Rameses II.** On the upper part of the stele are cut the date, which is mutilated, the *utchats*, the names and titles of Rameses II within a cartouche, and a figure of Ḥui, making offerings to his ancestors, who are arranged in four groups. The text below contains a prayer to Osiris, Ḥeru-nekht-netch-tef-f, Isis, Anubis, and other gods, for sepulchral offerings. This stele was set up by Ḥui in memory of his father, mother, brethren, and all his forefathers whose names are cut thereon, and he prays that they may live on what the god lives on 

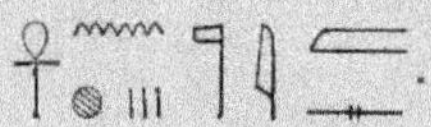. Salt Collection. XIXth dynasty. Height 3 ft. 8 in., width 2 ft. 5 in. [No. 166.]

611. (*Bay* **20.**)—Limestone **sepulchral stele**, with rounded top, of **Ptaḥ-em-uȧa** 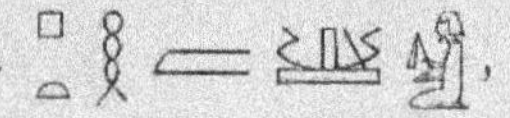, the overseer of the royal stables, scribe of royal chamber, and royal envoy to foreign lands, who flourished in the reign of **Rameses II.** On it are sculptured the following: 1. The winged disk, from which project human hands and arms embracing the name of Rameses II. 2. The deceased adoring Osiris, Isis, and Horus. 3. The deceased making offerings to his ancestors, the figures of whom are arranged in three rows. Salt Collection. XIXth dynasty. Height 2 ft. 9½ in., width 1 ft. 4 in. [No. 167.]

612. (*Bay* **19.**)—Limestone **sepulchral stele**, with rounded top, of **Bak-āa** 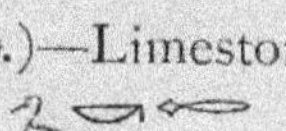, the son of the councillor Hau-nefer 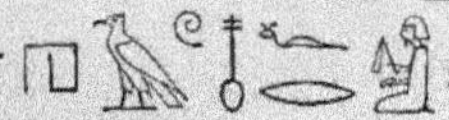, who died in the thirty-eighth year of the reign of **Rameses II**, *i.e.*, about B.C. 1290. On it are cut the following: 1. The date. 2. Ȧnpu of the North and Ȧnpu of the South. 3. The bull's skin. 4. The titles of Rameses II within a cartouche. 5. The deceased adoring ten gods and goddesses. 6. The deceased making offerings to his deceased kinsfolk. 7. A hymn of praise to Osiris and prayers to this god. The deceased held the office of "superintendent of the "*āḥu* chamber," 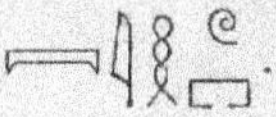. XIXth dynasty. Salt Collection. Height 3 ft. 9 in., width 2 ft. 3 in. [No. 164.]

613. (*Bay* **20.**)—Limestone **sepulchral stele**, with rounded top, of **Nefer-ḥrà** , a "scribe of the house of books of "Pharaoh," who died on the twenty-ninth day of the first month of the summer in the sixty-second year of the reign of **Rameses II.** On the stele are sculptured the following scenes: 1. The deceased adoring Osiris, Isis, Nephthys, and Horus. 2, 3. The deceased making offerings to his kinsfolk, figures of whom are arranged in two rows. Salt Collection. XIXth dynasty. (**Plate XXIII.**) Height 2 ft. 4 in., width 1 ft. 8 in. [No. 163.]

614. (*Central Saloon.*)—Limestone seated **statue** of **Pi-Àai** , the son of the lady Àst 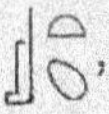, a royal scribe, councillor, and overseer of the seal, who flourished in the reign of **Rameses II.** On the front of the figure are cut prayers to Osiris, Anubis, Ptaḥ, and Seker for sepulchral offerings. XIXth dynasty. Height 2 ft. 4 in. [No. 46.]

615. (*Bay* **18.**)—Flint agglomerate **statue of Khā-em-Uast** , the eldest son of **Rameses II**, king of Egypt, about B.C. 1300. The deceased wears a short heavy wig and a tunic, and holds to his sides with his arms two standards. The standard on the right was surmounted by a mummied form and a figure of the prince; that on the left by an object which appears to represent the box which held the head of Osiris at Abydos. In the front of this object are two uraei. On the standard on the right is cut the prenomen of **Rameses II**, and on that on the left the name of this king. From Asyûṭ. XIXth dynasty. Height, including base, 4 ft. 8 in. [No. 947.]

Presented by Samuel Sharpe, Esq., 1866.

Sepulchral stele of Nefer-ḥrā, a scribe in the Library of Rameses II.
[Bay 20, No. 613.]

616. (*Bay* 21.)—Quartzite sandstone seated **statue of User-kheperu-Rā-meri-Åmen, Seti II Mer-en-Ptaḥ (II)**

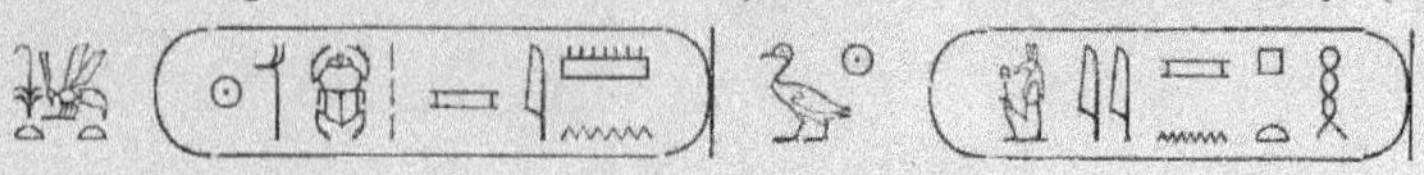,

king of Egypt, about B.C. 1250, holding a small shrine, surmounted by the head of the Ram of Åmen. The king's prenomen is cut on the right shoulder, and his nomen on the left, and his names and titles are repeated on the pedestal and base. The sides of the throne are decorated with the symbol of the union of the countries of the South and the North. Salt Collection. From Karnak. Height 5 ft. 4½ in. [No. 26.]

617. (*Central Saloon.*)—Portion of a group of limestone slabs inscribed with fragments of four lines of a funerary text containing prayers to the gods on behalf of **Seti II Mer-en-Ptaḥ,** remains of whose prenomen, User-kheperu-Rā-meri-Åmen 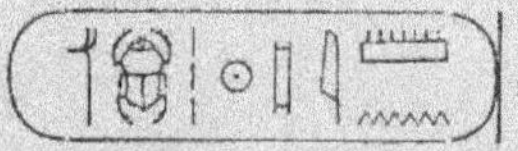, are still visible. From the tomb of Seti II at Thebes. XIXth dynasty, about B.C. 1250. Height 6 ft. 4 in. [No. 1378 (167*).]

618. (*Central Saloon.*)—**Head** from a black granite **statue of a king,** or prince, wearing the uraeus, symbol of royalty, over the forehead. XIXth dynasty. Height 1 ft. 2 in. [No. 487.]

619. (*Central Saloon.*)—Sandstone standing figure of the dog-headed **Ape-god,** who was the associate of Thoth, the Scribe of the gods. He is often seen sitting on the standard of the Balance in which the souls of the dead are weighed in the Hall of Judgment, and he reports to Thoth when the beam is exactly horizontal. Salt Collection. From Abû Simbel. XIXth dynasty. Height 2 ft. 11 in. [No. 40.]

620. (*Bay* 10.)—Limestone **sepulchral stele,** in the form of the door of a tomb, with palm-leaf cornice and a raised flat border, surmounted by a pyramidion. On the upper part of the border are cut , with the figure of a jackal on each side, and on the flat surface enclosed by the border is a well-cut figure of the deceased **Khart-âh . . . . . . -i (?)**

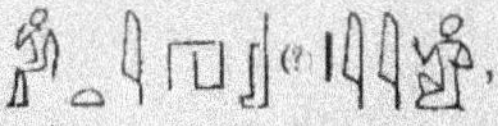, seated on a chair of state and smelling a lotus. Before him is a table of offerings, at which stands his brother Ȧnni 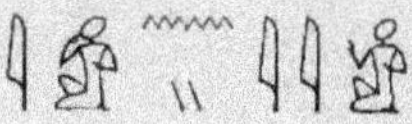, who set up this stele to his brother's memory. Anastasi Collection. XIXth dynasty. Height 2 ft., width 1 ft. 4½ in. [No. 308.]

621. (*Bay* 10.)—Limestone **sepulchral stele,** with rounded top, of **Māi** 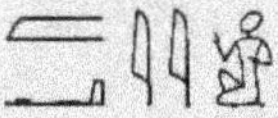, a royal official. On the upper portion of the stele are cut figures of Māi and his father standing in adoration before Osiris, Isis, and Horus, and below, in two rows, seated in adoration, are figures of twelve of their relatives, two males and ten females. Sabatier Collection. XIXth dynasty. Height 2 ft. 1 in., width 1 ft. 6 in. [No. 656.]

622. (*Bay* 13.)—Painted limestone **sepulchral stele,** with rounded top, of **Neb-Nefer** , a judge, sculptured with kneeling figures of the deceased, and Karu, Nefer-ḥetep, Neb-Ȧmenti, Uatchmes, and other sons kneeling in adoration before the gods Ptaḥ, Khnemu, Sati, and Ȧnqet, who are seated on thrones with a table of offerings before them. Belmore Collection. XIXth dynasty. Height 1 ft. 9½ in., width 1 ft. 2 in. [No. 267.]

623. (*Bay* 13.)—Limestone **sepulchral stele,** cut on a slab with a pyramid top, of **Neb-Nefer** 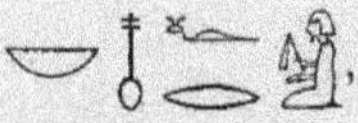, a member of the royal bodyguard. On the flat portion of the slab, above the stele, are cut the utchats, etc. , and below, in three registers, are the following scenes:—1. Neb-nefer kneeling in adoration before Osiris, Ḥeru-sa-Ȧsȧr, and Isis. 2 and 3. Neb-nefer pouring out a libation and offering incense to kinsfolk. XIXth dynasty. Height 2 ft. 1 in., width 1 ft. 3 in. [No. 1184.]

624. (*Bay* 13.)—Limestone **sepulchral stele,** with rounded top, of **Pa-sheṭ** , a judge, sculptured with scenes representing the deceased, his wife, and their daughter and son Àmen-mes, adoring Ptaḥ, lord of Maāt, who stands within a shrine, before which are two altars laden with flowers. Belmore Collection. XIXth dynasty. Height 1 ft. 1 in., width 9½ in. [No. 262.]

625. (*Bay* 13.)—Sandstone **sepulchral stele,** with rounded top, of **Pa-sheṭ** , sculptured with figures of the deceased and his wife, **Bakpupi** , making adorations to Àmen-Rā and Horus of Behen. XIXth dynasty. From Wâdî Ḥalfah. Height 1 ft., width 9 in. [No. 950.]

626. (*Bay* 13.)—Limestone **relief,** from the wall of a tomb, on which is sculptured a figure of the jackal-god Anpu, or Àp-uat, *couchant,* upon the roof of a funerary temple. Salt Collection. XIXth dynasty. Height 1 ft. 5 in., width 2 ft. 1 in. [No. 455.]

627. (*Bay* 14.)—Limestone **tablet for offerings** of **Bu-qent-f** , a judge in the Seat of Law, and his wife **Nub-em-usekh** , inscribed with a prayer to Rā-Harmachis-Temu and Osiris Khenti Àmenti for sepulchral offerings. Belmore Collection. XIXth dynasty. Length 7½ in., breadth 7 in. [No. 424.]

628. (*Bay* 15.)—Lower portion of a seated sandstone **statue** of the goddess **Isis suckling Horus,** which was dedicated to one of the temples in Thebes by **Ḥui** , queen and high-priestess of Àmen. On one side of the throne is cut a prayer to Àmen-Rā and Mut for sepulchral offerings, and on the other are sculptured figures of three princes and three princesses, Rā-men-kheper, Àmen-meri (in a cartouche) Àmen-Meri (without a cartouche), Àst, etc. From Thebes **XIXth** dynasty. Height 2 ft. [No. 1280.]

629. (*Bay* 17.)—Upper portion of a limestone **sepulchral stele,** with rounded top, on which are sculptured figures of

Amen-Rā and his consort Mut, and of Ḥeru-khuti and Isis, seated, with an incense stand in their midst. XIXth dynasty. Height 1 ft. $3\frac{1}{2}$ in., width 1 ft. 9 in. [No. 646.]

630. (*Bay* **17.**)—Painted limestone **sepulchral stele,** with rounded top, of **Khā-Bekhnet** [hieroglyphs], a judge,

Sepulchral stele of Khā-Bekhnet, with scenes representing the deceased worshipping Rā and Hathor.
[Bay 17, No. 630.] XIXth dynasty.

sculptured with the following scenes:—1. The Boat of Rā-Harmachis, accompanied by the [hieroglyph] and [hieroglyph]. 2. The deceased adoring the cow of Hathor, the head of which emerges from the funeral Mountain. 3. The god (?) [hieroglyphs].

4. The deceased and his wife kneeling in adoration. The text contains a prayer for sepulchral offerings. Belmore Collection. XIXth dynasty. Height 2 ft. 1 in., width 1 ft. 4 in. [No. 555.]

631. (*Bay* 17.)—Limestone **sepulchral stele,** with rounded top, sculptured with scenes representing **Ḥui** and his wife and son making offerings to Osiris, and a daughter and three sons pouring out a libation to **Reb**, and his wife **Nebt-Nefert**. Above are the utchats, etc. XIXth dynasty. Height 1 ft. 1 in., width 11 in. [No. 354.]

632. (*Bay* 17.)—Limestone **sepulchral stele,** with rounded top, of **Qen-ḥer-khepesh-f**, a judge in the "place of Maāt," sculptured in relief with a figure of the deceased kneeling in adoration before the goddess Hathor, who is accompanied by the Ka of Àmentet. The text contains the names and titles of the goddess and prayers to Hathor, Àmen-Rā and his consort Mut. From Thebes. Belmore Collection. XIXth dynasty. Height 1 ft. 1 in., width 9 in. [No. 278.]

633. (*Bay* 17.)—Upper portion of a limestone **sepulchral stele,** with rounded top, of **Unen-neferu**, an official, which was set up by his son Sent-thu (?) (?). Below the short lines of text is sculptured a scene in which Sent-thu (?) is represented pouring out a libation to his father and mother who are seated on chairs of state, and wearing "cones" on their heads. Belmore Collection. From Thebes. XIXth dynasty. Height 9 in., width 11½ in. [No. 285.]

634. (*Bay* 17.)—Portion of a painted limestone **relief,** on which is sculptured the figure of a man standing in adoration before a seated figure of Rā. XIXth dynasty. Height 10 in., width 9 in. [No. 329.]

635. (*Bay* 17.)—Limestone **relief,** with cornice, from the tomb of **Mes**, a priest of the KA, sculptured with two scenes in each of which the deceased is represented sitting upon a stool with elaborately carved legs and seat-frame, and receiving the homage of his wife Bak-ānkhet, a priestess of Isis, who is making an offering of flowers to him. Fine work. From Memphis. XIXth dynasty. Length 7 ft. 1 in., breadth 2 ft. 6 in. [No. 1465.]

Sepulchral stele of Åmen-Rā-mes, a priest of the statue of Mer-en-Ptaḥ, about B.C. 1250. [Bay 20, No. 636.]

636. (*Bay* 20.) — Limestone **sepulchral stele,** with rounded top, of **Åmen-Rā-mes**, a priest of the statue of **Mer-en-Ptaḥ,** king of Egypt, about B.C. 1250; it was made and set up by Khā-em-thert, the son of the deceased, who was a scribe of the soldiers, or military secretary. On it are sculptured the following:—1. The winged disk. 2. The sacred standard of Osiris at Abydos being held in position by Isis and Horus; on one side is the deceased, and on the other his son. 3, 4. Khā-em-thert offering incense to his kinsfolk. 5. A scribe of the altar offering incense to his kinsfolk. From Thebes. XIXth dynasty. Height 2 ft. 6 in., width 1 ft. 2 in. [No. 139.]

637. (*Central Saloon.*)—Painted limestone seated **statues of Māḥu** 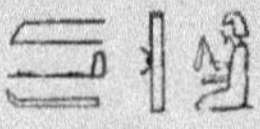, director of the works of Åmen-Rā at Thebes, and **Sebta** , a priestess of Hathor and Åmen-Rā. The inscriptions down the figures, and on the sides of the pedestal, and on the back, contain prayers to Åmen, Mut, Ptaḥ-Seker-Åsår, Anubis, Åp-uat, Hathor, Rā-Harmachis, Tem, etc., for sepulchral offerings. Anastasi Collection. XIXth dynasty, about B.C. 1350. Height 2 ft. [No. 460.]

638. (*Central Saloon.*)—Seated granite **figure of Rui** 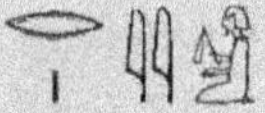, a high-priest of Åmen. In front of his knees is sculptured a Hathor-headed sistrum, and on the plinth behind are cut two lines of text, in which he prays to Åmen-Rā to make his name permanent in the hall of the lord of Heaven, and to Mut, the lady of Åsheru, that he may sail in peace and safety into the "temple of eternity." From Karnak. XIXth dynasty. The legs and pedestal are broken away. Height 3 ft. [No. 81.]

Presented by His Majesty King George III, 1801.

639. (*Bay* 12.)—Limestone **sepulchral stele,** with rounded top, of **Ta-måit** 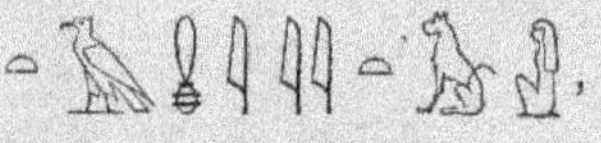, sculptured with a scene representing her daughter Kiåu , standing in homage before her. Above the scene are the utchats, etc. . XIXth dynasty. Height 1 ft. 2½ in., width 1 ft 3 in. [No. 644.]

640. (*Bay* 17.)—Limestone **sepulchral stele,** with rounded top, of **Pa-ren-nefer** , a judge, on which are cut, in outline, scenes representing the deceased kneeling in adoration before the ram of Åmen-Rā, and his wife, and daughter, and two members of the family, making offerings to Hathor. The texts contain a prayer to Åmen-Rā and Mut, and a list of the titles of Àmen-Ra. Belmore Collection. XIXth dynasty. Height 1 ft. 8 in., width 1 ft. 2 in. [No. 283.]

641. (*Bay* **17**.)—Portion of a limestone **sepulchral stele,** with rounded top, on which are sculptured a figure of Rā-Harmachis, seated in his boat, and the utchats . Belmore Collection. XIXth dynasty. Height 7½ in., width 7 in. [No. 260.]

642. (*Central Saloon.*)—Rectangular limestone **sepulchral stele of Ptaḥ-mes** , a veritable royal scribe and overseer of the grain supply of the Lord of the Two Lands. On the upper portion is sculptured a figure of the deceased, with his hands raised in adoration, and below is a scene in which is represented the performance of the ceremony of "Opening the Mouth" of the deceased. A relative, or wife, called Rui  is mentioned in the text. Found near the pyramids of Gîzah. Salt Collection. XIXth dynasty. Height 4 ft. 9 in., width 1 ft. 9 in. [No. 160.]

643. (*Central Saloon.*)—Massive limestone **sepulchral stele,** with rounded top, of **Pa-ser** , a royal scribe and superintendent of the builders of the "Lord of the "Two Lands." On the upper part is sculptured a scene in which the deceased and his brother Thunrei 
, are represented adoring Osiris, Isis, and Hathor. Below is a second scene, showing Pa-ser and his wife Pipui , receiving offerings and adoration from members of their family. Between the two scenes are five lines of text containing prayers to Osiris, Ptaḥ-Seker, and Ànpu, for sepulchral offerings. Salt Collection. XIXth dynasty. Height 5 ft. 5 in., width 2 ft. 9 in. [No. 165.]

644. (*Central Saloon.*)—Painted limestone seated **figure of Pa-mer-áḥau** 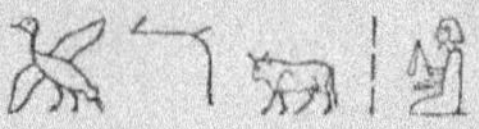, a royal scribe and general of troops, holding before him a shrine. Above the door of the shrine is cut the winged disk, and on each door-post is the Ṭeṭ, emblem of stability, surmounted by horns, disk, and plumes. In the doorway, sculptured in relief, is a figure of Osiris, "Lord of Ta-Tchesert"; the text contains a prayer to Osiris for sepulchral offerings. XIXth dynasty. Height, including original base, 2 ft. 4 in. [No. 853.]

645. (*Central Saloon.*)—Sandstone **sepulchral stele,** with pyramidal top, of **Mer-netchem** (?) , the son of Khnemu-mes , the overseer of the gold-workers, and the lady Seneterḥeth 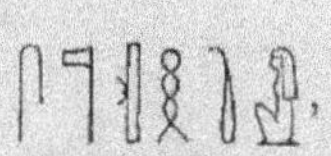, the superintendent of all the priests of the Land of the South. On it are sculptured the following scenes: 1. The Sun's disk in a boat, adored by Ape-gods. 2. The deceased adoring Àp-uat and Anubis. 3. The deceased worshipping Osiris, Isis, Nephthys, and Horus. 4, 5. Members of the family of the deceased worshipping him. From Wâdî Ḥalfah. XIXth dynasty, about B.C. 1330. Height 6 ft. 1 in., width 3 ft. 1 in. [No. 1188.]

Presented by General Sir Charles Holled Smith, K.C.B., 1887.

646. (*Bay* 10.)—Limestone **sepulchral stele,** with rounded top, of **Qaḥa** 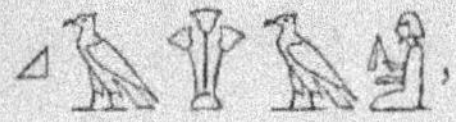, a master-craftsman. On the upper portion are sculptured in relief: 1. A figure of the goddess **Kent** 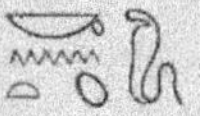, who stands, full-face, on the back of a lion. In her right hand she holds a bunch of lotus flowers, with long stalks, and in the left two serpents. 2. The god **Reshpu** , who holds a spear in his right hand, and  in his left; from beneath his head-covering projects the head of a gazelle. He stands on a shrine. 3. The ithyphallic god **Menu** 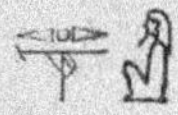, "the great "one, whose plumes are lofty, who lifteth his hand." He wears the plumes of Ȧmen, and has his right hand and arm raised. He stands on  which rests on a shrine. On the lower portion the deceased is seen accompanied by his wife Tui , and his son Nai , making adorations to the goddess **Ānthȧt,** or Anaitis, who is seated on a throne. She wears the White Crown, with the feathers of Maāt attached, and holds a spear and buckler in her right hand, and a club in her left. XIXth dynasty. Height 2 ft. 5½ in., width 1 ft. 7 in. [No. 191.]

647. (*Bay* 17.)—Limestone **sepulchral stele,** with rounded top, on which is cut the figure of the god **Reshpu** , who wears the White Crown, with bandlet, and a tunic reaching to the knees, and holds a mace in his right hand, and a spear and buckler in his left. Before him is a table of offerings. The name of the deceased is not given. Belmore Collection. From Thebes. XIXth dynasty. Height 1 ft. 2 in., width 9½ in. [No. 263.]

648. (*Bay* 17.)—Limestone **sepulchral stele,** with rounded top, of **Seti** 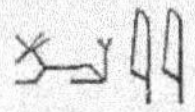, a scribe of Ȧmen, on which is cut, in outline, a scene representing the deceased and another person standing in adoration of the god Ȧmen, who is seated within a shrine, with the winged disk above. Below is a line of cursive writing which appears to contain the names of three scribes, or masons. Salt Collection. XIXth dynasty. Height 7½ in., width 6 in. [No. 217.]

649. (*Bay* 17.)—Portion of a fine limestone **relief,** or stele, on which is cut, in outline, a figure of the sacred boat of the goddess Hathor, resting on its sledge. XIXth dynasty. Height 7 in., width 10½ in. [No. 913.]

650. (*Bay* 17.)—Limestone **sepulchral stele,** with rounded top, of **Ḥeru**  a judge, on which are painted figures of the deceased and two members of his family, making offerings to the goddess **Qeṭeshit,** or Kent, who stands on a lion, and to Ȧmsu, or **Menu,** and **Reshpu.** Salt Collection. XIXth dynasty. Height 11 in., width 7 in. [No. 355.]

651. (*Bay* 18.)—Limestone **libation bowl,** dedicated to the goddesses Isis and Ta-urt (Thoueris) by **Ḥeru-Menu**, in memory and on behalf of his father and mother, whose names are wanting. On one side are the remains of three kneeling figures, which represented father, mother, and son. XIXth dynasty. Diameter 2 ft. [No. 465.]

652. (*Bay* 12.)—Upper portion of a black granite **sepulchral stele,** with rounded top, of **Ṭāṭā-àa**,

Sepulchral stele of Ṭāṭā-àa, superintendent of the Scribes of Àmen.
[Bay 12, No. 652.] XIXth dynasty.

a superintendent of the scribes of Àmen, the son of Ḥāt-àai, an overseer of scribes. On the upper portion are sculptured figures of the gods of the great triad of Thebes, Àmen, Mut, and Khensu, and facing them are two rows of figures of the gods Menu, or Ȧmsu, Isis, Thoth, Maāt, Hathor as a Cow-goddess, Un-nefer, Horus, Ȧnpu, Hathor in the form of a woman, Ȧpuat, and Nephthys. Below are cut a number of addresses to Ȧmen-Rā, Tem, Shu, Tefnut, Seb. Round the margin of the stele are cut two texts containing prayers to the gods for sepulchral offerings, and on its edge are two texts, one of which is a prayer addressed to the living, in which the deceased entreats them to make prayers on his behalf. From Thebes (Dêr al-Baharî). XIXth dynasty. Height 1 ft. 7 in., width 1 ft. 8 in. [No. 706.]

Presented by the Egypt Exploration Fund, 1905.

653. (*Bay* **15.**)—Lower portion of a seated sandstone **figure of Ȧāḥmes** , who was surnamed **"Thur"** , a superintendent of the "countries of the "South," *i.e.*, an officer in the Sûdân, who flourished probably under the XIXth dynasty. The text contains a prayer to Horus of Behen for sepulchral offerings. Found near Kermah, in the Sûdân. XIXth dynasty. Height 1 ft. 7 in., width 10 in. [No. 1279.]

Presented by G. Page, Esq., 1898.

654. (*Central Saloon and Bay* **17.**)—Massive red **granite coffin,** with cover, of **Pa-neter-ḥen** (?) , a high-priest 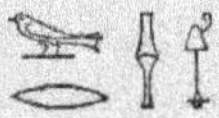, of Memphis, and SEM priest, in the form of a mummy. The deceased is bearded, and holds  in his right hand, and  in his left. On the breast is a figure of the goddess Nut, with outstretched wings and arms, holding 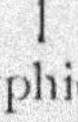 in each hand. Down the front is a single line of hieroglyphics, containing the name and titles of the deceased, and at right angles to it is inscribed the name of the deceased. The coffin appears to be unfinished. Anastasi Collection. From Memphis. XIXth dynasty. Height 7 ft. 4 in. [No. 18.]

655. (*Bay* 18.)—Painted limestone **sepulchral stele**, with rounded top, of **Ḥeru-mes**, sculptured with the following scenes:—1. The deceased making offerings to the god **Khensu-em-Uast** , who is in mummied form, bearded, and wearing the lock of youth, and seated with a table of offerings before him. 2. Three ladies of the family of the deceased making offerings to a seated goddess, who appears to be called "Tura , lady of heaven," and is probably Hathor. XIXth dynasty. Height 1 ft. 3 in., width 10½ in. [No. 1297.]

656. (*Bay* 18.)—Limestone **sepulchral stele**, with rounded top, of **Naia** 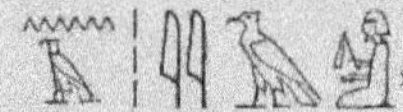, a royal ambassador, sculptured with the following scenes: 1. Naia kneeling in adoration before Osiris, Isis, Horus, and Khnemu. 2 and 3. Naia pouring out libations and offering incense to thirteen of his kinsfolk. XIXth dynasty. Height 1 ft. 9½ in., width 1 ft. 1½ in. [No. 795.]

Presented by Sir Thomas Phillips, 1858.

657. (*Bay* 18.)—Limestone **sepulchral stele**, with rounded top, of **Menthu-Menu** , a scribe of the altar, or table, of the Lord of the Two Lands, and his wife Åst-met (?) 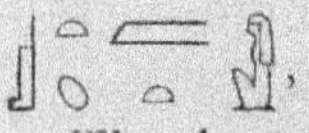, on which are sculptured the following scenes:—1. The deceased and family adoring Osiris, Isis, and Horus. 2. The deceased and his family adoring Menu of Coptos. 3. A sepulchral festival. Men and women sitting at a table of offerings. From Coptos. XIXth dynasty. Height 2 ft. 1 in., width 1 ft. 6½ in. [No. 304.]

658. (*Bay* 18.)—Limestone **sepulchral stele**, with rounded top, on which is sculptured a scene representing . . . . **mes** making offerings to the lady **Nefer-ȧn** 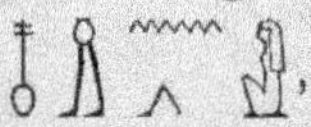, and her mother **Ȧpi** 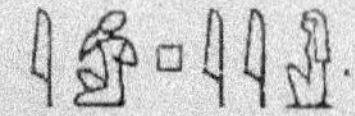. The text contains a prayer to Osiris for sepulchral offerings. XIXth dynasty. Height 1 ft. 4½ in., width 10½ in. [No. 367.]

659. (*Bay* 18.)—Limestone **sepulchral stele**, with pyramidal top, of **Pen-nub** , and his wife **Khamuiā** . On the upper portion are cut kneeling figures of Isis and Nephthys, and the standard (?), and below are figures of the deceased seated with a table of offerings between them. XIXth dynasty. Height 11 in., width 6½ in. [No. 372.]

Sepulchral stele of Naia, a king's messenger.
[Bay 18, No. 656.] XIXth dynasty.

660. (*Bay* 18.)—Limestone **sepulchral stele**, with rounded top, of **Ḥeruȧ** , sculptured with a scene representing the deceased and his wives and family kneeling in adoration before Osiris and Isis. XIXth dynasty. Height 1 ft. 2½ in., width 9½ in. [No. 327.]

661. (*Bay* 18.)—Fragment of a limestone **relief** from the wall of a tomb, on which are cut figures of three gods, or mythological beings. XIXth dynasty. Height 9 in., width 1 ft. 2 in. [No. 1323.]

Presented by Mrs. Hawker, 1901.

662. (*Bay* 18.)—Limestone **sepulchral stele**, with rounded top, of **Pa-ser**, a Ḥā prince of Thebes, sculptured in relief with a figure of the deceased kneeling in adoration before Āmen-Rā, Mut, and Khensu, and with a figure of another official kneeling in adoration before the goddess of the city of Thebes. XIXth dynasty. Height 1 ft. 4½ in., width 9½ in. [No. 1214.]

663. (*Bay* 18.)—Limestone **sepulchral stele**, with rounded top, of a judge whose name is illegible, sculptured with a scene in which the deceased is represented adoring **Sekhet**, the lady of heaven and mistress of the gods. The lower portion of the stele is wanting. XIXth dynasty. Height 1 ft. 1 in., width 9½ in. [No. 810.]

Presented by Lyttleton Annesley, Esq., 1854.

664. (*Bay* 18.)—Portion of a limestone **pyramid** on which are sculptured figures of two priests, kneeling, with their hands raised in adoration of the setting sun, Temu. XIXth dynasty. Height 6½ in., width 9 in. [No. 385.]

665. (*Bay* 18.)—Sandstone **sepulchral stele**, with rounded top, of **Āmen-er-ḥāt-f**, a judge, sculptured with a scene representing the deceased kneeling in adoration before Osiris Khenti Āmenti. The text contains a prayer to Osiris for sepulchral offerings. Salt Collection. XIXth dynasty. Height 10½ in., width 7 in. [No. 345.]

666. (*Bay* 18.)—Limestone **sepulchral stele**, with rounded top, sculptured, in relief, with a figure of a man adoring a seated goddess. XIXth dynasty. Height 5 in., width 4 in. [No. 343.]

667. (*Bay* 18.)—Limestone **sepulchral stele**, with rounded top, of **Ḥui**, son of the lady Māāu, a scribe and controller of the ecclesiastical revenues of all the gods, sculptured with a scene in which the deceased is represented adoring Osiris, Isis, and Horus. The scene and texts on the lower part of the stele have been damaged by water. XIXth dynasty. Height 1 ft. 6½ in., width 1 ft. 1 in. [No. 315.]

668. (*Bay* 18.)—Upper portion of a black granite **statue of a priestess,** wearing a heavy wig and a deep collar, or necklace, and holding an object of uncertain import in her left hand. XIXth dynasty. Height 1 ft. 5 in. [No. 484.]

669. (*Bay* 18.)—Painted limestone kneeling **figure of Ashamāruȧa** 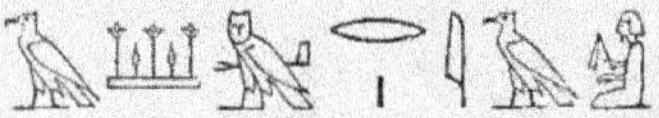, the superintendent of the offering-bearers of Ȧmen-Rā, the great god of Thebes, holding before him a tablet on which is sculptured a figure of the Boat of Rā-Harmachis. Below this is inscribed a portion of a Hymn to the Sun-god which forms part of Chapter XV of the Book of the Dead, and is addressed to Rā-Kheper-Tem. Down the back of the figure is cut a prayer to Ȧmen-Rā for "life, strength, health," etc., every day. Salt Collection. From Thebes. XIXth dynasty. Height 1 ft. 8 in. [No. 1382.]

670. (*Bay* 19.)—Limestone **sepulchral stele,** with rounded top, of **Kharu** , and his wife Ḥunru 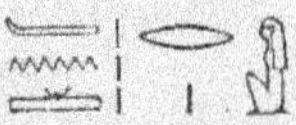, a priestess of Ȧmen, sculptured with the following scenes: 1. The deceased adoring Osiris and Isis. 2. Lamentation for the deceased, whose mummy is held by Ȧnpu, by Ḥunru and Ur-nefert , his wife and daughter. 3. The presentation of offerings to Kharu and Ḥunru by their sons and daughter. Salt Collection. XIXth dynasty. Height 3 ft. 3 in., width 1 ft. 3 in. [No. 549.]

671. (*Bay* 19.)—Limestone **sepulchral stele,** with rounded top, of **Unen-nefer** 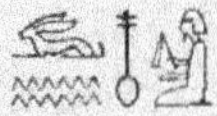, "the chief envoy of his majesty, "and messenger to every land"  , on which are cut the following scenes: 1. The deceased adoring Osiris, Hathor, Isis, and Horus.

Sepulchral stele of Un-nefer, a king's chief messenger.
[Bay 19, No. 671.] XIXth dynasty.

2. Un-nefer adoring his father Rui, his mother Bak-urn-ru, his brother Mer-en-Ptaḥ, a royal scribe, his two wives Ḥent-Ȧnnu, and Ȧui, etc. 3. The sons and daughters of Un-nefer adoring him. XIXth dynasty. (**Plate XXIV.**) Height 3 ft. 4 in., width 2 ft. 3 in. [No. 154.]

672. (*Bay* **19.**)—Portion of a limestone **relief** on which are cut figures of Osiris, Ȧnpu (Anubis), and Hathor, lady of Thebes. XIXth dynasty. Height 9 in., width 8½ in. [No. 319.]

673. (*Bay* **19.**)—Black granite group of four **seated figures** which represent **Renp-nefer,** a Ḥā prince of the South, and his wife **Sent-Nai,** a royal nurse. The inscriptions contain prayers to Ȧmen-Rā, Osiris, and Hathor for sepulchral offerings. On one end of the monument is a figure of Nefert-ȧri, daughter of Renp-nefer. XIXth dynasty. Height 1 ft. 7 in., width 1 ft. 11 in. [No. 113.]

674. (*Bay* **22.**)—Limestone **sepulchral stele,** in the form of a doorway of a tomb, with palm-leaf cornice and raised flat border, of **Ḥumes**, a *setem* priest. On the upper portion of the border are cut flanked by and figures of jackals, and below are sculptured the following scenes: 1. The deceased worshipping Osiris. 2. Members of the family making offerings to Ḥumes and his wife Thi. Salt Collection. From Abydos. XIXth dynasty. Height 3 ft. 1 in., width 2 ft. 4 in. [No. 158.]

675. (*Bay* **22.**)—Limestone **sepulchral stele,** with rounded top (broken), of **Ḥeru-à** 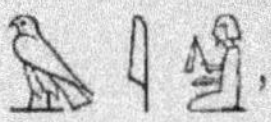, an estate steward  of the "Lord of the Two Lands," sculptured with the following scenes:—1. Ḥeru-à and his wife Thent-pa-ta  adoring Osiris, Horus, Isis, and Thoth. 2. Ḥeru-à making an offering to his father Rā-meri and his mother Àni. 3. Bak-en-Àmen, brother of Ḥeru-à, making an offering to Ḥeru-à and his wife. 4. Five brothers and two sisters of Ḥeru-à adoring him. From Thebes. XIXth dynasty. Height 2 ft. 11 in., width 1 ft. 9½ in. [No. 132.]

676. (*Bay* **22.**)—Limestone **sepulchral stele,** with rounded top, of **Àmen-mes** 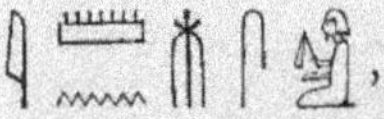, a judge, on which is sculptured a scene representing the deceased and his wife Mākhai , and their four daughters, standing in adoration before the goddesses **Taurt, Nekhebit,** the "White," of Nekhen, and **Hathor** of Thebes. From Thebes. XIXth dynasty. Height 1 ft. 10 in., width 1 ft. 2½ in. [No. 1388 (283*).]

677. (*Bay* **21.**)—Rectangular limestone **sepulchral stele** of **Àmen-mes** 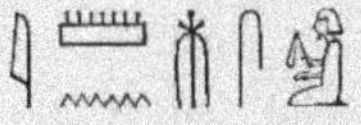, an official in the temple of Àmen, on which are sculptured figures of the deceased and his wife and daughter adoring Osiris, to whom the text contains an address. XIXth dynasty. Height 1 ft. 6½ in., width 1 ft. 2½ in. [No. 107.]

678. (*Bay* **20.**)—Limestone **sepulchral stele,** in the form of a door of a tomb, with a palm-leaf cornice and raised flat border, of **Māḥu** 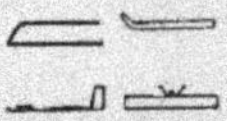, a superintendent of a part of a temple or palace. Within the border are sculptured scenes representing Māḥu adoring Osiris, who is seated in a shrine, with a table of offerings before him, and Māḥu's mother, who is making offerings to her son, and his two wives. On the border are inscribed texts containing prayers to Osiris and Ànpu for sepulchral offerings. XIXth dynasty. Height 2 ft. 5 in., width 1 ft. 5 in. [No. 1369.]

679. (*Bay* **20.**)—Limestone **sepulchral stele,** in the form of a door of a tomb, with a palm-leaf cornice and raised flat border, of **Stau-ān** (?) , a superintendent of the treasury of Àmen and director of festivals of that god. Within the border are sculptured two scenes representing the deceased adoring Rā and Isis, and pouring out a libation and offering incense to Osiris. On the border are inscribed prayers to Rā-Harmachis, Hathor, Ànpu, Àp-uat, and Thoth for sepulchral offerings. Salt Collection. XIXth dynasty. Height 2 ft. 5 in., width 1 ft. 9 in. [No. 556.]

680. (*Bay* **20.**)—Portion of a limestone **relief,** on which is sculptured the head of a female. XIXth dynasty. Height 8 in., width 9½ in. [No. 397.]

681. (*Bay* **20.**)—Limestone **sepulchral stele,** with rounded top, of **Àḥait** (?), a priest, and Àḥait, a superintendent of artizans, and Ur-Àmen-Nekht, and Àḥait, son of Àhait, sculptured with figures of the deceased persons adoring **Àmen-ḥetep I** and his wife **Nefert-àri.** XIXth dynasty. Salt Collection. Height 1 ft. 5 in., width 11 in. [No. 317.]

682. (*Bay* **20.**) — Limestone **sepulchral stele,** with pyramidal top, of **Khamui** , and his wife **Pen-nub** 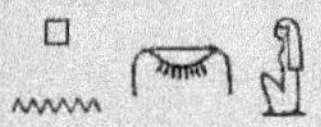, who are called "perfect spirits of "Rā," and are represented seated on chairs of state facing each other. Salt Collection. XIXth dynasty. Height 9 in., width 6 in. [No. 359.]

683. (*Bay* **20.**)—Portion of a limestone **column** from the tomb of a "scribe of the soldiers," sculptured with a figure of the deceased, kneeling in adoration before a figure of Osiris. Sams Collection. XIXth dynasty. Height 11½ in. [No. 357.]

684. (*Bay* **20.**)—Limestone **sepulchral stele,** with rounded top, of **Khamuiā** , on which are cut , and a figure of the deceased, who is called a "perfect spirit of Rā," seated on a chair of state. XIXth dynasty. Height 7 in., width 4½ in. [No. 344.]

685. (*Central Saloon.*)—**Wooden figure** of a king, or prince, in which the eyes and eyebrows were inlaid with obsidian, or coloured glass. The whole figure was originally covered with a layer of bitumen; one leg and both feet are restored. Salt Collection. From a tomb in the Valley of the Tombs of the Kings at Thebes. XIXth or XXth dynasty. About B.C. 1300–1200. Height, including restoration, 6 ft. 7 in. [No. 883.]

686. (*Central Saloon.*)—Corner of a grey **granite shrine,** or sepulchral coffer, on which are sculptured figures of Horus of Beḥuṭet, or Edfû, who is receiving a libation and the homage of a king, who is probably Rameses II or Rameses III. XIXth or XXth dynasty. Height 1 ft. 10 in., width 11 in. [No. 958.]

687. (*Central Saloon.*)—Large black **granite hawk,** with inlaid eyes, symbol of Horus, to whom the hawk was sacred. From Coptos. XIXth or XXth dynasty. Height 1 ft. 8 in. [No. 1226.]

688. (*Bay* 16.)—Black granite **libation bowl,** in the form of a cartouche, with two flattened kneeling figures holding it at one end. On their backs are six lines of hieroglyphics, containing a prayer for sepulchral offerings on behalf of **Mes** , **Penànen** , **Nekhtu** , etc. From Thebes. XIXth or XXth dynasty. Length 1 ft. 9 in. [No. 1301.]

689. (*Bay* 17.)—Painted limestone **sepulchral stele,** with rounded top, on which are sculptured figures of:—1. The winged disk. 2. The goddess Hathor. 3. A heart, with the face of Hathor, on a standard, and one cat seated to the right and another to the left of it. 3. Seven members of the family of the deceased, whose figure is broken away, headed by the lady **Buātnef** 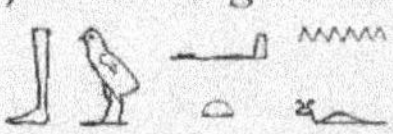. XIXth or XXth dynasty. Height 10 in., width 6½ in. [No. 369.]

690. (*Bay* 17.)—Limestone **sepulchral stele,** with rounded top, of **Neb-tchefaut** , a judge, on which is sculptured a scene representing the deceased and his son

U-nefer, kneeling in adoration before Ptaḥ, lord of Maāt, king of the Two Lands, and Thoth, lord of Khemennu (Hermopolis). From Thebes. XIXth or XXth dynasty. Height 1 ft. 3 in., width 10½ in. [No. 807.]

691. (*Bay* 18.)—Portion of a limestone **sepulchral stele,** of **Neb-tchefaut**, a judge, and his wife Hathor, sculptured with figures kneeling in adoration before the Boat of Rā. The text contains a prayer to the setting sun. From Thebes. Belmore collection. Height 1 ft., width 11½ in. [No. 268.]

692. (*Bay* 17.)—Limestone **sepulchral stele,** with rounded top, of **Ptaḥ-em-ḥeb**, a "scribe of the Lord of the Two Lands," son of Åmen-nekhtu, on which are sculptured, in three registers, figures of the deceased and thirteen members of his family, adoring Osiris, Isis, and Horus. XIXth or XXth dynasty. Height 1 ft. 8 in., width 1 ft. 2 in. [No. 314.]

693. (*Bay* 17.)—Limestone **sepulchral stele,** with rounded top, of **Nefer-Åāb**, on which are sculptured the following scenes:—1. Five women—two standing and three seated—lamenting before four mummied forms, whilst two priests are performing the ceremonies connected with the "Opening of the Mouths" of the deceased persons. Behind stand three women lamenting, and a girl. 2. The deceased lying on his bier with Anubis bending over him. 3. Two sons and two daughters of the deceased bearing offerings. 4. Extract from Chapter I of the Book of the Dead, and the title, "Chapter of going to the Tchatcha." This stele was set up by Nefer-renpet, son of the deceased. Salt Collection. XIXth or XXth dynasty. Height 2 ft., width 1 ft. 4 in. [No. 305.]

694. (*Bay* 18.)—Upper portion of a red granite **statue of a king,** or prince. XIXth or XXth dynasty. Height 1 ft. 10 in. [No. 125.]

695. (*Bay* 18.)—Portion of a **relief** sculptured with a figure of **Pa-sheṭ**, a judge, who stands with both hands raised in adoration before Rā. From Thebes. Belmore Collection. XIXth or XXth dynasty. Height 8½ in., width 1 ft. 4 in. [No. 261.]

696. (*Bay* 18.)—Rectangular **relief** from a temple wall, sculptured with a figure of the god Khnemu wearing the *atef* crown and holding a vase. XIXth or XXth dynasty. Length 1 ft. 9 in., height 1 ft. 7 in. [No. 635.]

697. (*Bay* 18.)—Fragment of a **painted relief** of a tomb, sculptured with figures of a scribe and a priestess making offerings. XVIIIth to XXth dynasty. Height 10 in., width 1 ft. 3 in. [No. 449.]

698. (*Bay* 18.)—Portion of a limestone **sepulchral stele,** of **Takhāt**, a priestess (?), sculptured with a scene representing the deceased, and her son Ḥui-nefer, and her daughters Mer-seḳert, Pa-sheṭu, Ptaḥ-mert, Nefert-àri, and Thent-àpt adoring a seated deity. XIXth or XXth dynasty. Height 1 ft. 3 in., width 11 in. [No. 818.]

Presented by Lyttleton Annesley, Esq., 1854.

699. (*Bay* 18.)—Sandstone **pyramid of Ḥeru-nefer**, a judge in the "seat of Maāt," on which are cut in outline the following:—

Side I.—Boat of Harmachis, and two figures of the deceased.

Side II.—Beetle with disk, and figures of the deceased and his sister Ubekht.

Side III.—Figures of the deceased and his son.

Side IV.—Isis and Nephthys and the standard of Àmentet, and two figures of the deceased.

XIXth dynasty. Height 1 ft. 6 in. [No. 479.]

Presented by Sir J. Gardner Wilkinson, 1834.

700. (*Bay* **19.**)—Rectangular limestone **relief** from the tomb of **Neb-nefer**, a high official in the "seat of Maāt," and his wife **Ii**, on which are sculptured two scenes, wherein their son **Nefer-ḥetep**, and their daughters **Ḥent-meḥit**, and **I-em-uauu**, are making offerings to their parents. XIXth or XXth dynasty. Height 1 ft. 2 in., width 3 ft. 4 in. [No. 447.]

Pyramid of Heru-nefer.
[Bay 18, No. 699.]

701. (*Bay* **20.**)—Limestone **sepulchral stele**, with rounded top, of **Åmen-em-uåa**, Ånḥer-nekht, his grandfather, Mut-em-uåa his mother, Parātabuba (?), his wife, Ḥui, his father, a priest of Mer-en-Ptaḥ, Pa-Rā-em-åpt, his brother, a royal envoy, and two other brothers. XIXth or XXth dynasty. Height 1 ft. 9½ in., width 1 ft. 1 in. [No. 1183.]

702. (*Bay* 20.)—Portion of a limestone **sepulchral stele,** with rounded top, on which are sculptured figures of **Menu**, god of generation, and the goddess **Qeṭshet**, lady of heaven ; on the missing portion was a figure of **Ȧmen.** On the right hand edge is a prayer to these gods that sepulchral offerings may be given to a person not named. XIXth or XXth dynasty. Height 1 ft. 1 in., width 9½ in. [No. 817.]

Presented by Lyttleton Annesley, Esq., 1854.

703. (*Bay* 20.)—Limestone **sepulchral stele,** of unusual shape, with rounded top, of **Nekhtu-Menu (?)-Nepan**, on which is sculptured a scene, in three registers, representing the deceased and his wife Ta-ān-ḥer-tuuset, five sons, five daughters, and one grand-daughter, adoring Osiris and Isis. XIXth or XXth dynasty. Height 1 ft. 8 in., width 1 ft. 2 in. [No. 292.]

704. (*Bay* 20.)—Limestone **sepulchral stele,** with rounded top, of **Iȧ**, a priestess, sculptured with figures of the deceased and her three daughters, Tuȧu, Nerȧut, and Mert-Seḳer, adoring a seated figure of the goddess **Ānqet**, "lady of Asia." XIXth or XXth dynasty. Height 10 in., width 5½ in. [No. 370.]

705. (*Bay* 20.)—**Head** from a painted limestone **statue of a goddess,** or lady of high rank, wearing a heavy wig and cone. From Thebes. XIXth or XXth dynasty. Height 1 ft. [No. 127.]

706. (*Bay* 20.)—**Head** from a painted limestone **statue of a goddess,** or lady of high rank, wearing a heavy wig. From Thebes. XIXth or XXth dynasty. Height 10 in. [No. 425.]

707. (*Bay* **20.**)—**Head** from a painted limestone **statue of a goddess,** or lady of high rank, wearing a heavy wig and a lotus flower over her forehead. From Thebes. XIXth or XXth dynasty. Height 10 in. [No. 435.]

708. (*Bay* **21.**)—Upper portions of **seated figures** of a priest, or official, and his wife. XIXth or XXth dynasty. Height 1 ft. 10½ in., width 2 ft. 11 in. [Nos. 126 + 432.]

709. (*Bay* **21.**)—Limestone **sepulchral stele,** with rounded top, of **Smen-taui** 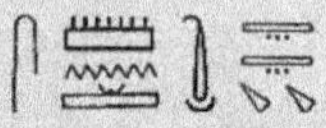, a superintendent of the royal miners, sculptured with a scene representing the deceased and four members of his family adoring Osiris and Isis. XIXth or XXth dynasty. Height 1 ft. 7 in., width 1 ft. 1 in. [No. 312.]

710. (*Bay* **22.**)—Limestone **sepulchral stele,** with rounded top, of **Rā-messu-em-per-Rā** 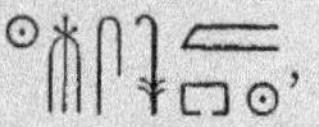, the chief guardian of the doors of the temple of Rameses II, in the House of Ȧmen, sculptured with scenes representing the deceased worshipping Osiris, Isis, Horus, and Thoth, and the deceased and his relatives worshipping Hathor in the persea tree. XIXth or XXth dynasty. Height 2 ft. 2 in., width 1 ft. 4 in. [No. 796.]

711. (*Bay* **22.**)—Sandstone **sepulchral stele,** with rounded top, of **Ȧmen-mes** 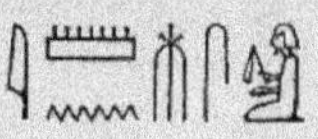, a royal scribe, on which is sculptured a scene, in three registers, representing the deceased and his family adoring Osiris, Isis, and Horus. XIXth or XXth dynasty. Height 2 ft. 3 in., width 1 ft. 3 in. [No. 351.]

712. (*Bay* **22.**)—White limestone **sepulchral stele,** with rounded top, of **Paiharui** , a superintendent of the stables, on which are sculptured the following scenes:—1. The deceased and his wife Nebtȧa , adoring Osiris. 2. The family of Paiharui adoring their father and mother. 3. Paiharui and relatives adoring his father Rā-mes and his mother Urti. XIXth or XXth dynasty. Height 1 ft. 10 in., with 1 ft. 1 in.

[No. 313.]

713. (*Bay* 22.)—Limestone **sepulchral stele,** with rounded top, of **Qaḥa**, a superintendent of workmen, on which are sculptured the following scenes:—1. Qaḥa adoring Osiris. 2. Qaḥa adoring Anubis. 3 and 4. Members of the family and relatives of the deceased making offerings at an altar, and adoring the deceased. A portion of the rounded top is broken, and the surface of the stele is damaged. XIXth or XXth dynasty. Height 3 ft., width 1 ft. 10 in.

[No. 144.]

Shrine of Ruka, overseer of the artificers of the temple of Horus of Mâmāt, in Nubia. [Central Saloon, No. 714.]

714. (*Central Saloon.*)—Rectangular limestone **shrine of Ruka**, the superintendent of the artificers of the temple of Horus, lord of Mâmāt. On the sides are figures of the deceased adoring Osiris, Isis, and Nephthys under the forms of serpents, and on the back is sculptured a scene in which Ruka and his wife Sen-seneb, are receiving the offerings and adoration of their relatives. The texts referring to a second scene have been cut, but the figures are wanting. XIXth or XXth dynasty. From Nubia (?). Height 2 ft. 2 in., width 1 ft. 10 in. [No. 476.]

NEW EMPIRE.

TWENTIETH DYNASTY.

715. (*Bay* 21.)—Limestone **sepulchral stele,** with rounded top, of **Āk-beru**, surnamed **Rā-mes-nekhtu**

Sepulchral stele of Ākberu, a doorkeeper of a temple of Rameses II.
[Bay 21, No. 715.]

, a doorkeeper of the third class of a temple of **Rameses II,** on which are sculptured scenes representing the deceased, and Māshakbu-Pentaur  , and Pen-Nāāt, and two women adoring Osiris, Isis, and Nephthys. XXth dynasty. Height 1 ft. 10 in., width 1 ft. 2 in. [No. 290.]

716. (*Bay* **18**.)—Circular limestone **base of a small pillar,** which stood in the sanctuary of **Rameses III,** at Karnak, inscribed with the prenomen and nomen of the king. The texts read :—

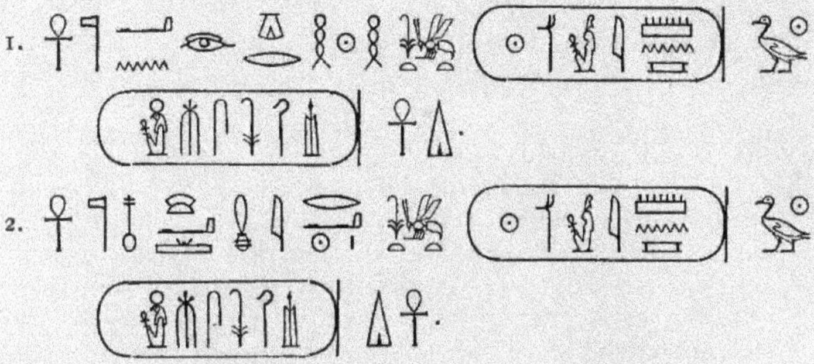

XXth dynasty, about B.C. 1200. Diameter 1 ft. 1 in. [No. 634.]

717. (*Central Saloon.*)—Rectangular limestone **lintel,** from the door of a chamber in a building of **Rameses III,** on which is sculptured, in low relief, a winged disk with pendent uraei. Below this are cut the names and titles of the king, arranged symmetrically. From Ṣaḳḳârah. XXth dynasty. Length 4 ft. 6 in., breadth 2 ft. 3 in. [No. 1344.]

718. (*Bay* **22**.)—Portion of a **wall-slab** of a public building, inscribed with parts of the cartouches of **Rameses III,** king of Egypt, about B.C. 1200. From Gîzah. Salt Collection. XXth dynasty. Height 1 ft. 8 in., width 1 ft. 7 in. [No. 442.]

719. (*Bay* **24**.)—Limestone **sepulchral stele,** with rounded top, fractured in places, of **Ḥeru-á** , an envoy, royal scribe, and royal inspector, the son of Ptaḥ-em-uáa and Ḥet-Ḥerṭ, who flourished in the reign of Rameses IV (?)

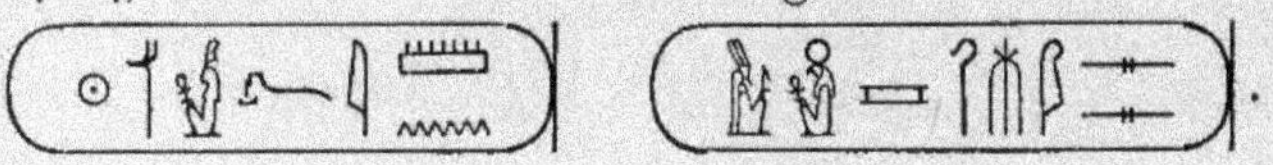

On the upper portion is sculptured a figure of the deceased standing in adoration before the king, behind whom is a figure of the goddess Maāt, and below these is a kneeling figure of the deceased. The text contains a list of the offerings made to the priesthood by the king. Belmore Collection. From Thebes. XXth dynasty, about B.C. 1150. Height 2 ft. 5 in., width 1 ft. 8 in. [No. 588.]

720. (*Bay* 19.)—Massive red granite **cover** of the **sarcophagus of Setau**, a royal scribe, a steward of the palace, and governor of the Sûdân, who flourished about B.C. 1200. The deceased is represented in mummied form, and wears a heavy wig; his hands are crossed over his breast, and in one is ☥ and in the other . On his breast is a figure of the goddess Nut, and below are sculptured four scenes in which he is making offerings to four great gods of the dead; over his feet are figures of Isis and Nephthys weeping. Down the front is a line of text in which Setau beseeches the goddess Nut to spread her wings over him, and on the sides are short inscriptions referring to Seb, or Ḳeb, Ȧnpu, Sep, the four sons of Horus, and two addresses to the deceased, one by Seb, and the other by Nut. XXth dynasty. Height 8 ft., width 2 ft. 8 in. [No. 78.]

721. (*Bay* 11.)—Lower portion of a seated grey **granite figure of Māiu**, the high priest of Mentu, lord of Ȧnnu Resu (Hermonthis), and overseer of the works in the temple of Nekhebet. He was the son of Ani, a scribe, and his mother was Nub-nefer, a priestess of Sebek. From Al-Ḳāb. XVIIIth to XXth dynasty. Height 1 ft. 1 in. [No. 1194.]

Presented by Somers Clarke, Esq., 1896.

722. (*Bay* 19.)—Sandstone **libation basin,** ornamented with a head of Hathor, which was dedicated to the goddess **Ta-urt,** or **Thoueris,** by **Ḥeru-nefer,** a judge, son of Neb-tchefa, and his wife Ḥunru, and **Ṭeḥuti-ḥer-māk-f**. On the sides of the basin and on a rectangular tablet cut on it are inscribed the names of the judges **Nai**, **Pa-sheṭ**, **Ḥui**, **Khā-em-Uast**, **Pen-nubi**, **Nā-ḥetep**. From Karnak. Salt Collection. XXth dynasty. Diameter 2 ft. 3½ in. [No. 28.]

723. (*Central Saloon.*)—Base of a black granite **statue of Nes-Ptaḥ-Senb**, an Erpā, and Ḥā prince, chancellor, Smer-uāt, and inspector of the priests, the son of Menthu-em-ḥāt, an Erpā, and Ḥā prince, and chief of the Ḥā princes. The text contains a prayer to Ȧmen-Rā, Mut, Khensu in Thebes Nefer-ḥetep, and Menthu for sepulchral offerings. XXth dynasty. Length 2 ft. 4 in., breadth 1 ft. 7 in. [No. 133.]

724. (*Bay* 14.)—Limestone rectangular **relief** on which is sculptured a tablet for offerings, with figures of bread-cakes, etc., cut in outline in the sunk surface. It was made and dedicated by Tutuȧa, and It-neferth, in memory of their father **Tchakaruthȧ**. XXth dynasty. Length 10½ in., breadth 7½ in. [No. 1379.]

725. (*Bay* 16.)—White marble **tablet for offerings** of **Nekht**, on which are cut, in outline, figures of bread-cakes, etc. On the margins are cut prayers to the Great and Little Companies of the Gods for sepulchral offerings, and in front are cut two shallow tanks. XXth dynasty. Length 1 ft., breadth 11½ in. [No. 1295.]

726. (*Bay* 17.)—Seated alabaster **figure of a king,** or prince, holding the sceptre in one hand, and the whip in the other. Uninscribed. XXth dynasty (?). Height 2 ft. 9 in. [No. 611.]

727. (*Bay* 17.)—Portion of a limestone **sepulchral stele,** on which is sculptured the figure of a man seated on a chair of state, with a table of offerings before him. XXth dynasty. Height 9½ in., width 5 in. [No. 850.]

728. (*Bay* 18.)—Grey granite seated **figures of Àmen-Rā,** the king of the gods, and the **goddess Mut,** his consort, the lady of Asher, a quarter of Eastern Thebes. From Thebes. XXth dynasty. Height 3 ft. 3½ in. [No. 1084.]

729. (*Bay* 18.)—Limestone **sepulchral monument** of **Khā-em-àpt**, a scribe of the offerings of the Lord of the Two Lands, in the form of a funerary coffer. Within the doorway is sculptured a figure of the deceased, holding in his right hand a sceptre, surmounted by the aegis of Osiris, wearing plumes, and in the other a sceptre, surmounted by an aegis of Horus. On the border is cut a prayer to Osiris for funerary offerings. Barker Collection. XXth dynasty. Height 1 ft. 8½ in. [No. 472.]

Sepulchral monument of Khā-em-àpt, a scribe.
[Bay 18, No. 729.]
XXth dynasty.

730. (*Bay* 18.) — Limestone **sepulchral stele,** with rounded top, of **Àa**, or **Ḥāt-àa**, sculptured with scenes representing the deceased pouring out libations to Osiris, Isis, and Horus, and making offerings to his ancestors, male and female. XXth dynasty. Height 1 ft. 10½ in., width 1 ft. 3 in. [No. 772.]

731. (*Bay* 18.)—Limestone **sepulchral stele of Àmen-ḥetep**, a divine father of Àmen and Khensu, and a royal scribe of the temple of Àmen, sculptured with a scene representing the deceased offering incense and pouring out a libation before Osiris, Horus, and Isis. The text contains a prayer to Osiris, Horus, Isis, Åp-uat, and Ånpu for sepulchral offerings. XXth dynasty. Height 1 ft. 1½ in., width 10½ in. [No. 799.]

732. (*Bay* 19.)—Upper portion of a granite standing **figure of an Erpā,** and Ḥā prince, holding by his left side a standard, surmounted by an aegis of the ram-god Khnemu. XXth dynasty. Height 1 ft. 2½ in. [No. 122.]

733. (*Bay* 19.)—Portion of a limestone **relief,** on which is sculptured the figure of a bull, with its four legs tied together for sacrifice. XXth dynasty. Height 7 in., width 8 in. [No. 298.]

734. (*Bay* 19.)—Limestone **sepulchral stele,** with rounded top, of **Åthu** 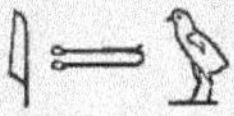, a chief reader and fan-bearer, and of his father **Māḥu** , an *åm Khent* priest, sculptured with scenes representing Åthu, Māḥu, and his grandson Nefer-ḥrå worshipping Osiris, Menu, or Åmsu, Ḥeru-nekht, and Åp-uat, who stand beneath the winged disk. The text contains a prayer to these gods for sepulchral offerings, and states that Åthu set up the stele to his father's memory. XXth dynasty. Height 1 ft. 7½ in., width 1 ft. 1 in. [No. 962.]

Presented by Wentworth Huyshe, Esq., 1875.

735. (*Bay* 20.)—Portion of a limestone **sepulchral stele of Åmen-mes** , the son of Rā-mes , and Nefert-åri 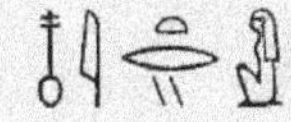, a royal scribe of the table (or altar) of the Lord of the Two Lands, overseer of Åmen, director of the temple of Rameses II, etc. The text contains a hymn of praise to a god, probably Osiris. Sams Collection. From Thebes. XXth dynasty. Height 1 ft. 11 in., width 2 ft. 6 in. [No. 142.]

736. (*Bay* 20.)—Limestone **sepulchral stele,** of unusual shape, with rounded top, of **Un-ta-uat** 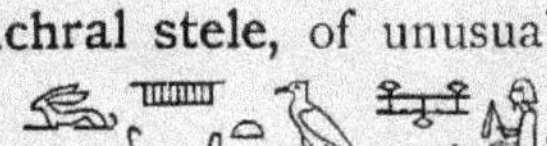, a "prince of Kash" (*i.e.*, Nubia), and high priest of Åmen,

Sepulchral stele of Un-ta-uat, a governor of the Sûdân.
[Bay 20, No. 736.] XXth dynasty.

Sepulchral stele of the scribes Àu-en-Àmen and Āḥauti-nefer, sculptured with scenes representing the deceased persons worshipping Osiris and Her-shefit.
[Bay 20, No. 737.] XXth dynasty.

sculptured with a scene representing the deceased, and his wife Ta-user-s, a priestess of Ȧp-uat, and two brothers and two sisters, adoring Osiris, Ḥeru-netch-tef, and Isis. The text contains a prayer to these gods for sepulchral offerings. XXth dynasty. (**Plate XXV.**) Height 1 ft. 10½ in., width 1 ft. 3½ in. [No. 792.]

737. (*Bay* **20.**)—Limestone **sepulchral stele,** with rounded top, of **Ȧu-en-Ȧmen**, a scribe, and of **Āḥauti-nefer**, a scribe of the altar, or table, of the "Lord of the two Lands," on which are sculptured two scenes:—1. Ȧu-en-Ȧmen adoring Osiris. 2. Āḥauti-nefer adoring the god Ḥer-shefit (Arsaphes). XXth dynasty. (**Plate XXVI.**) Height 1 ft. 6½ in., width 1 ft. 1 in. [No. 794.]

738. (*Bay* **20.**)—Limestone **sepulchral stele,** with pyramidal top, of **Pa-neter-ḥen**, high-priest of Memphis, **Ṭāṭā-ȧa**, high priest of Memphis, **Meriti**, the chief inspector of the cattle of Ȧmen, **Pai**, the chief bowman, and the five princesses, Nerȧ-Rā, Theti, Mut-nefert, Setmenthi, and Ḥunrui. On the stele are sculptured a figure of Ȧnpu and a scene representing the above mentioned adoring Osiris and Hathor. XXth dynasty. Height 2 ft. 5 in., width 1 ft. 6½ in. [No. 183.]

739. (*Bay* **21.**)—Limestone **sepulchral stele,** with rounded top, of **Neb-tchefaut**, a royal scribe and superintendent of the granaries of the South and North, *i.e.*, Upper and Lower Egypt, sculptured with a scene representing the deceased adoring Osiris. XXth dynasty. Height 1 ft. 10½ in., width 1 ft. 2 in. [No. 793.]

740, 741. (*Bay* **21.**)—Two limestone seated figures of the **dog-headed ape,** sacred to Thoth and Khensu, the scribe of the gods; each figure had on its head a disk and crescent, which symbolised the lunar character of the animal. They were placed on pedestals, one on each side of a doorway of the temple of Khensu at Thebes. XXth dynasty. Height 1 ft. 9 in. [No. 1232]; 1 ft. 8 in. [No. 1233].

Figure of the dog-headed ape sacred to Thoth.
[Bay 21, No. 740.]

742. (*Bay* **21.**)—Portions of a large limestone **sepulchral stele,** with rounded top, of **Nefer-āb**, a judge, son of the lady Maḥi, on which is sculptured a scene representing the deceased, his father, and a long series of relatives adoring the goddess **Mer-seḳert**. From Thebes. XXth dynasty. Height 5 ft. 9 in., width 3 ft. 11 in. [No. 150.]

743. (*Bay* **21.**)—Limestone **sepulchral stele,** with rounded top, of **Neḥi**, a priestly official (?), on which is sculptured a figure of **Ḥeru-ur**, who is seated on a chair of state, with a table of offerings before him. XXth dynasty. Height $7\frac{1}{2}$ in., width $5\frac{1}{2}$ in. [No. 373.]

744. (*Bay* **21.**)—Limestone **sepulchral stele,** with rounded top, of **Ȧmen-mes**, and **Bak-set**, sculptured with a scene representing the deceased persons adoring the standard of Hathor Nebt-pri-qer-qa (?)

 D'Athanasi Collection. XXth dynasty. Height 1 ft. 4½ in., width 9 in. [No. 323.]

745. (*Bay* **21.**)—Limestone **sepulchral stele,** with rounded top, of **Neḥebu-Khensu** , and his sister "the lady of the house, the *qemāt* of Åmen," **Ḥent-en-nebt** , sculptured with a winged disk and a scene in which the deceased and his sister are represented making offerings to Osiris. The text contains a prayer to Osiris and other gods for sepulchral offerings. XXth dynasty. Height 1 ft. 0½ in., width 8½ in. [No. 700.]

746. (*Bay* **21.**)—Portion of a slab inscribed with parts of four lines of hieroglyphic text, which mention the "lord of Åḳert," etc. From Akhmîm. XXth dynasty. Height 1 ft. 4 in., width 10 in. [No. 1052.]

747. (*Bay* **21.**)—Limestone **sepulchral stele,** with rounded top, of **Qåa** , a quarry official and the captain of the barge of Ḥeru-Beḥuṭet, sculptured with figures of the solar disk with one wing, the *utchat* , the cow-headed serpent of Hathor, and a scene representing the deceased making offerings to **Khensu in Thebes.** The text contains a prayer to Khensu, Ḥeru-Beḥuṭet, and Hathor of Denderah and Edfû for sepulchral offerings. From Edfû. XXth dynasty. Height 1 ft. 7 in., width 11 in. [No. 1366.]

748. (*Bay* **21.**)—Limestone **sepulchral stele,** with rounded top, of **Ur-Reshpu** , a royal scribe and steward, and **Åmen-mes,** a royal scribe and steward, on which are sculptured figures of the deceased persons and their families, arranged in three registers, adoring the standard, on the top of which was the box containing the head of that god. On one side of it are Horus and a ram-standard, and on the other Isis and a ram-standard. Salt Collection. From Abydos. XXth dynasty. Height 4 ft. 7 in., width 3 ft. [No. 161.]

749. (*Bay* 22.)—Sandstone **sepulchral stele,** with rounded top, of **Mer-Ptaḥ-per-Åmen** , on which are sculptured the following scenes:—Obverse: The deceased and his wife and sons adoring the Theban triad of Åmen-Rā, Mut, and Khensu. Reverse: The deceased and members of his family adoring Osiris, Isis, and Åmen-Rā. It is unusual to find stelae of this class with sculptures on both sides. D'Athanasi Collection. From Thebes. XXth dynasty. Height 1 ft. 8½ in., width 1 ft. 2 in. [No. 350.]

750. (*Bay* 22.)—Sandstone **sepulchral stele,** with rounded top of **Nefer** . . . . . . 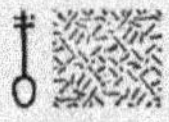 on which is sculptured a scene representing the deceased, her daughter, and six relatives adoring Osiris, "lord of Eternity," who is seated on a throne. Sams Collection. XXth dynasty. Height 1 ft. 9 in., width 1 ft. 3 in. [No. 306.]

751. (*Bay* 22.)—Sandstone **sepulchral stele,** with pyramidal top, of **Bak-en-Åmen** 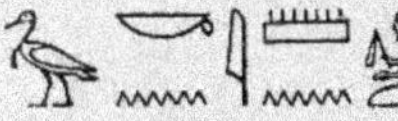, a scribe of the table and wine cellar, on which are sculptured the following:—1. Figure of Ånpu. 2. Figures of the deceased and his wife, Urt-uaḥ-su , adoring Osiris and Isis. 3 and 4. Åmen-em-åpt, son of the deceased, and his wife and relatives adoring Osiris and Isis. XXth dynasty. Height 2 ft. 3 in., width 1 ft. 2½ in. [No. 349.]

752. (*Bay* 22.)—Limestone **sepulchral stele,** with rounded top, of **Pai** , the overseer of the household of the "chief queen of the Lord of the Two Lands," on which are sculptured the following scenes:—1. Winged disk. 2. Pai adoring Osiris, Isis, and Ḥeru-netch-tef. 3 and 4. Members of the family of Pai bringing offerings and making adoration to himself and his wife Erpit 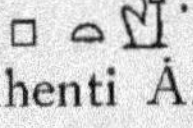. Below is a text containing a prayer to Osiris Khenti Åmenti Un-nefer, Horus, Åp-uat, Ånpu, and all the great gods of the Other World, for sepulchral offerings. D'Athanasi Collection. From Thebes. XXth dynasty. Height 3 ft. 4 in., width 1 ft. 10 in. [No. 156.]

753. (*Bay* 24.)—Portion of a limestone **sepulchral stele,** sculptured with a scene representing the deceased worshipping Rā-Harmachis. Sams Collection. XXth dynasty. Height 1 ft. 1 in., width 1 ft. 5 in. [No. 318.]

754. (*Bay* 17.)—Limestone **shrine,** in the form of a sepulchral coffer, of **Åmen-em-ḥeb** 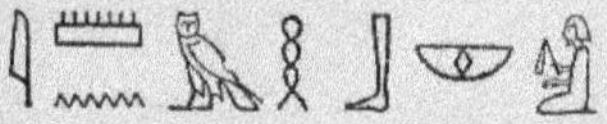, a scribe of the bowmen of the Lord of the Two Lands. Above the door are cut the utchats, the Boat of Rā, the symbol of Osiris of Abydos, etc., and in the door is sculptured in relief a figure of the deceased holding a standard, the head of which is in the form of that of a god wearing plumes. On each side of the door is a figure of the deceased. On the right side of the shrine are figures of Åmen-em-ḥeb, his wife Ta-nefer 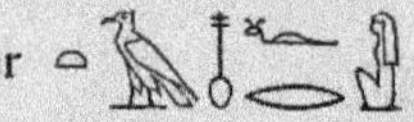, Neb-Åmen, and Bakuru; and on the left are figures of the deceased and his wife, and of two children. The scribe Neheri , is mentioned in the line of text which runs round the monument. Barker Collection. XXth to XXIInd dynasty. Height 2 ft. 3 in. [No. 474.]

755. (*Bay* 19.)—Limestone **sepulchral stele,** with rounded top, of **Māḥu** 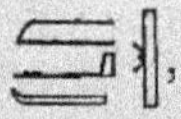, a scribe, on which are cut in outline a series of scenes representing Māḥu making offerings to Osiris and Isis, and to several pairs of ancestors. Sams Collection XXth to XXIInd dynasty. Height 2 ft. 8 in., width 1 ft. 1 in [No. 311.]

756. (*Bay* 19.)—Lower portion of a black granite kneeling **figure of Åmen-mes** 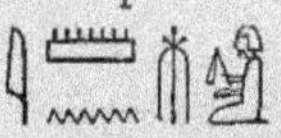, a royal scribe, the son of Pen-tcherti-Åni (?) , and the lady Ånit

. XXth to XXIInd dynasty. Height 1 ft. 7½ in. [No. 137.]

Presented by His Majesty King George III, 1801.

757. (*Bay* 24.)—Painted limestone **sepulchral stele,** with rounded top, of **Rā-uben** , a judge, sculptured with a winged disk and a figure of the deceased standing in adoration before Rā-Ḥeru-khuti . The text contains a prayer for sepulchral offerings. XXth to XXIInd dynasty. Height 1 ft. 1 in., width 8½ in. [No. 320].

758. (*Southern Gallery.*)—**Papyrus** inscribed in hieroglyphic characters with a series of Chapters of the Theban Recension of the **Book of the Dead,** with the accompanying vignettes, etc., for **Queen Netchemet** , the mother or wife of **Ḥer-Ḥeru** 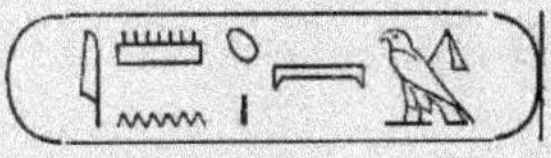, high-priest of Àmen and king of Egypt, about B.C. 1050.

Vignettes :—

1. Rā-Harmachis seated, with a table of offerings before him.
2. King Ḥer-Ḥeru and Netchemet.
3. King Ḥer-Ḥeru and Netchemet making offerings. They stand, with hands raised in adoration, before Osiris, who is seated within a shrine. In front of him are : (i) A pair of scales in which the deceased Netchemet is being weighed against the symbol of righteousness by the Ape-god Thoth. (ii) The four sons of Horus seated on a lily. (iii) The goddess Isis.
4. King Ḥer-Ḥeru and Netchemet adoring the setting sun.
5. The Sunrise. The solar disk adored by apes.
6. The Doors of the Ṭuat, or Other World.

7. The Funeral Procession. The body of the queen being drawn along on a sledge by the cows which are to be offered up as sacrifices.
8. A funeral coffer drawn by priests.
9. The priest burning incense.
10. Ministrant bearing offerings.
11. The queen playing draughts in the Other World.
12. The soul of Queen Netchemet.
13. The queen adoring the lion-gods of yesterday and to-morrow.
14. The Bennu bird of Heliopolis.
15. The mummy being watched over by two vultures, *i.e.* Isis and Nephthys.

Text:—

1. A Hymn to Rā when he rises.
2. Adorations to Osiris.
3. A Hymn to the setting sun.
4. Chapter XVII of the Book of the Dead.

From Thebes. XXIst dynasty. Length 13 ft. 7 in. [No. 10541.]
Presented by His Majesty King Edward VII, 1903.

759. (*Bay* **24.**)—Painted limestone **sepulchral stele,** with rounded top and raised border, of **Ȧst** 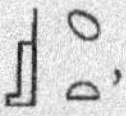, surnamed **Nenkasa** 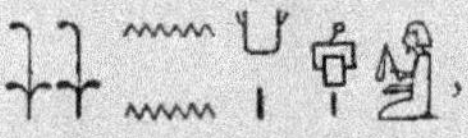, the daughter of Ānkh-Khensu, and Tcheṭ-Mut-ȧs-ānkh 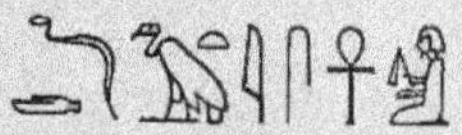, sculptured with a scene representing the deceased adoring Rā-Harmachis and Isis. Below is a prayer to Rā-Harmachis, Tem, and Ptaḥ-Seker, that the deceased's soul may "come forth to see the "disk." XXIst dynasty. Height 1 ft. 4 in., width 11 in. [No. 931.]

760. (*Bay* **22.**)—Portion of a **slab,** with deeply cut hieroglyphics, recording the name of a king . . . . . . **Mer-taui pen Ȧmen** . From Tarrāna. XXIst dynasty (?). Height 1 ft. 1½ in., width 1 ft. 3 in. [No. 653.]

761. (*Bay* **20**.)—Rectangular **sepulchral stele of Pa-ḥapt-ṭep-nekhtu** 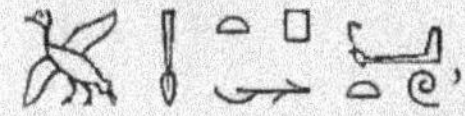, on which is cut a scene representing the deceased making an offering to the god Ptaḥ. Salt Collection. XXIst dynasty. Height 9½ in., width 5½ in. [No. 342.]

762. (*Bay* **22**.)—Limestone **sepulchral stele,** with rounded top, of **Pen-Åmen** 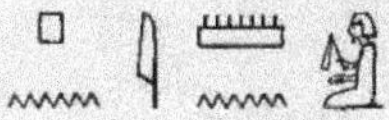, a royal scribe and Kher-ḥeb priest, the son of Mut-em-åpt, on which are sculptured scenes representing the deceased adoring Osiris, Isis, and Horus, and seated with relatives with tables of sepulchral offerings before them. Salt Collection. XXIst or XXIInd dynasty. Height 1 ft. 6½ in., width 1 ft. 1 in. [No. 309.]

763. (*Bay* **19**.)—Massive grey granite **seated statue of Sekhet,** a fire-goddess, in the form of a woman with the head of a lioness, with the solar disk on her head. She wears a deep wig, a necklace, bracelets, anklets, and a tunic which extends to her ankles. On the front of her throne are cut the prenomen and nomen of **Shashanq I**, the **Shishak** of the Bible (1 Kings xi, 40; xiv, 25–28; 2 Chron. xii, 2–13), king of Egypt, about B.C. 966:

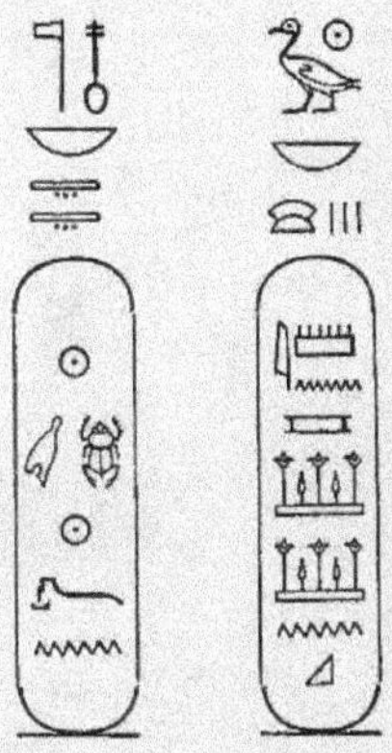

From Karnak. Belmore Collection. XXIInd dynasty. (**Plate XXVII.**) Height 7 ft. 7 in. [No. 517.]

764. (*Bay* **20**.)—Massive grey granite **seated statue of Sekhet,** a fire goddess, similar to No. 763. On the front of her throne are cut the prenomen and nomen of **Shashanq I,**

(*To face page* 210.)

PLATE XXVII.

Statue of Sekhet, a Fire-goddess. On the throne are cut the names of Shashanq I (Shishak), about B.C. 966.

[I:y 1ç, No. 763.]

king of Egypt, about B.C. 966, and on the sides are symbols of the union of the Two Egypts, North and South . From Karnak. Salt Collection. XXIInd dynasty. Height 6 ft. 8 in. [No. 63.]

765. (*Bay* 19.)—Fine limestone **base of a statue of Prince Åuputh** , the son of **Shashanq I** 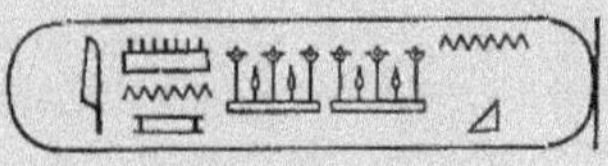, and high-priest of Åmen and commander-in-chief of the Egyptian army. The inscription on the upper surface and the sides contains the name and titles of Åuputh several times repeated. From Karnak. XXIInd dynasty. 1 ft. 5 in. by 1 ft. 3 in. by 4½ in. [No. 1307.]

766. (*Bay* 22.)—Quartzite sandstone **statue of Ḥāpi,** the Nile-god, who is represented standing in a meadow filled with plants, and holding on his outstretched hands an altar, or table of offerings, from which hang down bunches of grain, green herbs, flowers, water-fowl, etc. It was dedicated to Åmen-Rā, the king of the gods at Thebes, by **Shashanq (Shishak) meri-Åmen-Rā** , the son of **Uasarken-meri-Åmen,** and Maāt-ka-Rā, a daughter of **Pasebkhānut** , high-priest of Åmen-Ra. On the side of the plinth is cut a figure of Shashanq, with his hands raised in adoration. Salt Collection. XXIInd dynasty. From Karnak. Height 7 ft. 3 in. [No. 8.]

767. (*Bay* 22.)—Fine white limestone **sepulchral stele,** with rounded top, of **Paseb-khānut** , or Pasebenkhānut , a high-priest of Åmen-Rā, a divine father of Åmen-Rā, and the 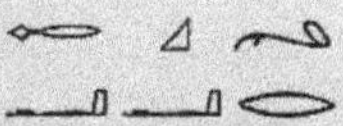, of Åmsu, or Menu, of Coptos, Horus and Isis, and the son of Rā-men-kheper

, a high-priest of Ȧmen-Rā, king of the gods. On the upper portion of the stele are sculptured the winged disk and a scene representing the deceased adoring Osiris, Horus, and Isis. Below these is cut a prayer to Osiris, Horus, Isis, Ȧp-uat, Thoth, Ptaḥ-ȧsti, and Ḥeqi for sepulchral offerings. XXIst or XXIInd dynasty. Height 3 ft., width 1 ft. 11 in. [No. 642.]

768. (*Bay* 16.)—Massive red granite **capital of a column** from the great temple built at Bubastis by **Osorkon (Uasarken) II,** king of Egypt, about B.C. 866, sculptured with a head of **Hathor.** Above the head of the goddess is a cornice of uraei, and on each side of her face is an uraeus, one representing Southern Egypt, and the other Northern Egypt; she has the ears of a cow. A portion of one side of the face has been restored. XXIInd dynasty. From Tall Bastah (Bubastis). Height 6 ft. 6 in., width 4 ft. 6 in. [No. 1107.]

Presented by the Egypt Exploration Fund, 1891.

769. (*Bay* 23.)—Red granite **relief** on which are sculptured: 1. A figure of **Osorkon II,** king of Egypt, about B.C. 866,

Granite relief from the temple of Osorkon II at Tall Bastah (Pibeseth, or Bubastis). [Bay 23, No. 769.] XXIInd dynasty.

wearing the Crown of the North, seated within a shrine resting on a platform with steps. 2. A figure of the goddess **Bast**

 3. A series of figures of priests and ministrants performing ceremonies. From the temple of Osorkon II at Bubastis. XXIInd dynasty. Height 3 ft. 6 in., width 5 ft. 1 in. [No. 1105.]

Presented by the Egypt Exploration Fund, 1891.

770. (*Bay* **26.**)—Red granite **relief** sculptured with figures of **Osorkon II,** king of Egypt, about B.C. 866, and his wife **Karāmā** 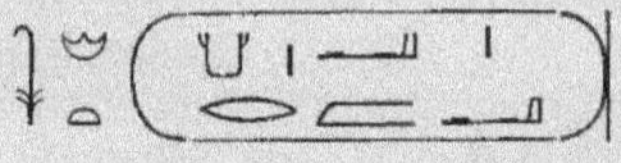, who stand in adoration

Relief sculptured with figures of Osorkon II and his wife Karāmā.

[Bay 26, No. 770.] XXIInd dynasty.

before a deity. From Bubastis. XXIInd dynasty. Height 5 ft. 9 in., width 3 ft. 6 in. [No. 1077.]

Presented by the Egypt Exploration Fund, 1891.

771. (*Bay* **23.**)—Portion of a granite **slab** on which is cut the Horus name  of **Khufu,** or **Cheops,** king of Egypt, about B.C. 3730. From the temple at Bubastis. Height 3 ft. 1 in., width 1 ft. 8 in. [No. 1097.]

Presented by the Egypt Exploration Fund, 1891.

772. (*Bay* **23.**)—Red granite **slab** on which is cut the name of **Khā-f-Rā,** or **Chephren,** 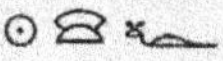, king of Egypt, about B.C. 3660. From the temple at Bubastis. Height 2 ft. 2 in., width 3 ft. 2 in. [No. 1098.]

Presented by the Egypt Exploration Fund, 1891.

773. (*Bay* **23.**)—Red granite **slab** on which are sculptured figures of kings **Åmen-ḥetep II** and Seti I presenting offerings to Åmen-Rā. From the temple at Bubastis. Height 3 ft., width 6 ft. 6 in. [No. 1103.]

Presented by the Egypt Exploration Fund, 1891

774. (*Bay* **22.**)—**Head** of the grey granite **seated statue** (No. 775) of **Åmen-em-ḥāt III** (?), whereon **Osorkon II** caused his names and titles to be inscribed. From Bubastis. XIIth–XXIInd dynasty. Height 2 ft. 6 in. [No. 1063.]

Presented by the Egypt Exploration Fund, 1889.

775. (*Bay* **20.**)—Portion of a grey granite **statue of a king** seated on a throne, the sides and pedestal of which are inscribed with the names and titles of **Uasarken,** beloved of Åmen, son of Bast 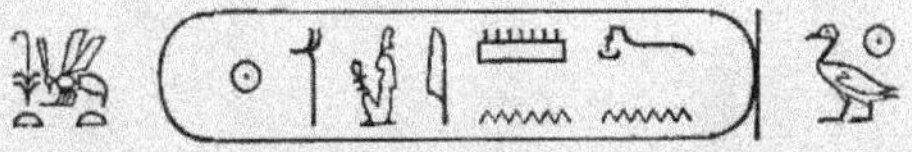

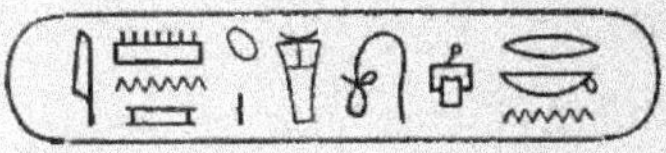, *i.e.*, **Osorkon II,** king of Egypt, about B.C. 866. There is good reason for believing that this statue was made for **Åmen-em-ḥāt III,** king of Egypt, about B.C. 2300, and that Osorkon II caused the names and titles of this king to be erased from the front of the throne, and his own to be cut upon the sides of the throne and the pedestal. XIIth–XXIInd dynasty. From Bubastis. Height 9 ft. [No. 1064.]

Presented by the Egypt Exploration Fund, 1889.

Sepulchral stele of Prince Ȧuuaruath, son of Osorkon II, sculptured with a scene representing the deceased and his sister worshipping Rā-Harmachis.
[Bay 22, No. 777.] XXIInd dynasty.

776. (*Bay* **21.**)—Red granite **seated figure of Ānkh-renp-nefer** , holding a small shrine containing a seated figure of Osiris, who flourished in the reign of **Osorkon II,** king of Egypt, about B.C. 866. The deceased was Deputy Governor of Succoth, inspector of the palace, and the "good recorder" , of Per-Tem, or Pithom. On one side are cut figures of the triad Àmen-Rā, Mut, and Khensu, and on the other figures of Harmachis, Shu, and Tefnut. On the head of Ānkh-renp-nefer is a beetle, symbol of the resurrection, on each side of the head is the figure of a god, and on the flat surface near his chin are the cartouches of **Osorkon II,**

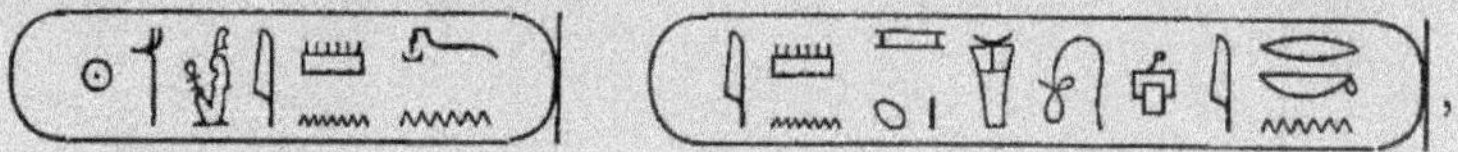,

and the figure of a man holding  and  in his hands. From Tall al-Maskhûṭah. XXIInd dynasty. Height 2 ft. [No. 1007.]

Presented by the Egypt Exploration Fund, 1883.

777. (*Bay* **22.**)—Limestone **sepulchral stele,** with rounded top, of **Àuuaruath** , or 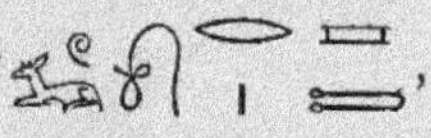, the son of **Uasarken (Osorkon II or III)** 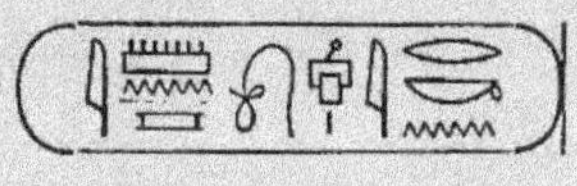, high-priest of Àmen, and chief of all the forces of Egypt. On the upper portion are sculptured figures of the deceased and his sister, **Shepset-ṭent**  (?), kneeling in adoration before the disk of Rā-Harmachis, which rests in its boat and is adored by apes. Under one end of the boat is a fish, and under the other is a frog. Below this scene are nine lines of hieroglyphics containing a prayer to the Sun-god. From Thebes. XXIInd or XXIIIrd dynasty. (**Plate XXVIII.**) Height 1 ft. 11 in., width 1 ft. 4 in.

[No. 1224.]

778. (*Bay* 21.)—Upper portions of seated **granite figures** of a priest of Ȧmen and his wife **Ānkh-s-en-Ȧst** 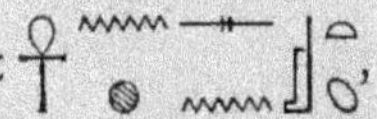,

a priestess of Mut, lady of Ȧsher, who flourished in the reign of Uasarken-sa-Ȧst (?) The names and titles of the king are cut upon the back of the male figure and across the breast; under his chin is a figure of Osiris, and on his right shoulder a figure of Horus. From Karnak. XXIInd or XXIIIrd dynasty. Height 2 ft. 1 in., width 1 ft. 9 in. [No. 110.]

779. (*Bay* 17.)—Portion of a red quartzite **sepulchral monument,** in the form of a rectangular stele, with a palm-leaf cornice. On the front, within a cavity, were sculptured figures of four goddesses, with a disk and a pair of cow's horns on the head of each; only one of these is now perfect. On the right is the figure of a priestess, and on the edge are figures of two priestesses. On the back are five lines of hieroglyphics. This stele was set up to commemorate the priestesses Ta-urt , Ta-Khā , and others. XXIInd dynasty. Height 1 ft. 9 in., width 1 ft. 4 in. [No. 473.]

780. (*Bay* 17.)—Limestone **truncated obelisk** of **Ptaḥ-erṭānȧ** , the son of Pesṭett 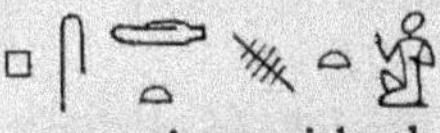, a captain of the soldiers employed in connection with the temples. The inscriptions contain prayers to Osiris, Ȧp-uat, and Ptaḥ-ȧneb-resu for sepulchral offerings. XXIInd dynasty. Height 1 ft. 10 in. [No. 177.]

781. (*Bay* 17.)—Sandstone kneeling **figure of Tchai** 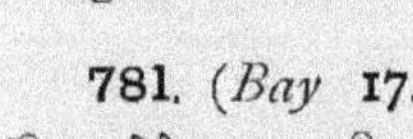, the chief bow-bearer and superintendent of all the workmen employed on the buildings of the king, inscribed with a prayer to Ȧmen-Rā for a long, prosperous and happy life, and for sepulchral offerings. XXIInd dynasty. Height 1 ft. 11 in. [No. 1381 (469*).]

782. (*Bay* 19.)—Limestone **sepulchral stele,** the upper part of which is in the form of a truncated pyramid, of **Bāḥri** , and his wife **Neferut** 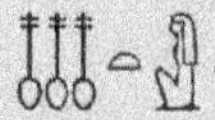. On the upper portion is cut a scene in which the deceased and his wife are represented adoring Osiris, the "lord of Eternity," Isis, etc., and below this are two other scenes wherein we see the children of the deceased bringing offerings to their father and mother, and adoring them. XXIInd dynasty. Height 3 ft. 3½ in., width 2 ft. 2 in. [No. 151.]

783. (*Bay* 20.)—Rectangular granite **sepulchral stele** of **Qemḥȧ** (?) , a priest of the goddess Hathor of Denderah, sculptured with the following scenes:—1. The deceased seated on a chair of state. 2. The son of the deceased adoring Ȧmsu, or Menu. 3 and 4. The members of the family of Qemḥȧ kneeling in adoration. D'Athanasi Collection. From Thebes. XXIInd dynasty. Height 10 in., width 7 in. [No. 506.]

784. (*Bay* 20.)—Granite **stele,** with rounded top, on which are cut in outline the figures of **Menu,** the god of generation and virility, and **Khnemu,** the Ram-god of the First Cataract and god of the Nile. From Wâdî Ḥalfah. XXIInd dynasty. Height 1 ft. 3½ in., width 11 in. [No. 1045.]
Presented by Colonel F. G. Plunkett, R.E., 1887.

785. (*Bay* 22.)—Painted limestone **sepulchral stele,** with rounded top, of **Bastet-ȧrt-ṭāts** 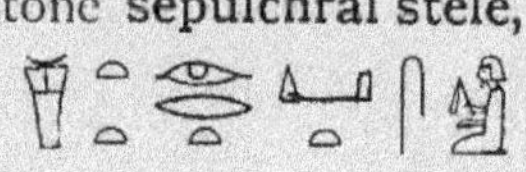, the daughter of P-māu  and Ȧnut 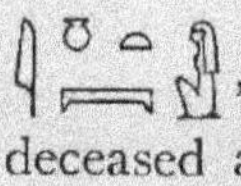, on which is sculptured a scene representing the deceased adoring the sun's disk in his boat beneath the winged disk. The text contains a prayer to Rā-Harmachis for sepulchral offerings. XXIInd dynasty. Height 1 ft. 4 in., width 10 in. [No. 917.]

786. (*Bay* 22.)—Limestone **sepulchral stele,** with rounded top, of **Nefer-ābu** , a judge. On the obverse are sculptured:—1. A figure of Ptah seated in a shrine, with a table of offerings before him. 2. Four ears

, the sign *Ka* 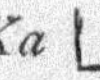, and two eyes 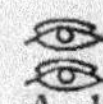. 3. A kneeling figure of the deceased Nefer-ābu. 4. A hymn of praise to Ptaḥ. On the reverse are cut ten lines of text containing addresses to Ptaḥ and his souls. Belmore Collection. XXIInd dynasty. Height 1 ft. 3 in., width 10½ in. [No. 589.]

787. (*Bay* 19.)—Portion of an arragonite **figure of a priest,** whose duty it was to array statues of the gods Ḥeru-khenti-khat, Ȧmsu, or Menu, and Ptaḥ and of the goddesses Isis and Sekhet, in their festival apparel, and to place their crowns and other ornaments upon them. Sams Collection. XXIInd to XXVIth dynasty. Height 1 ft. 4 in. [No. 121.]

788. (*Bay* 22.)—Limestone **sepulchral stele,** with rounded top, of **Paa-** ...... , and **Shemsu-Ḥeru-Menu** , on which are cut figures of the deceased, and certain of their relatives, adoring Osiris, Horus, and Isis. The text contains a prayer for sepulchral offerings. Sams Collection. XXIInd to XXVIth dynasty. Height 1 ft. 3 in., width 1 ft. 1½ in. [No. 321.]

789. (*Bay* 22.)—Upper portion of a dark granite **seated figure** of an Erpā, and Ḥā Prince, who was a priest of Ȧmen-Rā at Thebes. From Thebes. XXIInd to XXVIth dynasty. Height 1 ft. 2 in. [No. 1132.]

790. (*Bay* 26.)—Lower portion of a grey granite kneeling **figure of Nes-p-qa-shuti** , a chancellor, *smer uāti,* priest of the *ka,* etc., holding before him the sistrum of Hathor. From Edfû. XXIInd to XXVIth dynasty. Height 1 ft. 7 in. [No. 1225.]

791. (*Bay* 26.)—Limestone **sepulchral stele,** with rounded top, on the upper portion of which are sculptured ten figures of ichneumons, arranged in five pairs, with a vase of offerings between each pair. It was dedicated to the ichneumon god by **Khensu** , overseer of the king's stables, his wife Ta-ur, and their son Aȧ, a scribe of the offerings of the king, whose kneeling figures are sculptured below those of the ichneumons. XXIInd to XXVIth dynasty. Height 1 ft. 9½ in., width 1 ft. 2 in. [No. 1430.]

792. (*Bay* 19.)—Limestone **sepulchral stele,** with rounded top, of **Ḥui** 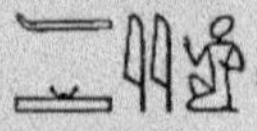, an offering bearer, on which are sculptured two scenes:—1. Ḥui, his son Åmen-em-åpt, and his daughter Pii , presenting offerings to Osiris. 2. Nekfi 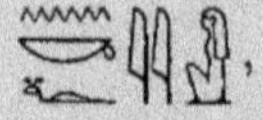, Ta-usert, and Mer-en-Ptaḥ, children of Ḥui and his wife Kefna 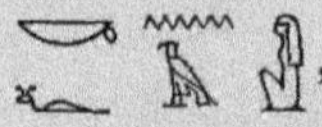, presenting offerings to their parents. Anastasi Collection. XIXth to XXIInd dynasty. Height 1 ft. 8 in., width 1 ft. [No. 364.]

793. (*Central Saloon.*)—**Cast** of the **stele of Piānkhi-meri-Åmen,** king of Nubia, about B.C. 750, set up at Napata, (Gebel Barkal), to commemorate his invasion and conquest of Egypt. Piānkhi heard that a great rebellion had broken out in Egypt, headed by a local chief called Tafnekhth, who had captured Memphis, and was sailing up the Nile, presumably to Thebes. As he sailed southwards, city after city submitted to him, and at length he arrived at Herakleopolis, which he besieged. Piānkhi ordered his generals who were in Egypt to stop the advance of Tafnekhth, and in a short time the troops which he sent made Tafnekhth raise the siege and take to flight. Soon afterwards, Piānkhi himself set out for Egypt, and having arrived at Thebes, and offered up sacrifices to Åmen-Rā and the other gods of the city, he sailed northwards with his troops to attack the foe. Hermopolis, Herakleopolis, and the Fayyûm submitted to him, and then he advanced on Memphis. Here he found the gates closed, and the people hostile, but he sailed his boats close up to the walls of the city, and his soldiers were able to drop from the bows, which projected over the tops of the walls, for it was the season of the inundation, into the city, and so "captured it like a water-flood." Piānkhi sacrificed to the gods of Memphis, and then crossed the Nile and went to Heliopolis, where he worshipped the gods, made offerings to them, and celebrated a feast in their honour. In a very short time he crushed the rebellion, and the leader Tafnekhth, having sued for pardon and presented gifts, was forgiven by Piānkhi. The Nubian king made no attempt to administer the country, but having filled his boats with the gifts made to him by the vanquished governors, he sailed southwards to Napata. The text is the fullest and clearest of all the Egyptian historical texts, and is the only record extant of the Nubian conquest of Egypt. The original stele is in the Egyptian Museum in Cairo. Height 5 ft. 9 in., width 4 ft. 7 in. [No. 1121.]

794. (*Bay* 20.)—Grey granite **tablet for offerings,** mounted on its original pillar stand, and large **bowl** of the same material, made to receive offerings of wine. On the face of the table are sculptured figures of offerings, cakes, fruit, joints of meat, vases, etc., and on the front edge are cut the cartouches of King **Kashta, Shep-en-ȧpt, Ȧmenȧrṭās,** etc. The bowl is ornamented with a head of Hathor, and on one side of it are sculptured figures of the two persons, one of whom appears to have been called NES-ȦMSU, who dedicated the bowl and the table of offerings to the temple of Ȧmen. The text on the bowl contains a prayer to Ta-urt and Hathor for sepulchral offerings, but it is badly cut and mutilated, and some portions of it are illegible. XXVth dynasty. Height of bowl 1 ft. 1 in., diameter 1 ft. 5½ in. Height of table and stand 3 ft. [Nos. 1258, 1259.]

795. (*Bay* 20.)—Grey granite **base,** or pedestal, of a **statue of Osiris** (?), dedicated to the god by **Ȧr-tchau** , an Erpā, Ḥā prince, and chancellor, who flourished about B.C. 700. In the front is a text of three lines containing an address to Osiris, and on the front edge are five cartouches, namely those of Princess P-ānkhi, the royal wife Shep-en-Ȧpt, the royal mother Ȧmenȧrṭās, the royal mother Shep-en-Ȧpt, and . These may have been cut on the base at a later date. XXIVth dynasty. Length 1 ft. 3 in., width 11 in. [No. 713.]

796. (*Bay* 20.)—Rectangular granite **libation vessel,** inscribed with the name of **Queen Ȧmenȧrṭās** 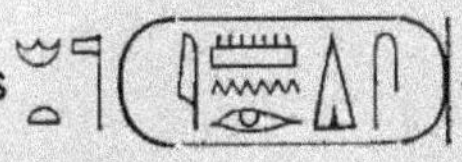. XXVth dynasty, about B.C. 700 (?). Length 1 ft. 2½ in., breadth 8 in. [No. 1380.]

797. (*Bay* 25.)—**Black basalt** rectangular **slab,** inscribed with a **mythological text,** which was copied from an old and partly obliterated document, by the order of **Shabaka,** king

of Egypt, about B.C. 700, and set up in the temple of Ptaḥ at Memphis. The text consists of two horizontal lines, which contain the names of Shabaka, and state the reason for cutting the inscription. Below these were sixty perpendicular lines of text, having reference to legends of Ptaḥ, Rā, Horus, Set, and other gods, but as one third of this number is wanting, it is impossible to give any complete account of their contents. This slab has been used as the nether stone of a mill, and grooves cut in it for the flour to run out. XXVth dynasty. Length 4 ft. 6 in., breadth 2 ft. 2 in. [No. 498 (135*).]

Presented by Earl Spencer, 1805.

798. (*Bay* **20.**)—Lower portion of a **seated figure of Na-menkh-Åmen** 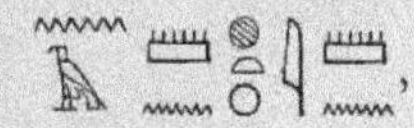, an Erpā, Ḥā prince, *Smer-uāt*, scribe and priest, who flourished in the reign of **Queen Åmen-årṭās,** about B.C. 700. XXVth dynasty. Height 1 ft. 1 in., 1 ft. 2½ in. square. [No. 908.]

799. (*Bay* **22.**)—**Cast** of the **stele of Ta-nuath-Åmen,** king of Nubia, or the Northern Sûdân, inscribed with an account of his dream, in which, according to the priests, his sovereignty over the whole country was foretold. Having received the kingship from Åmen-Rā of Napata, he set out for the North, invaded Egypt, and marched to Heliopolis, overcoming all opposition on his way. He made war upon the governors of the chief cities in the Delta, and claims to have defeated them, but, according to the Annals of Ashur-bani-pal, he was himself defeated by the Assyrians, and obliged to fly to his own country. The original stele was found at Gebel Barkal, opposite to the site of the ancient city of Napata, and is now in the Egyptian Museum in Cairo. Height 3 ft. 5 in. [No. 1124.]

TWENTY-SIXTH DYNASTY.

800. (*Bay* **24.**)—Black basalt **intercolumnar slab,** with deep cornice surmounted by uraei on the obverse and by hawks on the reverse. On the obverse is sculptured a scene wherein **Psammetichus I**  is represented kneeling and presenting offerings to Menthu, to two bull-headed gods, and to a serpent (Tem ?), and on the reverse is a mutilated scene of similar import. Found in the temple of Temu at Rosetta, wherein the "Rosetta Stone" (No. 960) was originally placed. XXVIth dynasty. Height 4 ft., width 3 ft. 4 in. [No. 20.]

Presented by His Majesty King George III, 1801.

801. (*Bay* **24.**)—Portion of a grey granite **statue of Psammetichus I** , king of Egypt, about B.C. **660.** From Karnak. XXVIth dynasty. Height 1 ft. 5 in. [No. 600.]

Presented by W. R. Hamilton, Esq., 1840.

802. (*Bay* **24.**)—**Shaft of a basalt column,** inscribed with the prenomen and titles of **Psammetichus I** , king of Egypt, about B.C. 660. XXVIth dynasty. From the temple of Temu at Rosetta. Height 3 ft. 5 in., diameter 1 ft. 2 in. [No. 964.]

803. (*Bay* **23.**)—Head of a colossal seated sandstone **statue of Psammetichus II,** king of Egypt, about B.C. 596. It was found, with the fragments of its throne, on which were cut the cartouches , near the southern end of the Suez Canal, in 1906. XXVIth dynasty. Height 2 ft. 9 in. [No. 1238.]

804. (*Bay* **22.**)—Portion of a limestone **stele,** on which is cut in outline a figure of **Uaḥ-àb-Rā** , king of Egypt, about B.C. 590, the **"Pharaoh Hophra"** of Jeremiah xliv, 30, and the "Apries" of Herodotus, making an offering of two vases of wine to a god. From Abydos. XXVIth dynasty. Height 2 ft. 2 in., width 1 ft. [No. 1358.]

Presented by the Egypt Exploration Fund, 1901.

805. (*Central Saloon.*)—Lower portion of a black granite kneeling **statue of Pef-ā-Net** 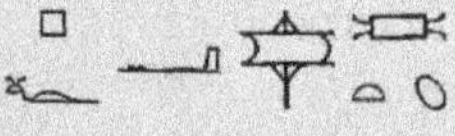, the son of Sebek , and the lady Nānes-Bast , a priestess of Saïs, holding a shrine, on which is sculptured a figure of Osiris. The deceased held the offices of chief physician to King **Uaḥ-ȧb-Rā,** *i.e.*, Apries, **Pharaoh Hophra** 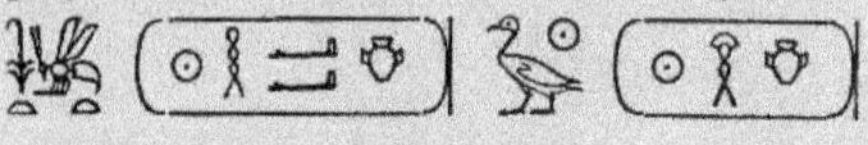, superintendent of the two Treasuries , chief councillor, and superintendent of the "Great House," or Palace, priest of Horus of Pe, Åmen of Thebes, etc. XXVIth dynasty, about B.C. 590. Height 2 ft. 4 in. [No. 83.]

806. (*Bay* 16.)—Black granite **tablet for offerings** of a king whose names and titles have been erased ; the traces of the signs in the first cartouche suggest that it was made for , *i.e.*, **Åāḥmes II,** who reigned about B.C. 570. On the tablet are sculptured figures of libation jars, vessels for wine and unguents, cakes, geese, etc., and round the edges is an inscription in which the deceased prays for thousands of loaves of bread, oxen, geese, thousands of vessels of beer, unguents, incense, wine, thousands of suits of linen garments, apparel, etc. Salt Collection. XXVIth dynasty. From Saïs. Length 2 ft. 8 in., breadth 2 ft. 5 in. [No. 94.]

807. (*Bay* 17.)—Massive red granite **tablet for offerings of Åāḥmes** (Amasis II) , king of Egypt about B.C. 570, sculptured on the margins with a text containing the names and titles of the deceased. On the face are sculptured figures of the usual objects presented, and at the back is cut a tank five inches deep. XXVIth dynasty. Length 1 ft. 7 in., breadth 1 ft. $10\frac{1}{2}$ in., depth 1 ft. 1 in. [No. 610.]

Presented by the Egypt Exploration Fund, 1902.

808. (*Bay* 24.)—Limestone **stele,** with rounded top, dated in the eighth year of **Khnem-àb-Rā Ȧāḥ-mes sa Net,** *i.e.,* **Amasis II,** king of Egypt, about B.C. 570, inscribed with a text recording the **dedication of a building,** etc., to the goddess Net, or Neith, of Saïs, and to Horus of Resenet, and Horus of Meḥenet. On the upper portion is sculptured a scene representing the king offering two vases to Neith, behind whom stand the two Horus gods; above is a winged disk with pendent uraei. From Saïs. XXVIth dynasty. (**Plate XXIX.**) Height 1 ft. 4$\frac{1}{2}$ in., width 10$\frac{3}{4}$ in. [No. 1427.]

809. (*Bay* 24.)—Limestone **stele,** with rounded top, on the upper portion of which is cut a scene representing **Ȧāḥmes (Amasis II)** , king of Egypt, about B.C. 570, making an **offering of a field** to Rā, or Horus, and Isis. Above is the winged disk. The dedication took place in the first year of the king's reign. Height 1 ft. 10 in., width 1 ft. 0$\frac{1}{2}$ in. [No. 952.]

810. (*Bay* 24.)—**Cast of the inscription of Psemthek** , an official who flourished in the reign of **Ȧāḥmes II** (Amasis), about B.C. 570, containing a prayer for funerary offerings. Height 1 ft. 7$\frac{1}{2}$ in., width 8$\frac{1}{2}$ in. [No. 655.]
Presented by the Society of Antiquaries of London, 1870.

811. (*Bay* 24.)—Rectangular black limestone **sarcophagus of Ānkh-nes-nefer-àb-Rā** 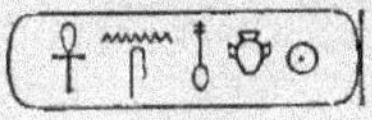, daughter of Psammetichus II, king of Egypt, about B.C. 596, and Queen Thakhauath 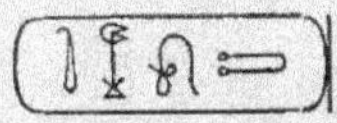, and wife of Amasis II. On the outside of the cover is sculptured, in relief, a figure of the queen wearing the vulture head-dress surmounted by the disk and horns of Hathor and the plumes of Ȧmen-Rā. She is arrayed in a garment which reaches to her ankles, and holds the sceptre . On the inside of the cover is a full length figure of the goddess Nut, and on the bottom of the sarcophagus is another of Hathor-Ȧmenti. The whole sarcophagus, both inside and outside, is covered with well-cut hieroglyphic inscriptions, containing prayers and addresses to the various gods of the dead. The body of the queen was removed from the

Stele recording the dedication of a building to the goddess Neith by Àāḥmes (Amasis) II, about B.C. 572.

[Bay 24, No. 808.]

Sarcophagus of Ānkh-nes-nefer-ȧb-Rā, daughter of Psammetichus II and Queen Thakhauath.
[Bay 24, No. 811.] XXVIth dynasty, B.C. 570.

sarcophagus in very early times, probably during the reign of Cambyses, and burnt. Subsequently the sarcophagus seems to have been occupied by a royal scribe called **Ȧmen-ḥetep,** or **Pi-Menth** 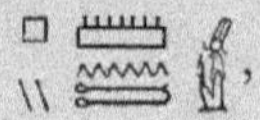, who had his name inserted in the cartouches of the queen, and caused the feminine suffixes to be made masculine, in order that the prayers, etc., might be his. The sarcophagus was found at the bottom of a pit, one hundred and twenty-five feet deep, behind the Ramesseum at Thebes; it was removed to Paris, but was subsequently purchased by the Trustees of the British Museum. XXVIth dynasty. (**Plate XXX.**) Length 8 ft. 6 in., breadth 3 ft. 9½ in., height when closed 3 ft. 8 in., weight about 5¾ tons. [No. 32.]

812. (*Bay* **24.**)—Sandstone **relief,** sculptured with a scene representing the high-priestess of Ȧmen Queen **Ānkh-nes-nefer-ȧb-Rā Net-ȧqert** 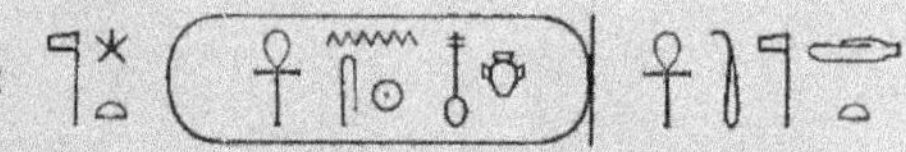 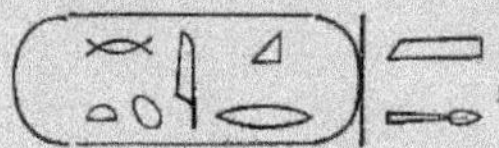, accompanied by Shashanq 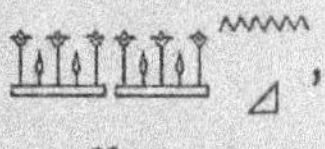, the chief steward of the high-priestess, making offerings to Ȧmen-Rā. From Thebes. XXVIth dynasty. Anastasi Collection. Height 1 ft. 9 in., width 1 ft. 4 in. [No. 835.]

813. (*Bay* **24.**)—Portion of a sandstone **slab,** inscribed with the name of Queen **Ānkh-nes-nefer-ȧb-Rā** 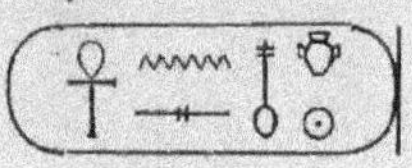 high-priestess of Ȧmen, daughter of Psammetichus II, and wife of Amasis II, king of Egypt, about B.C. 570. XXVIth dynasty. From Thebes. Height 3 ft. 2 in. [No. 907.]

814. (*Bay* **24.**)—Upper portion of a grey granite **statue of Ta-Kharṭ-Ȧst** , a princess, the daughter of **Ȧmasis II,** king of Egypt, about B.C. 570. XXVIth dynasty. Height 2 ft. 4 in. [No. 775.]

815. (*Bay* **18.**)—**Cast of the stele of Ḥeru-sa-ȧtef,** king of Nubia, or the Northern Sûdân, dated in the thirty-fourth (?) year of his reign, about B.C. 580. The text contains an account of the military expeditions which this king made against the tribes in the Southern and Eastern Sûdân in the 3rd, 5th, 6th, 11th, 16th, 18th, 23rd and 33rd years of his reign, and records the restoration of the temples of Åmen-Rā of Napata, and of other gods, and gives a list of the properties with which he endowed them. The original stele was found at Gebel Barkal, opposite to the site of the ancient city of Napata, and is now in the Egyptian Museum in Cairo. Height 6 ft. 7 in. [No. 1125.]

816. (*Bay* 20.)—**Cast of a stele** inscribed with an account of the **Coronation of Åspelta,** king of Nubia, at Napata, in the sixth century before Christ. The text records that the chief officers of state presented the "Royal Brethren" before Åmen-Rā, and expected him to indicate which of them was to be king by touching him. When the Royal Brethren had passed before the god, who made no sign, they brought into his presence Åspelta, whose mother had been high-priestess of Åmen. Then Åmen-Rā touched him, and declared that he should be king, and should rebuild the temples in the lands of the South and North, and bestowed upon him the sceptre and crown of sovereignty. Thereupon the priests and soldiers cast themselves down before Åspelta, and paid him homage. The inscription concludes with a statement that Åspelta established two annual festivals, and enumerates the gifts which he bestowed upon the priests of Åmen. The original stele was found at Gebel Barkal, opposite to the site of the ancient city of Napata, in the Sûdân, and is now in the Egyptian Museum at Cairo. Height 5 ft. 4 in. [No. 1122.]

817. (*Bay* 20.)—**Cast of a stele** inscribed with an account of the passing of an **edict of excommunication** by a king of Napata in the sixth century before Christ. This edict was directed against a Sûdânî sect, or tribe, which appears to have been in the habit of eating raw meat, probably cut from the animal whilst still alive. It seems that the sect also determined to slay all those who cooked their meat before eating it. The edict strictly prohibits any eater of raw meat from entering the temple of Åmen-Rā of Napata, and invokes a curse upon all the members of the sect and their posterity. The original stele was found at Gebel Barkal, opposite to the site of the ancient city of Napata, in the Sûdân, and is now in the Egyptian Museum at Cairo. Height 4 ft. [No. 1126.]

818. (*Bay* 21.)—Black basalt **kneeling statue of Uaḥ-àb-Rā**, holding a shrine containing a figure of Osiris. The deceased was the son of Pef-ā-Net, and Ta-sheb-en-Net, was an Erpā, a Ḥā prince, a *Smer uāt,* governor of the Eastern and Western desert lands, commander-in-chief of the army in the South and North, and director of the temples and priests of Ḥeru-ur of the Two Lands. Found near Lake Mareotis, about fifty miles from Rosetta, in 1785. XXVIth dynasty, about B.C. 575. Height 5 ft. 11 in. [No. 111.]

Presented by E. Fletcher, Esq., 1844.

819. (*Bay* 23.)—Portion of a black basalt **kneeling statue of Henta**, who was also called **Khnem-àb-Rā-men**, prefect of the temples and chief reader of the goddess Neith of Saïs, holding a shrine containing a figure of Neith sculptured in relief. On the base of the shrine is cut a petition to Neith that she will make the name of the deceased to flourish for ever, and on the base of the statue is inscribed a prayer for sepulchral offerings. XXVIth dynasty. [For the black basalt **sarcophagus of Henta,** see No. 828 (86).] Height 2 ft. [No. 134.]

Presented by Matthew Duane, Esq., 1771.

820. (*Bay* 24.)—Portion of a white limestone **figure of Ānkh-p-khart̥**, a divine father of Àmen, a libationer of Menu-Àmen-em-khut in Àbtet, and of Khensu-pa-khart̥, the son of the lady Khart̥-Menu, a sistrum bearer of Àmen, and of Tchet-Khensu-àf-ānkh, a priest and scribe. The deceased holds before him a shrine containing a figure, in relief, of Khensu-p-khart̥, the third member of the Theban triad. In the inscription the deceased says that he ministered in the temple for eighty years, and he begs Àmen to set up his house in the land of the living, and to grant him posterity, son following son for ever. XXVIth dynasty. Height 2 ft. 2 in. [No. 92.]

821. (*Bay* 22.)—Circular, black granite **libation bowl,** ornamented with a figure of the head of Hathor in relief, and inscribed with prayers for sepulchral offerings to Mut and Hathor. It was dedicated for use in the temple of Ȧmen-em-Apt, or Karnak, by **Mentu-em-ḥāt** , or **Mentu-em-ḥāt-senb** , an Erpā, Ḥā prince, chancellor, and *Smer uāt,* who was the second priest of one god, and fourth priest of another. XXVIth dynasty. From Thebes. Height 1 ft. 1 in., diameter 2 ft. 3 in. [No. 1292.]

822. (*Bay* 22.)—Massive black basalt **libation bowl,** ornamented with heads of the goddess Hathor, cut in sunk relief. After the XXVIth dynasty. Height 6 in., diameter 2 ft. 6 in. [No. 1386 (28*).]

Presented by R. Goff, Esq., 1848.

823. (*Bay* 25.)—**Cast** of a green basalt figure of the **Cow of Hathor,** wearing her characteristic head-dress, necklace, *menȧt,* etc., dedicated to a shrine of the goddess by **Psemthek (Psammetichus),** a *Smer uāt,* governor of the temple, inspector, councillor, superintendent of the palace, seal-bearer, and priest of the goddess Hathor. Under the chin of the cow stands a figure of Psammetichus, whose name and titles are cut upon his tunic. The original belongs to the period of the XXVIth dynasty, and is in the Egyptian Museum, Cairo. Height 3 ft. 2 in., length 3 ft. 2 in. [No. 1076.]

Presented by the Egyptian Government, 1890.

824. (*Bay* 26.)—**Cast** of a green basalt figure of the **hippopotamus goddess Smeṭsmeṭ** 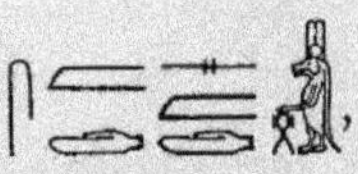, or Rert-rert 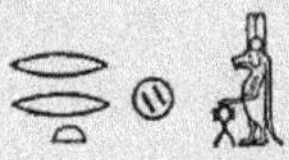, dedicated by **Pabasaȧ** , the son of Peṭā-Bast when Net-Ȧqert, the daughter of Psammetichus I, was high-priestess of Ȧmen. The deceased held the rank and offices of Erpā, Ḥā prince, chancellor, *Smer uāt,* priest of Ȧmen, superintendent of the prophets of the

South and the North, chief steward of the high priestess of Ȧmen, etc. The original is in the Egyptian Museum in Cairo. Height 3 ft. 4 in. [No. 1075.]

Presented by the Egyptian Government, 1890.

825. (*Bay* 26.)—Massive grey **granite sarcophagus** and cover, with one end rounded, of **Nes-qeṭiu** 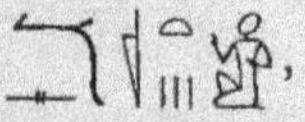, an Erpā, Ḥā prince, chancellor, *Smer uāt*, scribe in the library of Ȧmen-Rā, royal herald, libationer of the gods of the temples of Memphis, overseer of the treasury, etc., son of Ȧāḥmes, a priest of Uatchit, and the lady Ta-sa-en-ānkh 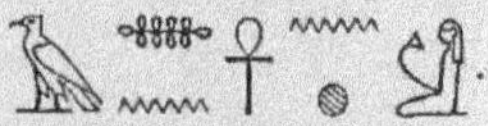. On the cover is sculptured, in relief, a bearded face, and down it are seventeen lines of text containing speeches of the four sons of Horus and addresses to the deceased. On the breast are figures of Nut, Isis, and Nephthys, and the four sons of Horus; on the foot is the figure of Isis. On the outside of the sarcophagus are cut figures of twenty-two protecting gods with appropriate inscriptions, on one end the boat of Ȧfu-Rā, and on the other two serpents, gods, etc. Found in Campbell's Tomb near the Pyramids of Gîzah. XXVIth dynasty. Length 8 ft. 2 in., breadth 3 ft. 6 in., height 4 ft. 8 in., weight about 5½ tons. [No. 3.]

Presented by Colonel Howard Vyse, 1839.

826. (*Bay* 25.)—Grey granite **sarcophagus of Ḥāp-men** 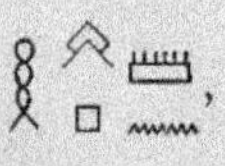, who was surnamed **Khensu-tef** 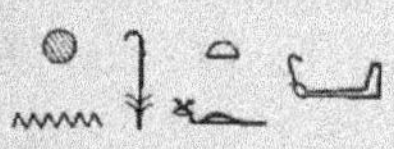, son of the lady Ḥetep-Ȧmen-ȧtef-s 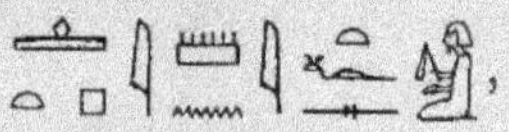, an Erpā, a Ḥā prince, *Smer uāt*, scribe of the revenues of Egypt, chief of the royal scribes, overseer of the scribes of the taxes, director of the granaries, general of the army, etc. On the outside of the sarcophagus are sculptured figures of Nephthys, Isis, the four sons of Horus, Anubis, , etc. On the bottom, inside, is a full length figure of the goddess of Ȧmenti, and on the sides and ends are cut figures of the twenty-one gods and goddesses who protected the various members of the body of the deceased. This sarcophagus was found in Cairo, where it was used as a water tank, and a hole was drilled at one end to empty it when necessary. XXVIth dynasty. Length 9 feet, width 4 ft. 7 in., height 3 ft. 11 in., weight about 7 tons 4 cwts. [No. 23.]

Presented by His Majesty King George III, 1801.

827. (*Bay* 27.)—Grey **basalt coffin of Uaḥ-åb-Rā,** overseer of the scribes of the *Ḥat*, inspector of scribes, and overseer of royal scribes, in the form of a bearded, mummied man, wearing a heavy wig and necklace. On the front of the cover are three lines of large well-cut hieroglyphics, containing the deceased's "beautiful name" and titles, and the statement that he "shall rise like a lily in the beautiful lake of Nefer-Tem," and shall "see the gods daily." Round the upper edge of the coffin is a line of text in which it is declared that Horus shall come and embrace the deceased, who shall appear in the sky, be born in heaven, and live with the gods. From "Campbell's Tomb" at Gîzah. XXVIth dynasty. (**Plate XXXI.**) Length 8 ft. 3 in., breadth 3 ft. 10 in., height 3 ft. 6 in., weight about 4 tons 9 cwt. [No. 1384.]

828. (*Bay* 27.)—Black **basalt coffin of Henta**, or **Henåatå**, who was also called **Khnem-åb-Rā-men**, prefect of the temples, and chief reader of the goddess Neith of Saïs, inscribed on the upper edge, outside, with two texts describing his felicity in the Other World. Found on the bank of the Nile at Bûlâḳ. XXVIth dynasty. [For the **statue of Henta** see No. 819 (134).] Height 7 ft. 6 in. [No. 86.]

Presented by His Majesty King George III, 1801.

829. (*Bay* 28.)—Grey **basalt coffin of Psemthek,** son of Pathenf, in the form of a bearded, mummied man, wearing a heavy wig and an elaborate pectoral with hawks' heads. On the front of the cover are eight lines of large well-cut hieroglyphics, containing a series of short sentences which refer to the happiness of the deceased in heaven with the gods, and round the upper edge of the coffin is a line of text in which it is asserted that the deceased shall never perish.

(*To face page* 230.)

[Grey basalt sarcophagus of Uaḥ-āb-Rā, an inspector of scribes.
[Bay 27, No. 827.] XXVIth dynasty, or later.

The phrases are extracted from texts which are as old as the Pyramids. XXVIth dynasty, or later. Length 8 ft. 3 in., breadth 3 ft. 3 in., height 2 ft. 8 in., weight about 3 tons 16 cwt. [No. 1047.]

Presented by the Egypt Exploration Fund, 1888.

830. (*Bay* 14.)—Grey granite **tablet for offerings** of a high ecclesiastical official who was priest of Neith, Horus, Sebek, and several other gods, on which are cut, in outline, two lakes of water, and a tablet for offerings , on which are two trees (sycamores), loaves of bread, cakes, etc. Near the edges is a well-cut channel by which the libations ran off the altar to the ground. XXVIth dynasty. Length 1 ft. 10 in., breadth 2 ft. 2 in. [No. 1340.]

831. (*Bay* 14.)—Grey granite **tablet for offerings of Ānkh-p-kharṭ** , the son of Àsàr-ser , and the lady Nes-p-Ḥeru-Rā , a scribe, chancellor, and priest of several gods. In it is sunk a rectangular tank, with a channel leading to the spout, and on it are sculptured figures of four bread-cakes and two libation jars. On the margins are cut a text containing the names and titles of the deceased and prayers for sepulchral offerings. XXVIth dynasty. Length 2 ft. 4 in., breadth 1 ft. 11 in. [No. 1284.]

832. (*Bay* 14.)—Schist **tablet for offerings of Tai-nekht-en-Uast** , the son of Bak-ref and Utcha-pes, sculptured with figures of birds, cakes, vases, etc., and inscribed with prayers to Osiris of the Staircase 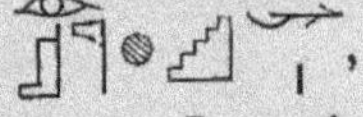, Àmsu, and Osiris of Qebti. XXVIth dynasty. Length 1 ft. 0½ in., breadth 10½ in. [No. 1202.]

833. (*Bay* 14.)—Limestone **tablet for offerings**, on the margins of which is a hieroglyphic inscription of which only a few signs are legible. Found near the temple of Ptaḥ at Memphis. XXVIth dynasty (?) Length 10 in., breadth 1 ft. 1 in. [No. 703.]

834. (*Bay* 16.)—Black granite **tablet for offerings,** inscribed on the face and sides with extracts from Chapters of the Book of the Dead which relate to funeral offerings. In the centre are sculptured, in relief, figures of a vase and two cakes of bread, and on each side of these is sunk a "tank," in the form of a cartouche. XXVIth dynasty. Length 2 ft. 2 in., breadth 2 ft. 1 in. [No. 1354.]

835. (*Bay* 16.)—Uninscribed sandstone **tablet for offerings,** on which are sculptured two libation vases, two water-fowl, a vessel of wine, and eight bread-cakes, four on each side of the wine jar. XXVIth dynasty. Length 2 ft. 4 in., breadth 1 ft. 10 in. [No. 596.]

836. (*Bay* 16.)—Black granite **tablet for offerings of Basa** , the son of Ȧmen-em-Ȧnt , and the lady Nefer-Net , inscribed with prayers to Rā-Harmachis and Ȧsȧr Khenti-Ȧmenti for sepulchral offerings. On the surface are sculptured in relief, figures of bread-cakes, geese, libation vases, etc.; the spout is wanting. XXVIth dynasty. Length 1 ft. 8 in., breadth 1 ft. 1 in. [No. 967.]

837. (*Bay* 17.)—Seated black granite **figure of Neser-Ȧmen** 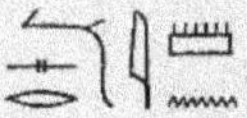, the son of Ānkh-f-en-Khensu and the lady Nes-khensu. In front of him is sculptured a figure of Rā-Harmachis, and the sides are decorated with scenes in which the deceased is represented adoring Osiris, Ȧmen, Mut, Khensu, and Isis and Nephthys (in the form of woman-headed winged serpents), the Ṭeṭ, etc. The deceased held several priestly offices. XXVIth dynasty. Height 1 ft. 3 in. [No. 1197.]

838. (*Bay* 19.)—Fragment of an inscribed limestone **slab** from a temple. XXVIth dynasty. Height 3½ in., width 9 in. [No. 787.]

839. (*Bay* 19.)—Portion of an **inscribed limestone slab** from the tomb of the chief *Kher-heb* priest **Peṭā-Ȧmen-Ȧpt** at Assasîf, in Western Thebes. XXVIth dynasty. Height 7 in., width 1 ft. 3 in. [No. 786.]

Presented by Sir J. Bowring, 1848.

840. (*Bay* 19.)—Portion of an **inscribed limestone slab** from the wall of a tomb; the hieroglyphics and dividing lines are deeply cut and painted, the former in dark green and the latter in red. From Ṣaḳḳârah. XXVIth dynasty. Height 1 ft. 2½ in., width 1 ft. 3½ in. [No. 458.]

841. (*Bay* 19.)—Rectangular limestone **slab** from the tomb of **Nakhi** , a judge, and his wife **Nefert-ȧri** 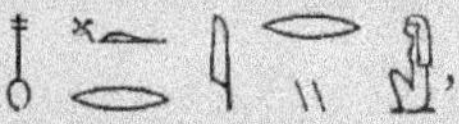, on which are sculptured two scenes. In the first the deceased and his wife are standing in adoration before Rā-Ḥeru-Khuti and praising the "lord of the gods," and in the second they are adoring Osiris Khenti Ȧmenti Unnefer, the lord of Abydos. From Thebes. Belmore Collection. Height 9½ in., width 2 ft. 9 in. [No. 281.]

842. (*Bay* 19.)—Dark green granite **stele**, with rounded top, of **Nekau** , a high ecclesiastical and civil official who flourished at Saïs in the reign of one of the Psammetichus kings. In the centre, at the top, is the upper portion of the framework of a niche in the form of a sepulchral coffer; on the right is a hollow, the purpose of which is unknown, and on the left are sculptured, in relief, figures of the deceased and his brother **Nekht-Ḥeru-ḥeb** 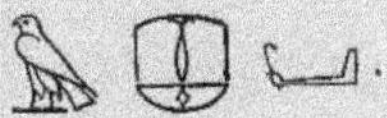. Their mother was a royal kinswoman. From the collection of Sir Hans Sloane. XXVIth dynasty. Height 1 ft. 5 in., width 1 ft. 7 in. [No. 511.]

843. (*Bay* 20.)—Painted limestone **sepulchral stele**, with rounded top, of **Tchaiu-taiu** , the son of Pa-ba , on which are cut figures of:—
1. The winged disk. 2. The deceased adoring Rā-Harmachis. 3. His son 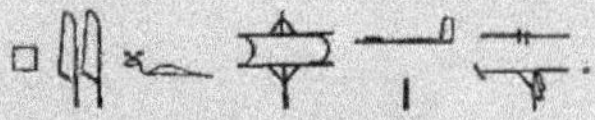. 4. A prayer to Rā-Harmachis for sepulchral offerings. The deceased was the

"chief barber of the temple of Osiris" = . From Akhmîm. XXVIth dynasty. Height 1 ft. 4 in., width 11 in. [No. 1317.]

844. (*Bay* 20.)—Sandstone **sepulchral stele,** with rounded top, of **Utcha-rens** , the daughter of Meḥi , on which are painted figures of:—1. The

Sepulchral monument of Nekau and Nekht-Ḥeru-ḥeb.
[Bay 19, No. 842.] XXVIth dynasty.

winged disk. 2. The deceased adoring Rā in his boat and Temu, Isis, and Nephthys. 3. A prayer addressed to Rā-Ḥeru-Khuti and the gods for sepulchral meals. Belmore Collection. XXVIth dynasty. Height 1 ft. 2 in., width 9½ in. [No. 331.]

845. (*Bay* 20.)—Limestone **sepulchral stele,** with rounded top, of **Khā-em-ȧpt**, a scribe, son of the lady Ḥunru, on which are cut figures of four deities, and an inscription in which the deceased prays for "glory "before Rā, strength before Sab, and the word of power in the "Other World." After the XXVIth dynasty. Height 9 in., width 6 in. [No. 877.]

Presented by Sir J. Bowring, 1848.

846. (*Bay* 21.)—Limestone **sepulchral stele,** with rounded top, of **Ka . . . s-Bast**, the daughter of Ḥeru and Nefert, on the upper part of which is cut a figure of the deceased adoring Rā, Kheperȧ, Isis, and Nephthys, who are seated in a boat under the winged disk, and followed by the ape Beḥuṭet. Below are a row of *khakeru* ornaments, and a text containing a prayer to the gods for sepulchral offerings. Sams Collection. XXVIth dynasty. Height 1 ft. 1½ in., width 8½ in. [No. 330.]

847. (*Bay* 21.)—Portion of **stele,** or slab, from the wall of a tomb of an official, who flourished under the IVth dynasty, and is represented seated on a chair of state, receiving the adoration of his son. The inscription was partly erased under the XXVIth dynasty, and the name and titles of **Pa-ȧu**, a priest of Neith, were inscribed by his eldest son Nema (?), who was also a priest of Neith. From the Fayyûm. Height 1 ft. 1 in., width 1 ft. 8 in. [No. 1042.]

Presented by H. Martyn Kennard, Esq., 1888.

848. (*Bay* 21.)—Limestone **sepulchral stele,** with rounded top, of **Katchakatcha**, a priestess of Menu, the daughter of Ḥeru-sa-Ȧst (whose forefathers for five generations had been priests) and the lady. On the upper portion are cut figures of the winged disk of Ḥeru-Beḥuṭet, the deceased adoring Rā-Harmachis, and the disk of Rā in his boat supported by a god, on one side of which stands the Soul of Rā, and on the other the Soul of Àtem. The text contains a prayer to Rā-Harmachis and Àtem for sepulchral offerings. From Akhmîm. XXVIth dynasty. Height 2 ft. 2 in., width 1 ft. 4 in. [No. 1138.]

849. (*Bay* 21.)—Sandstone **sepulchral stele,** with rounded top, of **Nes-pa-āa-tcharu** 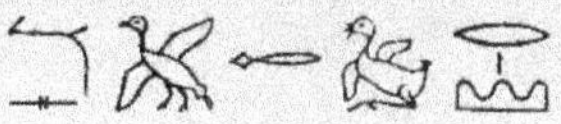, son of Ānkh-àuf , on which are cut figures of:—1. The winged disk. 2. The deceased adoring Rā in his boat. 3. A prayer to Rā-Harmachis, Khnemu-Rā, Sepṭ, and Ānqet, for a happy burial in Àmentet. XXVIth dynasty. Height 1 ft. 3 in., width 8 in. [No. 912.]

850. (*Bay* 21.)—Portion of a **relief** from the tomb of a chancellor and *Smer uāt*, on which is sculptured the figure of a *sem* priest, etc. XXVIth dynasty. Height 1 ft. 8 in., width 6 in. [No. 836.]

851. (*Bay* 24.)—Painted limestone **stele,** with rounded top, on which are sculptured figures of four women, Nes-Ḥeru-p-Kharṭ, Tcha-Ḥet-Ḥert-mu, Nes-urit, and another, standing in adoration before Rā-Harmachis. XXVIth dynasty. Height 1 ft. 1 in., width 10½ in. [No. 798.]

852. (*Bay* 21.)—Granite **sepulchral stele,** with rounded top, of **Tai-seshep-pet . . . . àbth** 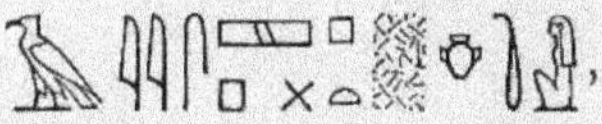, daughter of Ta-Bes 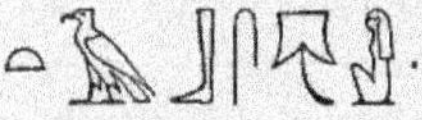. On the upper portion are cut a figure of the winged disk, with pendent uraei, and two scenes in which the deceased is represented adoring Horus and Temu, the rising and setting sun respectively. XXVIth dynasty. Height 1 ft. 2½ in., width 8 in. [No. 1086.]

853. (*Bay* 21.)—Portion of an **inscribed slab** from the wall of a tomb at Ṣaḳḳârah. Sams Collection. XXVIth dynasty. Height 1 ft. 1 in., width 1 ft. 3½ in. [No. 457.]

854. (*Bay* 21.)—Rectangular portion of a **slab** from the tomb of the royal kinsman **Ḥapi-mer**, the son of Peṭā-Ḥeru. XXVIth dynasty. Height 1 ft. 5 in., width 1 ft. 5 in. [No. 452.]

855. (*Bay* 21.)—Limestone **stele,** with rounded top, of **Ḥeru-qebḥ**, on which is sculptured, in high relief, a figure of Osiris; on one side of him, in flat relief, is a figure of Isis, and on the other, a figure of Nephthys. Above is the winged disk. XXVIth dynasty, or later. Height 1 ft. 10½ in., width 1 ft. 1 in. [No. 336.]

856. (*Bay* 21.)—Limestone **relief** from the wall of a tomb, on which are sculptured twelve figures of men and women who follow a funerary coffer borne upon staves on the shoulders of four ministrants, and form part of a funeral procession. D'Athanasi Collection. From Abydos. XXVIth dynasty. Length 2 ft. 10 in., height 1 ft. [No. 326.]

857-866. (*Bays* 22, 24.)—Series of limestone **slabs** from the tomb of **Uaḥ-åb-Rā-em-khut**, a chancellor, who flourished under the XXVIth dynasty, about B.C. 550, inscribed with extracts from Chapters of the Book of the Dead and vignettes illustrating the same. Anastasi Collection :—

857. Length 3 ft. 10 in. [No. 537.]
858. „ 3 ft. 6½ in. [No. 538.]
859. „ 3 ft. [No. 539.]
860. „ 2 ft. 4 in. [No. 540.]
861. „ 3 ft. 8½ in. [No. 541.]
862. „ 3 ft. [No. 542.]
863. „ 3 ft. 9½ in. [No. 543.]
864. „ 4 ft. [No. 544.]
865. „ 2 ft. 1 in. [No. 545.]
866. „ 2 ft. 9½ in. [No. 546.]

Average width 11 in.

867. (*Bay* 22.)—Lower portion of a black seated granite **figure of an official,** holding before him a Hathor-headed sistrum, the symbol of Hathor. The deceased was the governor of a city and a priest in the service of the "Lord of the Two Lands." His mother's name was Rā-merit, Feet restored. XXVIth dynasty. Height 1 ft. [No. 510.]
Presented by the Earl of Bute, 1767.

868. (*Bay* 22.)—Portion of a kneeling granite **figure of Ḥer-Bes**, or **Ḥar-Bes**, the son of Pif-māu, and Shebt-Ȧst, an official who was attached to the service of the throne, or throne chamber, holding before him an aegis of the goddess Hathor. Salt Collection. XXVIth dynasty. Height 10 in. [No. 514.]

869. (*Bay* 22.)—Limestone **sepulchral stele,** with rounded top, on which are cut a figure of the goddess Bast and a prayer to the goddess for sepulchral offerings. XXVIth dynasty. Height 1 ft. 1½ in., width 6 in. [No. 1017.]

870. (*Bay* 22.)—Painted limestone **sepulchral stele,** with rounded top, of **Ta-ḥes**, a priestess of Mut, on which are sculptured a winged disk and a figure of the deceased offering a mirror to Rā-Harmachis. XXVIth dynasty. Barker Collection. Height 1 ft. 2½ in., width 10½ in. [No. 347.]

871. (*Bay* 22.)—Limestone **figure,** of unusual shape, **of Mut-em-Ȧnt**, a sistrum-bearer of Ȧmen, Mut, and Khensu at Thebes. The deceased wears the head-dress of Hathor, and on her neck is cut the name of the double goddess Mut-Tefnut. XXVIth dynasty. From Thebes. Height 1 ft. 8 in. [No. 1198.]

872. (*Bay* 22.)—Red granite **head of a statue** of Neith, goddess of Saïs, wearing the Red Crown. From Memphis. XXVIth dynasty. Height 1 ft. 4 in. [No. 659.]

873. (*Bay* 23.)—Head of a green basalt **figure of the god Osiris,** wearing the White Crown, or of a king in the character of Osiris. XXVIth dynasty. Height 1 ft. 6 in. [No. 986.]

874. (*Bay* 24.)—Limestone **sepulchral stele,** with rounded top, of **Khā-nekhtu-en-Ḥeru**, the son of Tcha, on which is sculptured a scene representing the deceased adoring Osiris, Isis, and Horus, and several of his kinsfolk. Sams Collection. XXVIth dynasty. Height 1 ft. 2 in., width 10½ in. [No. 340.]

875. (*Bay* 24.)—White limestone **sepulchral stele,** with rounded top, of **Uaḥ-åb-Rā**, son of Ahen, and Her-åb-Net, on which are sculptured figures of the winged disk and the deceased adoring Osiris and Isis. Harris Collection. XXVIth dynasty. Height 1 ft. 7 in., width 10½ in. [No. 961.]

876. (*Bay* 24.)—Limestone **sepulchral stele,** with rounded top, of **Thi**, an Erpā, Hā prince, chancellor, *Smer uāt*, *sem* priest, high priest of Ptaḥ of Memphis, "the eyes of the king of the South and the ears of the king of the North." On it is sculptured a scene representing the deceased seated on a chair of state and receiving offerings from his son Sai, a *kher ḥeb* priest in the temple of Bast. XXVIth dynasty. Height 2 ft. 4 in., width 1 ft. 6 in. [No. 972.]

877. (*Bay* 24.)—**Torso** of a grey granite **figure of Nefer-renpit**, an Erpā, Hā prince, royal deputy and governor of a city, who held several priestly offices. XXVIth dynasty. Height 1 ft. 10 in. [No. 909.]

878. (*Bay* 25.)—Limestone **sepulchral stele,** with rounded top, of **Åsår-mes**, the son of Nes-Ḥeru, and the lady

Aṭepu , on which is sculptured a scene representing the deceased adoring Osiris and Isis, above whom is the winged disk. Salt Collection. XXVIth dynasty. Height 2 ft. 1 in., width 1 ft. 2½ in. [No. 548.]

879. (*Bay* **26.**)—Lower portion of a limestone, kneeling **figure of Ḥeru** , or **Ḥeru-á** , an Erpā, a Ḥā prince, and high-priest of Ptaḥ, holding before him a shrine in which is sculptured in relief a figure of Ptaḥ. The inscriptions contain prayers to Ptaḥ and Hathor for sepulchral offerings, etc. XXVIth dynasty. Height 1 ft. 1½ in., width 7 in. [No. 845.]

880. (*Bay* **28.**)—Portion of a **relief** from the wall of a temple sculptured with the face of a king, or prince, holding a Hathor-headed sistrum. Salt Collection. From a tomb near the Pyramids. XXVIth dynasty. Length 1 ft. 4 in., breadth 9 in. [No. 595.]

881. (*Bay* **28.**)—Black basalt **coffin of Sebek-sa** , or **Sa-Sebek,** a priest of Ptaḥ, director of the temples and governor of a city, inscribed with prayers to Ptaḥ-Seker-Ȧsár and Osiris, Lord of Ṭaṭṭu and Abṭu, for "glory in heaven "before Rā, power on earth before Seb, and triumph in Neter-"khert before Osiris," and for sepulchral offerings. Anastasi Collection. From Memphis (?). After the XXVIth dynasty. Length 7 ft. 6 in. [No. 17.]

882, 883. (*Bay* **23.**)—Portions of the grey granite **sarcophagus of Pep-ȧri-. . . .-sep** (?) (?), an Erpā, a Ḥā prince, chancellor, *Smer-uāt*, prefect of the temples, royal herald, overseer of the bowmen, chief of the scribes of the palace, etc., son of Nekht-Ḥeru-ḥeb, a prefect of the temples, and the lady Her-ȧb-Net . On the outside is cut a series of mythological figures, "circles," etc., from the Book "Ȧm-Ṭuat," and on the inside are several figures of gods and goddesses in the forms in which they were represented from the XXVIth dynasty onwards. XXVIth dynasty, or later. Length 5 ft. 4 in. [No. 66.] Length 7 ft. [No. 1387.]
No. 882 *was presented by His Majesty King George III*, 1801.

884. (*Bay* 25.)—Limestone **sepulchral stele,** with rounded top, of **Àn-ḥer-nekht** 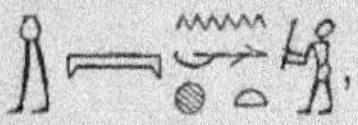, an *Ȧm ȧst* and Ka-priest, the son of Ḥeru-sa-Ȧst, and grandson of Tcheṭ-Ȧn-ḥer-ȧuf-āṅkh; his mother was 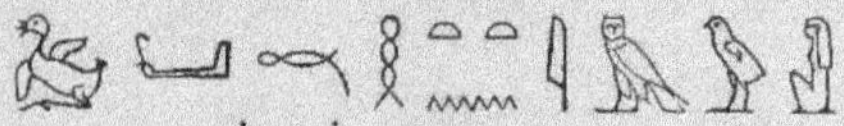, and was the daughter of the priest Ȧn-Ȧmen-nef-neb. On the upper portion are cut a winged disk and a scene representing the deceased and his father and mother adoring the symbol of the box which held the head of Osiris at Abydos. XXVIth dynasty, or later. Height 2 ft., width 1 ft. 4 in. [No. 809.]

885. (*Bay* 27.)—White limestone **sepulchral stele,** with rounded top, of **Ḥeru-nekht** , the daughter of Nes-Ḥeru, a priest, and Nes-Teft 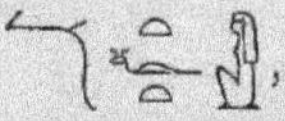, a sistrum-bearer of Menu, on which are sculptured:—1. Winged disk. 2. The jackal-gods Ȧnpu and Ȧp-uat. 3, 4. The deceased adoring Rā in his boat in the morning and evening, 5. Anubis and Osiris. 6. The souls of the deceased. 7. Horus and Osiris. Below are sixteen lines of text containing hymns to the rising and setting sun. From Akhmîm. XXVIth dynasty, or later. Height 2 ft. 1½ in., width 1 ft. 6½ in. [No. 1148.]

886. (*Bay* 28.)—Rectangular limestone **sepulchral stele** of **Un-nefer** 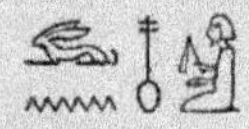, a priest of Menu, the son of Thent-Ȧmen, inscribed with thirty-six lines of hieroglyphic text. The first twenty-four lines contain prayers by the deceased against the attacks of the great serpent-fiend **Nāi** 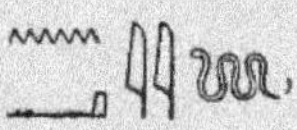, or Nāȧu , and the great Worm 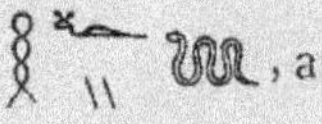, and a monster called **Sȧu** 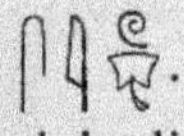. In line twenty-five begins the chapter of Ȧm-ā-f, and in line thirty-three another chapter, the recital of which was believed to keep away scorpions, snakes, and other noxious reptiles. The formulae resemble those found on the Metternich Stele. XXVIth dynasty, or later. Height 3 ft. 6 in., width 2 ft. 2 in. [No. 190.]

887. (*Bay* 24.)—Limestone **stele** sculptured with a representation of a man, whose name is not given, kneeling in adoration before the jackal-god Àp-uat and an uraeus on a standard, and the four jackals who tow the Boat of the Sun. Below are figures of fifty-nine jackals. XXVIth dynasty, or later. Height 1 ft. 8 in., width 9½ in. [No. 873.]

888. (*Bay* 24.)—Limestone **sepulchral stele,** with rounded top, of **Ptaḥ-nekhtu** 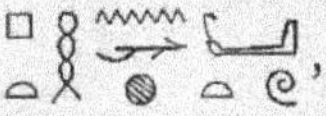, keeper of the library of Ptaḥ, on which are sculptured figures of the deceased and eighteen of his kinsfolk adoring Osiris and Isis. Salt Collection. From Abydos. XXVIth dynasty, or later. Height 1 ft. 7 in., width 11½ in. [No. 288.]

889. (*Bay* 25.)—Limestone **sepulchral stele,** with rounded top, of **Ḥeru-sa-Àst** 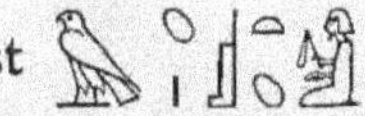, a priest, on which are sculptured in relief a figure of the winged disk, and two scenes in which the deceased is represented adoring Rā Ḥeru-khuti, the rising sun, and Temu, the setting sun. Below are two texts containing hymns of praise to these gods. XXVIth dynasty, or later. From Akhmîm. Height 3 ft. 4 in., width 1 ft. 11 in. [No. 624.]

890. (*Bay* 25.)—Limestone **sepulchral stele,** with rounded top, on which is sculptured a scene representing the deceased **Bastet (?) Ḥeru-khebit-sa** , son of Net-Àrṭāt , worshipping Ptah-Seker-Àsàr and Isis. Sams Collection. XXVIth dynasty, or later. Height 1 ft. 5 in., width 11 in. [No. 333.]

891. (*Bay* 16.)—Limestone **tablet for offerings of Àṭi** , which was made to his memory by his beloved son Àṭ . On the face are sculptured figures of cakes and libation vases, and at each end is cut a small rectangular tank. A deep channel runs to the spout from both ends. After the XXVIth dynasty. Length 1 ft. 5½ in., breadth 1 ft. 1½ in. [No. 1309.]

892. (*Bay* 16.)—Basalt **tablet for offerings**, on which are sculptured in relief a table with bread-cakes and flowers upon it, two libation jars, and clusters of water-lilies and papyrus plants. Above the table are two rectangular cavities. Anastasi Collection. After the XXVIth dynasty. Length 1 ft. 3 in., breadth 1 ft. 3 in. [No. 502.]

893. (*Bay* 19.)—Portion of a **relief** from the side of a grey granite sarcophagus on which are cut figures of several of the gods who assisted in the reconstruction of the morning sun by bringing arrows of light and disks. The scene forms part of the illustration of the XIth Division of the BOOK OF GATES. After the XXVIth dynasty. Height 1 ft., width 1 ft. 1 in. [No. 516.]

Head from the statue of a king, or prince.
[Bay 25, No. 895.]
XXVIth dynasty, or later.

894. (*Bay* 25.)—**Head** from a grey granite statue of an Egyptian official. From Benha. After the XXVIth dynasty. Height 1 ft. [No. 1316.]

895. (*Bay* 25.)—**Head** from a grey granite statue of an Egyptian prince. From Benha. After the XXVIth dynasty. Height 1 ft. [No. 633.]

896. (*Bay* 29.)—Limestone **sepulchral stele,** with rounded top, of **Pentebḥi** 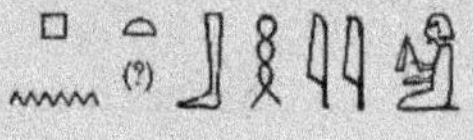, son of Ptaḥ-ārtās , on which are sculptured the winged disk and figures of Osiris, Isis, and of deceased persons making offerings. After the XXVIth dynasty. Height 1 ft. 3½ in., width 10 in. [No. 395.]

897. (*Bay* 29.)—Grey granite **statue of a king** or prince, uninscribed. From Benha. After the XXVIth dynasty. Height 3 ft. [No. 1209.]

898. (*Bay* **31.**)—Colossal limestone **hawk,** sacred to Horus and Rā-Harmachis. After the XXVIth dynasty. Height 3 ft. [No. 1420 (59*).]

Presented by T. Philipe, Esq., 1805.

Statue of a king or prince. [Bay 29, No. 897.]

899. (*Bay* **14.**)—Limestone libation **tablet** with deep channel on all sides leading to the spout. Salt Collection. Late Period. Length 9 in., width 11 in. [No. 423.]

900. (*Bay* **14.**)—Limestone **tablet for offerings,** uninscribed. In the face of the tablet are cut three rectangular tanks, with sloping sides, and figures of a haunch of beef, a cake, etc. Late Period. Length 1 ft. 5½ in., breadth 1 ft. 1 in. [No. 704.]

901. (*Bay* **14.**)—Black stone **tablet for offerings of Seqin** , or , the son of the lady Qersh , inscribed with a prayer to Rā-Harmachis, Shu, Tem, and Osiris for sepulchral offerings. On the face are sculptured in relief figures of bread-cakes, geese, vegetables, etc., and a deep channel to carry the libations to the spout is provided. Anastasi Collection. Late Period. Length 1 ft. 10½ in., breadth 2 ft. [No. 509.]

902. (*Bay* **14.**)—Green schist **tablet for offerings,** sculptured in relief with figures of geese, bread-cakes, vases, etc., and inscribed with a prayer to Osiris for sepulchral offerings. Late Period. Length 9 in., breadth 9½ in. [No. 1310.]

903. (*Bay* **14.**)—Red terra-cotta **tablet for offerings,** on which are stamped figures of four cakes. Late Period. Length 10 in., breadth 1 ft. [No. 181.]

904. (*Bay* 15.)—Portion of a black granite kneeling **statue** of a high ecclesiastical official, whose father and grandfather were high-priests of Memphis. The pedestal is restored. Late Period. Height 3 ft. 8 in. [No. 25.]

Presented by His Majesty King George III, 1801.

905. (*Bay* 16.)—Uninscribed limestone **tablet for offerings,** sculptured in relief with a table of offerings, *i.e.*, bread, cakes, flowers, vessels of wine, etc., flanked by clusters of papyrus and lily plants. Above the table are two cavities into which the libations were poured. Sams Collection. Length 1 ft. 5½ in., breadth 1 ft. 5 in. [No. 418.]

906. (*Bay* 16.)—Uninscribed sandstone **tablet for offerings,** with cavities for libations, on which are sculptured libation vases, etc. From Akhmîm. Rough work of a Late Period. Length 2 ft., breadth 1 ft. 1 in. [No. 1051.]

907. (*Bay* 16.)—Uninscribed sandstone **tablet for offerings,** with a rectangular cavity, intended to represent a tank of water, on each side of which is a flight of steps. The face is ornamented with palm branches. Belmore Collection. Late Period. Length 8 in., breadth 10 in. [No. 554.]

908. (*Bay* 16.)—Uninscribed sandstone **tablet for offerings,** on which are sculptured, in three divisions, libation jars, flowers, loaves of bread, etc. From Aswân. Late Period. Length 1 ft. 5½ in., breadth 1 ft. 1½ in. [No. 1050.]

909. (*Bay* 17.)—Sandstone **libation tank,** in the form of a table, with a massive solid support at each end. The front is decorated with a cornice, below which is sculptured a row of lotus flowers, or lilies, some in full bloom and others in bud. Late Period. Length 2 ft. 8 in., breadth 1 ft. 2½ in., height 1 ft. 4 in. [No. 800.]

Presented by W. R. Hamilton, Esq., 1839.

910. (*Bay* 16.)—Limestone **tablet for offerings,** to which are attached two large deep circular receptacles, in the place of tanks, for libations. On the face of the tablet are sculptured figures of cakes, a libation vase, etc. On one end are figures of the deceased and his wife, seated on chairs of state, receiving offerings from their son; and on one side of the spout are figures of their relatives, Ȧrit-ru, Tcheṭ-āb (?), Tcheṭ-Khensu, etc. Late Period. Length 1 ft. 1 in., breadth 1 ft. 4½ in., depth 9 in. [No. 1302.]

911. (*Bay* 17.)—Portion of a limestone **relief,** on which are sculptured the figures of a priest and his wife with their hands raised in adoration. Sams Collection. Late Period. Height 8½ in., width 10 in. [No. 450.]

912. (*Bay* 19.)—Limestone **sepulchral stele,** with rounded top, on the upper part of which are sculptured in high relief the busts of a man and a woman. Below, traced in black outline, is the upper portion of a figure of the deceased (?), seated with a table of offerings before him. Late Period. Belmore Collection. Height 9 in., width 6 in. [No. 270.]

913. (*Bay* 20.)—Sandstone **coffin and cover** of a woman, whose name is illegible, ornamented on the sides with figures of the four sons of Horus, Anubis, Ȧp-uat, Nephthys, and other gods of the dead. It was found by Belzoni, who "restored" the painted figures. Late Period. Length 6 ft. 8 in. [No. 39.]

Presented by the Earl of Belmore, 1820.

914. (*Bay* 24.)—Limestone **stele,** with rounded top, on which are cut, in outline, figures of twenty-three ibises. Late Period. Height 1 ft., width 10½ in. [No. 927.]

915. (*Bay* 24.)—Limestone **stele,** with rounded top, on which is sculptured a representation of a deceased person paying homage to a figure of the jackal-god Ȧp-uat and to an uraeus on a standard, and to four jackals, which are called the "jackals of Pharaoh" 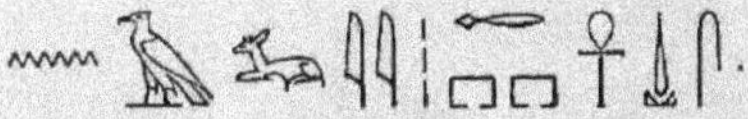. Late Period. Height 11 in., width 8 in. [No. 891.]

916. (*Bay* 24.)—Painted limestone **stele,** on which are cut the figures of a man and a woman standing in adoration at a table of offerings; which they present to the four jackals that towed the Boat of Rā. Late Period. Height 1 ft. 1 in., width 9 in. [No. 896.]

917. (*Bay* 28.)—Grey granite **sepulchral stele,** with rounded top, of a "royal mother" , sculptured with a scene representing the deceased adoring Osiris, Isis, and Anubis, and a winged disk. Below is cut a text containing a prayer for sepulchral offerings. The hieroglyphics in the cartouche containing the queen's name are uncertain, for they are badly cut, and the surface of the stone has been damaged. From Philae. Late Period. Height 3 ft., width 1 ft. 10 in. [No. 1289.]

918. (*Bay* 29.)—Portion of a sandstone **relief**, on which is sculptured the figure of the god of "hundreds of thousands of "years." On his head is the solar disk, with uraei, and in each hand he holds the notched palm branch, resting on , the symbol of eternity. He is seated on the sign for gold , and above his head is , the sky. Late Period. Height 1 ft., width 8½ in. [No. 894.]

919, 920. (*Bays* 31 and 32.)—Two black **basalt obelisks** (pyramidions wanting) which were dedicated to "Thoth, "the Twice-great" , by **Nekht-Ḥeru-ḥebt**

,

the **Nektanebês** of the Greeks, king of Egypt, about B.C. 378. The inscriptions record the names and titles of this king, and state that the obelisks were set up by the doorway of the shrine chamber of the temple of Thoth. These obelisks were removed at some period during the eighteenth century from the ruins of a town in the Delta, and were taken to Cairo, where for many years they stood before one of the mosques. They passed into the possession of the British in 1801, and were brought to London in 1802. XXXth dynasty. Height 9 ft. [No. 523.] Height 8 ft. 5 in. [No. 524.]

Presented by His Majesty King George III, 1802.

921. (*Bay* 30.)—Portion of a black granite seated **statue** of the god **Åmen** (?) holding before him a standing figure of **Nekht-Ḥeru-ḥebt** (the Nektanebês of the Greeks), king of Egypt, about B.C. 378. Height 3 ft. 5 in. [No. 1421 (*70b*).]

922. (*Bay* 25.)—Side of a red **granite shrine**, on which are sculptured:—1. Figures of the Golden Horus and cartouches containing the prenomen and nomen of **Nekht-Ḥeru-ḥebt**, the **Nektanebês** of the Greeks, king of Egypt, about B.C. 378. 2. A figure of the king adoring Bast, and his names and titles. 3. Figures of the king performing a religious ceremony. From Bubastis. XXXth dynasty. Height 5 ft. 7 in., width 3 ft. 2 in. [No. 1106.]

Presented by the Egypt Exploration Fund, 1891.

923. (*Bay* 25.)—Massive agglomerate **sarcophagus of Nekht-Ḥeru-ḥebt** , the Nektanebês of Greek writers, king of Egypt, about B.C. 378. The **inside** is decorated with figures of gods of the dead, all now, more or less, effaced; among them being the four sons of Horus—Mesthȧ, Ḥāpi, Ṭua-mutef, and Qebḥsennuf—and Anubis. At the head and foot are figures of Isis and Nephthys, with outstretched arms, kneeling upon signs for "gold" , and above, all round the edge, is a border formed of the symbols for "stability" and "protection" . The **outside** is covered with series of texts and vignettes from the Ist, IInd, IIIrd, VIth, VIIIth and IXth Sections of the Book entitled "That which is in the Ṭuat" (or Other World). This work illustrates the passage of the Night Sun through the twelve Sections of the Ṭuat, and was intended to form a guide to that region, and to help the souls of the dead to pass from this world to the next in safety. The **First Section** is cut on the rounded head of the sarcophagus, and it describes the region of the Ṭuat which was passed through by the Sun-god during the first hour of the night. The region is called Net-Rā. In the two centre registers we see the Boat of Rā with his attendant gods, and the Boat of Osiris with his attendant gods. Above and below are figures of the gods who sang praises to Rā as he travelled onwards. The **Second Section**, which represents the region of Urnes, is cut on the right side of the sarcophagus, and contains the "fairy boats" with which Rā travelled; they contain the moon, the Hathor fetish, the Lizard-god, and the Grain-gods. Above and below are the various gods who preside over the seasons of the year, the harvest, etc., and those who minister to the needs of the Sun-god, and light his way and destroy his enemies. The **Third Section**, which

PLATE XXXII.

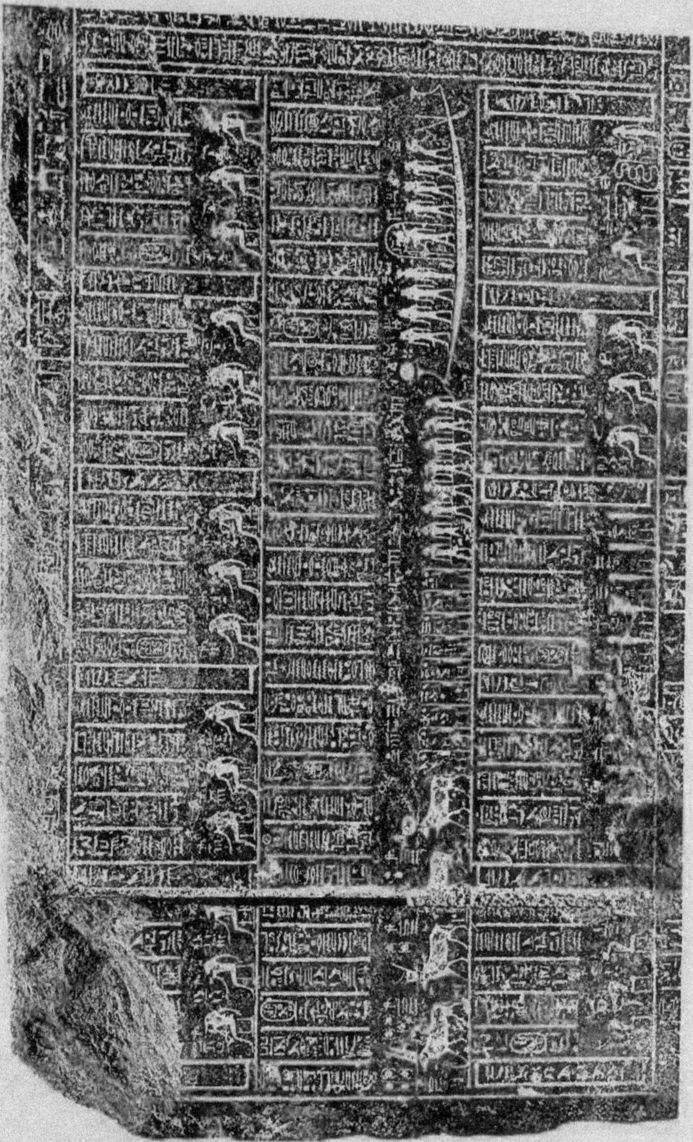

The journey of the Sun-god through the Eighth Section of the Other World. From the sarcophagus of Nekht-Ḥeru-ḥebt, king of Egypt, B.C. 378. [Bay 25, No. 923.]

The journey of the Sun-god through the Third Section of the Other World. From the sarcophagus of Nekht-Ḥeru-ḥebt, king of Egypt, B.C. 378.
[Bay 25, No. 923.]

represents the region of Net-neb-uā-kheper-âut, is cut on the left side of the sarcophagus, and contains three boats, wherein are gods who assisted the Sun-god. Above and below are the gods who destroyed the Sebâ fiend and his attendants, and who burned up with the fire from their bodies all those who tried to block the path of the Sun-god, These gods also made the Nile to flow. The **Sixth Section,** which represents the region Metchet-mu-nebt-Ṭuat, is cut on the right side of the sarcophagus near the foot. It contained the abode of kings and of the spirits of the great, and the chambers of Rā. The beings who were therein came to life when they heard the words of the Sun-god, and rendered him service. The **Eighth Section,** which represents the region Tebat-neteru-s, is cut on the left side of the sarcophagus, near the foot; it contained a series of "circles," or abodes of gods, who came into life when the Sun-god appeared, and performed their service, and wailed loudly when he departed from them. The **Ninth Section,** which represents the region Best-âru-ānkhet-kheperu, is cut upon the foot of the sarcophagus. In it dwelt the gods who provided new light and fire for the Sun-god, and prepared his material form for new birth. The remaining six sections of the book "That which is in the Ṭuat" were probably cut upon the cover of the sarcophagus, which was destroyed in ancient days. The lower portion of each side of the sarcophagus, and of the head and foot, contains a selection from the "Book of Praises" of the Seventy-five Forms of the Sun-god Rā, with figures of thirty-seven of these Forms. This sarcophagus was found in the courtyard of a building at Alexandria, dedicated to St. Athanasius, where it is said to have been used for some hundreds of years as a bath. To facilitate the removal of the sediment of the muddy Nile water, twelve holes were drilled through the sides and ends of the sarcophagus on a level with the bottom inside. (**Plates XXXII, XXXIII.**) Weight about 6 tons 17 cwt., length 10 ft. $3\frac{1}{2}$ in., breadth 5 ft. $3\frac{3}{4}$ in., height 3 ft. $10\frac{3}{4}$ in. [No. 10.]

924. (*Bay* 29.)—Upper portion of a dark granite **statue of Nekht-neb-f,** the Nektanebos of the Greeks, the last native king of Egypt, who reigned about B.C. 358. The king's prenomen , is cut on the front of his girdle. From Memphis. XXXth dynasty. Height 2 ft. 6 in. [No. 44.]

Presented by Colonel Howard Vyse, 1839.

925. (*Bay* 27.)—Portion of a grey granite **statue of Nekht-neb-f,** the **Nektanebos** of the Greeks, the last native king of Egypt, about B.C. 358. On the plinth behind is an inscription recording his names and titles, and mention is made of Sepṭ and Ḥeru Bakha, gods of the Eastern Delta. XXXth dynasty. Height 2 ft. 3 in. [No. 1013.]

926. (*Bay* 27.)—Black basalt **intercolumnar slab,** from a temple built near the modern city of Alexandria by **Nekht-neb-f,** the **Nektanebos** of the Greeks, the last native king of Egypt, about B.C. 358. On the obverse is sculptured a kneeling figure of the king presenting an offering to a god, and above are inscribed his names and titles. On the reverse the king's names and titles are repeated. From Alexandria. XXXth dynasty. Height 4 ft., width 3 ft. 2 in. [No. 22.]

Presented by His Majesty King George III, 1766.

927. (*Bay* 28.)—Black basalt **intercolumnar slab,** with a deep cornice ornamented with a row of hawks, sculptured with a figure of **Nekht-neb-f,** or **Nektanebos,** king of Egypt, about B.C. 358, who is represented kneeling and making offerings to a god. Found in the ruins of the temple at Rosetta. XXXth dynasty. Height 4 ft., width 2 ft. 6 in. [No. 998.]

Presented by His Majesty King George III, 1766.

928. (*Bay* 23.)—Cover of the limestone **coffin of the lady Khartʼ-Ȧst** 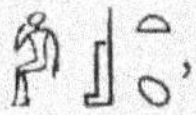, with painted head-dress, eyes, and eye-brows. Down the front are three lines of hieroglyphics, inlaid with green paste, containing the names and titles of Osiris, and a short address to the gods of the dead. XXXth dynasty (?) Height 6 ft. [No. 1331.]

929. (*Bay* 24.)—Limestone **sepulchral stele,** with rounded top, of **Ȧser** (?)  (?) on which are painted a winged disk and a scene representing two men and a woman adoring Rā-Harmachis. From Akhmîm. XXXth dynasty. Height 1 ft. 6 in., width 1 ft. [No. 337.]

930. (*Bay* 29.)—Portion of a **relief,** on which is sculptured the head of a king, or prince, wearing the lock of youth on the right side of his head. From Elephantine. XXXth dynasty, or later. Height 5 in., width 4 in. [No. 862.]

931. (*Bay* 24.)—Limestone **sepulchral stele,** with rounded top, of **Un-nefer-å** , a scribe and priest, on which is sculptured a scene representing the deceased standing on the top of the steps leading to a shrine containing a standard with a top in the form of the box which held the head of Osiris at Abydos, and two other holy standards. His right hand is raised towards the shrine, and in his left he holds a censer. His mother's name was Utchat-ren-s, and that of his father Rer. XXXth dynasty. Height 1 ft. 4 in., width 11 in. [No. 808.]

932. (*Bay* 24.)—Limestone **stele,** with rounded top, of **Pkhar-Khensu** , the son of Tcheṭ-ḥrå, on which are sculptured in relief:—1. The winged disk. 2. Twelve votive ears. 3. A figure of Menu-Åmen-Rā-ka-mut-f standing in a sacred tree. XXXth dynasty. Height 2 ft., width 1 ft. 3½ in. [No. 911.]

933. (*Bay* 24.)—Limestone **sepulchral stele,** with rounded top, of **Nes-Åmen** 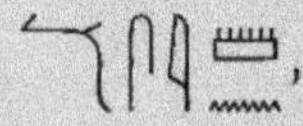, a priest of Ån-Ḥer, overseer of the prophets, *Ka* priest, etc., son of Ṭāt-Åmen-ḥeb and Ta-khaā-en-Bastet, sculptured with figures of the deceased adoring Rā-Harmachis and Temu under a winged disk. XXXth dynasty. Height 1 ft. 9 in., width 1 ft. 2½ in. [No. 1333.]

934. (*Bay* 25.)—Cover of a fine white **marble coffin,** in the form of a man, wearing a wig, necklace, pectoral, etc., of **Peṭā-Ḥeru-Ḥap-ḥap** , son of Ren-rut. Down the front are six lines of hieroglyphics in which the deceased is adjured to "live, become renewed, and be young," and is promised the help of the gods in the Other World. On the sides are figures of ten gods, viz.: Åmseth, Ḥāpi, Ṭuamutef, Qebḥsennuf, Ḥeq, Maa-tef, Årmāuai, Åri-ren-f, Kher-beq-f, and Ḥeru-ån-maati. On the foot are figures of Isis, Nephthys, and the jackal-gods Åp-uat and Ånpu. XXXth dynasty. Height 6 ft. 5 in. [No. 790.]

Presented by the Marquis of Northampton, 1852.

935. (*Bay* 25.)—Limestone **sepulchral stele,** with rounded top, of a priest or official whose name is illegible, on which are traced in black outline a figure of a winged disk, and a scene representing the deceased making offerings to Rā, Ȧnpu, Isis, and Nephthys. Below are the remains of five lines of text containing a prayer for funerary offerings. XXXth dynasty. Height 1 ft. 1 in., width 9½ in. [No. 1180.]

936. (*Bay* 25.)—Sandstone **sepulchral stele,** uninscribed, with rounded top, on which are cut in outline a figure of the winged disk, , the jackals of Ȧnpu and Ȧp-uat, and a scene representing the deceased and two members of his family adoring Rā - Harmachis. Sams Collection. XXXth dynasty. Height 1 ft. 6 in., width 1 ft. 1½ in. [No. 352.]

The god Ȧn-Ḥer, spearing an animal, symbol of evil.
[Bay 25, No. 937.]

937. (*Bay* 25.)—Limestone **stele,** on which is sculptured, in relief, an entrance to a shrine, with pillars having lotus capitals, a cornice with uraei, a winged disk, and a figure of the god **Ȧn-Ḥer** spearing an animal. XXXth dynasty. Height 1 ft. 7½ in., width 9 in. [No. 1217.]

938. (*Bay* 25.)—Portion of a limestone **sepulchral stele of Peṭā-ās** (?), a scribe chancellor, and priest of Khensu - em - Uast Nefer-ḥetep, Hathor, Ȧmen-em-Ȧpt, etc., inscribed with a prayer for funerary offerings. Sams Collection. XXXth dynasty. Height 9½ in., width 7½ in. [No. 396.]

939. (*Bay* **25.**)—Limestone **sepulchral stele,** with rounded top, on which are the remains of about twelve lines of hieroglyphics, and of two or three lines of demotic; these appear to describe the felicity which the person for whom the stele was made would enjoy in the Other World. Salt Collection. From Ṣaḳḳârah. XXXth dynasty. Height 1 ft. 9 in., width 1 ft. [No. 382.]

940. (*Bay* **25.**)—Sandstone **sepulchral stele,** with rounded top, of **Pa-Sab-en-Ḥeru** , an *Ȧm-ȧs* priest, *Ka* priest, and scribe of the treasury of Osiris, son of . . . . tebḥa, who held the same offices. On the upper portion are cut a winged disk, the utchats, and a scene representing the deceased adoring Rā-Harmachis and Isis. Salt Collection. XXXth dynasty. Height 1 ft. 6 in., width 11 in. [No. 338.]

941. (*Bay* **26.**)—Limestone **sepulchral stele,** with rounded top, of **Nes-Ḥeru** , an *Utcheb*, *Ȧm-ȧst*, priest of the *Ka*, royal kinsman, councillor, etc., the son of Tcheṭ-ḥrȧ, and the lady Ȧru-ru 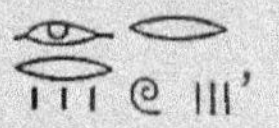, a sistrum-bearer of Menu, grandson of Maat-Ḥeru-ru, great-grandson of Tcheṭ-ḥrȧ, great-great-grandson of Ḥeru-em-sa-f, great-great-great-grandson of Tcheṭ-ḥrȧ, great-great-great-great-grandson of Pa-nes-qa-shuti. On the upper part are sculptured the following scenes:—1. The deceased worshipping the solar disk. 2. The deceased adoring Rā in his boats. 3. The deceased adoring Osiris. From Akhmîm. XXXth dynasty. Height 1 ft. 8½ in., width 1 ft. 1½ in. [No. 1018.]

942. (*Bay* **26.**)—Portions of painted limestone **reliefs** from the tomb of **Nes-Menu** 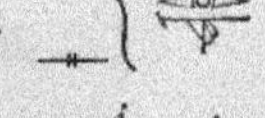, the son of **Maat-Ḥeru-ru** , an *Ȧm-ȧs* priest, a *Ka* priest, and an *Utcheb* priest, on which are sculptured figures of Thoth and Horus pouring out libations. From Akhmîm. XXXth dynasty. Height 4 ft. 6 in., width 4 ft. 10 in. [No. 1235.]

943. (*Bay* 26.)—Painted limestone **relief** from the tomb of **Nes-Menu**, the son of **Maat-Ḥeru-ru**, on which is sculptured a scene representing the deceased standing at a table of offerings and adoring Osiris and Isis. From Akhmîm. XXXth dynasty. Height 3 ft. 10 in., width 4 ft. 9 in. [No. 1306.]

944. (*Bay* 27.)—White limestone **sepulchral stele,** with rounded top, of **Pa-ṭā-Bast** , the son of Maat-u-ru , sculptured with:—
1. The solar disk on the horizon between two winged serpents.
2. The sky . 3. Scene representing deceased, who is styled 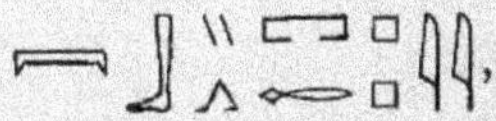, adoring Osiris, Isis, and Nephthys. In the last line the "father" of the Osiris is said to be Nekhth-sa pa-mes, his mother Ta-Khar, and her mother Thent-ȧsha . Anastasi Collection. XXXth dynasty. Height 2 ft., width 1 ft. 5 in. [No. 302.]

945. (*Bay* 27.)—**Head of a** limestone **sphinx,** wearing a heavy wig with uraeus, symbol of sovereignty. From the temple in front of the Sphinx. XXXth dynasty. Height 9 in. [No. 464.]

Presented by Captain Caviglia, 1814.

946. (*Bay* 27.)—Sandstone **figure of the god Bes,** bearded and wearing plumes, and brandishing a knife. XXXth dynasty. Height 2 ft. 2 in. [No. 463.]

947. (*Bay* 27.)—Upper portion of an arragonite **statue of a king of Egypt,** perhaps one of the Ptolemies. Ptolemaïc Period. Height 1 ft. 11 in. [No. 941.]

Presented by Her Majesty Queen Victoria, 1854.

948. (*Bay* 29.)—Portion of a black stone circular vessel, which was used as a **clepsydra,** or water clock, inscribed with the prenomen and nomen of **Alexander the Great** , king of Egypt, about B.C. 332. On the outside are cut figures of the king making offerings to the god **Khensu** and the goddess **Åpt**; on the inside are the signs 𓋹 𓊽, and 𓎬, and above each is a series of small holes which were originally filled with pegs. From Tell al-Yahûdîyyah. Height 1 ft. 2½ in., width 1 ft. 3 in. [No. 933.]

949. (*Bay* 29.)—Portion of a black stone circular vessel which was used as a **clepsydra,** or water clock. On the outer face are sculptured scenes representing King **Philip Arrhidaeus**

making offerings to Åmsu, or Menu, and another deity. Behind the king, in one scene, stands the goddess Sekhet. On the top edge are cut the letters OCT. (October), with four demotic characters below them; further to the right is the letter N (for NOV., *i.e.*, November). Inside are cut the signs 𓋹, 𓎬, and 𓊽; and above each 𓎬 and 𓊽 is a series of twelve small holes, arranged at an average distance of ¾ in. from each other. Height 1 ft., width 11 in. [No. 938.]

950. (*Bay* 28.)—**Cast** of a black granite stele of **Alexander,** son of Alexander the Great, with rounded top, on which are sculptured a winged disk and two scenes representing a king making offerings to the goddess Uatchit and the god Ḥeru-netch-tef-f. The cartouches above the king's head are empty. Below is a hieroglyphic inscription in eighteen lines, dated in the first month of the season *Shat*, or Akhet, in the seventh year of Ḥāā-åb-Rā setep-en-Åmen 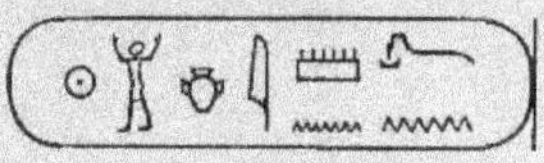, *i.e.*, **Alexander IV** of Macedon, or **Alexander II** of Egypt. The stele was set up to commemorate the restoration of the property of the priests of Pe and Tep, which had been alienated from them by Xerxes when Ptolemy I was satrap of Egypt, about B.C. 312. The original is in the Egyptian Museum in Cairo. Height 6 ft. 2 in., width 3 ft. 10 in. [No. 1127.]

PTOLEMAIC PERIOD.

951. (*Bay* 25.)—Portion of an **inscription of Ptolemy I, Soter**, mentioning Hathor, Lady of Măfket (the Sinai Peninsula), and Heru-sma-taui. From Tarrâna (Terenouthis). About B.C. 300. Length 1 ft. 10 in. [No. 652.]

Presented by the Egypt Exploration Fund, 1889.

952. (*Bay* 25.)—Fragment of a limestone **relief** on which are cut the name and titles of **Ptolemy I, Soter**, governor of Egypt, about B.C. 300. From Tarrâna (Terenouthis). Height 1 ft. 1 in., width 1 ft. 2 in. [No. 651.]

Presented by the Egypt Exploration Fund, 1889.

953. (*Bay* 25.)—Rectangular limestone **relief**, on which are sculptured figures of **Ptolemy II, Philadelphus**, king of Egypt B.C. 287, and **Queen Arsinoë**. The cartouches are:

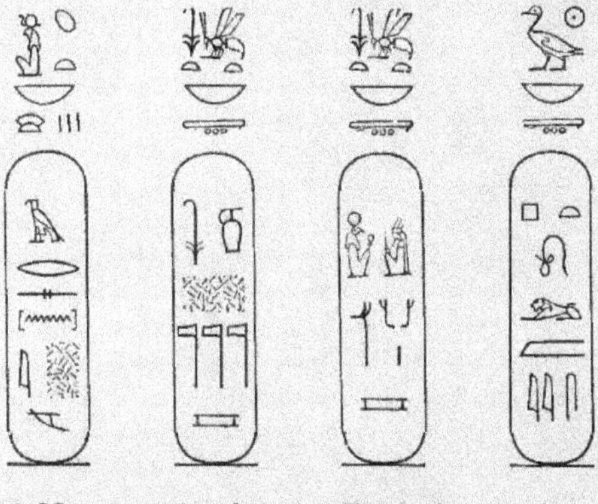

From Ṣân al-Ḥagar. Ptolemaïc Period. Height 1 ft. 4½ in., width 1 ft. 1½ in. [No. 1056.]

Presented by the Egypt Exploration Fund, 1885.

954. (*Bay* 25.)—Upper portion of a limestone **stele**, with rounded top, on which are sculptured the winged disk, and two scenes wherein **Ptolemy II, Philadelphus**, is represented making offerings to Menu and Queen Arsinoë, and to the goddess Uatchit (Buto) and Harpokrates. From Tanis. About B.C. 260. Height 2 ft. 4 in., width 1 ft. 5 in. [No. 1057.]

Presented by the Egypt Exploration Fund, 1885.

955. (*Bay* **29**.)—Limestone stele, with rounded top, sculptured with a scene representing **Ptolemy II, Philadelphus,** and **Queen Arsinoë,** adoring Menu, Harpokrates, and the goddess Uatchit. Above is the winged disk with pendent uraei. From Ṣân al-Ḥagar (Tanis). About B.C. 260. Height 2 ft. $3\frac{3}{4}$ in., width 1 ft. $7\frac{1}{4}$ in. [No. 1054.]

Presented by the Egypt Exploration Fund, 1885.

Ptolemy II, Philadelphus, and Queen Arsinoë adoring Menu, or Åmsu, Harpokrates, and Uatchit. About B.C. 260.
[Bay 29, No. 955.]

956. (*Bay* **28**.)—Upper portion of a black granite **stele,** with rounded top, of **Ptolemy II, Philadelphus** 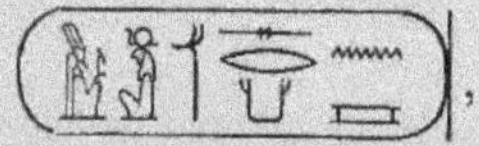, king of Egypt, from about B.C. 286 to B.C. 247, inscribed with the text of an edict. On the rounded portion, a winged disk, with pendent uraei, has been partially worked, and below it

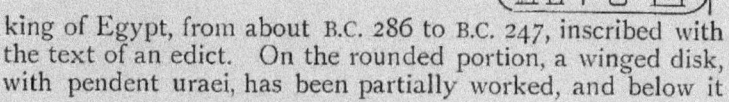

is left blank a space upon which it was intended to cut the figures of the king and the gods whom he worshipped. Height 1 ft. 7 in., width 2 ft. [No. 616.]

957. (*Bay* **28.**)—**Cast** of a limestone stele, with rounded top, inscribed in hieroglyphics, demotic, and Greek, with copies of the **Decree** promulgated by the priests **of Canopus,** on the seventeenth day of the first month of the season *Pert,* in the ninth year of the reign of **Ptolemy III, Euergetes I** (B.C. 238). In it reference is made to the king's successful expedition to Persia, to the righteousness of his rule and his benevolence, to the remission of taxes, to the death of the Princess Berenice, etc. And the priests decreed that, with a view of regulating the observance of festivals, in future one day should be added to the year every fourth year, *i.e.*, every fourth year should contain three hundred and sixty-six days, and that the day so added should be kept as a festival in honour of the king and queen. Further it was ordered that a copy of this decree should be cut on stone or bronze, and set up in the most public place in each temple of the first, second, and third class, throughout Egypt. The original was found at Tanis in 1866 and is in the Egyptian Museum in Cairo. Height 7 ft. 4 in., width 2 ft. 7 in. [No. 1081.]

Presented by H.H. the Khedive, Ismâ'îl Pâshâ, 1871.

958. (*Bay* **26.**)—Rectangular limestone **slab,** inscribed in Greek with a dedication to the god Ares by **Alexandros,** general of the elephant-hunt in the Sûdân, and his soldiers, in the reign of **Ptolemy IV, Philopator,** king of Egypt, B.C. 222–205. From the Eastern Desert. Height 1 ft. 3 in., width 1 ft. 8 in. [No. 1207.]

959. (*Bay* **26.**)—Limestone **stele,** with rounded top, of **Ptolemy IV,** Philopator I, king of Egypt from B.C. 222 to 205, sculptured with the following:—1. The winged disk, with the uraei of Uatchit and Nekhebit. 2. The king making an offering of Maāt , to Menu, Ḥeru-sa-Ȧst, Isis, a form of Sekhet, and a Horus-god. 3. The king offering vases to two Horus gods. Below these scenes was a demotic inscription which has been erased. (**Plate XXXIV.**) Height 1 ft. $10\frac{1}{2}$ in., width 1 ft. 3 in. [No. 1431.]

960. (*Southern Egyptian Gallery.*)—The **Rosetta Stone.** This slab of hard black basalt was found by a French artillery officer, called Boussard, among the ruins of Fort St. Julien, near the Rosetta mouth of the Nile, in 1798, but subsequently

Stele sculptured with a scene representing Ptolemy IV, adoring Menu, or Ȧmsu, Isis, Ḥeru-sa-Ȧst, and other deities.
[Bay 26, No. 959.] About B.C. 220.

came into the possession of the British Government at the capitulation of Alexandria. It is inscribed with portions of fourteen lines of hieroglyphics, thirty-two lines of demotic, and fifty-four lines of Greek text. Portions of the slab have been broken off from the top and the right hand bottom corner. The missing portion from the top was probably about fifteen inches high, and it was, no doubt, rounded and sculptured with a winged disk, having pendent uraei wearing the crowns of the South  and North  like the **Canopus Stone.** (See the cast in Bay 28, No. 957.)

The Rosetta Stone is inscribed with a copy of the Decree promulgated in the ninth year of the reign of **Ptolemy V. Epiphanes,** by the priests of Memphis, who had assembled in that city to celebrate the first commemoration of the coronation of the king who was not crowned until the eighth year of his reign. This decree was first drawn up in the Egyptian language, and was written in the cursive writing in general use at that time, now known as **demotic.** In the Decree the priests set forth the good deeds of Ptolemy V, and enumerate the benefits which he had conferred upon Egypt, and, as a mark of their great appreciation of these acts of goodness, they decreed that:—1. Additional honours be paid to the king and his ancestors. 2. An image of the king be set up in every temple in Egypt, and worshipped three times a day. 3. A statue of the king in a shrine be set up in the sanctuary of every temple, and both statue and shrine to be specially dressed and carried in processions on sacred days. 4. A monthly festival to be established on the king's birthday and coronation day. 5. The first five days of the month *Thoth* to be observed as a festival, and garlands worn. 6. The priests who carry out these instructions to have a special title, and their names to appear in official documents and on their rings. 7. Private citizens to be allowed to establish a shrine and to keep all festivals, yearly and monthly. 8. This Decree to be inscribed upon a hard stone stele in (*a*) the **writing of the priests,** (*b*) in the **writing of books,** and (*c*) in the **writing of the Greeks,** and set up in every temple of the first, second, and third class throughout Egypt, by the side of the statue of the king.

In accordance with these orders, slabs of basalt were prepared and copies of the Decree cut upon them in the Egyptian and Greek languages. The Egyptian version was written in the "writing of the priests" (*i.e.*, hieroglyphics), and in the "writing of books" (*i.e.*, demotic), and the Greek version in ordinary uncials. Thus each copy became a **bilingual document** in Egyptian and Greek, though it contained *three* kinds of writing. The Rosetta Stone was one of the stelae inscribed with the Decree of the priests of Memphis, which were set up in the temples as a result of this Decree, and its original home was probably the temple of Temu at Rosetta, whence came the intercolumnar slab of Nekht-neb-f in Bay 28, No. 927. Other stelae inscribed with the hieroglyphic text of the Decree are known, *e.g.*, the Stele of Damanhûr, now in the Egyptian Museum in Cairo, and another has been discovered in recent years. For an account of the great importance of the Rosetta Stone for the decipherment of Egyptian hieroglyphics, and methods by which Young and Champollion used the texts cut upon it in connection with the bilingual Egyptian and Greek inscription on the famous Obelisk at Philae, see the "Guide to the Collections of Egyptian Antiquities in the British Museum," pages 44, 45. (**Plate XXXV.**) Length 3 ft. 9 in., breadth 2 ft. 4½ in., thickness 11 in. [No. 24.]

961. (*Bay* **27.**)—White limestone **stele,** with rounded top, sculptured with a scene representing **Ptolemy VII** and the two Cleopatras standing in adoration before Âmen-Rā, Mut and Khensu, the great triad of Thebes. Above is the winged disk, with pendent uraei, etc.; the text contains the names and titles of Ptolemy VII and the two Cleopatras. From Karnak. About B.C. 181. (**Plate XXXVI.**) Height 2 ft., width 1 ft. 7 in. [No. 612.]

962. (*Bay* **30.**)—Grey granite **monolithic shrine,** with a rectangular cavity in the upper portion, wherein was kept a figure of a sacred hawk, or of one of the gods or goddesses. Above the cavity are sculptured, in relief, a cornice of uraei and three winged disks with uraei, and down the sides are inscriptions containing the names and titles of **Ptolemy IX** (?), **Euergetes II,** and his wife **Cleopatra,** B.C. 147. Below the cavity are sculptured a palm-leaf cornice, winged disks, and figures of two gods who bear up the sky on their raised hands. On each side of the lower portion of the cavity are flat projections, with sockets, into

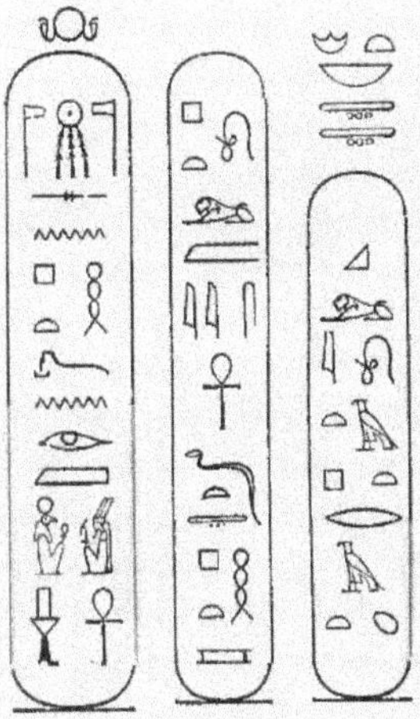

Hieroglyphic Text. | Demotic Text. | Greek Text.

Ptolemy VII and the two Queens Cleopatra adoring Åmen-Rā, Mut, and Khensu, the triad of Thebes.

[Bay 27. No. 961.] About B.C. 181.

which the bolts of the doors of the shrine worked. Found under the ruins of a Christian church on the Island of Philae in 1886. Height 8 ft. 3 in. Weight about 3 tons 12 cwt. [No. 1134.]

963. (*Bay* 29.)—Central portion of a **red granite monument,** consisting of three slabs, which was set up in a temple at Syene, the modern Aswân, to commemorate the endowments and benefactions which had been made to the gods of the First Cataract, Khnemu, Sati, etc., and the priesthood of the Island of Elephantine, by **Ptolemy X, Soter II,** king of Egypt, about B.C. 117. On the upper portion are sculptured figures of the king making offerings to the gods of Elephantine. From Aswân. Height 9 ft., width 1 ft. 10 in. [No. 1020.]

964. (*Bay* 28.)—Grey schist **statue** of the goddess **Isis** holding before her a figure of Osiris, whom she protects with her wings. It was dedicated to the goddess by **Shashanq** 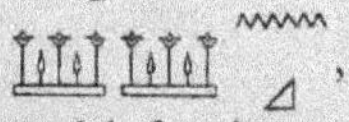, an official who was high in the service of the chief-priestess of Åmen-Rā at Thebes. Ptolemaïc Period. Height 2 ft. 8 in. [No. 1162.]

965. (*Central Saloon.*)—Massive green **granite beetle,** or model of the **scarabaeus sacer,** which was the symbol of **Kheperå** , a god who, according to the Egyptians, was self-produced, and who was the creator of the universe and of all therein. At a very early period the beetle became the symbol of renewed life and the type of the resurrection. Brought from Constantinople by Lord Elgin. Ptolemaïc Period. Length 5 ft., height 3 ft. Weight about 43 cwt. [No. 74.]

966. (*Bay* 32.)—Stone **figure of a serpent,** with the breasts of a woman and the head raised ready to strike, supported by the trunk of a tree. From Benha. Ptolemaïc Period. Height 2 ft. [No. 1157.]

967. (*Bay* 29.)—Green **basalt coffin,** in the form of a bearded, mummied man, with pedestal and plinth. Down the front are cut three lines of hieroglyphic texts containing prayers on behalf of the lady **Ānkhet** 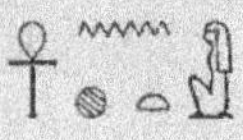, the daughter of the lady Neb[t] Ḥait , although the coffin was originally intended for a man. Above the texts is cut the sign for "heaven" , on each side are cut figures of two of the children of Horus, and over the feet are two figures of the jackal-gods Ȧnpu and Ȧp-uat. Ptolemaïc Period. Height 6 ft. 6 in. [No. 33.]

968. (*Bay* 26.)—White **limestone coffin,** in the form of a man, of **Ḥes-Peṭān-Ȧst** 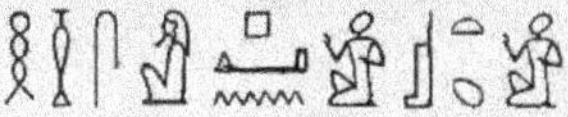, son of the lady T-kharṭ-Menu , inscribed with an address to the "Lords of Law" in which the deceased entreats them to deliver him from the Crocodile, and to give him his mouth to speak with, and sepulchral meals to eat. Sams Collection. From Thebes. Ptolemaïc Period. Height 6 ft. [No. 2.]

969. (*Bay* 24.)—Fine white **limestone coffin** in the form of a mummied man, with rectangular base and plinth up the back. The two portions of this coffin were fastened together by a raised edge in one half fitting into a groove in the edge of the other. This is a good example of the coffins which were kept in private houses in the latter part of the Dynastic Period. From Tana, near Hermopolis. Salt Collection. Ptolemaïc Period. Height 6 ft. 2 in. [No. 47.]

970. (*Bay* 21.)—White limestone **cover of the coffin of Ȧsȧr-Pa-ser-Ṭuat** (?) , the son of the lady Thitu 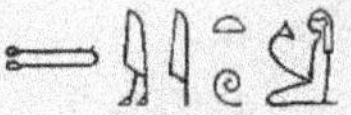. On the right shoulder are cut the three hawk-gods, and on the left the three uraei goddesses, who protect the deceased by day and by night. On the breast is cut a deep pectoral, with heads of hawks surmounted by solar disks, and below these are five lines of hieroglyphics containing prayers to Osiris Khenti Ȧmenti and Osiris Khenti Mekes, that the deceased may make a successful passage through the Ṭuat to the kingdom of Osiris. On the right are cut figures of Mesthȧ and Ṭuamutef, and on the left figures of Ḥāpi and Qebḥsennuf. Ptolemaïc Period. Height 5 ft. 8 in. [No. 1343.]

971. (*Bay* 28.)—Portion of the **cover of the** white limestone **coffin of I-em-ḥetep** 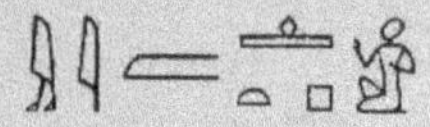, the son of Ḥeru-sa-Àst and Tat-Ḥert , with painted head-dress and necklace. Down the front are painted in outline three lines of hieroglyphic text, containing an address to the great gods of the dead. Ptolemaïc Period, about B.C. 300. Height 4 ft. 2 in. [No. 1303.]

972. (*Bay* 25.) — Fine limestone **window** from the clerestory of the temple of Denderah, with mullions in the form of pillars with Hathor-headed capitals. On the upper part of the frame are cut, in relief, winged disks with uraei; on the right side is the serpent of the North, Uatchit, and on the left that of the South, Nekhebit. Ptolemaïc Period. Height 2 ft. 1 in., width 2 ft. 3 in. [No. 1153.]

973. (*Bay* 17.)—Limestone seated **figure of a priestly official,** inscribed with prayers to Seker and other gods for sepulchral offerings. On the front of it is sculptured in relief a figure of Osiris; on the right, cut in outline, is a figure of Isis, and on the left a figure of Horus. The work is poor, and the inscription is much damaged, being in many places illegible. Ptolemaïc Period. Height 1 ft. 2 in. [No. 1085.]

974. (*Bay* 27.)—Marble **head** from the statue **of a queen** or princess of the Ptolemaïc Period (Berenice ?). From Alexandria. Harris Collection. Height 1 ft. 6 in. [No. 982.]

975. (*Bay* 29.)—Portion of a granite **statue of Ptualmā** , a priestess, the daughter of Ptolemy. Ptolemaïc Period. From Alexandria. Height 1 ft. 5 in. [No. 985.]

976. (*Bay* 29.)—Marble **sun-dial,** resting on a flight of seven steps; the twelve hours were marked by the letters of the alphabet, A—IB, but of these only six remain. Found during the excavation made on the site where stood "Cleopatra's Needle," in Alexandria. Ptolemaïc Period. Height 1 ft. 3 in., width 1 ft. 5 in. [No. 778.]

977. (*Bay* 27.)—Portion of a **relief** from the wall of a temple, on which is sculptured a scene representing a king making offerings to Isis-Hathor. Ptolemaïc Period. Length 3 ft. 2 in., breadth 1 ft. [No. 649.]

978. (*Bay* 27.)—Portion of a limestone **relief** from a Ptolemaïc temple, on which is sculptured in sunk relief the head of a king or prince. Height 1 ft. 1½ in., width 1 ft. 10 in. [No. 650.]

979. (*Bay* 26.)—Rectangular grey **granite pedestal** of a Stele of Horus, inscribed with a magical text. From Denderah. Ptolemaïc Period. Length 11½ in., breadth 7½ in., depth 5 in. [No. 1433.]

980. (*Bay* 29.)—Portion of a limestone **relief**, on which is sculptured a figure of a god having the head of a man, the body of a beetle, and the tail of a hawk. Ptolemaïc Period. Height 1 ft. 2 in., width 11 in. [No. 895.]

981. (*Bay* 29.)—Fragment of a sandstone **relief** from a wall of a temple, inscribed with a portion of a line of hieroglyphics. Ptolemaïc Period. Height 10 in., width 1 ft. 4 in. [No. 881.]

982. (*Bay* 31.)—Limestone **Canopic jar**, with a cover in the form of the head of Mesthȧ, one of the four sons of Horus, who presided over the South, and who protected the portion of the intestines of the deceased which was placed inside the jar. Ptolemaïc Period. Height 2 ft. 4 in. [No. 1154.]

983. (*Bay* 27.)—Limestone **sepulchral stele**, with rounded top, broken across the middle, of **Th-nefer-ḥrȧ**  a sistrum-bearer of Ptaḥ, daughter of Ḥrȧ-ānkh, sculptured with the following:—1. A winged disk. 2. A scene representing the deceased being presented to Osiris, Isis, and Nephthys by Horus and Anubis; behind him is the bull-headed god Ḥāp Ȧsȧr or **Serapis.** The hieroglyphic and demotic inscriptions below are illegible. Anastasi Collection. From Ṣaḳḳârah. Height 2 ft. 5 in., width 1 ft. 8 in. [No. 184.]

984. (*Bay* 27.)—Sandstone **sepulchral stele,** with rounded top, on which is sculptured a scene representing Anubis presenting a man and his wife to Osiris, who stands beneath a winged disk with his head-box by his side. Below are three lines of demotic text. Anastasi Collection. Ptolemaïc Period. Height 10½ in., width 8 in. [No. 837.]

985. (*Bay* **27.**)—Limestone **sepulchral stele,** with a short inscription in the demotic character. Ptolemaïc Period. Height 8½ in., width 9 in. [No. 698.]

986. (*Bay* **27.**)—Rectangular limestone **sepulchral stele,** on which are sculptured, in relief, a winged disk, and a scene representing the deceased, attended by Anubis, standing in the presence of Osiris and Isis. Below are two lines of text in the demotic character. Ptolemaïc Period. Height 1 ft., width 8 in. [No. 1003.]

987. (*Bay* **27.**)—Limestone **sepulchral stele,** with rounded top, on which is cut a funerary inscription in the demotic character. Height 7½ in., width 5½ in. [No. 654.]

988. (*Bay* **27.**)—Limestone **sepulchral stele,** with rounded top, on which is traced in black ink a funerary inscription in the demotic character. Ptolemaïc Period (?) Height 1 ft. 1½ in., width 10 in. [No. 394.]

989. (*Bay* **27.**)—Limestone **sepulchral stele,** with rounded top, on which is cut a funerary text in the demotic character. Ptolemaïc Period. Height 1 ft. 3½ in., width 10 in. [No 1088.]

990. (*Bay* **27.**)—Limestone **sepulchral stele,** with rounded top, sculptured with a scene representing Anubis standing by the bier of the deceased; above is a short inscription in the demotic character. Ptolemaïc Period. Height 1 ft. 8½ in., width 8 in. [No. 433.]

991. (*Bay* **29.**)—Limestone **sepulchral stele,** with rounded top, on which are cut the winged disk and a scene representing a woman, wearing the feather of Maāt, standing in adoration before Osiris and Anubis. Between the winged disk and the scene is a line of inscription in the demotic character. Anastasi Collection. Ptolemaïc Period. Height 2 ft. 2 in., width 1 ft. 6 in. [No. 841.]

992. (*Bay* **30.**)—Limestone **sepulchral stele,** with rounded top, on the upper part of which are painted the winged disk and a scene representing the deceased standing in the presence of Osiris, Apis, Anubis, Horus, etc. Below is an illegible inscription of nineteen or twenty lines in the demotic character. Ptolemaïc Period. Height 1 ft. 7 in., width 1 ft. 1 in. [No. 392.]

993. (*Bay* 27.)—Sandstone **sepulchral stele,** with rounded top, inscribed in the demotic character with a decree (?) of one of the Ptolemies, or one of the Roman emperors. On the upper portion is sculptured a figure of the solar disk, with three pairs of wings and pendent uraei, between which is a beetle. Below are two scenes: in the one the king is represented making an offering to Menu, or Âmsu, and Isis, and in the other, to Temu and Sebek. The inscription of thirty-one lines is coloured red. From Karnak. Ptolemaïc Period. Height 2 ft. 5 in., width 1 ft. 9 in. [No. 1325.]

994. (*Bay* 29.)—Limestone **sepulchral stele,** with rounded top, of **Euonymos,** son of Hierakion, who died aged twenty-seven years. On the upper portion are cut a winged disk, with pendent uraei, and a scene in which we see the deceased being led into the presence of Osiris and Isis by Anubis. Below is a bilingual Greek and demotic inscription. Roman Period. Height 1 ft. 9 in., width 1 ft. [No. 838.]

995. (*Bay* 30.)—Portion of a limestone **sepulchral stele,** with rounded top, of **Her-âbu** , a priest of the gods Ptaḥ, Mut, Serapis, scribe of several orders of priests, and the son of Aāḥmes, who held similar offices. The deceased was a guardian of the statues of 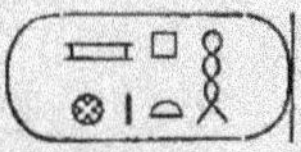, and priest of Saḥu Rā (?) 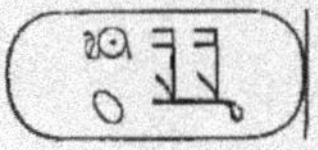; his embalmment occupied seventy days , and he died aged 50 years, 7 months, and 5 days. Salt Collection. Ptolemaïc Period. Height 1 ft. 9 in., width 1 ft. 2½ in. [No. 378.]

996. (*Bay* 27.)—Portion of the limestone **sepulchral stele** of **Ta-mut-sher** , a sistrum-bearer and priestess of Isis and Nephthys, the daughter of Peṭā-Nefer-ḥetep, a priest and herald of Hathor Nefer-ḥetep, and the lady Shep-en-Âmen, who died at the age of 97 years 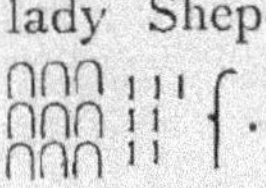. Sams Collection. Ptolemaïc Period. Height 10 in., width 11 in. [No. 386.]

997. (*Bay* 25.)—Limestone **sepulchral stele,** with rounded top, of **Khā (?) -em-ḥrȧ**, son of Tche-ḥrȧ, a priest. On the upper portion of the stele is traced in black ink a figure of the deceased adoring Osiris and Isis, who stand beneath a winged disk with pendent uraei. Beneath are eight lines of hieroglyphics and two lines of demotic. The deceased was buried on the 23rd day of the 4th month of Pert in the 22nd year [of Ptolemy Physkon]; his embalming occupied seventy days, and he died aged 74 years, 9 months, and 7 days. Ptolemaïc Period. Height 1 ft. 2½ in., width 9½ in. [No. 393.]

998. (*Bay* 29.)—Limestone **sepulchral stele,** with rounded top, of **Barnetaḳet** (?) (**Berenice** ?), the daughter of Ptaḥ-meri, a priest of Ptaḥ, and the lady Ȧrsentai (**Arsinoë**), who died aged 64 years, 8 months, and 26 (?) days. On the upper portion were traced in outline a winged disk and a scene representing the deceased adoring Osiris, and on the lower, in red ink, are four lines of hieroglyphic text, and, in black, a rendering of the same in demotic. Ptolemaïc Period. Height 1 ft. 6 in., width 1 ft. [No. 383.]

999. (*Bay* 32.)—Portion of a limestone **sepulchral stele** of a person whose name is illegible. At the top is a part of a line of hieroglyphics which probably contained the name and the number of years of the life of the deceased, and below this is an inscription of twenty-eight lines in demotic, dated in the ninth (?) year of Ptolemy IX. From Ṣaḳḳârah. Height 1 ft. 10½ in., width 1 ft. 4 in. [No. 377.]

1000. (*Bay* 27.) — Limestone **sepulchral stele,** with rounded top, of **Ḥeru-em-khut**, an Erpā, Ḥā prince, and high-priest of Memphis, the son of Ȧnem-ḥrȧ and Neb-ḥrȧ-ānkh, sculptured with a scene representing Ȧnem-ḥrȧ pouring out a libation before Osiris. The text states that the funerary ceremonies were performed by Nes-qeṭi, "his eldest son," the son of the lady Nefer-itet.

In the text spaces are left blank for the date of the death of the deceased, and his age, etc.; his son was a priest of Philopator (Ptolemy IV). Salt Collection. From Ṣakkârah. Height 2 ft., width 1 ft. 2½ in. [No. 391.]

1001. (*Bay* 26.) — Limestone **sepulchral stele,** with rounded top, of **Ta-sherȧ-Menu**, the son of Ṭeḥuti-mes and the priestess Utchat-Shu, on which are sculptured:—1. The winged disk. 2. Rā, in the form of a ram, in his boat. 3. Kheperȧ in his boat. 4. The deceased adoring Osiris, Anubis, Horus, and Isis. 5. The deceased adoring Menu, Horus, Isis, Mest-ḥent- . . . . (?) Below, in eleven lines, is cut the text of a prayer to these gods for sepulchral offerings. From Akhmîm. Ptolemaïc Period. (**Plate XXXVII.**) Height 1 ft. 9½ in., width 1 ft. 4 in. [No. 1139.]

1002. (*Bay* 22.) — Limestone **sepulchral stele,** with rounded top, of **Ḥeru-sa-Ȧst**, an *Ȧm-ȧs* priest and priest of the Ka, on which are sculptured, and a scene representing the deceased adoring Rā-Harmachis and Isis. Below are five lines of text containing a prayer to Osiris and a statement of the genealogy of the deceased. Ptolemaïc Period. Height 1 ft. 4 in., width 10 in. [No. 325.]

1003. (*Bay* 24.) — Limestone **sepulchral stele,** with rounded top, on which are painted a winged disk, with, and a scene representing Ṭā- . . . . . en-meḥ (?), a woman wearing on her head, and two men **Peṭāt-Ȧnḥer**, and **Maat-Ḥeru-** . . . . .

Sepulchral stele of Ta-sherȧ-Menu, son of Ṭeḥuti-mes and Utchat-Shu.
[Bay 26, No. 1001.] Ptolemaïc Period.

each wearing  on his head, adoring Rā-Harmachis. From Akhmîm. Ptolemaïc Period. Height 1 ft. 3 in., width 11 in. [No. 641.]

1004. (*Bay* 25.) — Limestone **sepulchral stele,** with rounded top, of **P-sher-meḥt** , an *Utcheb* priest, and priest of Ḥāp (the Nile), on which are sculptured a figure of the winged disk and two scenes representing the deceased adoring Osiris and Isis, and Menu and Isis. From Akhmîm. Ptolemaïc Period. Height 1 ft. 3 in., width 11½ in. [No. 1365.]

1005. (*Bay* 25.) — Limestone **sepulchral stele,** with rounded top, of **P-sher-meḥt** , an *Utcheb* and *Ȧm-ȧs*, priest of the Ka, etc., sculptured with a figure of the winged disk, and with a scene representing the deceased adoring Menu, Horus, and Isis, and Osiris, Horus, and Isis. Below are fourteen lines of text containing a prayer that sepulchral offerings may be given by the above-mentioned gods to the deceased, whose pedigree is set out at length. From Akhmîm. Ptolemaïc Period. Height 1 ft. 11 in., width 1 ft. 1½ in. [No. 1349.]

1006. (*Bay* 26.) — Limestone **sepulchral stele,** with rounded top, of **Peṭā-nefer-ḥetep** 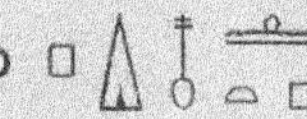, a priest, on which are cut the following scenes :—1. The jackal-gods of the South and North, *couchant*, beneath the winged disk. 2. The deceased adoring Osiris, Ptaḥ - Seker - Ȧsȧr, Isis, Nephthys, Ḥeru-netch-tef-f, and Hathor. 3. The deceased in the boat of Rā with attendant ape-gods and jackals. 4. Two seated figures of the deceased. The text contains a prayer for sepulchral offerings. Ptolemaïc Period. Height 1 ft. 6 in., width 1 ft. 0½ in. [No. 934.]

1007. (*Bay* 27.) — Limestone **sepulchral stele,** with rounded top, of **Peṭāt-Ḥeru** , the son of Maat-Ḥeru-Ru and Nini, on which are painted the utchats and a figure of the deceased adoring Rā-Harmachis. From Akhmîm. Ptolemaïc Period. Height 1 ft. 3 in., width 10½ in. [No. 640.]

1008. (*Bay* 27.)—Limestone **sepulchral stele,** with rounded top, of **Theṭā-Åsår**, the daughter of Ḥāpi-menḥ, on which is painted a scene representing the

Sepulchral stele of Peṭāt-Ḥeru.
[Bay 27, No. 1007.] Ptolemaïc Stele.

deceased adoring Rā-Harmachis. From Akhmîm. Ptolemaïc Period. Height 1 ft., width 8½ in. [No 637.]

1009. (*Bay* 28.)—Limestone **sepulchral stele,** with rounded top, of **Ḥeru**, on which are sculptured a winged disk and a scene representing the deceased adoring Rā-Harmachis. From Akhmîm. Ptolemaïc Period. (**Plate XXXVIII.**) Height 1 ft. 3 in. width 1 ft. [No. 639.]

Sepulchral stele of Ḥeru.

[Bay 28, No. 1009.]

1010. (*Bay* 24.)—Limestone **sepulchral stele,** with rounded top, of **Kerāsher Nefer-ḥetep Peṭā-Khensu** . On the upper portion are sculptured:—1. The winged solar disk, with pendent uraei. 2. The jackals of the South and North. 3. The disk . 4. The deceased standing in adoration before Osiris, Isis, Nephthys, Horus, and Anubis. Below the text, which contains prayers to these gods, is sculptured a figure of the Boat of Rā, with the god standing in it, accompanied by Horus and Anubis. A jackal tows the boat of the god along, and four ape-gods acclaim him. Ptolemaïc Period. Height 2 ft. 3½ in., width 1 ft. 4 in. [No. 1428.]

1011. (*Bay* 29.)—Limestone **sepulchral stele,** with rounded top, of **Ruru** , an *Àm-às* priest and priest of the Ka, the son of Ḥeru-khebit , a man who held similar offices, and the lady Nesthet-Utchat . On the upper portion are cut in outline:—1. The winged disk. 2. The deceased making an offering to Osiris, who appears in the form of a bull's skin attached to a jackal-headed standard. On the one side stand Anubis and Isis, and on the other Horus, Nephthys, standards, etc. Below this are: 1. A text, in five lines, addressed to Osiris and Qebḥsennuf. 2. The souls of the deceased adoring the solar disk in his boat. Ptolemaïc Period. Height 1 ft. 2¾ in., width 10¾ in. [No. 699.]

1012. (*Bay* 29.)—Limestone **sepulchral stele,** with rounded top, of **Peṭā-Ḥeru-p-khart** , an *Utcheb* priest of Ḥeru-ur, scribe of Menu, or Àmsu, son of the scribe Peḥāi (?), and of Àst-resht , a sistrum-bearer of Menu. On the upper portion are sculptured:—1. Winged disk. 2. Scene representing the deceased adoring Menu, Horus, and Nephthys. 3. Scene representing **Th-sheret-meḥt** , wife of the deceased, adoring Osiris

Anubis, and Isis. Beneath are cut two inscriptions, one on behalf of the deceased, and the other on behalf of his wife. From Akhmîm. Ptolemaïc Period. Height 1 ft. 9½ in., width 1 ft. 1½ in. [No. 1141.]

1013. (*Bay* 29.)—**Relief,** on which are sculptured four figures of the god Bes holding swords in their right hands. Ptolemaïc Period. Height 1 ft. 2½ in., width 1 ft. 5 in. [No. 1178.]

1014. (*Bay* 29.)—Limestone **sepulchral stele,** with rounded top, of **Ḥeru** , an *Utcheb* priest, priest of the Ka, and an *Ȧm-ȧs* priest, son of the lady Theḥi 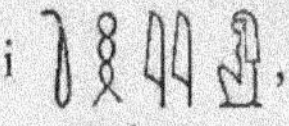, on which are sculptured:—1. A winged disk with pendent uraei. 2. The two boats of Rā, with figures of the god seated in them. 3. The deceased adoring Menu, Horus, Isis, and Nephthys. 4. The deceased adoring Osiris, Anubis, Ȧn-Ḥer, and Bast. Below is cut an inscription of fifteen lines containing prayers. From Akhmîm. Ptolemaïc Period. Height 2 ft. 3¼ in., width 1 ft. 6 in. [No. 1158.]

1015. (*Bay* 29.)—Limestone **sepulchral stele,** with rounded top, of **Ta-set** , the daughter of **Tche-Menu** 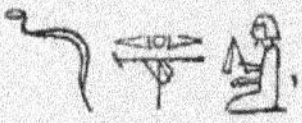, and the lady Nebt-utchat , on which are sculptured:—1. The winged disk. 2. The two boats of the Sun-god, one containing Rā in the form of a ram, and the other Rā in the form of a beetle. 3. A heaven of stars. 4. The deceased adoring Osiris, Horus, Rā, Isis, and Nephthys. Below is an inscription of fourteen lines containing prayers. From Akhmîm. Ptolemaïc Period. Height 2 ft. 3½ in., width 1 ft. 5 in. [No. 1160.]

1016. (*Bay* 32.)—Grey granite **sepulchral stele,** with rounded top, of **Takem** , the daughter of Ta-nefer 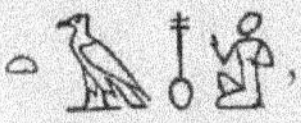, on the upper part of which are cut the winged disk, with pendent uraei, and a scene representing the deceased standing in adoration before the Boat of Rā, in which are seated Rā-Harmachis, Osiris, Isis, and Nephthys. The text contains a prayer to Rā-Harmachis and the gods for sepulchral offerings. Ptolemaïc Period. Height 1 ft. 2½ in., width 8 in. [No. 1311.]

1017. (*Bay* 27.)—Grey granite **sepulchral stele,** with rounded top, on which are sculptured:—1. Winged disk. 2. The jackals of Ȧnpu and Ȧp-uat. 3. A heaven of stars. 4. A figure of the deceased adoring Osiris, Horus, Anubis, Hathor, Isis, and Nephthys. Below are cut twelve lines of text, six in hieroglyphics and six in the demotic character, containing a prayer to several gods for sepulchral offerings, and the genealogy of the deceased. From Akhmîm. Ptolemaïc Period. Height 1 ft. 7 in., width 1 ft. 0½ in. [No. 711.]

1018. (*Bay* 27.)—Limestone **sepulchral stele,** with rounded top, on which is painted a scene representing the deceased and his wife adoring Rā-Harmachis. Above are figures of the winged disk , and . From Akhmîm. Ptolemaïc Period. Height 1 ft. 2 in., width 9½ in. [No. 638.]

1019. (*Bay* 27.)—Limestone **sepulchral stele,** with rounded top, on which is painted a scene representing the deceased, a woman, adoring a bearded serpent, which wears the crown  and a feather 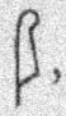, and Osiris, Isis, and Horus. The inscription is illegible. Ptolemaïc Period. Height 1 ft. 1 in., width 8 in. [No. 988.]

1020. (*Bay* 28.)—Limestone **sepulchral stele,** with rounded top, on which is sculptured, in relief, a figure of a dog-headed ape, the animal sacred to Thoth, wearing on his head the crescent moon and the lunar disk, and holding in his paws the Eye of Horus . Before him is a table of offerings, and above him are the winged solar disk, with uraei, and the winged solar disk symbolic of the sun in his strength. Ptolemaïc Period. Height 1 ft. 2 in., width 10½ in. [No. 1425.]

1021. (*Bay* 28.)—Limestone **sepulchral stele,** with rounded top, on which is sculptured, in relief, a figure of an ibis, the sacred bird of Thoth, with the crescent moon and the full moon on its head, standing with a table of offerings before it. Above are the winged solar disk, with pendent uraei, and a winged disk emblematic of the sun in his strength. Ptolemaïc Period. Height 1 ft. 2 in., width 1 ft. 0½ in. [No. 1424.]

1022. (*Bay* 24.)—Limestone **sepulchral stele,** with rounded top, of , an *Utcheb* and *Ȧm-ȧs* priest. On the upper portion are sculptured:—1. The winged disk. 2. The two boats of the Sun-god, with Harpokrates sitting between them. 3. The deceased worshipping Menu, Isis, and Nephthys. 4. The deceased worshipping Osiris, Horus and Isis. Below are ten lines of text containing a prayer to Osiris, Menu, and other deities for sepulchral offerings. From Akhmîm. Ptolemaïc Period. Height 2 ft. 2½ in., width 1 ft. 4 in. [No. 1426.]

1023. (*Bay* 30.)—Portion of a limestone **tablet,** with rounded top, and an illegible hieroglyphic inscription. Ptolemaïc Period. Height 1 ft. 2 in., width 10 in. [No. 180.]

1024. (*Bay* 30.)—Limestone **sepulchral stele,** with rounded top, which seems to have been inscribed in hieroglyphics with the text of a Chapter from the Book of the Dead, and to have been made for a priest of Memphis. The characters, figures, etc., have now all but disappeared. Ptolemaïc Period. Salt Collection. Height 1 ft. 7 in., width 1 ft. [No. 388.]

1025. (*Bay* 29.)—Limestone **sepulchral stele,** with rounded top, of **I-em-ḥetep** 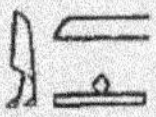, a priest of Ptaḥ, Sekhet, and other gods, and a scribe, son of **Ānkh-Ḥāpi** , and the lady **Nefert-i** 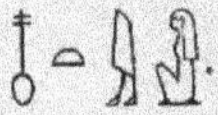. On the rounded portion are cut nine perpendicular lines of hieroglyphics, in the first of which is mentioned the lady **Ḥrȧ-ānkh,** wife of the deceased; an *utchat*  is drawn on each side. Below is an inscription in eighteen lines, containing the genealogy of the deceased, etc.; portions of twelve lines are wanting. Salt Collection. From Ṣakkârah. Ptolemaïc Period. Height 2 ft. 5¼ in., width 1 ft. 3¾ in. [No. 380.]

1026. (*Bay* 27.)—Limestone **sepulchral stele,** with rounded top, of **Pa-sher-en-Ptaḥ** , high-priest of Memphis, Erpā, Ḥā prince, *Smer-uāt*, chancellor, superintendent of the priests of the gods, etc., the son of Peṭā-Bast, high-priest of Memphis, and of the sistrum-bearer Ḥrȧ-ānkh. On the upper portion is sculptured a scene representing the deceased kneeling in adoration before Osiris, Serapis, Isis, Nephthys, Horus, Anubis, I-em-ḥetep, and Ȧmentet, above them is the solar disk with three pairs of wings, on one side is the sceptre , and on the other the palm branch , symbolic of many years. The deceased was born in the reign of **Ptolemy XIII** 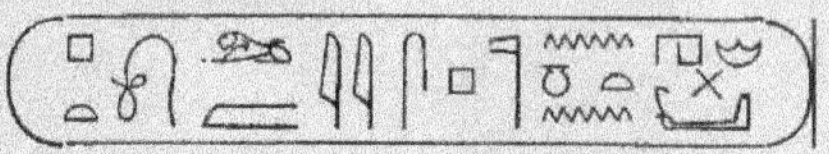. At the age of thirteen years he was made high-priest of Memphis. Height 2 ft. 4½ in., width 2 ft. [No. 886.]

1027. (*Bay* 29.)—Limestone **sepulchral stele,** with rounded top, of **Th-I-em-ḥetep** 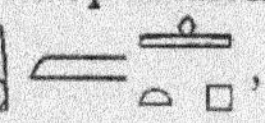, a lady of high rank, the daughter of **Ḥrȧ-ānkh.** On the upper portion are sculptured a winged disk and a scene representing the deceased adoring Osiris, Serapis, Isis, Nephthys, Horus, Anubis, and the emblem of Ȧmentet, and below are cut twenty-one lines of hieroglyphic text, in which is given the genealogy of the deceased, etc. She was born in the ninth year of the reign of **Ptolemy XIII,** about B.C. 71, and thirteen years later she became the wife of the high-priest of Memphis, Pa-sher-en-Ptaḥ, the son of Peṭā-Bast; she had a son, I-em-ḥetep, surnamed Peṭā-Bast, and died in the tenth year of the reign of Cleopatra. From Ṣaḳḳârah. Ptolemaïc Period. Height 2 ft. 10½ in., width 1 ft. 5½ in. [No. 147.]

1028. (*Bay* 25.)—Limestone **sepulchral stele,** with rounded top, of **That-I-em-ḥetep** 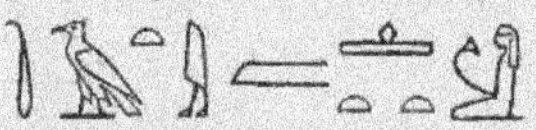, daughter of a lady of the same name, and priestess of Ptaḥ of Memphis and Isis. On the upper portion of the stele is traced, in black ink, a figure of the deceased adoring the gods Osiris and Isis, who stand beneath a winged disk with pendent uraei. Beneath this are seven lines of hieroglyphics and two lines of demotic, traced in black ink. The text states that the deceased was buried on the 17th day of the 1st month of Pert, in the 29th year [of Ptolemy Physkon], that her embalming occupied seventy days, and that her age was 36 years, 3 months, and 20 days. Ptolemaïc Period. Height 1 ft., width 8½ in. [No. 387.]

1029. (*Bay* **24.**)—Portions of a limestone **sepulchral stele,** with rounded top, of **Nes-qeṭi**, who was surnamed **Peṭā-ḥrȧ-ka**, high-priest of Memphis, priest of the temple of King Rameses in Memphis, priest of the Princess **Philotera**, and of Queen **Arsinoë**, son of the lady Nefer-renpet. On the upper portion of the stele were a winged disk and a figure of the deceased adoring a god; the figures and text are traced in black ink. Salt Collection. From Ṣakkârah. Ptolemaïc Period. Height 2 ft. 1 in., width 1 ft. 3½ in. [No. 379.]

1030. (*Bay* **27.**)—Limestone **sepulchral stele,** with rounded top, of **Peṭā-Bast**, an Erpā, Ḥā prince, and high-priest of Ptaḥ of Memphis, the son of the lady Th-I-em-ḥetep, sculptured with the following:—1. A winged disk. 2. A scene representing the deceased being presented to Osiris, Isis, and Nephthys, by Horus and Anubis; behind stands I-em-ḥetep, the son of Ptaḥ. Below are two nearly obliterated inscriptions, one in hieroglyphics and one in the demotic character. Anastasi Collection. From Ṣakkârah. Height 2 ft. 4½ in., width 1 ft. 8 in. [No. 188.]

1031. (*Bay* **27.**)—Limestone **sepulchral stele,** with rounded top, of **Ḥra-sānkh**, the daughter of the lady

Ḥrâ-ānkh, who died in the twenty-second year of the reign of one of the Ptolemies, aged 66 years, 5 months, and 5 days. On the upper portion is cut a scene representing the deceased adoring Osiris under a disk with three pairs of wings and pendent uraei. The funerary ceremonies, which lasted seventy days, were carried out by her son Nes-qeṭi, a SEM priest, and priest of Ptaḥ. From Ṣaḳḳârah. Ptolemaïc Period. Height 1 ft. 6½ in., width 11½ in. [No. 389.]

1032. (*Bay* 27.)—Limestone **sepulchral stele,** with rounded top of **Khensu-iu**, a priest and scribe, the son of Nes-qeṭi, high-priest of Ptaḥ of Memphis, and the lady Renpit-Nefert, on which are drawn in black ink the following:—1. A heaven of stars. 2. A winged disk. 3. The sceptres of East and West. 4. A figure of the deceased adoring Osiris. 5. An inscription of four lines in the demotic character. Salt Collection. From Ṣaḳḳârah. Height 1 ft. 4½ in., width 1 ft. 0½ in. [No. 375.]

1033. (*Bay* 29.)—Limestone **sepulchral stele,** with rounded top, of . . . . **-Ḥāp**, a scribe, on which is traced in black ink a hieroglyphic inscription of eighteen lines, the greater part of which is illegible. Salt Collection. Ptolemaïc Period. Height 1 ft. 5½ in., width 11½ in. [No. 390.]

1034. (*Bay* 14.)—Red granite **tablet for offerings of Ḥeru-sa-Ȧst**, a scribe and priestly official, on which are cut in outline: 1. A tablet for offerings, on which are bread-cakes, libation vases, etc. 2. The Nile-god of the South and the Nile-god of the North, bearing tables on which are vessels of water, fruits, flowers, etc. 3. Nut, or Hathor, in the Sycamore Tree pouring out water for the soul of the deceased. 4. Nut, or Hathor, in the Sycamore Tree pouring out water on the hands of the deceased. From Panopolis. Ptolemaïc Period. Length 1 ft. 9 in., breadth 1 ft. 9½ in. [No. 1227.]

1035. (*Bay* 14.)—Limestone **tablet for offerings,** on which are sculptured in relief figures of libation vases, bread-cakes, and a vine (?); at each end is a small tank in the form of a cartouche. Ptolemaïc or Roman Period. Length 11 in., breadth 10 in. [No. 416.]

1036. (*Bay* 14.)—White limestone **tablet for offerings** of **Ṭuṭu** 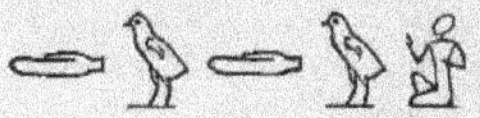, an *Utcheb* priest, and priest of the "Beneficent Gods," *i.e.*, Ptolemy IV and Arsinoë, the son of Peṭā-khens-àat 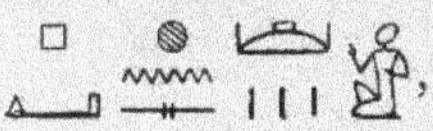, a priest who held the same offices, and Àst-urt , a sistrum-bearer of Menu. In one corner is sculptured a figure of the goddess Nut standing in the Sycamore Tree of heaven, and pouring out the water of life upon the hands of the deceased. The other portion of the face of the altar is inscribed with an address to the Sycamore Tree, the text of Chapter XXIII of the Book of the Dead (Saïte Recension), and the text beginning: "Let "the doors of heaven be opened for me, let the gates of the "earth be unclosed for me," etc. Ptolemaïc Period. Length 1 ft. 5½ in., breadth 1 ft. 5½ in. [No. 1215.]

1037. (*Bay* 14.)—Limestone **tablet for offerings** of **Ḥu-utchat-shu** , the daughter of Ḥeru, a royal scribe, and the lady Ānkh-set 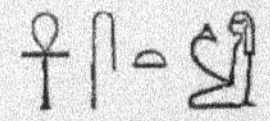, on which are sculptured figures of libation and unguent vases, bread-cakes, the Tree of Nut, or Hathor, from which project human hands holding bread-cakes and a vase of water, and the figure of a female pouring out libations. The inscription gives the genealogy of the deceased. Ptolemaïc Period. Length 1 ft. 5 in., breadth 1 ft. 4 in. [No. 1364.]

1038. (*Bay* 14.)—Grey **granite tablet** for offerings, on which are cut in outline figures of libation vases, a table of offerings, flowers, etc.; near the spout are sunk two tanks in the form of cartouches. Ptolemaïc Period. Length 1 ft. 6 in., breadth 1 ft. 6 in. [No. 592.]

1039. (*Bay* 14.)—Limestone **tablet for offerings** of **Taset** 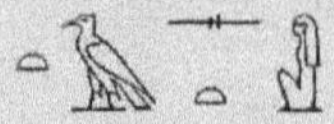, the daughter of Nes-Àmsu (or Nes-Menu) and Nebt-Utchat, inscribed with prayers to Osiris for funerary offerings, and ornamented with two figures of the deceased receiving water from deities in sycamore trees. Ptolemaïc Period. Length 1 ft. 1½ in., breadth 1 ft. 2 in. [No. 1253.]

1040. (*Bay* 16.)—Uninscribed limestone **tablet for offerings,** on which are sculptured two libation vases, a loaf of bread, and two oval cavities to receive libations. Ptolemaïc Period. Length 1 ft. 3½ in., breadth 1 ft. 3 in. [No. 419.]

1041. (*Bay* 16.)—Fine limestone **tablet for offerings** of **Sheret-ānkh** 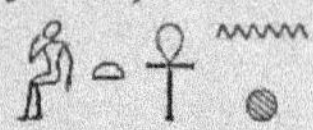, on which are cut in outline a table laden with bread-cakes, lilies, etc., flanked by libation vases. Above each vase is a hawk, with human head, arms, and hands, representing the soul of the deceased. From Akhmîm. Ptolemaïc Period. Length 1 ft. 3½ in., breadth 1 ft. 2 in. [No. 1137.]

1042. (*Bay* 16.)—Uninscribed limestone **tablet for offerings,** on which is sculptured a stand laden with bread-cakes, etc., flanked by libation vases from the spouts of which water flows. From Akhmîm. Ptolemaïc Period. Length 1 ft. 2½ in., breadth 1 ft. 2½ in. [No. 1058.]

1043. (*Bay* 17.)—Limestone **libation tablet,** with two spouts and a channel running round the four sides. In it is sunk a tank with flights of steps at the sides, which is perforated in three places. From the temple at Berenice on the Red Sea. Ptolemaïc Period. Length 1 ft. 9 in., breadth 1 ft. 3 in. [No. 135.]

Presented by Sir J. Gardner Wilkinson, 1834.

1044. (*Bay* 29.)—Limestone **sepulchral stele,** with sunk panel on which is sculptured in relief the figure of a man bidding farewell to a woman. Ptolemaïc Period. Height 1 ft. 2 in., width 8½ in. [No. 1004.]

Presented by F. G. Hilton Price, Esq., 1882.

1045. (*Bay* 27.)—Limestone **sepulchral stele,** with rounded top, of Tallous (?), on which are rudely cut the outline of a winged disk and a scene representing Anubis leading the deceased into the presence of Osiris and Nephthys. Ptolemaïc Period, or later. Height 1 ft. 3 in., width 1 ft. 1 in. [No. 400.]

1046. (*Bay* 25.) — Sandstone **sepulchral stele,** with rounded top, of **Aspidous** (?), daughter of Dionysius, on which are cut:—1. Winged disk. 2. Mummy of the deceased in a boat. 3. Anubis presenting the deceased before Osiris and Isis. Ptolemaïc Period. Height 1 ft. 2½ in., width 9½ in. [No. 843.]

1047. (*Bay* 32.)—**Head** from a **terra-cotta cover of a coffin** of a female; uninscribed. Salt Collection. From the Desert of Zobah. Ptolemaïc Period. Height 1 ft. 5 in. [No. 429.]

1048. (*Bay* 25.)—**Head** from a **terra-cotta cover of a coffin** of a female, who is represented with her hands crossed over her breast. Salt Collection. From the Desert of Zobah. Ptolemaïc Period. Height 1 ft. 10 in. [No. 431.]

ROMAN PERIOD.

1049. (*Bay* **31.**)—**Relief from the south wall** of the innermost chamber of the funerary temple which stood on the east side of the pyramid of one of the queens called **Candace,** in the great pyramid-field, near the site of the city of Meroë, the capital of the Island of Meroë, about 150 miles to the north of Kharṭûm. On the right is sculptured in relief a figure of the queen, who is seated under a canopy and holds in her hands sceptres symbolic of sovereignty and dominion; by her side is seated her Consort, whose feet rest upon a group of men representing conquered tribes. By the side of his throne are figures of members of the royal family, and behind him stands the goddess Isis pouring out a libation. Immediately in front of the knees of the large figure of the queen is another figure of the queen, who is standing by the side of a table of offerings and pouring out a libation. She stands above a seated figure of Osiris, who wears the *atef* crown. Arranged in rows before the god and the queen are vases of wine, beer, and unguents, animals bound for sacrifice at the funeral feast, baskets of figs, four bulls for sacrifice, bread-cakes, fruit, etc. Above these is a group of gods and goddesses who are making offerings at altars, and performing funerary ceremonies on behalf of the dead queen. The remaining portions of the relief are filled with figures of priests, officials, relatives, friends, and representatives of tribes, bearing offerings, palm branches, etc. Though broken in places, this relief is a very fine example of the wall decoration of funerary temples in the Sûdân during the Roman Period. It was originally painted, and traces of red colour still remain. From the Pyramid Group A. Height 8 ft. 3 in., width 15 ft. 10 in. [No. 719.]

Presented by the Government of the Egyptian Sûdân, 1905.

1050. (*Bay* **30.**)—Sandstone **tablet for offerings,** or altar, inscribed in the **Meroïtic character** with a sepulchral (?) text of twenty lines. From the Island of Faras in the Sûdân. A.D. 100 to 300. Length 1 ft. $8\frac{1}{2}$ in., breadth 1 ft. $3\frac{1}{2}$ in. [No. 892.]

Presented by A. H. Rhind, Esq., 1863.

1051. (*Bay* 30.)—Sandstone **tablet for offerings,** or altar, inscribed in the **Meroïtic character** with a sepulchral text of twelve lines. Traces of red paint still remain in some of the characters. From the Sûdân (?). A.D. 100 to 300. Length 1 ft. $2\frac{1}{2}$ in., breadth 1 ft. 1 in. [No. 901.]

Presented by the Rev. Greville Chester, B.A., 1865.

1052. (*Bay* 27.)—Reddish sandstone **sepulchral stele,** with rounded top, inscribed with a text recording the building of additions to the temple of Mut, lady of Asher and consort of Amen-Rā in Thebes, by the Roman Emperor **Tiberius Caesar,** about A.D. 20. On the upper portion are sculptured the winged disk and a scene representing the emperor kneeling before the goddess Mut, her son Khensu, and Khensu-p-khart, and presenting to them an offering. From Thebes. Roman Period. Height 2 ft. 2 in., width 1 ft. $5\frac{1}{2}$ in.

[No. 617.]

1053. (*Bay* 29.)—Sandstone **sepulchral stele,** with rounded top, set up to commemorate the erection of a statue to the goddess Mut, and the restoration of certain buildings connected with her sanctuary at Thebes, and their re-endowment by **Tiberius Caesar** 

 about A.D. 20. On the upper part is sculptured a scene representing the emperor kneeling and making an offering to the goddess Mut and to her son Khensu, beneath a winged disk, and below are cut seven lines of hieroglyphics describing his work. Salt Collection. From Karnak. Height 2 ft. 2 in., width 1 ft. 5 in. [No. 398.]

1054. (*Bay* 26.)—Sandstone **stele,** with rounded top, of the Roman Emperor **Tiberius** (A.D. 14 to 37). On the upper portion are sculptured :—1. The solar disk, with three pairs of

 (*To face page* 283.)

Stele sculptured with a scene representing the Emperor Tiberius making offerings to the gods of Thebes.

[Bay 26, No. 1054.]

wings and pendent uraei. 2. A scene in which the emperor is represented making an offering of Maāt  to the gods Ȧmen, Mut, Khensu, and Khensu-pa-kharṭ. Below are cut seven lines of text. (**Plate XXXIX.**) Height 2 ft. 2 in., width 1 ft. 5 in. [No. 1432.]

1055. (*Bay* **27.**)—Sandstone **stele,** with rounded top, on which is sculptured a winged disk, and a scene representing the Roman Emperor **Trajan** (?) making offerings to a cow wearing the horns and plumes of Isis or Hathor. Below are eleven lines of hieroglyphic text, recording the presentation of gifts to the goddess by the king. From Thebes. Roman Period. Height 2 ft. 6½ in., width 1 ft. 8½ in. [No. 709.]

1056. (*Bay* **25.**)—Massive limestone **stele,** in the form of the door of a tomb, with palm-leaf cornice, surmounted by uraei with disks, and ornamented with a winged disk, supported on lotus pillars, cut in relief. Within this door is a second door, similar to the first, and on the flat, sunk surface are sculptured two scenes in which a Roman Emperor is represented adoring the gods Seb (?), Rā, Ḥeru-Beḥuṭet and Isis. Roman Period. Height 4 ft. 1 in., width 2 ft. 6½ in. [No. 789.]

Presented by the Marquis of Northampton, 1852.

1057. (*Bay* **32.**)—Limestone **stele,** with rounded top, sculptured with a figure of the winged disk with pendent uraei, and inscribed with thirty-five lines of Greek text. It was set up near the Sphinx by the inhabitants of the villages of the Letopolite nome, in honour of **F. Claudius Balbillus,** governor of Egypt, and as a token of their gratitude to the Emperor **Nero,** who had appointed him to rule over Egypt. From the Temple of the Sphinx at Gîzah. First century A.D. Height 3 ft. 11 in., width 2 ft. [No. 192.]

1058. (*Bay* **32.**)—Limestone **stele,** with rounded top, inscribed in Greek with a text recording the repairs of the walls which surrounded the **Sphinx** at Gîzah, in the sixth year of the reign of the Emperors **Marcus Aurelius Antoninus** and **Lucius Verus** (*i.e.,* A.D. 166), when Fl. Titianus was

Prefect of Egypt, and Lucceius Ophellians was general of the army, and Theon was Nomarch. Dated on the 15th day of the month Pakhôn. Found in front of the Sphinx. Height 2 ft. 3 in., width 1 ft. 2 in. [No. 438.]

Presented by Captain Caviglia, 1817.

1059. (*Bay* **26.**)—Sandstone **slab,** inscribed with the names of Diocletian and Constantine. From Philae. Roman Period. Length 2 ft. 6 in., breadth 1 ft. 2 in. [No. 1359.]

1060. (*Bay* **29.**) — Limestone **sepulchral stele,** with rounded top, of **P-ḥā** , the son of Qeprer , on which are sculptured :—1. The winged disk. 2. The jackals of Ȧnpu and Ȧp-uat. 3. The deceased adoring Rā-Harmachis. 4. The deceased adoring Rā in his boat. Below are cut sixteen perpendicular lines of hieroglyphics containing praises of the gods. Roman Period (?) Height 2 ft. 2 in., width 1 ft. 7½ in. [No. 710.]

1061. (*Bay* **29.**) — Limestone **sepulchral stele,** with rounded top, of . . . . . **Menu** . . . . , an *Utcheb* priest, and Ka-priest, on which are sculptured :—1. The winged solar disk, with pendent uraei. 2. The jackals of Ȧnpu and Ȧp-uat. 3. The deceased adoring Menu, Horus, Isis, and Nephthys. 4. The deceased adoring Ȧn-ḥer, Tefnut, and Osiris. Below are cut nineteen perpendicular lines of hieroglyphic text, containing praises and prayers to the gods, and the genealogy of the deceased. Roman Period. Height 2 ft. 1 in., width 1 ft. 6 in. [No. 1155.]

1062. (*Bay* **29.**)—Painted limestone **sepulchral stele,** with rounded top, of **Ḥeru-bȧk (?)-shep (?)-Menu-āa (?)** on which are sculptured the solar disk, with four pairs of wings, the jackals of Ȧnpu and Ȧp-uat, and a scene representing the deceased adoring Osiris, Horus, and Anubis. The name of the deceased is in hieroglyphics, and on the lower portion of the stele is an inscription of six lines in the demotic character. Roman Period. Height 2 ft., width 1 ft. 4½ in. [No. 1298.]

1063. (*Bay* 29.)—Limestone **sepulchral stele,** with rounded top, of **Ḥeru-sa-Ȧst** , on which are sculptured a winged disk, the boat of Rā drawn by the jackal of Ȧp-uat, and a scene representing the deceased adoring Osiris, Horus, Isis, and Nephthys. Below is cut a prayer for sepulchral offerings. Roman Period. Height 1 ft. 2 in., width $9\frac{1}{2}$ in. [No. 1294.]

1064. (*Bay* 14.)—Marble **tablet for offerings,** sculptured in relief with figures of ten bread-cakes, a stand of wine vases, libation jars, lilies, etc.; at the back is a tank, and a channel runs round all four margins. On the back edge is a demotic inscription in one line. Roman Period. Length 10 in., breadth 10 in. [No. 1251.]

1065. (*Bay* 16.)—Grey granite **tablet for offerings,** sculptured in relief with figures of bread-cakes, etc. A shallow channel is cut on all four sides, and on the front edge is a demotic inscription in one line. Roman Period. Length 1 ft., breadth 1 ft. [No. 1252.]

1066. (*Bay* 16.)—Sandstone **tablet for offerings,** unsculptured, on two edges of which is an inscription in demotic. Roman Period. Length 1 ft. 1 in., breadth 1 ft. 1 in. [No. 415.]

1067. (*Bay* 16.)—Limestone **tablet for offerings,** in the centre of which is sunk a small tank, with flights of steps; on each side of it is sculptured the figure of a libation vase, and on the spout is cut a flower. Roman Period. Length 11 in., breadth $9\frac{1}{2}$ in. [No. 717.]

1068. (*Bay* 16.)—Rectangular black basalt **libation tank,** in the form of a temple building, with deep cornice. On the front, in relief, is sculptured the head of a lion. Roman Period. Length 1 ft. 7 in., breadth 1 ft. $1\frac{1}{2}$ in., height $8\frac{1}{2}$ in. [No. 1281.]

1069. (*Bay* 29.)—Limestone **sepulchral stele,** with rounded top, on which are sculptured a winged disk, two jackals, and a scene representing Anubis leading the deceased into the presence of Osiris. The demotic inscription on the lower part is illegible. From Memphis. Roman Period. Height 1 ft. 4 in., width 10½ in. [No. 399.]

1070. (*Bay* 27.)—Green basalt **head** from the statue of a youth, or man. From Alexandria. Harris Collection. Roman Period. Height 9 in. [No. 970.]

Sepulchral stele of the Roman Period.
[Bay 29, No. 1069.]

1071. (*Bay* 26.)—Limestone **stele,** with rounded top, sculptured in relief with a scene representing a king making offerings to the gods Sebek and Khnemu, who are seated on thrones, and wear disks, plumes, and uraei, and hold sceptres in their hands. Above are figures of the winged disk, and two crocodiles, each wearing the crown. Roman Period. Height 1 ft. 7 in., width 1 ft. 3½ in. [No. 1073.]

1072. (*Bay* 28.)—Rectangular limestone **stele**, sculptured with a relief representing a man-headed sphinx standing with a table of offerings, wine-jars, etc., before him. On his head he wears the crown . Behind him is the winged disk , with pendent uraeus, symbolizing renewed youth and strength. Roman Period. Height 10½ in., width 1 ft. 1½ in. [No. 959.]

1073. (*Bay* 29.)—Dark basalt **head** from a statue, or sphinx, wearing the uraeus of royalty above the forehead. From the Towneley Collection. Roman Period, 1st or 2nd century A.D. Height 1 ft. 2 in. [No. 97.]

1074. (*Bay* 29.)—Limestone sepulchral **relief**, on which is sculptured a figure of a man lying on a bier. Roman Period. Height 1 ft. 7 in., width 1 ft. 9 in. [No. 885.]

1075. (*Bay* 29.)—Limestone sepulchral **relief**, on which is sculptured a scene representing two Anubis gods presenting to Osiris two deceased persons. Roman Period. Height 2 ft., width 1 ft. 10 in. [No. 189.]

1076. (*Bay* 29.)—Limestone **stele**, sculptured with a shrine in which, in relief, is a figure of an uraeus wearing the solar disk. D'Athanasi Collection. Roman Period. Height 1 ft. 2 in., width 10 in. [No. 401.]

1077. (*Bay* 29.)—Sandstone **stele**, sculptured with a shrine, having pillars with lotus capitals, a cornice of uraei, etc., and a niche containing a figure of the hawk of Horus. Roman Period. Height 1 ft. 5 in., width 1 ft. [No. 1363.]

1078. (*Bay* 30.) — Grey granite **obelisk**, uninscribed. Roman Period. Height 4 ft. 4 in., width of sides at base 5 in. [No. 1205.]

1079. (*Bay* 32.)—Limestone **slab**, on which is a representation of a human foot, in sunk relief; above it are the letters πεκφ, and on one side of it is cut a palm branch. Found in front of the Sphinx. Roman Period. Length 1 ft. 9½ in., width 9 in. [No. 436.]

Presented by Captain Caviglia, 1817.

1080. (*Bay* 32.)—Fluted, lotus-shaped **capital of a basalt pillar,** resting on a stone taken from the ruins of the building in which it was found. Roman Period, or later. Height of capital, with abacus, 1 ft. 9 in., height of stone, 2 ft. 8 in. [Nos. 136, 136A.]

Presented by Earl Spencer, 1805.

1081. (*Bay* 30.)—Limestone **portrait figure,** mounted in the form of a **term,** or boundary figure, of Hermes. Roman Period. Height 3 ft. 1 in. [No. 1218.]

1082. (*Bay* 30.)—Black granite **portrait figure,** mounted in the form of a **term,** or boundary figure, of Hermes. Roman Period. Height 2 ft. 2 in. [No. 1219.]

1083. (*Bay* 26.)—Limestone **sepulchral stele of Politta,** a child, inscribed with a Greek metrical text, and ornamented with a portico and pediment in relief. From Memphis. First century A.D. Height 1 ft. 8 in. [No. 1206.]

1084. (*Bay* 26.)—Portion of a **sepulchral stele,** inscribed in Greek with a prayer by **Artemidorus,** son of Auximes (?) and others to their gods. First century A.D. Height 7 in., width 1 ft. 2½ in. [No. 661.]

1085. (*Bay* 29.)—Rectangular limestone **sepulchral stele,** in the form of a shrine, on the upper portion of which is sculptured in relief a figure of the deceased reclining on a bed, with two cushions under the left elbow, and holding a wine cup in the right hand. At the foot of the bed is a figure of a man standing with both hands raised. Below this are cut in outline two jackals, two wine-jars on stands, a chest, etc. The inscription, in Greek, is illegible; it appears to be dated on the twenty-fifth day of the month of Thoth. Roman Period. Height 1 ft. 1½ in., width 1 ft. 1 in. [No. 821.]

Presented by Lyttleton Annesley, Esq., 1854.

1086. (*Bay* 31.)—Column, or **pillar altar,** inscribed in Greek with a dedication to the god **Serapis,** in the city of Canopus. Found at Abûķîr. Height 4 ft. 2 in. [No. 99.]

Presented by Dr. Bancroft, Junr., 1807.

1087. (*Bay* 26.)—Square sandstone **slab,** inscribed in Greek with a text recording the cleansing and restoration of some public building near the town of Kom Ombo in Upper

Egypt, by **Arsenius,** the governor. The work was carried out at the suggestion of the bishop, the whole population assisting, during the rule of Gabriel, Duke of the Thebaïd. Found on the south side of the temple of Kom Ombo. Sixth or seventh century A.D. 1 ft. 5 in. square. [No. 1196.]

1088. (*Bay* 28.)—Portion of a limestone **cylindrical monument,** inscribed with a dedication to Isis, in Greek. Height 8 in. [No. 1043.]

1089. (*Bay* 30.)—Rectangular limestone **sepulchral stele,** broken at three of its corners, inscribed with an epitaph in Greek. From Upper Egypt. Period doubtful. Height 1 ft. 1 in., width 10 in. [No. 923.]

1090. (*Bay* 30.)—Rectangular limestone **sepulchral stele,** inscribed in Greek with a text recording the restoration of a gate by certain officials; it was set up on the eleventh day of the month Paophi, in one of the years of the XIVth Indiction. Length 1 ft. 2½ in., breadth 8 in. [No. 603.]

1091. (*Bay* 26.)—Sandstone **sepulchral stele,** inscribed in Greek, of **Souaei,** who died on the tenth day of the month Phaophi, in the sixth year of an Indiction. From Thebes (?). Height 7½ in., width 5 in. [No. 409.]

1092. (*Bay* 26.)—Sandstone **sepulchral stele,** inscribed in Greek, of **Peter,** a deacon, who died in the month of Pharmuthi, in the fourth year of an Indiction. Height 7½ in., width 5½ in. [No. 1360.]

1093. (*Bay* 26.)—Sandstone **sepulchral stele,** inscribed in Greek, of **Mena,** who died on the third day of the month Phamenôth, in the fourteenth year of the Indiction. From Kalâbshah. Eighth or ninth century A.D. Height 7 in., width 5 in. [No. 823.]

Presented by Lyttleton Annesley, Esq., 1854.

1094. (*Bay* 26.)—Sandstone **sepulchral stele of Isis** (?), inscribed in Greek, with a prayer addressed to the "God of Spirits" that the deceased may find rest with Abraham, Isaac, and Jacob in heaven. Seventh to ninth century A.D. Height 1 ft. 8 in. [No. 939.]

Presented by the Royal Institution, 1870.

1095. (*Bay* 26.)—Sandstone **sepulchral stele,** inscribed in Greek, of **Aideosa,** who died on the fifteenth day of the month Pakhôn, in the tenth year of an Indiction. From Kalâbshah. Eighth or ninth century A.D. Height 7½ in., width 5½ in. [No. 822.]

Presented by Lyttleton Annesley, Esq., 1854.

1096. (*Bay* 26.)—Sandstone **sepulchral stele,** inscribed in Greek, of **Nikea,** who died on the nineteenth day of the month Payni, in the fifth year of an Indiction. From Kalâbshah. Eighth or ninth century A.D. Height 7 in., width 5½ in. [No. 824.]

Presented by Lyttleton Annesley, Esq., 1854.

1097. (*Bay* 28.) — Limestone **sepulchral stele,** with pyramidal top, decorated with flowers (?) etc., sculptured in relief, and inscribed in Greek, of **Moses,** a centurion, son of Paul, who died on the first day of the month Epiphi, in the second year of an Indiction, aged 35 years. Sams Collection. Height 1 ft. 1 in., width 11½ in. [No. 1362.]

1098. (*Bay* 26.)—Sandstone **sepulchral stele,** inscribed in Greek, of **Akkendarpe,** who died on the sixteenth day of the month Khoiak, in the first year of the Indiction. From Kalâbshah. Height 10 in., width 7½ in. [No. 602.]

Presented by Lyttleton Annesley, Esq., 1854.

1099. (*Bay* 30.) — Limestone **sepulchral stele,** with rounded top and cornice, inscribed in Greek with a prayer for the repose of the soul of **Theodore.** Below the inscription is sculptured a cross between two pillars. Christian Period. Height 1 ft. 5 in., width 1 ft. 0½ in. [No. 405.]

1100. (*Bay* 28.)—Portion of the sandstone **sepulchral stele of Marcus,** inscribed in Greek with a prayer that the deceased might rest in the bosom of Abraham, Isaac, and Jacob. He died on the fifth day of Phamenôth, in the second year of the Indiction, in the Year of Diocletian 472, *i.e.*, A.D. 756. Height 8½ in., width 10½ in. [No. 408.]

1101. (*Bay* 28.)—Rough-hewn sandstone **sepulchral stele of Talsia.** The inscription, which is cut within a line border, is in Greek, and states that she died on the first day of the month Khoiak, in the fourteenth year of an Indiction. Height 5½ in., width 1 ft. 1½ in. [No. 407.]

1102. (*Bay* 28.)—Rectangular limestone **sepulchral stele of Deido,** a Christian lady. The inscription is in Greek, and states that she died on the eighteenth day of the month Phamenôth, in the first year of an Indiction. Sixth or seventh century A.D. Height 8 in., width 1 ft. 5 in. [No. 1046.]

1103. (*Bay* 30.)—Limestone **tablet,** which was set up in a church to commemorate **Apa Paḥomo,** the Father of a monastic settlement, **Apa Victor, Apa Iônas, Apa Asa Antseinou, Anup,** and their mother and young brother **Phoibamôn.** In the centre are sculptured a cross and crown; on the right is a figure of the military saint **Victor,** and on

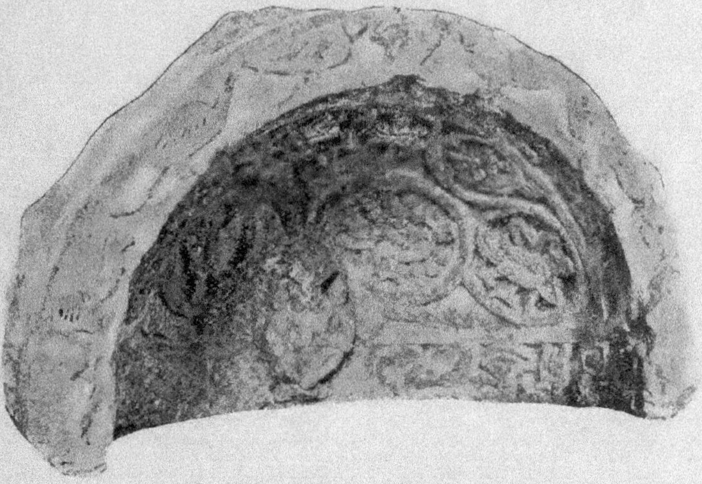

Apse of a shrine of a Saint from a Coptic church.
[Bay 32, No. 1104.]

the left a figure of the military saint **Apa Kene.** From Suhâḳ. Seventh to tenth century A.D. Length 6 ft. 5 in., breadth 1 ft. 1 in. [No. 1276.]

1104. (*Bay* 32.)—Portion of a limestone **pillar,** probably from an ancient Egyptian temple, which has been cut and hollowed out to form the **apse of the shrine** of a saint in a Coptic church. On the edge are sculptured the figures of birds (doves ?), and on the inside, springing from a shell in the centre, is a design formed of vine branches with doves perched among the grapes and leaves, the whole being enclosed within a border of leaves, flowers, shells, fish, etc. From Esnah. Diameter 2 ft. 7 in. [No. 1423.]

1105. (*Bay* 30.)—Rectangular limestone **sepulchral stele of John the Deacon,** inscribed with a text in which the deceased is made to lament the bitterness of death, and to state that he died and was buried in the city of Kôs. Height 1 ft. 4 in., width 1 ft. 1 in. [No. 900.]

Presented by J. Manship Norman, Esq., 1865.

1106. (*Bay* 32.) — Limestone **panel,** which was fixed immediately above the altar in a Coptic church, sculptured with five circular ornaments, three large and two small. The central ornament contains a cross and four vine leaves, and the large ones on the right and left contain vine leaves and a rectangle and circle interlaced. In each of the two small connecting circles is a rosette. From Ṣûhâḳ. Length 4 ft. 10 in., breadth 1 ft. 7½ in. [No. 1334.]

1107. (*Bay* 32.)—Portion of a limestone **sepulchral stele,** of Apa **Jôsêph Pegosh,** a native of Terôt-en-Shoone, who died on the twenty-first day of the month of Mesore. The inscription is in Coptic, and contains an invocation to Saints Biktôr (Victor), Phêbamôn, Mêna, George, Cyriacus, Philotheos, Sergius and his brethren, and other saints. Round the inscription is a raised flat border ornament with diamond and leaf patterns. Height 1 ft. 7½ in., width 1 ft. 6 in. [No. 676.]

1108. (*Bay* 30.)—Upper portion of a rectangular limestone **stele,** inscribed in Coptic with an address, or **invocation,** to Jeremiah, Enoch, Mary the Virgin, and other saints. Height 11 in., width 11 in. [No. 672.]

1109. (*Bay* 30.)—Portion of a limestone **sepulchral stele,** inscribed in Coptic with an invocation of Michael, Gabriel, and other saints. From Abydos. Height 9½ in., width 9½ in. [No. 995.]

1110. (*Bay* 28.)—Upper portion of a rectangular limestone **sepulchral stele,** inscribed in Coptic with an address, or **invocation,** to Michael, Gabriel, Adam, Mary the Virgin, Victor, Phoebamon, Mêna, George, Cyriacus, and other saints and martyrs. Height 10 in., width 1 ft. [No. 673.]

1111. (*Bay* 30.)—Rectangular limestone **sepulchral stele,** inscribed in Coptic with a text commemorating Apa **Phoibammon,** who died on the twenty-fifth day of the month Paope, Mêna, John, and other brethren. Height 1 ft. 2 in., width 2 ft. 8 in. [No. 702.]

1112. (*Bay* 30.)—Sandstone **sepulchral stele,** inscribed in Coptic with a prayer on behalf of **Hetosê,** who died on the tenth day of the month Mesore. Height 1 ft. 2 in., width 10 in. [No. 607.]

1113. (*Bay* 30.)—Sandstone **apse,** from a small shrine which held a figure of Mary the Virgin, or a Coptic saint, on which are sculptured, in relief, a cross and other religious symbols. From the ruins of a Coptic church on the Island of Philae. Coptic Period. Height 2 ft., width 2 ft. 3 in. [No. 1422.]

1114. (*Bay* 28.)—Rectangular limestone **sepulchral stele** of a woman, who appears to have died in the month of Khoiak, in the 335th (?) year ⲧⲗⲉ, of the Era of the Martyrs, *i.e.*, A.D. 619. The inscription is in Coptic. Height 7½ in., width 6½ in. [No. 182.]

1115. (*Bay* 30.)—Limestone **sepulchral stele of Hélenê,** the daughter of Peter, the deacon and steward of the Church of St. John at Esnah. From Esnah. Height 1 ft. 4½ in., width 10½ in. [No. 1336.]

1116. (*Bay* 32.)—Limestone **sepulchral stele,** with rounded top, of **Sara,** a Coptic lady, sculptured with figures of an altar, or pillar, with a floreated capital, a dove, a cross, etc., within an ornamented border. Inscribed "One God, our Helper." Height 1 ft. 3½ in., width 1 ft. [No. 667.]

1117. (*Bay* 32.)—Limestone **sepulchral stele,** with rounded top, of **Rachel,** a Christian, sculptured with the figure of a dove, standing between pillars, a cross, a shell, and semicircular bands of beaded and leaf ornaments. Inscribed "One God, our Helper." Height 1 ft. 8 in., width 1 ft. 2½ in. [No. 680.]

1118. (*Bay* 32.)—Rectangular sandstone **sepulchral stele of Teucharis,** a Christian lady, who died in the month of Mesore, in a year not stated. Below the Coptic text is a sunk panel, on which are cut in relief the Cross ☩, the letters Alpha and Omega, and vine leaves. On the border are cut a zig-zag pattern, vine leaves, crosses ✠ ✠, etc. Height 1 ft. 6½ in., width 1 ft. 1 in. [No. 1300.]

1119. (*Bay* 32.)—Octagonal marble **sepulchral stele of Troïs,** the wife of Parashe, who died on the twenty-eighth day of the month Mesore, in the 457th year of the Era of the Martyrs, *i.e.*, A.D. 741. The inscription is in Coptic. Height 1 ft. 5½ in., width 1 ft. 5½ in. [No. 1208.]

1120. (*Bay* 32.)—Sandstone **sepulchral stele of Rebecca,** a nun, inscribed in Coptic and sculptured with a representation of a pediment, with circle and vine leaves, and two *ānkh* crosses, ☥ ☥. Height 2 ft. 1 in., width 1 ft. 2 in. [No. 1299.]

1121. (*Bay* 32.)—Limestone **sepulchral stele,** inscribed in Greek, of **Eutychousa,** who died on the twenty-fifth day of the month Khoiak, in the eighth year of an Indiction. Height 2 ft., width 1 ft. [No. 660.]

1122. (*Bay* 30.)—Limestone **sepulchral stele,** with rounded top, of **Tsia,** who died on the twelfth day of the month Phamenôth, in the tenth year of the Indiction. Height 1 ft. 1 in., width 10 in. [No. 1328.]

1123. (*Bay* 32.)—Limestone **sepulchral stele of Mary,** a child, who died on the tenth day of the month Tybi. On the upper portion is a sculptured panel containing a cross and crown, and below this, enclosed within a leaf-border, is a second panel containing the Coptic inscription and the figure of a dove standing on scrolls ornamented with crosses. Both panels are enclosed within a scroll border. From Ṣûhâḳ. Height 4 ft. 4 in., width 1 ft. 6 in. [No. 618.]

1124. (*Bay* 32.)—Limestone **sepulchral stele,** with rounded top, of **Theutora,** sculptured with a representation of the front of the shrine, or temple, having a pediment and pillars with floreated capitals, and with figures of a dove, vine leaves, etc. Height 1 ft. 4½ in., width 1 ft. 1 in. [No. 669.]

1125. (*Bay* 32.)—Limestone **sepulchral stele,** with rounded top, of **Tapia,** who died on the fourth day of the month Pharmuthi, in the sixth year of an Indiction. The upper portion is decorated with a rosette within concentric circles, cut in relief. Height 1 ft. 4 in., width 9½ in. [No. 620.]

1126. (*Bay* 32.)—Limestone **sepulchral stele,** with rounded top, of **Taia,** who died on the seventeenth day of the month

Sepulchral stele of Mary, a child.
[Bay 32, No. 1123.] Coptic Period.

Mekheir, on which are sculptured a representation of the front of a shrine, or temple, figures of doves holding the Egyptian symbol of "life," ☥, etc. Height 1 ft. 4½ in., width 10 in. [No. 1327.]

1127. (*Bay* 32.)—Rectangular limestone **sepulchral stele of Manna,** who died on the seventh day of the month Tybi, in the third year of an Indiction. The Greek inscription is cut on the lower part of the monument, on three sides of it are rosettes and the meander ornament, and on the fourth side

Sepulchral monument in the form of a cross.
[Bay 32, No. 1128.] Coptic Period.

is a raised ornament. Between the inscription and the border are cut two crosses and two crowns, and between these is a rectangular cavity, with an ornament above it. Height 1 ft. 4 in., width 1 ft. 4½ in. [No. 677.]

1128. (*Bay* 32.)—Limestone cross which was set up in memory of **Abariouna** and **Eulekia.** Height 1 ft. 9½ in., width 8 in. [No. 1339.]

1129. (*Bay* 30.)—Limestone **sepulchral stele of George,** a Copt, who died in the month of Mekhir, in the fourth year of the third Indiction. Below the Coptic inscription are sculptured two figures, who stand full-faced, with their hands raised. Height 2 ft. 4 in., width 1 ft. [No. 924.]

1130. (*Bay* 32.)—Portion of the sandstone **sepulchral stele of George,** a monk, who died on the seventeenth day of the month Thoth, in the fifth year of an Indiction. The inscription is in Coptic. Height 1 ft. 2½ in., width 11 in. [No. 604.]

Presented by Sir J. Bowring, 1854.

1131. (*Bay* 30.)—Limestone **sepulchral stele of Sabinos,** inscribed in Greek, and sculptured with a rough representation of the front of a gabled shrine, or temple, with the sacred symbols ☧ and ☥, and the letters Alpha and Omega. Height 1 ft. 4½ in., width 1 ft. [No. 1352.]

1132. (*Bay* 30.) — Limestone **sepulchral stele,** with rounded top, of **Biktôr** (Victor), sculptured with figures of the eight-rayed cross, and a crown. Height 1 ft. 4½ in., width 1 ft. 0½ in. [No. 716.]

1133. (*Bay* 30.)—Rectangular limestone **sepulchral stele of Porieuthes,** who died aged 12 years, on which is sculptured a representation of the front of a shrine, or temple. Between the pillars, in high relief, are sculptured a cross and crown. Height 2 ft., width 1 ft. 1½ in. [No. 1254.]

1134. (*Bay* 30.)—Limestone **sepulchral stele of Moses,** on the upper part of which are sculptured, in relief, the representation of a pediment and vine leaves. Below these are the name of the deceased, a cross, and two palm branches. On the lower part, within a double frame, are the cross ☥, the letters Alpha and Omega, and four small crosses. Top left hand projection broken. Height 1 ft. 11½ in., width 1 ft. 1½ in. [No. 1255.]

1135. (*Bay* 32.)—Limestone **sepulchral stele,** with rounded top, of **Moses,** who died on the fifteenth day of the month Pharmuthi, in the sixth year of an Indiction. On the upper portion are sculptured representations of fronts of shrines, with pillars, semi-circular ornamental bands, figures of a dove, animals, etc. Height 1 ft. 8½ in., width 1 ft. 3½ in. [No. 664.]

1136. (*Bay* 30.)—Rectangular sandstone **sepulchral stele of Abraam,** the "perfect monk," on which is sculptured a representation of the front of a shrine, or temple. Between the pillars are a tablet bearing the name of the deceased, the cross ☥, the letters Alpha and Omega, and ☥ ☥. Height 1 ft. 11 in., width 1 ft. 1½ in. [No. 1257.]

1137. (*Bay* 32.)—Limestone **sepulchral stele,** with rounded top, of **John,** who died on the fifth day of the month Phamenôth, in the fourteenth year of an Indiction. On the upper portion is sculptured a representation of the front of a shrine, or temple, surrounded by an ornamental border. On each side of the pediment is a dove, and between the pillars is a cross. Height 2 ft. 0½ in., width 1 ft. 2½ in. [No. 665.]

1138. (*Bay* 32.) — Sandstone **sepulchral stele,** with pyramidal top, of **John,** the son of Euprepios, sculptured with a representation of a pediment with vine leaf, a cross within a crown, a cross between palm branches, annules, etc. Height 2 ft. 3 in., width 10½ in. [No. 1326.]

1139. (*Bay* 32.)—Sandstone **sepulchral stele of John,** who died on the fourteenth day of the month Tybi, in a year of the tenth Indiction. This monument is sculptured with representations of a gable, or pediment, bosses, a cross and crown, etc., and is inscribed in Greek with an address to the mourners, who are entreated not to grieve for the deceased. Seventh or eighth century A.D. Height 1 ft. 9½ in., width 11 in. [No. 1250.]

1140. (*Bay* 32.)—Sandstone **sepulchral stele of Peter,** a deacon and monk, who died on the twenty-fifth day of the month Khoiak, in the eighth year of an Indiction. The inscription is in Coptic. Height 1 ft. 3 in., width 1 ft. 0½ in. [No. 601.]

1141. (*Bay* 32.)—Limestone **sepulchral stele,** with rounded top, of **Paḥaê,** sculptured with a representation of a shrine, or temple, in relief. Height 1 ft. 3½ in., width 10 in. [No. 666.]

1142. (*Bay* 32.)—Rectangular **sepulchral stele,** with pyramidal top, of **Abraam,** who died on the twenty-second day of the month Mekhir, in a year not stated. On the upper portion is sculptured a vine branch, and on the middle are a cross and crown. Height 1 ft. 10½ in., width 1 ft. 0½ in. [No. 1351.]

1143. (*Bay* 32.)—Sandstone **pyramidal stele of Abraam,** a monk, sculptured with figures of a cross and crown, a dove, annules, and a vine leaf within a triangle; by the dove are cut the letters Alpha and Omega. Height 2 ft. 2 in., width 9½ in. [No. 619.]

1144. (*Bay* 32.) — Alabaster **circular tablet of Apa Kurillos,** a presbyter of the Church of Abbâ Kuros, who died on the twenty-sixth day of the month Thoth, in the seventh year of an Indiction. Diameter 1 ft. 8½ in. [No. 411.]

1145. (*Bay* 32.)—Limestone **sepulchral stele of Plêïnôs,** an *anagnôstês*, or "reader," on which are sculptured, in relief, the representation of the front of a shrine, or temple, the cross ☧ and crown, the letters Alpha and Omega, the cross ✠, and two *ānkh* crosses ☥ ☥, etc. Height 2 ft., width 1 ft. 3 in. [No. 679.]

1146. (*Bay* 32.)—Limestone **sepulchral stele,** with pyramidal top, of **Paulos Heliodoros,** who was at one time an officer in the army, and died on the twenty-ninth day of the month Pharmuthi, in the third year of an Indiction. On the upper portion is sculptured a vine leaf, and below the Greek inscription are a cross, crown, and four annules, in relief. Height 2 ft. 4 in., width 11 in. [No. 1335.]

1147. (*Bay* 32.)—Portion of the limestone **sepulchral stele of Phoibamon,** a monk, inscribed in Coptic with an invocation to the Trinity, and to the saints Jeremiah and Enoch. The year of his death is not stated. Height 1 ft. 6½ in., width 11½ in. [No. 404.]

1148. (*Bay* 32.)—Rectangular limestone **sepulchral stele of Philotheos,** who died on the eleventh day of the month Paône, in a year not stated. Height 1 ft., width 7½ in. [No. 622.]

1149. (*Bay* 32.)—Limestone **sepulchral stele of Apa Abeg** and **Apa Serine,** the former of whom died on the twenty-second day of the month Pharmuthi in a year not stated The inscription is in Coptic. Height 1 ft. 8 in., width 1 ft. 5½ in. [No. 1256.]

1150. (*Bay* 32.)—Limestone **sepulchral stele,** with rounded top, of **Anup,** sculptured with a rosette. The inscription is in Coptic. Height 1 ft. 5 in., width 9½ in. [No. 670.]

1151. (*Bay* 28.)—Portion of a limestone **sepulchral stele,** inscribed in Coptic with parts of three lines of text, a cross ✠, etc. Sams Collection. Height 7 in., width 1 ft. 6 in. [No. 1361.]

1152. (*Bay* 28.)—**Mural ornament,** sculptured with a cross in relief. From a Coptic Church on the Island of Philae. 11 in. square. [No. 1039.]

Presented by Captain Handcock, 1886.

1153. (*Bay* 30.) — Limestone **sepulchral stele,** with rounded top, on which are sculptured figures of a cross and crown and two circles containing crosses; below are three lines of rudely cut Coptic text. Height 1 ft. 5 in., width 1 ft. [No. 714.]

1154. (*Bay* 30.) — Limestone **sepulchral stele,** with rounded top, on which are sculptured a representation of the front of a shrine, with rounded roof and pillars, and a bird (dove?) with its wings raised. The name of the deceased is erased. Height 1 ft. 2 in., width 8½ in. [No. 671.]

1155. (*Bay* 30.)—Portion of a **sepulchral stele,** inscribed in Coptic, with prayers on behalf of a deceased person, whose name is illegible, that he may rest in the bosom of Abraham, and may hear the "sweet voice saying, 'Come, good and "'faithful servant.'" From Kalâbshah. Height 1 ft. 1 in., width 1 ft. 2 in. [No. 825.]

Presented by Lyttleton Annesley, Esq., 1854.

1156. (*Bay* 30.)—Portion of a limestone **sepulchral stele,** with rounded top, on which is sculptured, in relief, a representation of the front of a shrine, or temple, with pediment. Between the pillars are figures of two doves, facing each other, and on the sides of the roof are figures of animals. Below is an interlaced ornament. The raised semi-circular border, which rests on four pillars with floreated capitals, is sculptured with a floral pattern, leaves, and semi-circles. Height 1 ft., width 1 ft. 1 in. [No. 176.]

1157. (*Bay* 30.) — Limestone **sepulchral stele,** with rounded top, of a person whose name is wanting, sculptured on the upper part with a shell, bead and other ornaments, and on the lower with figures of two lions in combat (?), between two pillars. Height 1 ft. 2 in., width $10\frac{1}{2}$ in. [No. 621.]

1158. (*Bay* 28.)—Upper portion of the sandstone **sepulchral stele of Maria** (?), inscribed in Coptic. Sams Collection. Height 7 in., width $8\frac{1}{2}$ in. [No. 403.]

1159. (*Bay* 30.) — Limestone **sepulchral stele,** with rounded top, of **Ammonios,** sculptured with a representation of an elaborately decorated front of a shrine, or temple, with four pillars, gable, etc. Christian Period. Height 1 ft. 2 in., width 9 in. [No. 1337.]

1160. (*Bay* 30.)—Limestone **sepulchral stele,** with rounded top, of **David,** who died on the ninth day of the month Pakhon, in the twelfth year of an Indiction. On the upper portion is sculptured an eight-rayed cross enclosed within a crown. Height 1 ft. 10 in., width 1 ft. [No. 675.]

1161. (*Bay* 30.)—Limestone **sepulchral stele,** with rounded top, sculptured with figures of a cross and crown. The name of the deceased is wanting. Height 1 ft. 3 in., width 10 in. [No. 1338.]

1162. (*Bay* 32.) — Limestone **stele,** uninscribed, with rounded top, on which are sculptured figures of doves, palm branches, a cross and crown, and a representation of the front of a shrine, or temple. Height 1 ft. 5 in., width 1 ft. [No. 674.]

1163. (*Bay* 32.) — Limestone **stele,** uninscribed, with rounded top, sculptured with a representation of the front of a shrine, or temple, the figure of a dove, etc., within a decorated border. Height 1 ft. 5 in., width 11 in. [No. 668.]

1164. (*Bay* 32.)—Rectangular limestone **relief,** ornamented with herring-bone and rope patterns, and crosses, vine leaves, and other ornaments. Height 2 ft. $2\frac{1}{2}$ in., width 10 in. [No. 678.]

1165. (*Bay* 32.)—Portion of an alabaster **sepulchral stele** inscribed ✠ ⲙⲏ ⲡⲣⲟⲭ . . . . . Sams Collection. Length 8 in. [No. 410.]

1166. (*Bay* 32.)—Sandstone **sepulchral stele** of a person whose name is wanting, sculptured with figures of a cross and crown, a dove, and four annules. By the sides of the dove are cut the letters Alpha and Omega. Height 2 ft. 2 in., width 11 in. [No. 1350.]

1167. (*Bay* 32.)—Stone sculptured with a **rosette** in relief. From the ruins of an ancient Coptic church at Philae. Length 1 ft. 6 in., height 1 ft. [No. 1040.]

Presented by Captain Handcock, 1886.

1168. (*Bay* 32.)—Limestone **sepulchral stele**, with pyramidal top and unfinished inscription, sculptured in relief with figures of vine leaves, annules, a cross and crown, etc. Height 1 ft. 11½ in., width 10½ in. [No. 663.]

ADDITIONS.

1169. (*Central Saloon.*)—Massive limestone jamb from a doorway in the temple of King **Mer-en-Ptaḥ Ḥetep-ḥer-Maāt,** B.C. 1266, at Memphis. On the side are cut in large, bold hieroglyphics the king's cartouche and titles, and below is a scene representing the Nile-gods of the South and North tying papyrus and lily stems round the symbol , typifying the "Union of the Two Lands." From Memphis. XIXth dynasty. Height 6 ft. 9 in., width 1 ft. 5 in., thickness 2 ft. 9 in. [No. 1469.]

Presented by the Egyptian Research Account, 1908.

1170. (*Bay* 18.)—Massive limestone cornice from the ruins of a temple built by **Sa-Ȧmen,** a king of the XXIst dynasty (Tanite), at Memphis. In the centre are the king's cartouches, and on each side of these is his Horus name—

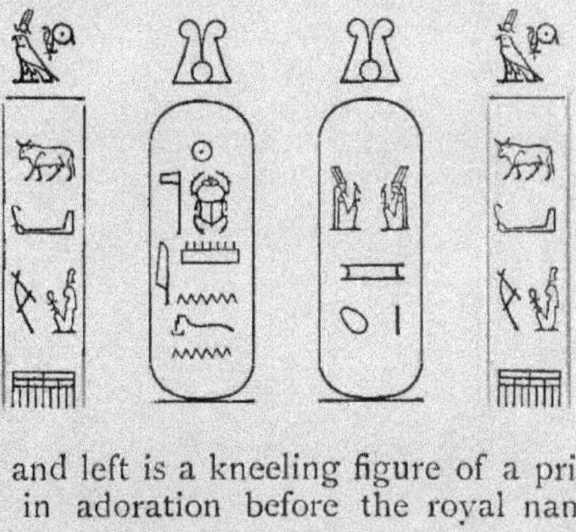

To the right and left is a kneeling figure of a priest with one hand raised in adoration before the royal names, and the other holding a fly-flapper. From Memphis. Length 7 ft. 3 in. [No. 1470.]

Presented by the Egyptian Research Account, 1908.

1171. (*Bay* 20.)—Limestone stele, with rounded top, down the centre of which is a line of hieroglyphics, which reads "Adoration to the Ka of Ptaḥ, Lord of Maāt, mighty one of "two-fold strength, the Hearer," 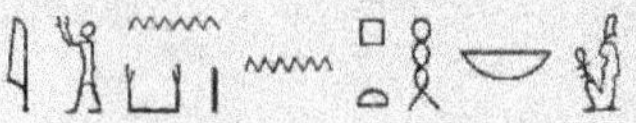 . On each side of this line were formerly twenty-two human ears, and at right angles to it, at the bottom of the stele, is a line of hieroglyphics which, when complete, probably contained the name of the man who dedicated this stele to Ptaḥ. From Memphis. XXIst dynasty. Height 8½ in., width 6½ in. [No. 1471.]

Presented by the Egyptian Research Account, 1908.

1172. (*Bay* 20.)—Limestone stele, with rounded top, on which is cut in outline a scene representing a man making offerings to the god Ptaḥ, who is here called "chief of all the "gods" 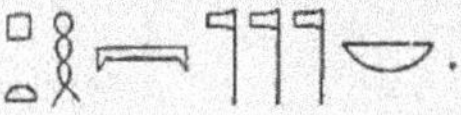. The god is in mummied form, and stands on the *maāt* pedestal ; he holds in his hand the sceptre , and from the back of his neck hangs a *menàt* . On each side of the god's head is a human ear . From Memphis. XXIst dynasty. Height 8½ in., width 5 in. [No. 1472.]

Presented by the Egyptian Research Account, 1908.

1173. (*Bay* 17.)—Painted limestone stele, with rounded top, of **Penbui** , a priestly official. On the upper portion is painted a figure of the god Ptaḥ seated within his shrine, and holding a sceptre formed of . Above the shrine are three human ears, and behind it are four human ears; in front of it is a table of offerings. The title of the god is 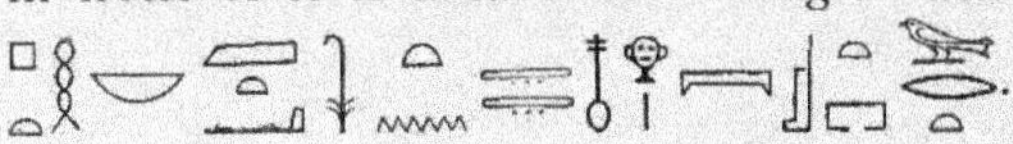.

On the lower part are painted a large , and a kneeling figure of the deceased with his hands raised in adoration. The text reads :—

From Memphis. XIXth or XXth dynasty. Height 1 ft. 3 in., width 10 in. [No. 1466.]

1174. (*Bay* 15.)—Massive black diorite libation bowl, with ears. From Thebes. XIXth dynasty. Height 1 ft. 7 in., diameter 1 ft. 11 in. [No. 1467.]

1175. (*Bay* 15.)—Massive black diorite libation bowl, with ears. From Thebes. XIXth dynasty. Height 1 ft. 4 in., diameter 1 ft. 7 in. [No. 1473.]

1176. (*Bay* 26.)—Fine white painted limestone stele of the priest of Horus  (var. 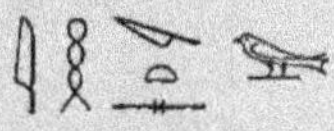 ), whose mother's name was Khenket . On the upper portion are cut a solar disk, with three pairs of wings and pendent uraei, and a scene representing the deceased standing in adoration before Osiris, Ḥeru-netch-tef-f, and Isis. Below are six lines of text containing a prayer to Osiris Un-Nefer for funerary offerings. From Akhmîm. Ptolemaïc Period. Height 1 ft. 4 in., width 11 in. [No. 1474.]

I.

INDEX OF EXHIBITION AND REGISTRATION NUMBERS.

Exhibition Number.	Registration Number.	Place.	Exhibition Number.	Registration Number.	Place.
1	1192	Vestibule.	46	531	Vestibule.
2	691	Vestibule.	47	528	Vestibule.
3	171	Vestibule.	48	870	Vestibule.
4	1212	Vestibule.	49	1112	Vestibule.
5	1267	Vestibule.	50	1385	Vestibule.
6	1266	Vestibule.	51	1143	Vestibule.
7	1228	Vestibule.	52	1275	Vestibule.
8	1324	Vestibule.	53	1383	Vestibule.
9	1345	Vestibule.	54	864	Vestibule.
10	490	Vestibule.	55	865	Vestibule.
11	491	Vestibule.	56	866	Vestibule.
12	492	Vestibule.	57	867	Vestibule.
13	1114	Vestibule.	58	868	Vestibule.
14	1181	Vestibule.	59	869	Vestibule.
15	1288	Vestibule.	60	1161	Vestibule.
16	1173	Vestibule.	61	1166	Vestibule.
17	1174	Vestibule.	62	1277	Vestibule.
18	1282	Vestibule.	63	1156	Vestibule.
19	1111	Vestibule.	64	1165	Vestibule.
20	1204	Vestibule.	65	1223	Vestibule.
21	58	Vestibule.	66	1278	Vestibule.
22	1269	Vestibule.	67	199	Vestibule.
23	1268	Vestibule.	68	1273	Vestibule.
24	157*b*	}	69	1274	Vestibule.
25	157*a*	} Bay 1.	70	430	Vestibule.
26	157*c*	}	71	1186	Vestibule.
27	1110	Vestibule.	72	994	Bay 2.
28	1113	Vestibule.	73	1170	Vestibule.
29	1117	Vestibule.	74	626	Vestibule.
30	1115	Vestibule.	75	1341	Vestibule.
31	1272	Vestibule.	76	1342	Vestibule.
32	682	Vestibule.	77	627	Vestibule.
33	1239	Bay 1.	78	1263	Vestibule.
34	35	Vestibule.	79	212	Vestibule.
35	1144	Vestibule.	80	718	Assyrian
36	1116	Vestibule.			Saloon.
37	993	Vestibule.	81	1136	Bay 1.
38	1185	Vestibule.	82	1287	Vestibule.
39	992	Vestibule.	83	658	Vestibule.
40	1242	Vestibule.	84	647	Vestibule.
41	1169	Vestibule.	85	1191	Vestibule.
42	1171	Vestibule.	86	128	Vestibule.
43	1168	Vestibule.	87	1011	Vestibule.
44	130	Vestibule.	88	1330	Vestibule.
45	527, 529,	Vestibule.	89	112	Vestibule.
	530, 532-5		90	1293	Vestibule.

Exhibition Number.	Registration Number.	Place.	Exhibition Number.	Registration Number.	Place.
91	1264	Vestibule.	145	828	Bay 6.
92	1262	Vestibule.	146	574	Bay 1.
93	1175	Bay 14.	147	839	Bay 1.
94	1176	Bay 14.	148	1236	Bay 5.
95	1179	Bay 14.	149	497	Bay 1.
96	159	Vestibule.	150	567	Bay 1.
97	203	Vestibule.	151	583	Bay 7.
98	1429	Vestibule.	152	829	Bay 5.
99	1208	Bay 4.	153	256	Bay 3.
100	614	Bay 4.	154	576	Bay 1.
101	614*c*		155	257	Bay 9.
102	614*b*	Bay 4.	156	573	Bay 1.
103	614*a*		157	1010	Vestibule.
104	720	Bay 3.	158	684	Bay 1.
105	1397	Bay 3.	159	685	Bay 1.
106	721	Bay 3.	160	686	Bay 3.
107	722	Bay 3.	161	608	Bay 1.
108	731	Bay 3.	162	692	Bay 1.
109	730	Bay 3.	163	1145	Vestibule.
110	752	Bay 3.	164	1146	Vestibule.
111	729	Bay 3.	165	1069	Vestibule.
112	750	Bay 3.	166	1099	Bay 23.
113	742	Bay 3.	167	1102	Bay 23.
114	732	Bay 3.	168	575	Bay 1.
115	745	Bay 3.	169	852	Bay 3.
116	724	Bay 3.	170	831	Bay 5.
117	753	Bay 3.	171	1072	Bay 5.
118	754	Bay 3.	172	688	Bay 2.
119	628	Bay 4.	173	1120	C.S.
120	1372	Bay 4.	174	1135	Bay 1.
121	643	Bay 3.	175	101	Bay 2.
122	1313	Bay 2.	176	1290	Vestibule.
123	187	Vestibule.	177	557	Bay 1.
124	1312	Bay 2.	178	827	Vestibule.
125	1260	Vestibule.	179	694	Bay 3.
126	451	Bay 5.	180	695	Bay 3.
127	100	Vestibule.	181	233	Bay 5.
128	152	Bay 1.	182	625	Vestibule.
129	579	Bay 1.	183	462	Bay 1.
130	131	Bay 1.	184	777	Bay 1.
131	1172	Vestibule.	185	143	Bay 1.
132	1315	Bay 4.	186	559	Bay 1.
133	582	Vestibule.	187	577	Bay 1.
134	1164	Bay 4.	188	774	Bay 1.
135	1261	Vestibule.	189	568	Bay 1.
136	963	Bay 5.	190	571	Bay 1.
137	615	Bay 1.	191	253	Bay 2.
138	586	Bay 3.	192	228	Bay 2.
139	489	Bay 3.	193	566	Bay 2.
140	572	Bay 1.	194	162	Bay 2.
141	562	Bay 3.	195	832	Bay 2.
142	461	Bay 3.	196	1177	Bay 4.
143	569	Bay 1.	197	581	Bay 7.
144	570	Bay 1.	198	1147	Bay 2.

Exhibition Number.	Registration Number.	Place.	Exhibition Number.	Registration Number.	Place.
199	1152	Bay 2.	253	363	Bay 7.
200	1151	Bay 2.	254	585	Bay 7.
201	1150	Bay 7.	255	830	Bay 7.
202	693	Bay 1.	256	361	Bay 9.
203	580	Vestibule.	257	928	Bay 9.
204	587	Vestibule.	258	469	Bay 6.
205	560	Vestibule.	259	413	Bay 14.
206	1149	Vestibule.	260	553	Bay 14.
207	193	Bay 1.	261	414	Bay 14.
208	129	Bay 1.	262	980	Bay 14.
209	584	Bay 1.	263	417	Bay 14.
210	578	Bay 1.	264	976	Bay 14.
211	561	Bay 1.	265	973	Bay 16.
212	564	Bay 1.	266	974	Bay 16.
213	565	Bay 1.	267	990	Bay 16.
214	558	Bay 1.	268	929	Bay 14.
215	252	Bay 2.	269	590	Bay 17.
216	903	Bay 2.	270	975	Bay 14.
217	334	Bay 2.	271	997	Bay 14.
218	243	Bay 2.	272	420	Bay 14.
219	258	Bay 3.	273	991	Bay 14.
220	205	Bay 3.	274	977	Bay 16.
221	222	Bay 3.	275	978	Bay 16.
222	971	Bay 3.	276	871	Bay 1.
223	240	Bay 3.	277	1346	Bay 2.
224	198	Bay 3.	278	1060	Bay 5.
225	471	Bay 4.	279	1348	Bay 5.
226	362	Bay 4.	280	1163	Bay 1.
227	223	Bay 4.	281	969	Bay 3.
228	230	Bay 4.	282	630	Bay 4.
229	232	Bay 4.	283	833	Bay 5.
230	219	Bay 4.	284	1100	Bay 23.
231	788	Bay 4.	285	201	Bay 1.
232	215	Bay 4.	286	861	Bay 2.
233	914	Bay 4.	287	636	Bay 2.
234	225	Bay 4.	288	1237	Bay 2.
235	1322	Bay 4.	289	1229	Bay 2.
236	1367	Bay 5.	290	507	Bay 3.
237	202	Bay 5.	291	208	Bay 3.
238	254	Bay 5.	292	904	Bay 3.
239	805	Bay 5.	293	224	Bay 3.
240	209	Bay 5.	294	851	Bay 4.
241	237	Bay 5.	295	239	Bay 4.
242	241	Bay 5.	296	504 (216*)	Bay 4.
243	238	Bay 5.	297	213	Bay 4.
244	98	Bay 6.	298	145	Bay 7.
245	235	Bay 7.	299	141	Bay 7.
246	247	Bay 7.	300	905	Bay 7.
247	220	Bay 7.	301	563	Bay 7.
248	227	Bay 7.	302	1246	Bay 7.
249	1213	Bay 7.	303	226	Bay 7.
250	1059	Bay 7.	304	221	Bay 7.
251	1201	Bay 7.	305	255	Bay 7.
252	244	Bay 7.	306	206	Bay 9

Exhibition Number.	Registration Number.	Place.	Exhibition Number.	Registration Number.	Place.
307	1061	Bay 3.	361	55	Bay 5.
308	196	Bay 3.	362	949	Bay 5.
309	195	Bay 3.	363	12	Bay 2.
310	207	Bay 4.	364	943	Bay 12.
311	231	Bay 4.	365	1019	Bay 10.
312	204	Bay 4.	366	1109	Bay 6.
313	249	Bay 4.	367	1108	C.S.
314	930	Bay 4.	368	1021	Bay 11.
315	242	Bay 5.	369	153	Bay 12.
316	791	Bay 7.	370	1015	Bay 11.
317	1244	Bay 7.	371	1199	Bay 10.
318	197	Bay 7.	372	701	Bay 8.
319	251	Bay 7.	373	840	Bay 9.
320	248	Bay 7.	374	1131 (51*a*)	Bay 9.
321	234	Bay 9.	375	31	Bay 4.
322	477	Bay 18.	376	890	Bay 12.
323	844	Bay 7.	377	902	Bay 11.
324	1245	Bay 7.	378	148	Bay 8.
325	1247	Bay 7.	379	1434	Bay 7.
326	806	Bay 7.	380	43	Bay 7.
327	1370	Bay 9.	381	76	Bay 1.
328	236	Bay 9.	382	80	Bay 1.
329	1371	Bay 9.	383	50	Bay 1.
330	846	Bay 9.	384	71	Bay 1.
331	250	Bay 9.	385	72	Bay 2.
332	246	Bay 9.	386	60	Bay 2.
333	245	Bay 9.	387	53	Bay 3.
334	229	Bay 9.	388	49	Bay 5.
335	210	Bay 11.	389	69	Bay 6.
336	1314	Bay 9.	390	65	Bay 7.
337	1318	Bay 11.	391	62	Bay 10.
338	310	Bay 11.	392	45	Bay 7.
339	1101	Bay 23.	393	84	Bay 8.
340	987	Bay 5.	394	41	Bay 9.
341	478	Vestibule.	395	519	Bay 12.
342	631	Bay 4.	396	520	Bay 13.
343	1142	Bay 16.	397	87	Bay 10.
344	1133	Bay 12.	398	85	Bay 10.
345	916	Bay 20.	399	599	Bay 14.
346	683	Bay 3.	400	521	Bay 11.
347	690	Bay 9.	401	77	Bay 11.
348	598	Bay 7.	402	522	Bay 13.
349	277	Bay 9.	403	52	Bay 16.
350	815	Bay 10.	404	79	Bay 4.
351	186	Bay 11.	405	88	Bay 4.
352	448	Bay 8.	406	57	Bay 5.
353	1347	Bay 8.	407	68	Bay 8.
354	816	Bay 10.	408	37	Bay 9.
355	297	Bay 10.	409	518	Bay 11.
356	811	Bay 10.	410	16 and 73	Bay 6.
357	446	Bay 11.	411	657 (138*)	Bay 6.
358	274	Bay 13.	412	14	Bay 8.
359	594	Bay 14.	413	21	Bay 9.
360	15	Bay 5.	414	105	Bay 11.

Exhibition Number.	Registration Number.	Place.	Exhibition Number.	Registration Number.	Place.
415	30	Bay 6.	469	356	Bay 9.
416	6	Bay 4.	470	689	Bay 9.
417	4	Bay 5.	471	773	Bay 9.
418	140	C.S.	472	293	Bay 9.
419	64	Bay 7.	473	910	Bay 9.
420	1001	Bay 12.	474	149	Bay 9.
421	503	Bay 6.	475	826	Bay 9.
422	123	Bay 7.	476	956	Bay 10.
423	1210	Bay 5.	477	1220	Bay 10.
424	1182	Bay 10.	478	264	Bay 10.
425	365	Bay 11.	479	819	Bay 10.
426	813	Bay 12.	480	346	Bay 10.
427	687	Bay 13.	481	381	Bay 10.
428	1068	Bay 12.	482	597	Bay 10.
429	38	Bay 11.	483	291	Bay 10.
430	1	Bay 11.	484	294	Bay 10.
431	34	Bay 10.	485	265	Bay 10.
432	138	Bay 10.	486	266	Bay 10.
433	194	Bay 9.	487	307	Bay 10.
434	834	Bay 13.	488	1012	Bay 10.
435	1000	Bay 13.	489	271	Bay 11.
436	880	Bay 13.	490	272	Bay 11.
437	1083	Bay 13.	491	932	Bay 11.
438	324	Bay 10.	492	368	Bay 11.
439	211	Bay 12.	493	332	Bay 11.
440	1002	C.S.	494	353	Bay 11.
441	75	Bay 13.	495	427	Bay 11.
442	5	Bay 12.	496	804	Bay 11.
443	1222	Bay 2.	497	1016	Bay 11.
444	29	Bay 3.	498	358	Bay 11.
445	124	Bay 5.	499	280	Bay 11.
446	200	Bay 5.	500	214	Bay 11.
447	893	Bay 5.	501	348	Bay 11.
448	632	Bay 6.	502	906	Bay 11.
449	1200	Bay 6.	503	1332	Bay 11.
450	1119	Bay 6.	504	860	Bay 12.
451	453	Bay 6.	505	547	Bay 12.
452	1022	Bay 7.	506	812	Bay 12.
453	1195	Bay 8.	507	1248	Bay 12.
454	456	Bay 8.	508	339	Bay 12.
455	282	Bay 8.	509	366	Bay 12.
456	803	Bay 8.	510	316	Bay 12.
457	295	Bay 8.	511	797	Bay 12.
458	1062	Bay 8.	512	623	Bay 12.
459	341	Bay 8.	513	1368	Bay 12.
460	155	Bay 8.	514	303	Bay 12.
461	551	Bay 8.	515	175	Bay 12.
462	552	Bay 8.	516	173	Bay 12.
463	550	Bay 8.	517	919	Bay 12.
464	279	Bay 8.	518	920	Bay 12.
465	322	Bay 8.	519	921	Bay 13.
466	300	Bay 9.	520	922	Bay 13.
467	276	Bay 9.	521	1373	Bay 12.
468	445	Bay 9.	522	1374	Bay 12.

Exhibition Number.	Registration Number.	Place.	Exhibition Number.	Registration Number.	Place.
523	1329	Bay 12.	577	61	C.S.
524	1291	Bay 12.	578	104	Bay 16.
525	876	Bay 12.	579	42	Bay 16.
526	968	Bay 12.	580	27	Bay 15.
527	1167	Bay 12.	581	109	Bay 14.
528	848	Bay 12.	582	67	Bay 14.
529	120	Bay 12.	583	119	Bay 12.
530	942	Bay 12.	584	96	Bay 17.
531	526	Bay 13.	585	1066	Bay 16.
532	275	Bay 13.	586	1104	Bay 23.
533	286	Bay 13.	587	697	C.S.
534	287	Bay 13.	588	858	C.S.
535	299	Bay 13.	589	1071	Vestibule.
536	814	Bay 13.	590	681	Bay 18.
537	269	Bay 13.	591	440	Bay 19.
538	284	Bay 13.	592	117	Bay 6.
539	360	Bay 13.	593	857	Bay 14.
540	371	Bay 13.	594	11	Bay 15.
541	374	Bay 13.	595	13	Bay 15.
542	218	Bay 13.	596	1006	C.S.
543	273	Bay 13.	597	9	Bay 16.
544	296	Bay 13.	598	1065	Bay 18.
545	289	Bay 13.	599	1123	Bay 17.
546	1243	Bay 13.	600	1355	Bay 16.
547	918	Bay 13.	601	93	C.S.
548	335	Bay 13.	602	948	C.S.
549	301	Bay 13.	603	1377	C.S.
550	7	Bay 14.	604	1376	C.S.
551	593	Bay 14.	605	108	Bay 14.
552	421	Bay 14.	606	954	C.S.
553	422	Bay 14.	607	645	Bay 11.
554	591	Bay 14.	608	1055	Bay 17.
555	103	C.S.	609	328	Bay 24.
556	48	C.S.	610	166	Bay 19.
557	444	Bay 17.	611	167	Bay 20.
558	707	Bay 18.	612	164	Bay 19.
559	493	Bay 18.	613	163	Bay 20.
560	468	Bay 18.	614	46	C.S.
561	467	Bay 18.	615	947	Bay 18.
562	915	Bay 20.	616	26	Bay 21.
563	454	Bay 11.	617	1378 (167*)	C.S.
564	179	C.S. wall.	618	487	C.S.
565	36	Bay 18.	619	40	C.S.
566	705	Vestibule.	620	308	Bay 10.
567	854	C.S.	621	656	Bay 10.
568	855	C.S.	622	267	Bay 13.
569	884	C.S.	623	1184	Bay 13.
570	856	C.S.	624	262	Bay 13.
571	609	Bay 8.	625	950	Bay 13.
572	1375	Bay 18.	626	455	Bay 13.
573	146	Bay 11.	627	424	Bay 14.
574	1189	Bay 13.	628	1280	Bay 15.
575	882	C.S.	629	646	Bay 17.
576	19	C.S.	630	555	Bay 17.

Exhibition Number.	Registration Number.	Place.	Exhibition Number.	Registration Number.	Place.
631	354	Bay 17.	685	883	C.S.
632	278	Bay 17.	686	958	C.S.
633	285	Bay 17.	687	1226	C.S.
634	329	Bay 17.	688	1301	Bay 16.
635	1465	Bay 17.	689	369	Bay 17.
636	139	Bay 20.	690	807	Bay 17.
637	460	C.S.	691	268	Bay 18.
638	81	C.S.	692	314	Bay 17.
639	644	Bay 12.	693	305	Bay 17.
640	283	Bay 17.	694	125	Bay 18.
641	260	Bay 17.	695	261	Bay 18.
642	160	C.S.	696	635	Bay 18.
643	165	C.S.	697	449	Bay 18.
644	853	C.S.	698	818	Bay 18.
645	1188	C.S.	699	479	Bay 18.
646	191	Bay 10.	700	447	Bay 19.
647	263	Bay 17.	701	1183	Bay 20.
648	217	Bay 17.	702	817	Bay 20.
649	913	Bay 17.	703	292	Bay 20.
650	355	Bay 17.	704	370	Bay 20.
651	465	Bay 18.	705	127	Bay 20.
652	706	Bay 12.	706	425	Bay 20.
653	1279	Bay 15.	707	435	Bay 20.
654	18	C.S.	708	126 and 432	Bay 21.
655	1297	Bay 18.	709	312	Bay 21.
656	795	Bay 18.	710	796	Bay 22.
657	304	Bay 18.	711	351	Bay 22.
658	367	Bay 18.	712	313	Bay 22.
659	372	Bay 18.	713	144	Bay 22.
660	327	Bay 18.	714	476	C.S.
661	1323	Bay 18.	715	290	Bay 21.
662	1214	Bay 18.	716	634	Bay 18.
663	810	Bay 18.	717	1344	C.S.
664	385	Bay 18.	718	442	Bay 22.
665	345	Bay 18.	719	588	Bay 24.
666	343	Bay 18.	720	78	Bay 19.
667	315	Bay 18.	721	1194	Bay 11.
668	484	Bay 18.	722	28	Bay 19.
669	1382	Bay 18.	723	133	C.S.
670	549	Bay 19.	724	1379	Bay 14.
671	154	Bay 19.	725	1295	Bay 16.
672	319	Bay 19.	726	611	Bay 17.
673	113	Bay 19.	727	850	Bay 17.
674	158	Bay 22.	728	1084	Bay 18.
675	132	Bay 22.	729	472	Bay 18.
676	1388 (283*)	Bay 22.	730	772	Bay 18.
677	107	Bay 21.	731	799	Bay 18.
678	1369	Bay 20.	732	122	Bay 19.
679	556	Bay 20.	733	298	Bay 19.
680	397	Bay 20.	734	962	Bay 19.
681	317	Bay 20.	735	142	Bay 20.
682	359	Bay 20.	736	792	Bay 20.
683	357	Bay 20.	737	794	Bay 20.
684	344	Bay 20.	738	183	Bay 20.

Exhibition Number.	Registration Number.	Place.	Exhibition Number.	Registration Number.	Place.
739	793	Bay 21.	793	1121	C.S.
740	1232	Bay 21.	794	1258, 1259	Bay 20.
741	1233	Bay 21.	795	713	Bay 20.
742	150	Bay 21.	796	1380	Bay 20.
743	373	Bay 21.	797	498 (135*)	Bay 25.
744	323	Bay 21.	798	908	Bay 20.
745	700	Bay 21.	799	1124	Bay 22.
746	1052	Bay 21.	800	20	Bay 24.
747	1366	Bay 21.	801	600	Bay 24.
748	161	Bay 21.	802	964	Bay 24.
749	350	Bay 22.	803	1238	Bay 23.
750	306	Bay 22.	804	1358	Bay 22.
751	349	Bay 22.	805	83	C.S.
752	156	Bay 22.	806	94	Bay 16.
753	318	Bay 24.	807	610	Bay 17.
754	474	Bay 17.	808	1427	Bay 24.
755	311	Bay 19.	809	952	Bay 24.
756	137	Bay 19.	810	655	Bay 24.
757	320	Bay 24.	811	32	Bay 24.
758	10,541	Bay 20.	812	835	Bay 24.
759	931	Bay 24.	813	907	Bay 24.
760	653	Bay 22.	814	775	Bay 24.
761	342	Bay 20.	815	1125	Bay 18.
762	309	Bay 22.	816	1122	Bay 20.
763	517	Bay 19.	817	1126	Bay 20.
764	63	Bay 20.	818	111	Bay 21.
765	1307	Bay 19.	819	134	Bay 23.
766	8	Bay 22.	820	92	Bay 24.
767	642	Bay 22.	821	1292	Bay 22.
768	1107	Bay 16.	822	1386 (28*)	Bay 22.
769	1105	Bay 23.	823	1076	Bay 25.
770	1077	Bay 26.	824	1075	Bay 26.
771	1097	Bay 23.	825	3	Bay 26.
772	1098	Bay 23.	826	23	Bay 25.
773	1103	Bay 23.	827	1384	Bay 27.
774	1063	Bay 22.	828	86	Bay 27.
775	1064	Bay 20.	829	1047	Bay 28.
776	1007	Bay 21.	830	1340	Bay 14.
777	1224	Bay 22.	831	1284	Bay 14.
778	110	Bay 21.	832	1202	Bay 14.
779	473	Bay 17.	833	703	Bay 14.
780	177	Bay 17.	834	1354	Bay 16.
781	1381 (469*)	Bay 17.	835	596	Bay 16.
782	151	Bay 19.	836	967	Bay 16.
783	506	Bay 20.	837	1197	Bay 17.
784	1045	Bay 20.	838	787	Bay 19.
785	917	Bay 22.	839	786	Bay 19.
786	589	Bay 22.	840	458	Bay 19.
787	121	Bay 19.	841	281	Bay 19.
788	321	Bay 22.	842	511	Bay 19.
789	1132	Bay 22.	843	1317	Bay 20.
790	1225	Bay 26.	844	331	Bay 20.
791	1430	Bay 26.	845	877	Bay 20.
792	364	Bay 19.	846	330	Bay 21.

Exhibition Number.	Registration Number.	Place.	Exhibition Number.	Registration Number.	Place.
847	1042	Bay 21.	901	509	Bay 14.
848	1138	Bay 21.	902	1310	Bay 14.
849	912	Bay 21.	903	181	Bay 14.
850	836	Bay 21.	904	25	Bay 15.
851	798	Bay 24.	905	418	Bay 16.
852	1086	Bay 21.	906	1051	Bay 16.
853	457	Bay 21.	907	554	Bay 16.
854	452	Bay 21.	908	1050	Bay 16.
855	336	Bay 21.	909	800	Bay 17.
856	326	Bay 21.	910	1302	Bay 16.
857	537	Bay 24.	911	450	Bay 17.
858	538	Bay 24.	912	270	Bay 19.
859	539	Bay 24.	913	39	Bay 20.
860	540	Bay 24.	914	927	Bay 24.
861	541	Bay 24.	915	891	Bay 24.
862	542	Bay 24.	916	896	Bay 24.
863	543	Bay 24.	917	1289	Bay 28.
864	544	Bay 22.	918	894	Bay 29.
865	545	Bay 22.	919	523	Bay 31.
866	546	Bay 24.	920	524	Bay 32.
867	510	Bay 22.	921	1421 (70*b*)	Bay 30.
868	514	Bay 22.	922	1106	Bay 25.
869	1017	Bay 22.	923	10	Bay 25.
870	347	Bay 22.	924	44	Bay 29.
871	1198	Bay 22.	925	1013	Bay 27.
872	659	Bay 22.	926	22	Bay 27.
873	986	Bay 23.	927	998	Bay 28.
874	340	Bay 24.	928	1331	Bay 23.
875	961	Bay 24.	929	337	Bay 24.
876	972	Bay 24.	930	862	Bay 29.
877	909	Bay 24.	931	808	Bay 24.
878	548	Bay 25.	932	911	Bay 24.
879	845	Bay 26.	933	1333	Bay 24.
880	595	Bay 28.	934	790	Bay 25.
881	17	Bay 28.	935	1180	Bay 25.
882	66	Bay 23.	936	352	Bay 25.
883	1387	Bay 23.	937	1217	Bay 25.
884	809	Bay 25.	938	396	Bay 25.
885	1148	Bay 27.	939	382	Bay 25.
886	190	Bay 28.	940	338	Bay 25.
887	873	Bay 24.	941	1018	Bay 26.
888	288	Bay 24.	942	1235	Bay 26.
889	624	Bay 25.	943	1306	Bay 26.
890	333	Bay 25.	944	302	Bay 27.
891	1309	Bay 16.	945	464	Bay 27.
892	502	Bay 16.	946	463	Bay 27.
893	516	Bay 19.	947	941	Bay 27.
894	1316	Bay 25.	948	933	Bay 29.
895	633	Bay 25.	949	938	Bay 29.
896	395	Bay 29.	950	1127	Bay 28.
897	1209	Bay 29.	951	652	Bay 25.
898	1420 (59*)	Bay 31.	952	651	Bay 25.
899	423	Bay 14.	953	1056	Bay 25.
900	704	Bay 14.	954	1057	Bay 25.

Exhibition Number.	Registration Number.	Place.	Exhibition Number.	Registration Number.	Place.
955	1054	Bay 29.	1009	639	Bay 28.
956	616	Bay 28.	1010	1428	Bay 24.
957	1081	Bay 28.	1011	699	Bay 29.
958	1207	Bay 26.	1012	1141	Bay 29.
959	1431	Bay 26.	1013	1178	Bay 29.
960	24	Bay 31.	1014	1158	Bay 29.
961	612	Bay 27.	1015	1160	Bay 29.
962	1134	Bay 30.	1016	1311	Bay 32.
963	1020	Bay 29.	1017	711	Bay 27.
964	1162	Bay 28.	1018	638	Bay 27.
965	74	C.S.	1019	988	Bay 27.
966	1157	Bay 32.	1020	1425	Bay 28.
967	33	Bay 29.	1021	1424	Bay 28.
968	2	Bay 26.	1022	1426	Bay 24.
969	47	Bay 24.	1023	180	Bay 30.
970	1343	Bay 21.	1024	388	Bay 30.
971	1303	Bay 28.	1025	380	Bay 29.
972	1153	Bay 25.	1026	886	Bay 27.
973	1085	Bay 17.	1027	147	Bay 29.
974	982	Bay 27.	1028	387	Bay 25.
975	985	Bay 29.	1029	379	Bay 24.
976	778	Bay 29.	1030	188	Bay 27.
977	649	Bay 27.	1031	389	Bay 27.
978	650	Bay 27.	1032	375	Bay 27.
979	1433	Bay 26.	1033	390	Bay 29.
980	895	Bay 29.	1034	1227	Bay 14.
981	881	Bay 29.	1035	416	Bay 14.
982	1154	Bay 31.	1036	1215	Bay 14.
983	184	Bay 27.	1037	1364	Bay 14.
984	837	Bay 27.	1038	592	Bay 14.
985	698	Bay 27.	1039	1253	Bay 14.
986	1003	Bay 27.	1040	419	Bay 16.
987	654	Bay 27.	1041	1137	Bay 16.
988	394	Bay 27.	1042	1058	Bay 16.
989	1088	Bay 27.	1043	135	Bay 17.
990	433	Bay 27.	1044	1004	Bay 29.
991	841	Bay 29.	1045	400	Bay 27.
992	392	Bay 30.	1046	843	Bay 27.
993	1325	Bay 27.	1047	429	Bay 32.
994	838	Bay 29.	1048	431	Bay 32.
995	378	Bay 30.	1049	719	Bay 31.
996	386	Bay 27.	1050	892	Bay 30.
997	393	Bay 25.	1051	901	Bay 30.
998	383	Bay 29.	1052	617	Bay 27.
999	377	Bay 32.	1053	398	Bay 29.
1000	391	Bay 27.	1054	1432	Bay 26.
1001	1139	Bay 26.	1055	709	Bay 27.
1002	325	Bay 22.	1056	789	Bay 25.
1003	641	Bay 24.	1057	192	Bay 32.
1004	1365	Bay 25.	1058	438	Bay 32.
1005	1349	Bay 25.	1059	1359	Bay 26.
1006	934	Bay 26.	1060	710	Bay 29.
1007	640	Bay 27.	1061	1155	Bay 29.
1008	637	Bay 27.	1062	1298	Bay 29.

Exhibition Number.	Registration Number.	Place.	Exhibition Number.	Registration Number.	Place.
1063	1294	Bay 29.	1117	680	Bay 32.
1064	1251	Bay 14.	1118	1300	Bay 32.
1065	1252	Bay 16.	1119	1208	Bay 32.
1066	415	Bay 16.	1120	1299	Bay 32.
1067	717	Bay 16.	1121	660	Bay 32.
1068	1281	Bay 16.	1122	1328	Bay 30.
1069	399	Bay 29.	1123	618	Bay 32.
1070	970	Bay 27.	1124	669	Bay 32.
1071	1073	Bay 26.	1125	620	Bay 32.
1072	959	Bay 28.	1126	1327	Bay 32.
1073	97	Bay 29.	1127	677	Bay 32.
1074	885	Bay 29.	1128	1339	Bay 32.
1075	189	Bay 29.	1129	924	Bay 30.
1076	401	Bay 29.	1130	604	Bay 32.
1077	1363	Bay 29.	1131	1352	Bay 30.
1078	1205	Bay 30.	1132	716	Bay 30.
1079	436	Bay 32.	1133	1254	Bay 30.
1080	136, 136*a*	Bay 32.	1134	1255	Bay 30.
1081	1218	Bay 30.	1135	664	Bay 32.
1082	1219	Bay 30.	1136	1257	Bay 30.
1083	1206	Bay 26.	1137	665	Bay 32.
1084	661	Bay 26.	1138	1326	Bay 32.
1085	821	Bay 29.	1139	1250	Bay 32.
1086	99	Bay 31.	1140	601	Bay 32.
1087	1196	Bay 26.	1141	666	Bay 32.
1088	1043	Bay 28.	1142	1351	Bay 32.
1089	923	Bay 30.	1143	619	Bay 32.
1090	603	Bay 26.	1144	411	Bay 32.
1091	409	Bay 26.	1145	679	Bay 32.
1092	1360	Bay 26	1146	1335	Bay 32.
1093	823	Bay 26.	1147	404	Bay 32.
1094	939	Bay 26.	1148	622	Bay 32.
1095	822	Bay 26.	1149	1256	Bay 32.
1096	824	Bay 26.	1150	670	Bay 32.
1097	1362	Bay 28.	1151	1361	Bay 28.
1098	602	Bay 26.	1152	1039	Bay 28.
1099	405	Bay 30.	1153	714	Bay 30.
1100	408	Bay 28.	1154	671	Bay 30.
1101	407	Bay 28.	1155	825	Bay 30.
1102	1046	Bay 28.	1156	176	Bay 30.
1103	1276	Bay 30.	1157	621	Bay 30.
1104	1423	Bay 32.	1158	403	Bay 28.
1105	900	Bay 30.	1159	1337	Bay 30.
1106	1334	Bay 32.	1160	675	Bay 30.
1107	676	Bay 32.	1161	1338	Bay 30.
1108	672	Bay 30.	1162	674	Bay 32.
1109	995	Bay 30.	1163	668	Bay 32.
1110	673	Bay 28.	1164	678	Bay 32.
1111	702	Bay 30.	1165	410	Bay 32.
1112	607	Bay 30.	1166	1350	Bay 32.
1113	1422	Bay 30.	1167	1040	Bay 32.
1114	182	Bay 28.	1168	663	Bay 32.
1115	1336	Bay 30.	1169	1469	C.S.
1116	667	Bay 32.	1170	1470	Bay 18.

Exhibition Number.	Registration Number.	Place.	Exhibition Number.	Registration Number.	Place.
1171	1471	Bay 20.	1174	1467	Bay 15.
1172	1472	Bay 20.	1175	1473	Bay 15.
1173	1466	Bay 17.	1176	1474	Bay 26.

II.

INDEX OF REGISTRATION AND EXHIBITION NUMBERS.

Registration Number.	Exhibition Number.	Place.	Registration Number.	Exhibition Number.	Place.
1	430	Bay 11.	47	969	Bay 24.
2	968	Bay 26.	48	556	C.S.
3	825	Bay 26.	49	388	Bay 5.
4	417	Bay 5.	50	383	Bay 1.
5	442	Bay 12.	52	403	Bay 16.
6	416	Bay 4.	53	387	Bay 3.
7	550	Bay 14.	55	361	Bay 5.
8	766	Bay 22.	57	406	Bay 5.
9	597	Bay 16.	58	21	Vestibule.
10	923	Bay 25.	60	386	Bay 2.
11	594	Bay 15.	61	577	C.S.
12	363	Bay 2.	62	391	Bay 10.
13	595	Bay 15.	63	764	Bay 20.
14	412	Bay 8.	64	419	Bay 7.
15	360	Bay 5.	65	390	Bay 7.
16 and 73	410	Bay 6.	66	882	Bay 23.
17	881	Bay 28.	67	582	Bay 14.
18	654	C.S.	68	407	Bay 8.
19	576	C.S.	69	389	Bay 6.
20	800	Bay 24.	71	384	Bay 1.
21	413	Bay 9.	72	385	Bay 2.
22	926	Bay 27.	74	965	C.S.
23	826	Bay 25.	75	441	Bay 13.
24	960	Bay 31.	76	381	Bay 1.
25	904	Bay 15.	77	401	Bay 11.
26	616	Bay 21.	78	720	Bay 19.
27	580	Bay 15.	79	404	Bay 4.
28	722	Bay 19.	80	382	Bay 1.
29	444	Bay 3.	81	638	C.S.
30	415	Bay 6.	83	805	C.S.
31	375	Bay 4.	84	393	Bay 8.
32	811	Bay 24.	85	398	Bay 10.
33	967	Bay 29.	86	828	Bay 27.
34	431	Bay 10.	87	397	Bay 10.
35	34	Vestibule.	88	405	Bay 4.
36	565	Bay 18.	92	820	Bay 24.
37	408	Bay 9.	93	601	C.S.
38	429	Bay 11.	94	806	Bay 16
39	913	Bay 20.	96	584	Bay 17.
40	619	C.S.	97	1073	Bay 29.
41	394	Bay 9.	98	244	Bay 6.
42	579	Bay 16.	99	1086	Bay 31.
43	380	Bay 7.	100	127	Vestibule.
44	924	Bay 29.	101	175	Bay 2.
45	392	Bay 7.	103	555	C.S.
46	614	C.S.	104	578	Bay 16.

Registration Number.	Exhibition Number.	Place.	Registration Number.	Exhibition Number.	Place.
105	414	Bay 11.	161	748	Bay 21.
107	677	Bay 21.	162	194	Bay 2.
108	605	Bay 14.	163	613	Bay 20.
109	581	Bay 14.	164	612	Bay 19.
110	778	Bay 21.	165	643	C.S.
111	818	Bay 21.	166	610	Bay 19.
112	89	Vestibule.	167	611	Bay 20.
113	673	Bay 19.	171	3	Vestibule.
117	592	Bay 6.	173	516	Bay 12.
119	583	Bay 12.	175	515	Bay 12.
120	529	Bay 12.	176	1156	Bay 30.
121	787	Bay 19.	177	780	Bay 17.
122	732	Bay 19.	179	564	C.S.
123	422	Bay 7.	180	1023	Bay 30.
124	445	Bay 5.	181	903	Bay 14.
125	694	Bay 18.	182	1114	Bay 28.
126 and 432	708	Bay 21.	183	738	Bay 20.
127	705	Bay 20.	184	983	Bay 27.
128	86	Vestibule.	186	351	Bay 11.
129	208	Bay 1.	187	123	Vestibule.
130	44	Vestibule.	188	1030	Bay 27.
131	130	Bay 1.	189	1075	Bay 29.
132	675	Bay 22.	190	886	Bay 28.
133	723	C.S.	191	646	Bay 10.
134	819	Bay 23.	192	1057	Bay 32.
135	1043	Bay 17.	193	207	Bay 1.
136 and *a*	1080	Bay 32.	194	433	Bay 9.
137	756	Bay 19.	195	309	Bay 3.
138	432	Bay 10.	196	308	Bay 3.
139	636	Bay 20.	197	318	Bay 7.
140	418	C.S.	198	224	Bay 3.
141	299	Bay 7.	199	67	Vestibule.
142	735	Bay 20.	200	446	Bay 5.
143	185	Bay 1.	201	285	Bay 1.
144	713	Bay 22.	202	237	Bay 5.
145	298	Bay 7.	203	97	Vestibule.
146	573	Bay 11.	204	312	Bay 4.
147	1027	Bay 29.	205	220	Bay 3.
148	378	Bay 8.	206	306	Bay 9.
149	474	Bay 9.	207	310	Bay 4.
150	742	Bay 21.	208	291	Bay 3.
151	782	Bay 19.	209	240	Bay 5.
152	128	Bay 1.	210	335	Bay 11.
153	369	Bay 12.	211	439	Bay 12.
154	671	Bay 19.	212	79	Vestibule.
155	460	Bay 8.	213	297	Bay 4.
156	752	Bay 22.	214	500	Bay 11.
157*a*	25	Bay 1.	215	232	Bay 4.
157*b*	24	Bay 1.	217	648	Bay 17.
157*c*	26	Bay 1.	218	542	Bay 13.
157	1010	Vestibule.	219	230	Bay 4.
158	674	Bay 22.	220	247	Bay 7.
159	96	Vestibule.	221	304	Bay 7.
160	642	C.S.	222	221	Bay 3.

Registration Number.	Exhibition Number.	Place.	Registration Number.	Exhibition Number.	Place.
223	227	Bay 4.	278	632	Bay 17.
224	293	Bay 3.	279	464	Bay 8.
225	234	Bay 4.	280	499	Bay 11.
226	303	Bay 7.	281	841	Bay 19.
227	248	Bay 7.	282	455	Bay 8.
228	192	Bay 2.	283	640	Bay 17.
229	334	Bay 9.	284	538	Bay 13.
230	228	Bay 4.	285	633	Bay 17.
231	311	Bay 4.	286	533	Bay 13.
232	229	Bay 4.	287	534	Bay 13.
233	181	Bay 5.	288	888	Bay 24.
234	321	Bay 9.	289	545	Bay 13.
235	245	Bay 7.	290	715	Bay 21.
236	328	Bay 9.	291	483	Bay 10.
237	241	Bay 5.	292	703	Bay 20.
238	243	Bay 5.	293	472	Bay 9.
239	295	Bay 4.	294	484	Bay 10.
240	223	Bay 3.	295	457	Bay 8.
241	242	Bay 5.	296	544	Bay 13.
242	315	Bay 5.	297	355	Bay 10.
243	218	Bay 2.	298	733	Bay 19.
244	252	Bay 7.	299	535	Bay 13.
245	333	Bay 9.	300	466	Bay 9.
246	332	Bay 9.	301	549	Bay 13.
247	246	Bay 7.	302	944	Bay 27.
248	320	Bay 7.	303	514	Bay 12.
249	313	Bay 4.	304	657	Bay 18.
250	331	Bay 9.	305	693	Bay 17.
251	319	Bay 7.	306	750	Bay 22.
252	215	Bay 2.	307	487	Bay 10.
253	191	Bay 2.	308	620	Bay 10.
254	238	Bay 5.	309	762	Bay 22.
255	305	Bay 7.	310	338	Bay 11.
256	153	Bay 3.	311	755	Bay 19.
257	155	Bay 9.	312	709	Bay 21.
258	219	Bay 3.	313	712	Bay 22.
260	641	Bay 17.	314	692	Bay 17.
261	695	Bay 18.	315	667	Bay 18.
262	624	Bay 13.	316	510	Bay 12.
263	647	Bay 17.	317	681	Bay 20.
264	478	Bay 10.	318	753	Bay 24.
265	485	Bay 10.	319	672	Bay 19.
266	486	Bay 10.	320	757	Bay 24.
267	622	Bay 13.	321	788	Bay 22.
268	691	Bay 18.	322	465	Bay 8.
269	537	Bay 13.	323	744	Bay 21.
270	912	Bay 19.	324	438	Bay 10.
271	489	Bay 11.	325	1002	Bay 22.
272	490	Bay 11.	326	856	Bay 21.
273	543	Bay 13.	327	660	Bay 18.
274	358	Bay 13.	328	609	Bay 24.
275	532	Bay 13.	329	634	Bay 17.
276	467	Bay 9.	330	846	Bay 21.
277	349	Bay 9.	331	844	Bay 20.

Registration Number.	Exhibition Number.	Place.	Registration Number.	Exhibition Number.	Place.
332	493	Bay 11.	388	1024	Bay 30.
333	890	Bay 25.	389	1031	Bay 27.
334	217	Bay 2.	390	1033	Bay 29.
335	548	Bay 13.	391	1000	Bay 27.
336	855	Bay 21.	392	992	Bay 30.
337	929	Bay 24.	393	997	Bay 25.
338	940	Bay 25.	394	988	Bay 27.
339	508	Bay 12.	395	896	Bay 29.
340	874	Bay 24.	396	938	Bay 25.
341	459	Bay 8.	397	680	Bay 20.
342	761	Bay 20.	398	1053	Bay 29.
343	666	Bay 18.	399	1069	Bay 29.
344	684	Bay 20.	400	1045	Bay 27.
345	665	Bay 18.	401	1076	Bay 29.
346	480	Bay 10.	403	1158	Bay 28.
347	870	Bay 22.	404	1147	Bay 32.
348	501	Bay 11.	405	1099	Bay 30.
349	751	Bay 22.	407	1102	Bay 28.
350	749	Bay 22.	408	1100	Bay 28.
351	711	Bay 22.	409	1091	Bay 26.
352	936	Bay 25.	410	1165	Bay 32.
353	494	Bay 11.	411	1144	Bay 32.
354	631	Bay 17.	413	259	Bay 14.
355	650	Bay 17.	414	261	Bay 14.
356	469	Bay 9.	415	1066	Bay 16.
357	683	Bay 20.	416	1035	Bay 14.
358	498	Bay 11.	417	263	Bay 14.
359	682	Bay 20.	418	905	Bay 16.
360	539	Bay 13.	419	1040	Bay 16.
361	256	Bay 9.	420	272	Bay 14.
362	226	Bay 4.	421	552	Bay 14.
363	253	Bay 7.	422	553	Bay 14.
364	792	Bay 19.	423	899	Bay 14.
365	425	Bay 11.	424	627	Bay 14.
366	509	Bay 12.	425	706	Bay 20.
367	658	Bay 18.	427	495	Bay 11.
368	492	Bay 11.	429	1047	Bay 32.
369	689	Bay 17.	430	70	Vestibule.
370	704	Bay 20.	431	1048	Bay 32.
371	540	Bay 13.	433	990	Bay 27.
372	659	Bay 18.	435	707	Bay 20.
373	743	Bay 21.	436	1079	Bay 32.
374	541	Bay 13.	438	1058	Bay 32.
375	1032	Bay 27.	440	591	Bay 19.
377	999	Bay 32.	442	718	Bay 22.
378	995	Bay 30.	444	557	Bay 17.
379	1029	Bay 24.	445	468	Bay 9.
380	1025	Bay 29.	446	357	Bay 11.
381	481	Bay 10.	448	352	Bay 8.
382	939	Bay 25.	449	697	Bay 18.
383	998	Bay 29.	450	911	Bay 17.
385	664	Bay 18.	451	126	Bay 5.
386	996	Bay 27.	452	854	Bay 21.
387	1028	Bay 25.	453	451	Bay 6.

Registration Number.	Exhibition Number.	Place.	Registration Number.	Exhibition Number.	Place.
454	563	Bay 11.	531	46	Vestibule.
455	626	Bay 13.	532	45	Vestibule.
456	454	Bay 8.	533	45	Vestibule.
457	853	Bay 21.	534	45	Vestibule.
458	840	Bay 19.	535	45	Vestibule.
460	637	C.S.	537	857	Bay 24.
461	142	Bay 3.	538	858	Bay 24.
462	183	Bay 1.	539	859	Bay 24.
463	946	Bay 27.	540	860	Bay 24.
464	945	Bay 27.	541	861	Bay 24.
465	651	Bay 18.	542	862	Bay 24.
467	561	Bay 18.	543	863	Bay 24.
468	560	Bay 18.	544	864	Bay 22.
469	258	Bay 6.	545	865	Bay 22.
471	225	Bay 4.	546	866	Bay 24.
472	729	Bay 18.	547	505	Bay 12.
473	779	Bay 17.	548	878	Bay 25.
474	754	Bay 17.	549	670	Bay 19.
476	714	C.S.	550	463	Bay 8.
477	322	Bay 18.	551	461	Bay 8.
478	341	Vestibule.	552	462	Bay 8.
479	699	Bay 18.	553	260	Bay 14.
484	668	Bay 18.	554	907	Bay 16.
487	618	C.S.	555	630	Bay 17.
489	139	Bay 3.	556	679	Bay 20.
490	10	Vestibule.	557	177	Bay 1.
491	11	Vestibule.	558	214	Bay 1.
492	12	Vestibule.	559	186	Bay 1.
493	559	Bay 18.	560	205	Vestibule.
497	149	Bay 1.	561	211	Bay 1.
498	797	Bay 25.	562	141	Bay 3.
502	892	Bay 16.	563	301	Bay 7.
503	421	Bay 6.	564	212	Bay 1.
504	296	Bay 4.	565	213	Bay 1.
506	783	Bay 20.	566	193	Bay 2.
507	290	Bay 3.	567	150	Bay 1.
509	901	Bay 14.	568	189	Bay 1.
510	867	Bay 22.	569	143	Bay 1.
511	842	Bay 19.	570	144	Bay 1.
514	868	Bay 22.	571	190	Bay 1.
516	893	Bay 19.	572	140	Bay 1.
517	763	Bay 19.	573	156	Bay 1.
518	409	Bay 11.	574	146	Bay 1.
519	395	Bay 12.	575	168	Bay 1.
520	396	Bay 13.	576	154	Bay 1.
521	400	Bay 11.	577	187	Bay 1.
522	402	Bay 13.	578	210	Bay 1.
523	919	Bay 31.	579	129	Bay 1.
524	920	Bay 32.	580	203	Vestibule.
526	531	Bay 13.	581	197	Bay 7.
527	45	Vestibule.	582	133	Vestibule.
528	47	Vestibule.	583	151	Bay 7.
529	45	Vestibule.	584	209	Bay 1.
530	45	Vestibule.	585	254	Bay 7.

Registration Number.	Exhibition Number.	Place.	Registration Number.	Exhibition Number.	Place.
586	138	Bay 3.	641	1003	Bay 24.
587	204	Vestibule.	642	767	Bay 22.
588	719	Bay 24.	643	121	Bay 3.
589	786	Bay 22.	644	639	Bay 12.
590	269	Bay 17.	645	607	Bay 11.
591	554	Bay 14.	646	629	Bay 17.
592	1038	Bay 14.	647	84	Vestibule.
593	551	Bay 14.	649	977	Bay 27.
594	359	Bay 14.	650	978	Bay 27.
595	880	Bay 28.	651	952	Bay 25.
596	835	Bay 16.	652	951	Bay 25.
597	482	Bay 10.	653	760	Bay 22.
598	348	Bay 7.	654	987	Bay 27.
599	399	Bay 14.	655	810	Bay 24.
600	801	Bay 24.	656	621	Bay 10.
601	1140	Bay 32.	657 (138*)	411	Bay 6.
602	1098	Bay 26.	658	83	Vestibule.
603	1090	Bay 26.	659	872	Bay 22.
604	1130	Bay 32.	660	1121	Bay 32.
607	1112	Bay 30.	661	1084	Bay 26.
608	161	Bay 1.	663	1168	Bay 32.
609	571	Bay 8.	664	1135	Bay 32.
610	807	Bay 17.	665	1137	Bay 32.
611	726	Bay 17.	666	1141	Bay 32.
612	961	Bay 27.	667	1116	Bay 32.
614	100	Bay 4.	668	1163	Bay 32.
614*a*	103	Bay 4.	669	1124	Bay 32.
614*b*	102	Bay 4.	670	1150	Bay 32.
614	101	Bay 4.	671	1154	Bay 30.
615	137	Bay 1.	672	1108	Bay 30.
616	956	Bay 28.	673	1110	Bay 28.
617	1052	Bay 27.	674	1162	Bay 32.
618	1123	Bay 32.	675	1160	Bay 30.
619	1143	Bay 32.	676	1107	Bay 32.
620	1125	Bay 32.	677	1127	Bay 32.
621	1157	Bay 30.	678	1164	Bay 32.
622	1148	Bay 32.	679	1145	Bay 32.
623	512	Bay 12.	680	1117	Bay 32.
624	889	Bay 25.	681	590	Bay 18.
625	182	Vestibule.	682	32	Vestibule.
626	74	Vestibule.	683	346	Bay 3.
627	77	Vestibule.	684	158	Bay 1.
628	119	Bay 4.	685	159	Bay 1.
630	282	Bay 4.	686	160	Bay 3.
631	342	Bay 4.	687	427	Bay 13.
632	448	Bay 6.	688	172	Bay 2.
633	895	Bay 25.	689	470	Bay 9.
634	716	Bay 18.	690	347	Bay 9.
635	696	Bay 18.	691	2	Vestibule.
636	287	Bay 2.	692	162	Bay 1.
637	1008	Bay 27.	693	202	Bay 1.
638	1018	Bay 27.	694	179	Bay 3.
639	1009	Bay 28.	695	180	Bay 3.
640	1007	Bay 27.	697	587	C.S.

Registration Number.	Exhibition Number.	Place.	Registration Number.	Exhibition Number.	Place.
698	985	Bay 27.	803	456	Bay 8.
699	1011	Bay 29.	804	496	Bay 11.
700	745	Bay 21.	805	239	Bay 5.
701	372	Bay 8.	806	326	Bay 7.
702	1111	Bay 30.	807	690	Bay 17.
703	833	Bay 14.	808	931	Bay 24.
704	900	Bay 14.	809	884	Bay 25.
705	566	Vestibule.	810	663	Bay 18.
706	652	Bay 12.	811	356	Bay 10.
707	558	Bay 18.	812	506	Bay 12.
709	1055	Bay 27.	813	426	Bay 12.
710	1060	Bay 29.	814	536	Bay 13.
711	1017	Bay 27.	815	350	Bay 10.
713	795	Bay 20.	816	354	Bay 10.
714	1153	Bay 30.	817	702	Bay 20.
716	1132	Bay 30.	818	698	Bay 18.
717	1067	Bay 16.	819	479	Bay 10.
718	80	A.S.	821	1085	Bay 29.
719	1049	Bay 31.	822	1095	Bay 26.
720	104	Bay 3.	823	1093	Bay 26.
721	106	Bay 3.	824	1096	Bay 26.
722	107	Bay 3.	825	1155	Bay 30.
724	116	Bay 3.	826	475	Bay 9.
729	111	Bay 3.	827	178	Vestibule.
730	109	Bay 3.	828	145	Bay 6.
731	108	Bay 3.	829	152	Bay 5.
732	114	Bay 3.	830	255	Bay 7.
742	113	Bay 3.	831	170	Bay 5.
745	115	Bay 3.	832	195	Bay 2.
750	112	Bay 3.	833	283	Bay 5.
752	110	Bay 3.	834	434	Bay 13.
753	117	Bay 3.	835	812	Bay 24.
754	118	Bay 3.	836	850	Bay 21.
772	730	Bay 18.	837	984	Bay 27.
773	471	Bay 9.	838	994	Bay 29.
774	188	Bay 1.	839	147	Bay 1.
775	814	Bay 24.	840	373	Bay 9.
777	184	Bay 1.	841	991	Bay 29.
778	976	Bay 29.	843	1046	Bay 27.
786	839	Bay 19.	844	323	Bay 7.
787	838	Bay 19.	845	879	Bay 26.
788	231	Bay 4.	846	330	Bay 9.
789	1056	Bay 25.	848	528	Bay 12.
790	934	Bay 25.	850	727	Bay 17.
791	316	Bay 7.	851	294	Bay 4.
792	736	Bay 20.	852	169	Bay 3.
793	739	Bay 21.	853	644	C.S.
794	737	Bay 20.	854	567	C.S.
795	656	Bay 18.	855	568	C.S.
796	710	Bay 22.	856	570	C.S.
797	511	Bay 12.	857	593	Bay 14.
798	851	Bay 24.	858	588	C.S.
799	731	Bay 18.	860	504	Bay 12.
800	909	Bay 17.	861	286	Bay 2.

Registration Number.	Exhibition Number.	Place.	Registration Number.	Exhibition Number.	Place.
862	930	Bay 29.	930	314	Bay 4.
864	54	Vestibule.	931	759	Bay 24.
865	55	Vestibule.	932	491	Bay 11.
866	56	Vestibule.	933	948	Bay 29.
867	57	Vestibule.	934	1006	Bay 26.
868	58	Vestibule.	938	949	Bay 29.
869	59	Vestibule.	939	1094	Bay 26.
870	48	Vestibule.	941	947	Bay 27.
871	276	Bay 1.	942	530	Bay 12.
873	887	Bay 24.	943	364	Bay 12.
876	525	Bay 12.	947	615	Bay 18.
877	845	Bay 20.	948	602	C.S.
880	436	Bay 13.	949	362	Bay 5.
881	981	Bay 29.	950	625	Bay 13.
882	575	C.S.	952	809	Bay 24.
883	685	C.S.	954	606	C.S.
884	569	C.S.	956	476	Bay 10.
885	1074	Bay 29.	958	686	C.S.
886	1026	Bay 27.	959	1072	Bay 28.
890	376	Bay 12.	961	875	Bay 24.
891	915	Bay 24.	962	734	Bay 19.
892	1050	Bay 30.	963	136	Bay 5.
893	447	Bay 5.	964	802	Bay 24.
894	918	Bay 29.	967	836	Bay 16.
895	980	Bay 29.	968	526	Bay 12.
896	916	Bay 24.	969	281	Bay 1.
900	1105	Bay 30.	970	1070	Bay 27.
901	1051	Bay 30.	971	222	Bay 3.
902	377	Bay 11.	972	876	Bay 24.
903	216	Bay 2.	973	265	Bay 16.
904	292	Bay 3.	974	266	Bay 16.
905	300	Bay 7.	975	270	Bay 14.
906	502	Bay 11.	976	264	Bay 14.
907	813	Bay 24.	977	274	Bay 16.
908	798	Bay 20.	978	275	Bay 16.
909	877	Bay 24.	980	262	Bay 14.
910	473	Bay 9.	982	974	Bay 27.
911	932	Bay 24.	985	975	Bay 29.
912	849	Bay 21.	986	873	Bay 23.
913	649	Bay 17.	987	340	Bay 5.
914	233	Bay 4.	988	1019	Bay 27.
915	562	Bay 20.	990	267	Bay 16.
916	345	Bay 20.	991	273	Bay 14.
917	785	Bay 22.	992	39	Vestibule.
918	547	Bay 13.	993	37	Vestibule.
919	517	Bay 12.	994	72	Bay 2.
920	518	Bay 12.	995	1109	Bay 30.
921	519	Bay 13.	997	271	Bay 14.
922	520	Bay 13.	998	927	Bay 28.
923	1089	Bay 30.	1000	435	Bay 13.
924	1129	Bay 30.	1001	420	Bay 12.
927	914	Bay 24.	1002	440	C.S.
928	257	Bay 9.	1003	986	Bay 27.
929	268	Bay 14.	1004	1044	Bay 29.

Registration Number.	Exhibition Number.	Place.	Registration Number.	Exhibition Number.	Place.
1006	596	C.S.	1100	284	Bay 23.
1007	776	Bay 21.	1101	339	Bay 23.
1010	157	Vestibule.	1102	167	Bay 23.
1011	87	Vestibule.	1103	773	Bay 23.
1012	488	Bay 10.	1104	586	Bay 23.
1013	925	Bay 27.	1105	769	Bay 23.
1015	370	Bay 11.	1106	922	Bay 25.
1016	497	Bay 11.	1107	768	Bay 16.
1017	869	Bay 22.	1108	367	C.S.
1018	941	Bay 26.	1109	366	Bay 6.
1019	365	Bay 10.	1110	27	Vestibule.
1020	963	Bay 29.	1111	19	Vestibule.
1021	368	Bay 11.	1112	49	Vestibule.
1022	452	Bay 7.	1113	28	Vestibule.
1039	1152	Bay 28.	1114	13	Vestibule.
1040	1167	Bay 32.	1115	30	Vestibule.
1042	847	Bay 21.	1116	36	Vestibule.
1043	1088	Bay 28.	1117	29	Vestibule.
1045	784	Bay 20.	1119	450	Bay 6.
1046	1102	Bay 28.	1120	173	C.S.
1047	829	Bay 28.	1121	793	C.S.
1050	908	Bay 16.	1122	816	Bay 20.
1051	906	Bay 16.	1123	599	Bay 17.
1052	746	Bay 21.	1124	799	Bay 22.
1054	955	Bay 29.	1125	815	Bay 18.
1055	608	Bay 17.	1126	817	Bay 20.
1056	953	Bay 25.	1127	950	Bay 28.
1057	954	Bay 25.	1131	374	Bay 9.
1058	1042	Bay 16.	1132	789	Bay 22.
1059	250	Bay 7.	1133	344	Bay 12.
1060	278	Bay 5.	1134	962	Bay 30.
1061	307	Bay 3.	1135	174	Bay 1.
1062	458	Bay 8.	1136	81	Bay 1.
1063	774	Bay 22.	1137	1041	Bay 16.
1064	775	Bay 20.	1138	848	Bay 21.
1065	598	Bay 21.	1139	1001	Bay 26.
1066	585	Bay 16.	1141	1012	Bay 29.
1068	428	Bay 12.	1142	343	Bay 16.
1069	165	Vestibule.	1143	51	Vestibule.
1071	589	Vestibule.	1144	35	Vestibule.
1072	171	Bay 5.	1145	163	Vestibule.
1073	1071	Bay 26.	1146	164	Vestibule.
1075	824	Bay 26.	1147	198	Bay 2.
1076	823	Bay 25.	1148	885	Bay 27.
1077	770	Bay 26.	1149	206	Vestibule.
1081	957	Bay 28.	1150	201	Bay 7.
1083	437	Bay 13.	1151	200	Bay 2.
1084	728	Bay 17.	1152	199	Bay 2.
1085	973	Bay 17.	1153	972	Bay 25.
1086	852	Bay 21.	1154	982	Bay 31.
1088	989	Bay 27.	1155	1061	Bay 29.
1097	771	Bay 23.	1156	63	Vestibule.
1098	772	Bay 23.	1157	966	Bay 32.
1099	166	Bay 23.	1158	1014	Bay 29.

1089-1096 are stelae in North Gallery.

Registration Number.	Exhibition Number.	Place.	Registration Number.	Exhibition Number.	Place.
1160	1015	Bay 29.	1219	1082	Bay 30.
1161	60	Vestibule.	1220	477	Bay 10.
1162	964	Bay 28.	1222	443	Bay 2.
1163	280	Bay 1.	1223	65	Vestibule.
1164	134	Bay 4.	1224	777	Bay 22.
1165	64	Vestibule.	1225	790	Bay 26.
1166	61	Vestibule.	1226	687	C.S.
1167	527	Bay 12.	1227	1034	Bay 14.
1168	43	Vestibule.	1228	7	Vestibule.
1169	41	Vestibule.	1229	289	Bay 2.
1170	73	Vestibule.	1232	740	Bay 21.
1171	42	Vestibule.	1233	741	Bay 21.
1172	131	Vestibule.	1235	942	Bay 26.
1173	16	Vestibule.	1236	148	Bay 5.
1174	17	Vestibule.	1237	288	Bay 2.
1175	93	Bay 14.	1238	803	Bay 23.
1176	94	Bay 14.	1239	33	Bay 1.
1177	196	Bay 4.	1242	40	Vestibule.
1178	1013	Bay 29.	1243	546	Bay 13.
1179	95	Bay 14.	1244	317	Bay 7.
1180	935	Bay 25.	1245	324	Bay 7.
1181	14	Vestibule.	1246	302	Bay 7.
1182	424	Bay 10.	1247	325	Bay 7.
1183	701	Bay 20.	1248	507	Bay 12.
1184	623	Bay 13.	1250	1139	Bay 32.
1185	38	Vestibule.	1251	1064	Bay 14.
1186	71	Vestibule.	1252	1065	Bay 16.
1188	645	C.S.	1253	1039	Bay 14.
1189	574	Bay 13.	1254	1133	Bay 30.
1191	85	Vestibule.	1255	1134	Bay 30.
1192	1	Vestibule.	1256	1149	Bay 32.
1194	721	Bay 11.	1257	1136	Bay 30.
1195	453	Bay 8.	1258 }	794	Bay 20.
1196	1087	Bay 26.	1259 }		
1197	837	Bay 17.	1260	125	Vestibule.
1198	871	Bay 22.	1261	135	Vestibule.
1199	371	Bay 10.	1262	92	Vestibule.
1200	449	Bay 6.	1263	78	Vestibule.
1201	251	Bay 7.	1264	91	Vestibule.
1202	832	Bay 14.	1266	6	Vestibule.
1203	99	Bay 4.	1267	5	Vestibule.
1204	20	Vestibule.	1268	23	Vestibule.
1205	1078	Bay 30.	1269	22	Vestibule.
1206	1083	Bay 26.	1272	31	Vestibule.
1207	958	Bay 26.	1273	68	Vestibule.
1208	1119	Bay 32.	1274	69	Vestibule.
1209	897	Bay 29.	1275	52	Vestibule.
1210	423	Bay 5.	1276	1103	Bay 30.
1212	4	Vestibule.	1277	62	Vestibule.
1213	249	Bay 7.	1278	66	Vestibule.
1214	662	Bay 18.	1279	653	Bay 15.
1215	1036	Bay 14.	1280	628	Bay 15.
1217	937	Bay 25.	1281	1068	Bay 16.
1218	1081	Bay 30.	1282	18	Vestibule.

Registration Number.	Exhibition Number.	Place.	Registration Number.	Exhibition Number.	Place.
1284	831	Bay 14.	1347	353	Bay 8.
1287	82	Vestibule.	1348	279	Bay 5.
1288	15	Vestibule.	1349	1005	Bay 25.
1289	917	Bay 28.	1350	1166	Bay 32.
1290	176	Vestibule.	1351	1142	Bay 32.
1291	524	Bay 12.	1352	1131	Bay 30.
1292	821	Bay 22.	1354	834	Bay 16.
1293	90	Vestibule.	1355	600	Bay 16.
1294	1063	Bay 29.	1358	804	Bay 22.
1295	725	Bay 16.	1359	1059	Bay 26.
1297	655	Bay 18.	1360	1092	Bay 26.
1298	1062	Bay 29.	1361	1151	Bay 28.
1299	1120	Bay 32.	1362	1097	Bay 28.
1300	1118	Bay 32.	1363	1077	Bay 29.
1301	688	Bay 16.	1364	1037	Bay 14.
1302	910	Bay 16.	1365	1004	Bay 25.
1303	971	Bay 28.	1366	747	Bay 21.
1306	943	Bay 26.	1367	236	Bay 5.
1307	765	Bay 19.	1368	513	Bay 12.
1309	891	Bay 16.	1369	678	Bay 20.
1310	902	Bay 14.	1370	327	Bay 9.
1311	1016	Bay 32.	1371	329	Bay 9.
1312	124	Bay 2.	1372	120	Bay 4.
1313	122	Bay 2.	1373	521	Bay 12.
1314	336	Bay 9.	1374	522	Bay 12.
1315	132	Bay 4.	1375	572	Bay 18.
1316	894	Bay 25.	1376	604	C.S.
1317	843	Bay 20.	1377	603	C.S.
1318	337	Bay 11.	1378	617	C.S.
1322	235	Bay 4.	1379	724	Bay 14.
1323	661	Bay 18.	1380	796	Bay 20.
1324	8	Vestibule.	1381	781	Bay 17.
1325	993	Bay 27.	1382	669	Bay 18.
1326	1138	Bay 32.	1383	53	Vestibule.
1327	1126	Bay 32.	1384	827	Bay 27.
1328	1122	Bay 30.	1385	50	Vestibule.
1329	523	Bay 12.	1386	822	Bay 22.
1330	88	Vestibule.	1387	883	Bay 23.
1331	928	Bay 23.	1388	676	Bay 22.
1332	503	Bay 11.	1397	105	Bay 3.
1333	933	Bay 24.	1420	898	Bay 31.
1334	1106	Bay 32.	1421	921	Bay 30.
1335	1146	Bay 32.	1422	1113	Bay 30.
1336	1115	Bay 30.	1423	1104	Bay 32.
1337	1159	Bay 30.	1424	1021	Bay 28.
1338	1161	Bay 30.	1425	1020	Bay 28.
1339	1128	Bay 32.	1426	1022	Bay 26.
1340	830	Bay 14.	1427	808	Bay 24.
1341	75	Vestibule.	1428	1010	Bay 24.
1342	76	Vestibule.	1429	98	Vestibule.
1343	970	Bay 21.	1430	791	Bay 26.
1344	717	C.S.	1431	959	Bay 26.
1345	9	Vestibule.	1432	1054	Bay 26.
1346	277	Bay 2.	1433	979	Bay 26.

Registration Number.	Exhibition Number.	Place.	Registration Number.	Exhibition Number.	Place.
1434	379	Bay 7.	1470	1170	Bay 18.
1465	635	Bay 7.	1471	1171	Bay 20.
10541	758	Bay 24.	1472	1172	Bay 20.
1466	1173	Bay 17.	1473	1175	Bay 15.
1467	1174	Bay 15.	1474	1176	Bay 26.
1469	1169	C.S.			

INDEX.

PUBLICATIONS

OF THE

DEPARTMENT OF EGYPTIAN AND ASSYRIAN ANTIQUITIES.

THE BOOK OF THE DEAD.

PHOTOGRAPHS OF THE PAPYRUS OF NEBSENI in the British Museum. 1876. Unmounted *2l. 2s.* (Mounted copies and copies in portfolios may be obtained on special terms.)

THE PAPYRUS OF ANI, THE BOOK OF THE DEAD. Facsimile. Second edition. 1894. Fol. Portfolio or half bound. *2l. 10s.*

THE PAPYRUS OF ANI, THE BOOK OF THE DEAD. The Egyptian Text, with interlinear transliteration and translation, a running translation, introduction, etc. By E. A. Wallis Budge, Litt.D. 1895. 4to. *1l. 10s.*

FACSIMILES OF THE PAPYRI OF HUNEFER, ANHAI, KERASHER, AND NETCHEMET, with supplementary text from the Papyrus of Nu. With transcripts, translations, etc. By E. A. Wallis Budge, Litt.D. 1899. Fol. *2l. 10s.*

EGYPTIAN TEXTS OF THE EARLIEST PERIOD, from the coffin of Amamu. 32 coloured plates. 1886. Fol. *2l. 2s.*

EGYPTIAN PAPYRI, ETC.

FACSIMILE OF THE RHIND MATHEMATICAL PAPYRUS in the British Museum. 21 plates. 1898. Fol. *18s.*

INSCRIPTIONS IN THE HIERATIC AND DEMOTIC CHARACTER. 1868. Fol. *1l. 7s. 6d.*

COPTIC AND GREEK TEXTS OF THE CHRISTIAN PERIOD, from Ostraka, Stelæ, etc., in the British Museum. By H. R. Hall. 100 plates. 1905. Foolscap. *2l.*

BABYLONIAN AND ASSYRIAN TEXTS, ETC.

INSCRIPTIONS IN THE CUNEIFORM CHARACTER, from Assyrian MONUMENTS discovered by A. H. Layard, D.C.L. 1851. Fol. 1*l.* 1*s.*

THE CUNEIFORM INSCRIPTIONS OF WESTERN ASIA, Vol. III. Prepared for publication by Major-General Sir H. C. Rawlinson, K.C.B., assisted by George Smith, Department of Antiquities, British Museum. 1870. Fol. 1*l.*

THE SCULPTURES AND INSCRIPTION OF DARIUS THE GREAT ON THE ROCK OF BEHISTÛN, IN PERSIA. A new collation of the Persian, Susian, and Babylonian Texts, with English translation, plates, etc. 1907. 8vo. 1*l.*

CUNEIFORM TEXTS FROM BABYLONIAN TABLETS, etc., in the British Museum. Parts I.–V., VII.–XXIII., 50 plates each; Part VI., 49 plates. 1896–1906. Foolscap. 7*s.* 6*d.* each part. Part XXIV. 50 plates. 1908. Foolscap. 10*s.*

ANNALS OF THE KINGS OF ASSYRIA. Cuneiform Texts, with translations, etc. By E. A. Wallis Budge, Litt.D., and L. W. King, M.A. Vol. I. 1903. 4to. 1*l.*

PHOTOGRAPH OF A BABYLONIAN TABLET (Sp. 3, 2). 1895. 1*s.* 6*d.*

THE TELL EL-AMARNA TABLETS IN THE BRITISH MUSEUM. Autotype Plates. 1892. 8vo. 1*l.* 8*s.*

CATALOGUE OF CUNEIFORM TABLETS IN THE KOUYUNJIK COLLECTION. By C. Bezold. Vol. I., 8vo, 1889, 15*s.*; Vol. II., 8vo, 1891, 15*s.*; Vol. III., 8vo, 1894, 15*s.*; Vol. IV., 8vo, 1896, 1*l.*; Vol. V., 8vo, 1899, 1*l.* 3*s.*

GUIDE BOOKS.

GUIDE TO THE EGYPTIAN COLLECTIONS. With 53 plates and 180 illustrations. 1909. 8vo. 1*s.*

GUIDE TO THE EGYPTIAN GALLERIES (SCULPTURE). With 39 plates and 46 illustrations. 1909. 8vo. 1*s.* 6*d.*

GUIDE TO THE FIRST AND SECOND EGYPTIAN ROOMS. With 32 plates and 28 illustrations. Second edition. 1904. 8vo. 1*s.*

GUIDE TO THE THIRD AND FOURTH EGYPTIAN ROOMS. With 8 plates and 131 illustrations. 1904. 8vo. 1*s.* 6*d.*

GUIDE TO THE BABYLONIAN AND ASSYRIAN COLLECTIONS. 2nd edition. With 45 plates and 45 illustrations. 1908. 8vo. 1*s.*

HIMYARITIC & PHŒNICIAN INSCRIPTIONS.

INSCRIPTIONS IN THE PHŒNICIAN CHARACTER, discovered on the site of Carthage during researches by Nathan Davis, 1856–58. 1863. Fol. 1*l.* 5*s.*

INSCRIPTIONS IN THE HIMYARITIC CHARACTER, discovered chiefly in Southern Arabia. 1863. Fol. 1*l.* 4*s.*

CPSIA information can be obtained
at www.ICGtesting.com
Printed in the USA
LVHW012104200821
695647LV00008B/237

9 781639 230471